*A Social History
of the Russian Empire
1650–1825*

A SOCIAL HISTORY OF EUROPE
General Editor: Raymond Pearson

A Social History of the Russian Empire 1650–1825 is the first volume to be published in a major new Longman series. Wide-ranging both geographically and chronologically, it will explore the history of the peoples of Europe in an ambitious programme of analytical surveys, each examining a nation, state or region in a key phase of its development. The books will be written by leading experts; and each, while synthesising the latest scholarship in the field, will be invigorated by the findings and preoccupations of the author's original research.

The series is designed for a wide audience: the volumes will be necessary reading for serious students and fellow scholars, but they are also written to engage and interest the non-specialist coming to the subject for the first time.

Inaugurated by the late Harry Hearder, the series is under the General Editorship of Professor Raymond Pearson, Professor of European History at the University of Ulster at Coleraine.

Many further volumes are in preparation.

A Social History
of the Russian Empire
1650–1825

Janet M. Hartley

LONGMAN
London and New York

Addison Wesley Longman Limited
Edinburgh Gate,
Harlow, Essex CM20 2JE, United Kingdom
and Associated Companies throughout the world.

Published in the United States of America by Addison Wesley Longman, New York.

First published 1999

ISBN 0–582–21528–5 CSD
ISBN 0–582–21527–7 PPR

Visit Addison Wesley Longman on the world wide web at http://www.awl-he.com

British Library Cataloguing in Publication Data

A catalogue entry for this title is available from the British Library

Library of Congress Cataloging-in-Publication Data

Hartley, Janet M.
    A social history of the Russian empire 1650–1825 / Janet Hartley.
        p.   cm. — (A social history of Europe)
    Includes bibliographical references and index.
    ISBN 0–582–21528–5. — ISBN 0–582–21527–7 (pbk.)
    1. Russia—Social conditions.   2. Russia—Economic conditions.
    3. Russia—History.   4. Russia—Civilization.   5. Russia—Politics
    and government.   I. Title.   II. Series.
    HN525.H37   1998
    306′.0947—dc21   98–7801
                                                                        CIP

Set by 35 in 10/12 pt Bembo
Produced by Addison Wesley Longman Singapore (Pte) Ltd.,
Printed in Singapore

Contents

Preface

This study concerns what eventually became the Russian empire, in which ethnic Great Russians became increasingly a minority. Nevertheless, I am mainly concerned with society within Great Russia. This emphasis has arisen from practical considerations. None of the non-Russian areas has been subject to the extensive, archive-based studies which have been made of society, the economy and government in Great Russia by Russian and western scholars. The result is that coverage of non-Russians in this book is uneven. Educational provision and self-governing institutions in the Ukraine, the Baltic provinces and the western provinces have been covered more extensively than, for example, land-holding patterns, household size and inheritance laws in these areas. Some territories which only became part of the Russian empire in the early nineteenth century – Georgia, the Grand Duchy of Finland, the Congress Kingdom of Poland – receive less attention than the Left-Bank Ukraine and the Baltic provinces, which were acquired earlier. The lifestyle and the social organizations of Siberian and nomadic peoples have only been touched on and the emphasis is on the relationship between these peoples and the Russian state. Footnotes have been kept to a minimum, and limited in the main to direct quotations, matters of historiographical debate, primary published and unpublished sources and secondary works not listed in the select bibliography. Dates are in New Style.

The following abbreviations of archive sources have been used in the text:

BL, Add. MS	British Library, Additional Manuscripts
RGADA	Moscow, Russkii gosudarstvennyi arkhiv drevnikh aktov
RGIA	St Petersburg, Russkii gosudarstvennyi istoricheskii arkhiv
SPgFIRI	St Petersburg, Sankt-Peterburg Filial Instituta russkoi istorii
TsGIA-SPg	St Petersburg, Tsentral'nyi gosudarstvennyi istoricheskii arkhiv – Sankt Peterburg

I am grateful to kind friends for their assistance with this book. In particular I should like to thank Roger Bartlett and Isabel de Madariaga for reading the first draft with such care and for their invaluable comments and suggestions.

I am also very grateful to Faith Wigzell and Lindsey Hughes for allowing me to see the texts of their books before publication. My husband, Will Ryan, read the final draft and bravely ventured further criticisms; the section in this book on magic is almost entirely drawn from his forthcoming publication on the subject. The book is dedicated to my children, Ben (aged seven) and Isabel (aged two), in the hope that it partly compensates for my frequent seclusion in the study doing 'Mummy's boring work'.

Janet Hartley

Any explanation of why period delimited by these years?

Acknowledgement

The publishers would like to thank Stanford University Press for permission to reproduce the figure of 'Basic plans of peasant houses' (page 177) from Wayne S. Vucinich (ed.), *The Peasant in Nineteenth Century Russia*. © 1968 by the Board of Trustees of the Leland Stanford Junior University.

TO BEN AND ISABEL

Introduction: society and state

Two major themes recur in this book: the relationship between society and the state and the degree of stratification and diversity between and within social groups. This book assesses the degree to which change took place as a result of government policies and the extent to which these changes affected distinctions between social groups.

STATE AND SOCIETY

There is no doubt that Russian rulers believed that they should, and could, change society. The extent to which they were successful is a major theme of this book.

Whole categories of social groups were eliminated, created and modified by tsarist legislation in this period. Amongst those eliminated were various categories of old servitors, slaves, elite urban groups and church and monastic peasants. Tsarist legislation created new social groups such as soldiers' children, the *raznochintsy* and teachers. In the late eighteenth century gypsies were categorized as state peasants and Jews in the lands of partitioned Poland had to register in one of the new urban categories. Individuals as well as groups had their status changed. Sons of priests were 'culled' to become soldiers, clerks, teachers and medical students. Whole villages of peasants were arbitrarily recategorized as artisans in the reign of Catherine II and as military colonists in the reign of Alexander I. At the same time, some social groups whose status seemed anomalous, such as *odnodvortsy* and postdrivers, were retained.

The extent to which the nobility was created and moulded by the tsars is a central issue in this study. The most dramatic legislative acts concerning the nobility were the Table of Ranks in 1722, the freedom of the nobility from compulsory service in 1762, and the promulgation of the Charter to the Nobles in 1785. Catherine also vastly expanded the number of posts in local government for nobles and created noble assemblies in the provinces. Tsarist legislation shaped the laws of inheritance for nobles and the status of hereditary and service land. The government also regulated economic relations between nobles

1

and merchants. Furthermore, the tsars played an important role in governing the way nobles looked, lived, and, to some extent, the way they thought. Peter I passed decrees on physical appearance, dress, social gatherings, marriage customs and on the ending of seclusion of noble women. The tsars also had a considerable influence on the syllabuses of elite noble schools and stimulated the development of the arts and the importation of western fashions and 'high' culture, which were eagerly assimilated by the noble elite. The implementation and implications of these policies are examined with a view to determining the extent to which the state transformed the Russian nobility in this period.

The tsars, and in particular Peter I and Catherine II, attempted to stimulate the urban life of Russia by establishing organs of municipal self-government, by recategorizing social groups within the urban community and by attempting to introduce craft guilds modelled on those of western and central Europe. The government specified which settlements should be reclassified as towns (and, in the process, which people should be recategorized as members of the urban community), decided which towns should be designated as district and provincial centres and legislated in the conflict between the urban community and the Church over property. It regulated the economic activities of the towns, determined the status of so-called 'trading' peasants in towns, set the fiscal and other obligations of the townspeople, passed decrees on town planning, street lighting and fire prevention and established police forces, schools, hospitals and welfare institutions. The extent of the success of these policies is analysed in this book.

The Law Code (*Ulozhenie*) of 1649 formally institutionalized serfdom in Muscovy. Thereafter the policies of the tsars defined who should be designated as serfs or state peasants. The introduction of the poll tax in the reign of Peter served to simplify the categories of peasant population and, in the process, to eliminate slaves and reduce the number of landless peasants. Church and monastic peasants became state peasants in the reign of Catherine II after the secularization of church lands. The government also intervened to a limited extent to force redivision of land amongst state peasants in north Russia in the late eighteenth and early nineteenth centuries. The calculation and extent of fiscal and other obligations imposed by the government had an impact not only on peasant prosperity but also on peasant household size and composition. The introduction of Russian institutions into non-Russian lands of the empire in the second half of the eighteenth century, and the absorption of many of the non-Russian nobility into the Russian nobility, led *inter alia* to further restrictions of movement on the peasantry and, in effect, the extension of serfdom. Nevertheless, areas in which the government failed to intervene, or did so effectively, are as important as, if not more important than, legislative activity and are reflected in the coverage of peasant issues in this book. Little attempt was made by the tsars to alter or alleviate the conditions of serfdom in this period, despite the professed distaste of Catherine II and Alexander I for the system. The autonomy of the peasant commune and the importance of customary law are both covered prominently; the state had little direct contact with either. Agricultural practices continued almost unchanged throughout this period. It is perhaps significant that even Peter I did not attempt to force peasants to shave their beards or change their dress. Nor could the state penetrate the minds of the peasants. Educational provision rarely reached the village (although some peasants attended national schools in towns) and pagan and magical beliefs were not fully superseded by Christianity, let alone by contact with new or foreign ideas.

The tsars determined the composition, size and structure of the armed forces. In the sixteenth century specialist groups of servitors were created, including musketeers (*strel'tsy*) and artillerymen (*pushkari*). In the mid-seventeenth century (in the reigns of Michael, 1613–45, and Alexis, 1645–76) so-called 'new model' infantry and cavalry regiments were established, modelled on the armies of western and northern Europe. Peter I created a proper standing army and a navy, and, in the process, influenced the composition of both the officer corps and the ordinary troops and sailors, making old categories of servitors redundant. Thereafter, tsars decided when recruit levies should take place, how many men should be raised and which social categories were liable for conscription. The role in the armed forces of groups of Muscovite servitors, such as *odnodvortsy*, and of irregular troops, such as the Cossacks and native forces, was also specified by the tsars. The state established the structure of command, and ranks, for the armed forces, controlled the level of wages and other rewards for all personnel, and set regulations for internal discipline, uniforms, food supplies, accommodation and medical care for officers and men. The direct encouragement of particular industries by the state and the levels of taxation were at least in part a consequence of perceived military needs. The tsars also created the elite schools for the training of future officers and were often personally responsible for the syllabuses of these schools.

The effect of tsarist policy on the Orthodox Church and the parish clergy was also of great significance. The policies of tsar Alexis were fundamental in creating the schism within the Russian Church in the mid-seventeenth century. Peter I in effect made the Church an arm of the state and the parish clergy into state servitors. The government was largely responsible for the composition of the clerical estate, controlling entry into the estate and, at various times, forcing or luring members of the clergy into other occupations. Russian rulers, in particular Peter I, Catherine II and Alexander I, played a crucial role by specifying the education the parish clergy should receive, while insisting that teachers in national schools should be secular (i.e. that they should renounce their clerical status if they were sons of priests). Government legislation also restricted entrance to monasteries and convents, determined the income and number of monks and nuns, established the welfare functions of monasteries and convents, secularized church lands and made church and monastic peasants into state peasants. In a broader context, however, this book is equally concerned with the lack of impact which the government, or, for that matter, the Church, had on the beliefs of the population. Tsarist

3

legislation could not counter the problem of the schism and neither persecution nor toleration served to lessen the appeal of Old Belief over time. Furthermore, neither the government nor the Church was able to eliminate the elements of paganism and magic within Christian practice and belief.

SOCIETY: STRATIFICATION AND DIVERSITY

The extent to which stratification *within* social groups existed and whether it increased or decreased over time is central to this study.

All social groups were heterogeneous. Divisions within the nobility remained and, to an extent, were deepened by the obsession with service. Wealthy and influential noble families were better able to take advantage of the new educational facilities, family connections and patronage to improve their service prospects. The freedom from compulsory service in 1762 merely accentuated the differences between the impoverished nobles who remained in the country on small estates and the wealthy nobles who took the most prestigious posts in military and civil service, resided in Moscow or St Petersburg and only visited their scattered estates for recreation. The extension of education for the nobility and their exposure to western culture served to deepen further the division between the sophisticated, well-travelled, few and the majority who acquired only the trappings of a western-style education and whose habits and lifestyle remained closer to those of their serfs. The government formally recognized the economic diversity within the urban community by categorizing townspeople according to wealth and occupation and by granting privileges to the elite merchantry. Stratification also existed within the peasantry, both between the different categories of peasants – state peasants regarded themselves as privileged compared with serfs, serfs regarded themselves as superior to houseserfs – and within peasant communities. The wealthier peasants often dominated village communes and controlled such matters as the division of households, fiscal and labour obligations and, most importantly, the selection of recruits. Nevertheless, differences of wealth within peasant communities should not be exaggerated; peasants were differentiated more by occupation (agrarian workers, trading peasants or houseserfs).

Distinctions *between* social groups also existed, and, to some extent, intensified during this period. A fundamental distinction existed between the privileged and non-privileged members of society and was determined by the nature of their service to the state. This was formalized in the reign of Peter I by the introduction of the poll tax. Payment of this tax (and other labour dues), as opposed to military or civil service for the state, came to signify membership of the non-privileged classes (which is why the *odnodvortsy* and wealthy merchants sought to be relieved of these burdens). The parish clergy were privileged in that they were exempt from the poll tax. After 1762, the nobility were marked as especially privileged in that they were no longer obliged to serve the state in any capacity although, in practice, financial need and the bond between service, rank and status meant that most nobles continued to serve the state for at least part of their adult life. The importance and advantages of noble status can be seen by the desperation with which this was claimed by the *odnodvortsy* and other former military servitors, the attempts by impoverished former nobleman to reclaim their status, the willingness of non-Russian nobles within the empire to enter the ranks of the Russian nobility from the late eighteenth century and the desire of wealthy merchants and industrialists to acquire noble status.

A further important division within society arose from the complexity of Russian law and legal institutions in this period. Most civil issues concerning peasants, be they state peasants or serfs, continued to be dealt with outside the legal system, being decided by the commune according to customary law. Serfs were subject to the jurisdiction of their noble landowner, or his agents, for all but the most serious criminal offences. Clergy were tried in separate clerical courts according to ecclesiastical law. Members of the armed forces – a category which included soldiers' children and military colonists – were also tried separately. Other social groups were subject to state law and legal institutions, but courts were segregated according to social estate, with separate courts established for townspeople, nobles and, after 1775, state peasants. Finally, the non-Russian population continued to be tried according to their local laws (although after 1775 the new judicial structure was extended to non-Russian parts of the empire).

During this period, education and lifestyle came to divide society. Education in the elite schools and with private tutors was largely the preserve of the nobility and even the slightest acquaintance with foreign languages (particularly French), history and culture marked the nobility as different from other members of society. Nobles themselves became aware that education gave them special advantages, and so tried to ensure that they were segregated from other members of society in schools and that elite establishments were reserved exclusively for them. In the same way, the isolation of the sons of the clergy from the rest of society in seminaries (where they were taught Latin) segregated this estate from other social groups, and from their own parishioners, and helped restrict entry into the clerical estate. By the second half of the eighteenth century society had become defined by its lifestyle. Nobles, and some richer townspeople, were eating, drinking, dressing and entertaining themselves differently from poorer townspeople and peasants.

The uneasy relationship between the military and civilians served both to divide and unite society. On the one hand, society was divided by the distinction between the 'unprivileged' groups which were liable for conscription, and which were obliged to quarter troops, and the 'privileged' groups which were exempt from these obligations. In addition, the armed forces were a separate group within society: Muscovite servitors such as *strel'tsy* became in effect social castes; the armed forces from the eighteenth century were regarded as a separate legal category, subject to their own laws; at the point of conscription soldiers shed their original social category and became legally 'free'; soldiers' children and colonists in the military colonies established in the reign of Alexander I became distinct social categories. On the other hand, military values and habits permeated society through the employment of army officers in the civil administration and by the application of military law (in particular the Code of Military Laws of 1716) in civil courts for certain offences. And all groups of society were affected by the disorders which were caused by army deserters, rebellious Cossacks and the passage of Russian and foreign troops through their lands.

Furthermore, this study demonstrates that the segregation of society according to estate, and the rigidity of the estate structure, should not be exaggerated. Social estates were never closed groups in Russia, Russian society could never in practice be neatly categorized into the four main groups of nobles, townspeople, clergy and peasants. Free-floating groups such as *raznochintsy*, various categories of military servitors such as *odnodvortsy*, clerks and junior office workers, retired soldiers who were 'free' citizens, and teachers (after 1786) complicated the structure of Russian society. The Russian empire was a multinational empire and the social structure was very different in the western borderlands, the Baltic provinces, Finland, the Ukraine, the Caucasus and amongst the non-Russian, and non-Christian, peoples of Siberia. Furthermore, all members of society shared certain experiences and values, irrespective of differences in status, wealth, occupation and education. At least until 1762, all members of society were expected to serve the state in some capacity. The lawlessness and violence of Russian life and the arbitrariness of justice and local officialdom affected all but the very privileged or the very fortunate. Most Russians, irrespective of social background, lived in large extended families. Courtship and betrothal, and the relationships between husbands and wives and parents and children did not differ markedly throughout society. All Russians suffered from poor hygiene, primitive medical facilities, and the general fragility of life, although town-dwellers fared worse than the rural population. Old Belief attracted peasants and townspeople rather than the nobility, but all Russians were Christian and worshipped the same God, usually in the same churches. Christenings, marriage and funeral ceremonies were essentially the same for all people and only differed in traditional rituals and cost but not in liturgical form. Finally, all members of society shared beliefs in magic and superstitions which education and exposure to foreign cultures had not eradicated.

CHAPTER 1

Land and people

Who lived in the vast lands of Muscovy and the Russian empire, and what was the ethnic, religious and social composition of this population? The period 1650–1825 is characterized by restlessness and change: a dynamic expansion of the boundaries of the Russian state was accompanied by a rapid population increase and extensive internal migration and resettlement. In the process the ethnic and religious composition of the empire underwent significant alteration. The social composition of the empire was a complex one and in part reflects the diversity of the lands in which people lived. In this chapter the main social groups which lived in the empire will be defined and some indication given of their size and changing composition during this period.

THE LAND: EXPANSION OF FRONTIERS

The Russian state underwent a substantial, if uneven and sometimes loosely defined, expansion in every direction from the mid-seventeenth to the early nineteenth centuries. During the reign of Alexis (1645–76) Muscovy made significant territorial gains in the west and south at the expense of Poland-Lithuania. The Treaty of Pereiaslavl' of 1654 bound the Ukrainian Cossacks, who were under Polish overlordship, to the tsar in a manner and to an extent which is still disputed by Ukrainian and Russian historians. In practice, by 1667 Muscovy exercised control over the eastern part of the Ukraine (the Hetmanate and Slobodskaia Ukraine), known as the Left-Bank Ukraine. The peace of Andrusovo in 1667 ceded the important towns of Smolensk and Kiev to Russia. The reign of Peter the Great (1682–1725) saw the acquisition of the eastern Baltic littoral from Sweden as a result of the success of the Russian forces in the Great Northern War of 1700–21. At the Treaty of Nystad in 1721 Sweden ceded Estonia, Livonia, Ingria and the district of Vyborg in southern Finland to Russia. Peter's successes in the north were not repeated in the south; the fort of Azov (giving access to the Black Sea) was won and then lost and was only ceded finally by the Ottoman empire in 1737 during the reign of Anna (ruled 1730–41). In 1721 Peter claimed the western-style title of

'Emperor' as well as 'tsar' (itself a title with claims to imperial dignity), a title which was gradually, and sometimes grudgingly, accepted by the other European powers in the course of the eighteenth century. I have used the term 'Russian empire' from this date, although in several important respects the Russian variant never accorded with the classical definition of empire. A further slice of southern Finnish territory (which became known as Old Finland until it was reunited by Alexander I with the Grand Duchy of Finland in 1812), including the towns of Fredrikshamn (Hamina), Villmanstrand (Lappeenranta) and Nyslott (Savonlinna), was ceded to Russia in 1743 during the reign of Elizabeth (1741–62).

The reign of Catherine II (1762–96) saw notable Russian expansion to the west and south, leading to the incorporation of over 112 million square kilometres of new territory. The three partitions of Poland-Lithuania (1772, 1793, 1795) extended the Russian frontier westwards and made Russia a direct neighbour of Prussia and Austria. Wars against the Ottoman empire yielded a strip of coast on the northern coasts of the Black Sea and the Crimean peninsula (annexed in 1783). The Napoleonic Wars in the reign of Alexander I (1801–25) resulted in further expansion for the Russian state – the rest of Finland was acquired in 1809 from Sweden, and Bessarabia was ceded by the Ottoman empire in 1812. The Congress of Vienna in 1815 created the Congress Kingdom of Poland (occupying a slightly smaller area than the land acquired by Prussia in the three partitions), which was bound to Russia in a dynastic union, the tsar of Russia being also the king of Poland (the territory was formally incorporated into the Russian empire after the Polish rebellion of 1830). Imperial Russia's westwards expansion had reached its limit by 1815.

Formal acquisition of territory by war, however, only accounts for Russian expansion at the expense of other major powers – namely Poland-Lithuania, Sweden and the Ottoman empire. Increase in Russian settlement was also a feature of this period. Russians advanced through Siberia from the second half of the sixteenth century onwards. The Pacific Ocean and the river Amur were reached by the mid-seventeenth century. Kamchatka was secured by the end of the century and settlements made on the coast of Alaska and as far down as California in the late eighteenth century; Alaska was finally sold to the United States in 1863. Expansion in the Caucasus started in the late eighteenth century. In 1783 Georgia placed herself under Russian protection and in 1801 was annexed to the Russian empire. The frontier in the south and the east was fluid and undefined and the relationship between military conquest, or some formal acquisition or claim to territory, and actual settlement of the area by Russian colonists was often complex and unclear. This has led historians to talk of 'moving frontiers' rather than clear boundaries as settlers gradually occupied the land secured and protected by the armed forces.

What were these lands like? The extreme north was Arctic tundra. South of this was an evergreen forest zone reaching from the provinces of Archangel and Vologda in the north down as far south as Nizhnii Novgorod on the Volga. This was an area of poor soil in a land of forest, lakes and swamps.

Below this was a belt of mixed forest covering most of central Russia, and extending almost to Kiev in the south-west and Vladimir in the east. South of this zone is the so-called 'black-earth' region which covers most of the Ukraine and the middle Volga area, mainly an area of flat steppe which includes some of the richest agricultural soil in Europe. The lower reaches of the Volga and the north Caucasus are areas of poorer soil and salt-marshes.

THE POPULATION: SIZE, DENSITY AND MOVEMENT

The period 1650–1825 was one of dynamic population growth. Figures before the censuses were taken can be only roughly estimated, but it is thought that the population rose from about 7 million people in 1646 to some 9 million by 1678 (excluding the Left-Bank Ukraine, the Don Cossack area and the non-Russian population of Siberia). The first census was taken in 1719. Census figures are neither complete nor accurate, and in any event only recorded the number of males (of every age from babies to grandfathers), but demonstrate the general growth of population. One historian has estimated the population to have been 15.5 million in 1719; a figure which rose to 18.2 million in 1744, 23.2 million in 1762, 28.4 million in 1782, 37.2 million in 1795, 41.7 million in 1811 and 43.1 million in 1815 (these figures exclude the Caucasus, the Polish provinces and Finland). The population rose throughout Europe in this period but the growth in the Russian empire was the most spectacular.

This increase, of course, was partly due to the acquisition of new territories. The population of the Left-Bank Ukraine was 1.3 million in 1762. Russia acquired over 6.5 million people as a result of the partitions of Poland and acquisitions of territory from the Ottoman empire in the late eighteenth century. The Grand Duchy of Finland (acquired in 1809) had a population of 1.4 million in 1834. Bessarabia (acquired in 1812) had a population at that time of some 240,000; by 1818 the population had risen to approximately 389,000 persons. The Congress Kingdom of Poland (acquired in 1815) contained approximately 3.3 million persons.

The population of the Russian empire was constantly on the move. Tens of thousands of peasants migrated to Siberia and the southern frontiers. The population of the Siberian provinces of Tobol'sk, Tomsk and Irkutsk rose from approximately 60,000 in 1699–1701 to 180,000 in 1719. Between the first census (1719) and the third census (1762–63) the population in the Siberian provinces increased by over 77 per cent while the population of European Russia rose by only 33.8 per cent within the same period. The southern provinces had been subject to intensive settlement; between 1744 and 1762 the population of New Russia (comprising Kherson, Ekaterinslav, Stavropol' and the Don Cossacks) increased by over 140 per cent. Land shortage in the early nineteenth century saw tens of thousands of Russian and Ukrainian peasants on the move; between 1805 and 1810 over 12,000 male adult state peasants settled in New Russia from the Ukrainian provinces. Peter I's new capital, St Petersburg, was founded in 1703 and built on Ingrian marshland on the

Gulf of Finland. Nobles, merchants and workers were first forced and then attracted to the new city. By 1750 the population of the new city numbered 74,383; by 1825 this had risen to 438,112.

Even within the fairly settled central provinces of European Russia there could be considerable fluctuations of population, partly due to natural causes and disasters, such as crop failures or epidemics, but also as a result of resettlement and movement of people. The population of Moscow province, for example, rose from 1,038,340 (both sexes) in 1719 to 1,166,044 in 1744. During this period 31,700 (males) had been recruited to the army, 30,638 people had fled and 54,702 had settled elsewhere. As 435,830 people had also died within the period one has to conclude that either the birth rate was extraordinarily high in this period or, more likely, that the losses of population were made up by constant replenishment from elsewhere. Furthermore, the population of the capitals – Moscow and St Petersburg – and, to a lesser extent, that of provincial towns, varied according to the seasons. The traveller Robert Ker Porter estimated that the population of Moscow decreased by about 50,000 people in the summer as members of the nobility and their households left for their estates. Peasants seeking work elsewhere or trading in local towns also led to constant fluctuation of the village population.

Population density within the empire was uneven. In 1719, the only province with a density of as many as 21–25 persons per square kilometre was Moscow. The next most populous provinces were those of Vladimir, Iaroslavl', Kursk and Tula. The most sparsely populated provinces at the time were those of Voronezh, St Petersburg, Novgorod, Olonets, Viatka, Vyborg, Livonia and Estonia. By 1795 the pattern had undergone some change, partly as a result of the acquisition of more populous territory in the south and west following the partitions of Poland. By this date, the provinces of Moscow, Kursk, Tula, Poltava and Podol'sk now had a density of 26–30 persons per square kilometre, followed by the provinces of Kaluga, Iaroslavl', Riazan', Orel, Vil'na and Kiev with a density of 21–25 persons. The lowest density (1–5 inhabitants per square kilometre) was recorded as before in the provinces of Novgorod, Olonets and Vyborg and also by this date in Perm', Orenburg, Kherson, the Taurida, while Viatka and St Petersburg now had a density of 6–10 inhabitants, and Voronezh, Livonia and Estonia a density of 11–15 inhabitants.

THE POPULATION: ETHNIC DIVERSITY

It has been estimated that the proportion of ethnic Russian population within the borders of 1719 stayed fairly constant at around 69 per cent. Acquisition of new territory, however, in particular through the partitions of Poland and expansion to the south, meant that by the fourth census (1782) the Russian percentage of the population had fallen overall to 48.9 per cent of the total in the empire and by 1833 (the seventh census) to 45.32 per cent. Ethnic Russians, inevitably, were less numerous in the borderlands of the empire, but here the ethnic mix was complex and partly an indication of occupation and status. In the Baltic provinces the peasants were Estonian and Latvian but the noble landowners and much of the urban elite were German (in 1795 ethnic Russians accounted for only 1.1 per cent of the population). Finland in 1834 comprised 86 per cent Finns, 12 per cent Swedes (mainly landowners or fishermen in the coastal areas) and only 2.2. per cent Russians. In Lithuania, the majority of the peasants were Lithuanian and Belorussian, the landowners and some of the peasants were Polish while commercial activities were largely carried out by Jews. Peasants and landowning classes were of the same ethnic group in the Left-Bank Ukraine (Ukrainian) and Bessarabia (Rumanian). In Georgia the upper classes and peasants were Georgian but the towns were dominated by Armenians. Chuvash people could be found mainly in Kazan' province. Finno-Ugric people such as the Mari (or Cheremiss) and Mordvins lived mainly in Simbirsk province, and Komi and Votiaks (or Udmurts) lived mainly in Vologda and Viatka provinces. Tatars could be found in large numbers along the river Volga down to the Caspian Sea. Beyond the Urals were Bashkir tribes (who predominated in Ufa province) and nomadic Kalmyks. As Russians penetrated east into Siberia and on to the coast of what is now Alaska they came into contact with Buriats, Ostiaks, Iakuts, Tungus, Koriaks, Kamchadals and Aleut peoples.

Statistics on ethnic composition have to be used with caution. Quite apart from the questionable accuracy of Russian census figures (and the need to guess the size of the female population), coupled with the particular difficulty of taking proper census returns of nomadic peoples and of inhabitants in distant and inaccessible areas, ethnic divisions were doubtless calculated on a rather simplistic basis (such as religious faith) with no allowance for mixed racial background. Nevertheless, the ethnic diversity of the population is clear. One Soviet demographer's estimate of the ethnic composition of the Russian empire in 1795 is as follows:

Total population:	41,174,800
Russians	20,117,700
Ukrainians	8,163,600
Belorussians	3,402,500
Poles	2,534,000
Finns	900,000
Lithuanians	818,800
Tatars	796,000
Latvians	721,900
Jews	576,200
Estonians	482,700
Chuvash	351,800
Mordvins	345,500
Germans	237,100
Rumanians	210,000
Bashkirs	191,600

Mari	145,200
Karelians	143,500
Votiaks	134,900
Swedes	127,600
Kalmyks	88,100
Komi	52,400
Others	631,700[1]

Russian and Ukrainian migration into the borderlands meant that the proportion of ethnic Russians grew steadily in these areas, to the disadvantage of non-Slav peoples. By the end of the eighteenth century the Russian population of Siberia had risen to almost 70 per cent and that of the North Caucasus had risen from 14.9 per cent in 1762 to over 50 per cent by 1795. In Ufa province the proportion of Bashkirs in the population decreased from 76.6 per cent in 1719 to 47.3 per cent in 1744. As the Russian and Ukrainian settlement of the north Caucasus and New Russia increased, the proportion of Tatars living there fell; in addition many Tatars emigrated to the Ottoman empire. In effect, Tatars in New Russia became confined to the Crimean peninsula.

Contacts with Russians could also cause enormous and irreversible damage to native populations. The native population of Kamchatka, which was estimated in the region of 7,000 in 1737, dropped to 3,000 by 1781, largely as a consequence of exposure to smallpox; by 1820 there were only 1,900 natives left. Death in battle and disease also led to the decline of the Koiak people in the far east of Siberia – from 12,910 in 1698 to 4,880 in the 1760s – and the Aleuts, in North America – from between 19,000 and 25,000 before the arrival of Russians to as few as 2,500 by the 1790s. In the 1770s, in one of the greatest and relatively unknown tragedies to befall an ethnic group, over 150,000 Kalmyks simply migrated east from Russia to China in a mass exodus in a desperate response to the pressure of Russian colonization in the Volga area. Of these almost 100,000 died in the course of the journey.

Non-Russians also settled in Russia. The second half of the eighteenth century and first third of the nineteenth century saw the influx of foreign colonists into Russia (although internal migration of Russian and Ukrainian peasants was far larger than the number of foreign colonists). Some of this migration was spontaneous but some was in response to invitations from the government, as the belief prevailed that an increase of population would lead naturally to increased wealth for the country. Armenians moved to Astrakhan', the Ukraine and the shores of the Caspian Sea, Serbs resettled in the Ukraine, Albanians moved to the Orenburg area and the Ukraine and Greeks and Bulgarians moved into New Russia. In the period 1754–58 approximately 1,500 Montenegrins settled in Russia. Colonists from the West were also encouraged to settle in Russia: between 1762 and 1775 30,623 were recruited, mainly from German lands.

1. V.M. Kabuzan, *Narody Rossii v XVIII veke. Chislennost' i etnicheskii sostav* (Moscow, 1990), p. 230.

Individual foreigners also sought their fortunes in Russia throughout this period in a variety of occupations, including mercenaries, officers in the armed forces, traders, ship-builders, industrialists, skilled artisans, estate managers, gardeners, doctors, tailors, performers and entertainers, tutors and hairdressers. Swedish prisoners of war were forcibly settled in Siberia during the Great Northern War. From the second half of the eighteenth century French tutors, cooks and hairdressers were particularly fashionable. 'Never was a land so overun with Locusts as this is with French,' commented Martha Wilmot tartly in 1806, her distaste doubtless linked to the fact that England had been at war with France.[2] Precise numbers of foreigners in Russia are unknown but they could constitute a significant number, particularly in St Petersburg, where 12,302 foreigners were listed in 1811 and 13,308 in 1821. As the Napoleonic forces entered Russia in 1812 a register was taken of foreigners in the provinces near to the invasion route. In the province of Kaluga 55 foreigners were listed, including Germans, Swiss, Englishmen, Danes, a Dutchman, a Pole, a Spaniard, a Portuguese, a Swede, an Italian and 24 Frenchmen and women. Kaluga was a provincial backwater but even here foreigners had found employment, mainly as tutors and estate managers.

Gypsies could also be found in the countryside, as S. Pleshcheev found in 1792:

About the Don, as well as in almost every part of Russia, from time to time are found gypsies, a race known every where by their cheating and pilfering. They have no fixed residence, but wander continually from one place to another, and exercise the trades of blacksmiths and farriers and horse-dealers, which last they generally do by exchanging instead of selling their horses.[3]

In 1759 Elizabeth passed a decree (which was still in force in 1917) banning gypsies from entering St Petersburg. One estimate in the mid-nineteenth century gave the total number of gypsies in the empire as 47,247.

Settlement and migration led to mixed composition of the areas at the periphery of the empire and on the main rivers. The Volga area was home to various ethnic groups, including Russians, Finno-Ugric peoples and Tatars. The inhabitants of Astrakhan', on the shores of the Caspian Sea, comprised 16,724 Russians, 5,116 Tatars, 2,000 Armenians, 179 Ukrainians, 103 Kalmyks, 89 Indians, 86 Georgians, 84 Germans and 79 Persians in 1783. Julius von Klaproth commented on his journey to the Caucasus in the early nineteenth century that:

The inhabitants of Mosdok are Russians, Armenians, Armenian Catholics, Georgians, Tatars, and Ossetes: there are also many baptized Tscherkessians. Owing to the concourse of so many different nations, most of the inhabitants

2. *The Russian Journals of Martha and Catherine Wilmot 1803–1808*, ed. by the Marchioness of Londonderry and H.M. Hyde (London, 1934), p. 274.
3. Quoted in David M. Crowe, *A History of the Gypsies of Eastern Europe and Russia* (London and New York, 1995), p. 157.

engaged in trade speak not only the Russian but also the Tatar, Armenian, Georgian, Tscherkessian, and Ossetian tongues, and have highly cultivated their capacity for learning languages.[4]

The traveller Edward Clarke characterized the diversity of the social composition of towns at the mouth of the river Don crudely, if wittily, as follows:

> The Tatars were fishing in the river, or driving cattle towards the town; the Turks were smoking in their coffee-houses; the Greeks, a bustling race, were walking about, telling lies, and bartering merchandize; the Cossacks were scampering in all directions on horseback; the Russians, as police officers, were scratching their heads; the Italians were Venetian and Neopolitan sailors; the Calmycks jabbering with each other; the Armenians, both men and women, airing in *droskis*; and the English staring at them all.[5]

THE POPULATION: RELIGIOUS DIVERSITY

Russia regarded itself as an Orthodox Christian country. Indeed, from the sixteenth century Russian Orthodoxy was seen as the only true heir to early Christendom, with Moscow as the 'Third Rome' following the fall of Constantinople in 1453. Precise figures of different faiths cannot be established; one estimate in the early nineteenth century was that there were 36,314,000 Christians (including Russian and Greek Orthodox, Uniates, Catholics and Protestants), 2,830,000 Muslims, 200,000 Jews, 305,000 Buddhists and 635,000 pagan shamanists within the empire. Yet although the vast majority of ethnic Russians and many Ukrainians were Orthodox Christians, the religious complexion of the whole empire was a complex mix in which faith was often a reflection of ethnic background, historical experience and social class. In Estonia, Livonia and Finland, the German and Swedish landowning classes and the Estonian, Livonian and Finnish peasantry in the main shared the Lutheran faith, despite their ethnic and linguistic differences. The mainly Polish landowners of Lithuania and Belorussia were Catholic, while the Lithuanian and Belorussian peasantry could be Catholic, Russian Orthodox or Uniate. Armenians and Georgians of all social classes were Christian, but they had converted before the Russians, and had their own, separate, autocephalous, Christian churches.

The Uniate faith was held by much of the population of the eastern provinces of what had been the Polish-Lithuanian state. In the late sixteenth and early seventeenth century, when these lands had been under Polish rule, these congregations had recognized the authority of the pope but had retained Orthodox liturgy and customs. It has been estimated that the population acquired by Russia through the partitions of Poland in the late eighteenth

4. Julius von Klaproth, *Travels in the Caucasus and Georgia, performed in the years 1807 and 1808, by Command of the Russian Government*, trans. by F. Shoberl (London, 1814), p. 305.
5. Edward Daniel Clarke, *Travels in Various Countries of Europe, Asia and Africa*, vol. I *Russia Tartary and Turkey* (London, 1810), p. 306.

century was approximately 40 per cent Uniate, 38 per cent Catholic, 6.5 per cent Russian Orthodox and 10 per cent Jewish. Precise figures of Uniates cannot be given. In the years 1794–96 alone it is estimated that 1,700,000 Uniates 'converted' to Russian Orthodoxy, but these conversions could have been forced or simply a consequence of Uniates being listed by the authorities as Orthodox. In 1839 the Uniates in the Ukraine were forced to become Russian Orthodox; in 1863 the same obligation was imposed on Uniates in the former Kingdom of Poland.

In the south and east of the empire there was a substantial non-Christian population. Bashkirs and Kazakhs were Sunni Muslims; Tatars on the whole were Shia Muslims. The Chuvash, Mari and Mordvins retained pagan beliefs well into the nineteenth century although many had been converted to Christianity (usually Russian Orthodoxy) or Islam. Most of the Komi and Votiaks had converted to Christianity by the eighteenth century. Buriats (in the vicinity of Lake Baikal) converted from paganism to Tibetan Buddhism in the late eighteenth century. Many of the native peoples of Siberia and the Alaskan coast continued to follow shamanistic pagan beliefs. Foreign settlers in the empire included Lutheran Swedes and Germans, Catholic Italians and French and Orthodox Greeks, Serbs and Bulgarians.

Jews had been resident in small numbers in the Russian lands from the mid-seventeenth century. They lived mostly in the Ukraine although a small Jewish community became established in Moscow. The government legislated to contain and control the Jewish population within the empire's borders. Both Catherine I (1725–27) and Elizabeth (1741–62) attempted to ban Jews from Russia; one estimate is that 35,000 Jews were banished in 1741. However, as a consequence of the three partitions of Poland, Russia acquired a far larger Jewish population, estimated by historians at anything between 155,000 and 900,000 persons, but probably closer to the lower figure. The empire acquired a further *c.* 250,000 Jews after the establishment of the Congress Kingdom of Poland in 1815. There was also a substantial Jewish population in Bessarabia (11.3 per cent of the population in 1863). In 1854, the Jewish population of the whole empire was estimated as 1,060,132.

Russian Orthodoxy was the main Christian religion in the Russian empire. But the Russian Orthodox Church had itself undergone a schism in 1667 (see Chapter 10). Those who dissociated themselves from the official Church and its liturgical reforms were known as Old Believers. Numbers of adherents to the Old Belief are impossible to gauge accurately. At times of persecution many people kept their faith privately while at other times some may have falsely claimed to be Old Believers to avoid recruitment (Old Believers paid a tax instead). A proper attempt to calculate the numbers of Old Believers was only made in the second half of the nineteenth century. The Ministry of the Interior quoted a figure of 8,220,000 Old Believers in 1863, but some historians regard this as a significant underestimate. P.N. Miliukov thought the real figure was nearer to 20 million by 1900. Old Believers were in the main found on the periphery of the empire, in the far north, Siberia, the Don Cossack

15

region and the Starodub district of Poland, but there were also substantial communities in Moscow.

In addition to the Old Belief, several small sects existed in Russia. The Dukhobor community (the 'spirit wrestlers', a priestless sect of 'spiritual' Christians) established communities in Tambov in the late eighteenth century. In the reign of Alexander I (1801–25) the Dukhobors were resettled in the province of Taurida (in the Crimea). In 1827 it was estimated that this community numbered 3,985 (800 households) in nine villages. Other sects included the Molokany or (or 'milk-drinkers', so-called because they drank milk on fast days), Khlysty ('flagellants') and Skoptsy ('self-castrators'). The membership of these groups cannot be ascertained accurately but in 1863 the Ministry of the Interior calculated that there were 110,000 molokans and dukhobors and 110,000 Khlysty and Skoptsy.

SOCIAL COMPOSITION: DEFINITIONS AND NUMBERS

The idea of a social estate with a defined legal status was unknown in seventeenth-century Muscovy. There were distinct social categories in pre-Petrine Russia but the groups were so numerous and complex that they defied simple classification. One Muscovite lexicon listed nearly 500 separate social categories to denote different ranks and statuses. The Law Code, or *Ulozhenie*, of 1649 contributed to the definition of social groups in that it institutionalized relationships between serf and master and attempted to designate the social categories which were allowed to trade. The actions of the rulers in the eighteenth century, however, served more decisively to define broader social categories. The major social groups which emerged are defined below. The number of people in each social group is difficult to estimate accurately, particularly before the first census, which took place in 1719, but some conclusions can be drawn about the relative size of groups and the extent to which changes took place during the period under review.

Nobles

The definition of the Russian nobility combines ancestry and service to the state. The oldest noble families were descended from the medieval princes who submitted to Muscovite rule or who were members of the personal retinue of the Muscovite rulers. In the second half of the seventeenth century the 'aristocracy' could be defined as those nobles (mostly, but not all, princes) who comprised the three ranks of nobles which were represented in the Boiar Duma (the boiar council), that is: the boiars, the senior and highest-ranking aristocrats; the *okol'nichie* (a word deriving from '*okolo*', or near, implying a person near the ruler), ranking immediately below the boiars; the *dumnye dvoriane* (or duma nobles). These magnates advised the tsar, occupied the highest posts in the army and supervised the administration and judicial organs of the state. Immediately below the noble elite was a large number of courtiers, including *stol'niki*, usually the sons of boiars, who carried out court, military or administrative tasks and the *striapchie* (estimated to number in the region of 800 men in the seventeenth century), who carried out miscellaneous duties at court. The lower ranks of the military servitors were, in turn, divided between those who were registered and mustered for military service in Moscow and those who were on 'provincial lists', whose status was lower. These military servitors were termed the *pomeshchiki* and received their land (their *pomest'e*) in order to enable them to carry out their military service to the tsar.

Until the late seventeenth century an elaborate system existed of 'placing by precedence' (*mestnichestvo*) according to clan, whereby nobles could refuse to serve under someone considered to be of inferior family, or clan, standing. The system led to many conflicts between members of the leading families as clan honour was seen to be at stake. Between 1613 and 1689 the 427 men who served in the Boiar Duma accounted for 294 precedence disputes (although the incidence declined after 1667). Historians have disputed whether *mestnichestvo* was more in the interest of the state or the aristocracy; some have seen it as an obstacle to the type of corporate development of the nobility which took place in western and central Europe. In practice, however, *mestnichestvo* did not prevent the rise of talented newcomers, particularly in the military sphere, and the tsar could always declare that appointments were exceptions and so avoid clashes of precedence. The aristocracy agreed to the abolition of *mestnichestvo* in 1682 but this did not reflect, or lead to, any lessening of their status vis-à-vis the rest of the nobility.

By the end of the reign of Peter I, and following the introduction of the Table of Ranks in 1722, some of these distinctions had become blurred and the collective term for the nobility – at first the *shliakhetstvo* and then the *dvorianstvo* – became more common. The definition and status of the nobility remained a complex mix of service and birth (discussed more fully in Chapter 3). The Charter to the Nobles in 1785 defined nobility as a hereditary status conferred by the ruler as a reward for service. The Charter classified nobles into six groups by a complex formula which included the means by which noble status had been acquired, nature of title and ancient lineage as follows: i) those whose noble status was due to a personal grant by the ruler within the last hundred years; ii) those whose status came through military service; iii) those whose status came through civil service; iv) those whose noble status was of foreign origin; v) those with titles of prince, count and baron; vi) those whose nobility had been established for more than a century. The last three groups regarded themselves as socially superior to those nobles whose status was acquired more recently as a result of their military or civil service.

The censuses in the eighteenth and early nineteenth centuries were primarily concerned with recording the number of the *tax-paying* males. This did not, of course, include the nobility, which means that it is difficult to be precise about its size. It is thought that the boiar aristocracy numbered some 1,000 males in the first half of the seventeenth century, a number which probably increased in the second half of the century. It was estimated in 1700 that the nobility numbered about 15,000 men, a figure which increased to over 37,000 in 1744 and which reached over 50,000 in the 1750s. Soviet demographers have estimated that numbers of male nobles in the empire (not including the lands of the former Poland-Lithuania) rose sharply from 108,255 in 1782 to 362,574 in 1795 and reached 429,226 in 1816. This meant a rise in the percentage of nobles in the total population from 0.79 to 2.05 per cent over this period. This meant that the nobility was proportionally larger than the nobility in Sweden or France but was small compared with other eastern European states such as Poland and Hungary.

The rise can be explained partly by additions from other social groups (see Chapter 2) but was mainly due to the assimilation of non-Russian nobles into the *dvorianstvo*, particularly in the late eighteenth and early nineteenth centuries. About 600,000 families claimed noble status in the partitioned lands of Poland-Lithuania (*c*.80,000 in the Belorussian lands acquired at the first partition); this compared with about 150,000 noble families in Russia in 1795. Even in the mid-nineteenth century the majority of the nobles in the Russian empire were Polish. The introduction of Russian institutions of provincial administration in 1775 and the Charter to the Nobles in 1785 made membership of the Russian *dvorianstvo* attractive for non-Russian nobles. In the Ukraine before the 1780s the elite wealthy magnates were known by the Polish term for the nobility, the *szlachta*, and numbered some 2,000 males. In 1781, an equalization of Ukrainian with Russian noble ranks took place in order to enable the Ukrainian nobility to take up posts created solely for the nobility in the provinces after the provincial reform of 1775. After the promulgation of the Charter to the Nobles the Ukrainian nobility was in effect co-opted into the Russian nobility in order to share these privileges and advance their careers. Ukrainians were notorious for their false claims of nobility. When Governor-General M.N. Krechetnikov insisted in 1795 that the credentials for nobility should be checked, almost half the Ukrainian nobles lost their noble status and were obliged to join the tax-paying classes.

The same pattern occurred for other non-Russian nobles. The Tatar nobles in the Crimea became members of the new Crimean Assembly of Nobility after 1785, and the Crimean nobility was made equivalent to Russian nobles, with the same privileges. In 1793 the traveller P.S. Pallas listed 570 male nobles and 465 female nobles in the Crimea. The Georgian nobility was strictly hierarchical, with royal princes at the apex, then clans of princes, below which was the vassal gentry (*aznauri*) who were dependent on the princes. At the time of annexation in 1801 approximately 5 per cent of the population of Georgia was noble. In 1827 all Georgian nobles and princes became members of the Russian nobility upon proof of their nobility. The Bessarabian aristocracy retained their privileges after annexation in 1812 but were given parity with Russian nobles. It was in the interest of the lesser nobility in Bessarabia in particular to claim membership of the Russian *dvorianstvo* in order to rise socially. The first list of the Bessarabian nobility in 1818 contained over 500 names; within a year 35 more families had been added. But following the examination of certificates of nobility in 1821, the number of noble families was reduced to 170.

Peasants

Serfs, or seigneurial peasants, were peasants who lived on the estates of a landowner (mostly noble). The development of serfdom is outside the chronological scope of this book. The Law Code or *Ulozhenie* of 1649 in the reign of Alexis (1645–76) institutionalized serfdom by abolishing the time limit for the recovery of fugitive peasants and by ending all freedom of movement for the peasant family. The right of the noble landowner to move his peasants within his properties was confirmed (initially landowners were not allowed to transfer peasants from service estates to hereditary estates but this distinction became meaningless in the eighteenth century). He had also almost full judicial control over his peasants (discussed more fully in Chapter 3).

Soviet demographers estimated that between 1678 and 1719 the number of male serfs rose from 2.3 million to just over 3.5 million. It is thought that by 1795 male serfs numbered 9,787,802. The proportion of serfs within the total population reached its apex at the time of the third census (1762–64) when 52.2 per cent of the *Russian* population was so classified; the proportion fell to 49.5 per cent in 1795. Serf ownership increased in the black-earth lands in particular during this period. The preponderance of serfs varied from province to province; it was highest in the central provinces (72 per cent of the inhabitants of Moscow province, 77 per cent in Smolensk province), lower further away from the centre (60 per cent in Nizhnii Novgorod province, 45 per cent in Voronezh, 32 per cent in Kazan') and virtually non-existent in Siberia. To a small extent the tsars contributed to the extension of serfdom by gifts of peasants to individuals. Between 1682 and 1710 Peter I granted over 170,000 serfs to individuals. According to the figures of the historian Semevskii, Catherine II granted a total of 398,973 peasants to individuals, most of whom were peasants from confiscated Church or noble lands in the former Polish lands granted after the partitions of Poland, although there is one recorded case of state peasants in Belorussia being transferred as serfs. Paul I gave away 80,000 peasants on the date of his coronation.[6] More significantly, the extension of Russian administrative and fiscal structures into non-Russian parts of the empire led in some cases to the *de facto* introduction of serfdom. Taxation of the peasantry in the Ukraine in the second half of the eighteenth century served to restrict their mobility and in effect enserfed them by 1783.

Court peasants lived on land owned by the imperial court. A separate category of 'sovereign's peasants', *gosudarevy krest'iane*, covered peasants on lands which were the personal possession of the tsars or their immediate family. From 1797, these peasants were known as 'appanage' peasants after Paul I

---

6. V.I. Semevskii, 'Razdacha naselennykh imenii pri Ekaterine II', *Otechestvennye zapiski* 13 (1877), pp. 204–27.

(1796–1801) set up an Appanage Department to deal with their affairs. The number of male court peasants rose slowly from 509,484 in 1719 to 520,840 in 1795. So-called 'falconers' from Vologda province supplied the court with falcons and numbered 1,079 in the 1780s. They were merged with other appanage peasants in the reign of Alexander I.

The term 'state peasants' was used to define several categories of peasants who were not seigneurial serfs; they lived on state land and were under the administration of the state, or treasury. The proportion of state peasants grew from 19 per cent in 1724 (1,049,287 males) to 40 per cent in 1781–82 (3,872,862 males) and then dropped back to 35 per cent in 1816 (5,774,823 males). Fluctuation in the size of this category was largely due to changes in the definition of which groups constituted state peasants. The 'true' state peasants were the so-called 'black' peasants (chernososhnye) in the north and Siberia, who lived on state lands where there had never been noble landowners (mainly in the provinces of Olonets, Archangel, Viatka, Vologda, Perm' and along the White Sea coast). Their numbers were estimated at 627,027 males in the 1760s.

In the course of the eighteenth and early nineteenth centuries it became common for smaller categories of non-seigneurial peasants to be classified as state peasants, including the following: 'servitors' (sluzhilye liudi), that is, descendants of low-ranking servitors, mainly found on what had been the southern frontiers of Muscovy (estimated at 40,000 males in 1762); postdrivers or coachmen (iamshchiki), a category of people who lived in villages near main roads and whose responsibility it was to supply horses for the post roads (numbering 57,105 males in 1806); share croppers (polovniki), who were landless peasants in Vologda province in the north who enjoyed some rights of movement (numbering 14,847 males in 1744 but only 11,277 males in 1762); ship forest peasants (iashmany), created by Peter I from tribesmen to work in the Admiralty forests (numbering 120,136 males in 1837); peasants who hauled boats through rivers in the north (numbering 1,386 in Novgorod province and 171 in Archangel province in 1835); servitors in monasteries and archbishops' residences (estimated as 4,000 males in 1764 and 5,091 males in 1853); freed serfs and so-called 'free tillers' who had been freed on a voluntary basis by noble landowners in 1803 in the reign of Alexander I (numbering some 47,153 persons in the early nineteenth century); foreign colonists (numbering 119,637 in 1835); various categories of free peasants in the land acquired as a result of the three partitions of Poland; veteran soldiers and their families; prisoners of war. Peasants in the Crimea were incorporated into the state peasantry after annexation in 1783.

The government also deliberately created new categories of state peasants. The most important of these were church and monastic peasants, who lived on land belonging to religious institutions, whose holdings were particularly large in northern European Russia. In 1759, it has been estimated there were almost 900,000 male church peasants divided as follows: 673,974 on monastic lands, 162,751 on the property of archbishops, 32,778 on synodal lands, and

24,560 attached to churches.[7] Church peasants became in effect state peasants after the secularization of Church lands in 1764, although they were classified as a separate category of state peasants: so-called 'economic' peasants. In 1786, the Economic College which handled the affairs of these peasants was closed down and the peasants became officially state peasants. Numbers of church/economic peasants rose sharply from 813,714 in 1719 to 1,465,469 in 1795. Of less significance were the so-called 'stable peasants' (*koniushennye*), who were reclassified as state peasants in 1786. These peasants were originally obliged to maintain 40,000 horses in the vicinity of Moscow in the second half of the seventeenth century and numbered between 30,000 and 40,000 males between 1738 and 1794. In 1783, during the reign of Catherine II, gypsies came to be regarded as state peasants, which meant they were subject not only to the same tax obligations but also to the same restrictions on movement. When, in 1794, a gypsy family attempted to register as townspeople in Moscow, permission was refused on the basis of this decree and the family were registered as economic (state) peasants in Moscow province.

Another group which came to be regarded as state peasants although its members vigorously opposed this, was the *odnodvortsy*, literally 'one-homesteaders'. These were the descendants of petty service men on what had been the lawless southern frontiers of Muscovy in the sixteenth and seventeenth centuries. They regarded themselves as nobles as they were also a military service class, owned land (albeit very small plots), and, in some cases, owned serfs, but their low social status was confirmed when Peter I made them subject to the poll tax, which classified them, in effect, as state peasants. The ambiguous status of this group can be seen in a law of 1823 which stated that 'the *odnodvortsy* form a middle estate between the nobles and the peasants, having the right to own estates of the former and the recruit obligations of the latter'.[8] It has been estimated that the number of *odnodvortsy* rose from 0.2 million people at the end of the seventeenth century to 0.3 million by 1719. By the beginning of the 1730s it was estimated that there were 394,000 male *odnodvortsy* and former serving people, most of whom could be found in the provinces of Voronezh, Kiev and Astrakhan'; in 1762–66 they numbered some 510,000 males. By the 1850s their numbers had risen to something in the region of 1,900,000 males.

Later in the eighteenth century, Cossacks also came to be viewed by the government as state peasants as they became subject to the poll tax. Cossacks were ethnically Ukrainian or Russian, and were originally mainly fugitive peasants, who, from the sixteenth century, had formed semi-autonomous military communities on lands between the Tatars and the Polish-Lithuanian

7. A.I. Komissarenko, 'Absoliutistskoe gosudarstvo Rossii i dukhovnye zemel'nye sobstvenniki v bor'be za zemliu, krest'ian i renty', in *Sotsial'no-politicheskoe i pravovoe polozhenie krest'ianstva v dorevoliutsionnoi Rossii* (Voronezh, 1983), p. 130.
8. Thomas Esper, 'The Odnodvortsy and the Russian Nobility', *Slavonic and East European Review* 45 (1967), p. 126.

Commonwealth. Cossacks 'defended' the borders by conducting raids against Tatars, the Ottoman empire and Poland. The Cossacks of the Hetmanate were divided into three groups: the rank and file (*vyborni*), poorer 'helpers' (*pidpomichnyky*), whose duties were auxiliary, and hired labour (*pidsusidky*), comprising Cossacks without land. In the 1760s there were approximately 176,000 (adult male) rank and file, 198,000 helpers and 80,000 labourers. To the south-east of the Hetmanate was the Sloboda Ukraine (*Slobodskaia Ukraina*), of which the major town was Khar'kov, which had its own form of Cossack self-administration. Beyond the borders of these settled lands were the 'Land of the Don Cossacks', the capital of which was Cherkassk, which had a population of about 200,000 in 1775, and the Zaporozhian host based on the left and right banks of the river Dnieper. In the 1760s the Zaporozhian population comprised between 18,000 and 22,000 adult males, of whom the majority were Cossacks proper and the rest *pospolity*, in effect people who were 'subjects' of the Cossacks. (The Zaporozhian host was dissolved in 1775.) Further east, the Iaik Cossacks were settled on the river Iaik (renamed the river Ural after the Pugachev rebellion); they could raise a force of about 12,000 Cossacks in the 1760s. Cossacks had settled in the Kuban' area of the north Caucasus from the sixteenth century; by the late eighteenth century this frontier was defended by the Black Sea host (made up of former Zaporozhian Cossacks) settled betwen the Eia and the Kuban', the Grebentsy host on the Kizliar-Mozdok line and the Terek host. There were also Cossacks stationed on the Volga, in Astrakhan' province and in Siberia.

The historian Richard Hellie has estimated that as many as 10 per cent of the population of Muscovy in 1649 were slaves (discussed further in Chapter 3). These slaves included Tatars or military captives but most were Russians who had fallen into slavery through debt. During the eighteenth century slavery largely disappeared, including the category of *kholop*, serf slaves or bondsmen, most of whom worked as domestics for the lord. Landless peasants or cotters (*bobyli*), however, remained in Russian villages in the eighteenth and even the early nineteenth centuries, but the equalization of their dues meant that they were regarded legally by the state as serfs or state peasants and not as a separate social or legal category.

The number of inhabitants, and their families, attached to and working in industrial enterprises increased sharply in this period. These people included state peasants and serfs who chose to work for a limited period in factories or mines to earn wages with which to pay their fiscal obligations to the state, runaway serfs and also state peasants, and their families, who had been temporarily or permanently attached to private or state enterprises (as opposed to being assigned to the owner of the enterprise). This latter group were termed 'assigned peasants' (*pripisnye*) (renamed possessional serfs in the early nineteenth century) and were obliged to work in the factory or to supply necessary raw materials, though they remained legally state peasants. Statistics on the social composition of workers in factories are particularly unreliable, because it is often impossible to distinguish between different categories of workers or to define sensibly the category of 'freely hired' labour. This could, in practice, include serfs who had been sent to the factory by their owners against their will, and state peasant and serf workers who had voluntarily chosen temporary employment as well as what would normally be understood as a genuine freely hired proletariat class. It has been estimated that in the mid-eighteenth century there were in the region of 50,000 workers and masters (including their families) in the Ural factories alone. One source concerning assigned peasants throughout the whole country indicated that there was a rise from 87,253 persons (both sexes) in 1744 to 188,594 in 1762, 263,899 in 1782 and 312,218 in 1795.

Townspeople *ref. p. 19*

The Law Code (*Ulozhenie*) of 1649 defined townsmen as those employed in trade and artisan activities within the town, with the exclusion of slaves. The word *posad* was used at this time to designate the whole legally defined, tax-paying, urban community. This designation was, however, a general term and in the second half of the seventeenth century the *posad* itself was split according to wealth into three groups – the 'best', the 'middle' and the 'younger', or poorer, *posad* members. But above these groups was a superior category – *gosti* or wealthy merchants. In 1691, 8.5 per cent of shop owners in the town of Iaroslavl' were classified as *gosti* and 79.8 per cent as ordinary townspeople. In Moscow in 1705 there were 27 families classified as *gosti*; this had declined to 10 by 1713. Below the *gosti* was a second category of wealthy merchants – the *gostinaia sotnia*. The numbers of members of the *gostinaia sotnia* in Moscow declined over the eighteenth century from over 80 in 1713–17 to 31 families by the end of the century.

The government constantly redefined urban society and introduced new legal and social categories. Peter I allowed the *gosti* to decline and recategorized urban society into two 'guilds' in 1721. These were not guilds in a west European sense but a broad division based as much on wealth as on occupation. Merchants (*kuptsy*), bankers, silversmiths and in general the higher echelons of urban society joined the first guild, while minor traders and artisans made up the second guild. The other, poorer and less skilled members of the town community were now known as the *posad*. The titles of *gosti* and *gostinaia sotnia* were retained but these wealthy merchants also had to register in the first guild. By the late 1720s merchants were divided into three guilds according to their declared capital, a division which was confirmed by a decree of 1742 in the reign of Elizabeth (with increased requirements of declared capital; from 10 roubles to enter the third guild to over 100 roubles to join the first guild).

Further significant changes were made to the categorization of the urban community in the reign of Catherine II. The taxation reform of 1775 increased the capital requirements for registration into the three guilds of the merchantry (500–1,000 roubles for the third guild; 1,000–10,000 for the second; over 10,000 roubles for the first). The Charter to the Towns of 1785 made a major attempt to redefine the townspeople who made up the urban community or 'society' (*obshchestvo gradskoe*). They were to register in the 'book of town inhabitants' in six categories (in parallel with the six categories of nobles registered in the Book of the Nobility) as follows: i) 'real citizens' (*nastoiashchie gorodovye obyvateli*), who owned property in the town; ii) merchants (*kuptsy*) registered in three merchant guilds according to their declared capital (now set at 1,000–5,000 roubles for registration in the third guild; 5,000–10,000 roubles for the second and 10,000–50,000 roubles for the first guild); iii) artisans (*meshchane*) registered in craft guilds (*tsekhi*); iv) foreign nationals and merchants from other towns; v) so-called eminent citizens (*imenitye grazhdane*), comprising those with over 50,000 roubles capital (that is, more than merchants in the first guild), bankers, shipowners, wholesale traders, townsmen who had served as elected town officials, artists and academics; vi) members of the *posad*, now defined as those who lived and worked in the town but lacked the skill or capital to register as artisans or merchants. Decline in membership of the merchant guilds in the early nineteenth century led to a further guild reform in 1824, which, among other things, obliged trading nobles to register in the first guild and made clearer distinctions concerning occupations between members of the third guild and the *posad* community.

The changes in definition of the meaning of the *posad*, in the amount of declared capital for membership of the merchant guilds, and in the qualifications for membership of the urban community in general make it impossible to draw meaningful conclusions from statistics on the size of each urban category. The number of merchants, in particular, decreased after Catherine's laws of 1775 and 1785 increased the capital qualifications for registration in the three guilds. (The composition of the urban community is discussed more fully in Chapter 7.)

The urban community as a whole grew slowly during this period. In the seventeenth century it rose from 22,861 persons (in 8,938 households) in 1646 to 88,768 persons (31,484 households) in 1678. The number of *males* in the urban community rose from 295,799 in 1719 to 355,340 in 1744 and then fell to 321,582 in 1762. From the late eighteenth century numbers of urban males rose steadily to 421,502 in 1782, 771,317 in 1795, 892,900 in 1811, 1,208,600 in 1815 and reached 1,690,000 in 1833. In percentage terms, this constituted a rise from 4.1 per cent of the total population in 1719 to 6.6 per cent in 1833. The largest urban communities in 1744 were as follows: Moscow, 13,458; Iaroslavl', 7,255; Kaluga, 6,416; Olonets, 3,912; Volkhov, 3,641; Orel, 3,632; St Petersburg, 3,741; Simbirsk 3,348; Eniseisk, 3,347; Kursk, 3,282; Tobol'sk, 3,184; Kazan', 3,014; Viaz'ma 2,940; Tver' 2,839; Tula, 2,726, Vologda, 2,670. The number of towns rose in Russia from 394 in 1745 to 507 in 1802 (over 216 new towns were founded in the period 1775 to 1785); by the mid-nineteenth century there were something in the region of 700 towns in the empire, the majority of them with fewer than 5,000 inhabitants.

The census material, however, only relates to the urban population as legally defined by its tax-paying and other obligations. This is misleading for in most towns in the empire these inhabitants could often be outnumbered by temporary or permanent residents of other social estates. Many towns had a garrison of soldiers, and ports, of course, had sailors. Provincial capitals and larger towns included resident nobles and their domestic servants. Administrative centres attracted large numbers of officials and clerks, while all towns included large numbers of peasants (see Chapter 7). Indeed, some towns had very few residents employed in traditional urban occupations.

Orthodox clergy

The Russian Orthodox clergy was divided into the black, or monastic, clergy, and the white, parish clergy. Bishops were drawn from the black clergy. There are no statistics on the numbers of clergy in the late seventeenth century, although it is thought that there were about 13,000 churches in Russia in the last quarter of the seventeenth century, a number which had increased to about 17,000 by 1722. In 1764, it has been estimated that there were 67,111 male members of the white clergy (priests, deacons and church servants). In 1824, there were 34,095 priests and archpriests, 15,081 deacons and 59,740 sacristans. In the seventeenth century 220 monasteries were founded. But the number of monasteries declined from 1,200 in 1700 to only 452 in 1800. Between 1724 and 1738 the number of monks, nuns and novices decreased from 25,207 to 14,282, mostly because of the restrictions on the number of people joining such communities. In 1825 there were 476 communities (377 monasteries and 99 convents) in which there lived 3,272 monks, 2,015 novice monks, 1,882 nuns and 3,456 novice nuns.

Raznochintsy and other 'social et ceteras'

A social category which is difficult to define is the *raznochintsy*, or 'people of different ranks', a term which came into use from about 1720, described by one historian as 'a sort of social *et cetera*'.[9] Early decrees concerning the *raznochintsy* concentrated on what they were *not* – for example not peasants (1718), not soldiers' children, peasants, postdrivers, craftsmen, slaves, foreigners or merchants (1736). Two decrees in 1724 defined the *raznochintsy* more precisely, one as lower ranking officials and the other as retired soldiers and they were described in a statute on bankruptcies in 1800 as 'lower court, civil, and retired military servants and the like, who are not enrolled in the merchant trading state'. Unranked and low-ranking officials in Tambov and Voronezh provinces asked if they could wear official dress and carry swords to distinguish them from the 'other *raznochintsy*'.[10] In practice, the *raznochintsy* were regarded as a useful 'catch-all' category which could include those who were

9. Christopher Becker, '*Raznochintsy*: The Development of the Word and the Concept', *American Slavonic and East European Review* 18, 1 (1959), p. 64.
10. Elise Kimmerling Wirtschafter, *Structures of Society. Imperial Russia's 'People of Various Ranks'* (DeKalb, 1994), p. 97.

hard to classify in other ways (see Chapter 2), and in official records at various times included children in almshouses, runaways, immigrants and even executioners and their children! After 1818 the *raznochintsy* included the children of personal nobles (that is, nobles who had not achieved the military or civil rank required for hereditary noble status; see Chapter 3). Teachers in national schools after 1786 (who were established as a separate social category, with ranks, by Catherine II) became categorized as *raznochintsy* in the nineteenth century. In the second half of the nineteenth century the *raznochintsy* became a general term to describe the non-noble intelligentsia.

The vagueness of the definition of the *raznochintsy*, and variations in applications of the term by census collectors, make it difficult to apply statistical material on this group usefully (the group was listed as a category in the first three censuses but not thereafter until the census of 1811). This might explain why statistics vary so much – according to church records the number of *raznochintsy* (both sexes) in towns in European Russia rose from 157,700 in 1737 to 897,000 in 1796 and then fell to 794,000 in 1825. Census material (males only) lists 74,000 *raznochintsy* in 1737–44, 298,600 in 1782 and 448,700 in 1811. In the city of St Petersburg alone 35,002 *raznochintsy* (of both sexes) were listed as residents in 1801 and 66,554 in 1811.[11]

The size of the army is difficult to estimate accurately. It is thought that by the 1680s the army comprised some 200,000 men, of whom about half were 'new model' infantry and cavalry forces, some 40,000 were privileged servitors and their dependants, some 20,000–30,000 were *strel'tsy* (although other estimates suggest there were as many as 55,000 *strel'tsy* in 1681), some 15,000 were Cossacks and some 7,000 were artillerymen and native troops. The reforms of Peter I created a standing army, which has been estimated to number about 100,000 men by 1720, with an additional 70,000 garrison troops and irregulars (Cossacks and native troops). The regular army (including garrison troops) is thought to have numbered around 200,000 men by 1725, supplemented by irregulars numbering some 85,000 men. By 1765 the army has been estimated at 303,529 men, which increased to 413,473 in 1795, 446,059 in 1801 and 597,000 in 1812. In 1725, the Baltic fleet of 34 ships was manned by 25,000 officers and men; by 1812 the Baltic fleet comprised 28,408 sailors, officers and coastal artillery, while the Black Sea fleet numbered some 12,000 sailors and officers.

Soldiers and sailors who survived service (which was only limited to 25 years in 1793), or who were invalided out of the armed forces, had the right to choose their own social status; in practice most became state peasants although some entered the ranks of the *raznochintsy*. Boys born after their father had become a soldier were considered as a separate social group of 'soldiers' children' (*soldatskie deti*). The state assumed that they would serve (which explains their exclusion from the poll tax), and obliged them to attend garrison schools, in

11. A.I. Kopanev, 'Naselenie Peterburga ot kontsa XVIII v do 1861', in *Ocherki istorii Leningrada* (Moscow-Leningrad, 1955) vol. I, p. 513.

the hope that this would lessen the burden of recruitment on other social groups. The number of soldiers' children in garrison school rose only slowly in the eighteenth century, from 6,002 in 1758 to 9,508 in 1763 and reaching 16,000 in 1801. Their numbers dramatically increased after Alexander I set up military colonies (see Chapter 2). The children of soldiers and peasants who had been obliged to settle in these colonies were supposed to form future military cadres and were termed 'cantonists' (*voennye kantonisty*). By 1822 there were 22,000 cantonists and 65,000 pupils in garrison schools; at the time of Alexander's death in 1825 it was estimated that 154,000 cantonists lived in military colonies. The legal category of soldiers' children was not abolished until 1856 when children were returned to their parents and relatives as members of the tax-paying population.

she's good at defining groups + cautious in estimating numbers

CHAPTER 2

The social estates: structure and composition

The concept of a social estate as a legally defined social group developed only slowly in Russia. In the second quarter of the nineteenth century the word *soslovie* came into use as a word to define a social group which incorporated some sense of a legal social estate with rights and obligations. By the late nineteeth century the word *soslovie* had taken on the negative connotations of 'caste' as some liberal contemporaries regarded the rigidity, as they perceived it, of Russia's social structure as a barrier to modern liberal development. In this chapter three major questions are posed concerning the Russian estate structure. First, how easy was it to move from one estate to another? Second, to what extent were some social groups set apart from this structure? Third, how homogeneous were the main social estates?

THE RUSSIAN NOBILITY – AN OPEN ESTATE?

The Russian nobility was never a closed estate. Exceptional service to the tsar led to ennoblement and the award of titles. The title of 'Prince' was procured by Peter I in 1705 from the Holy Roman Empire for his favourite, Aleksandr Menshikov. In 1741, Elizabeth ennobled 364 non-noble guards in the Pre-obrazhenskii regiment for their part in bringing her to power. The following year Mikhailo Serdiukov was ennobled for the rather less spectacular feat of 'clearing out the river Msta, and for constructing locks and other things'.[1] A small number of wealthy merchants and factory owners acquired noble status for themselves, or for their descendants. Some were ennobled by royal decree, and in the early eighteenth century these included A.G. Stroganov, who owned salt mines, and P.P. Shafirov, the son of a Jewish merchant from Smolensk who converted to Orthodoxy. A.A. Goncharov, originally an artisan from Kaluga, amassed enormous wealth as an industrialist and was ennobled by

---

1. A. Romanovich-Slavatinskii, *Dvorianstvo v Rossii ot nachala XVIII veka do otmena krepostnogo prava* (St Petersburg, 1870; reprint The Hague, 1968), p. 29.

Catherine II. During her reign, nobility was also granted to the merchant and manufacturing families of the Lukins, Khlebnikovs, Matveevs and Zubkovs. The manufacturer M.A. Miliutin was ennobled in 1814. Passage to the nobility through this route could, however, be a slow and painful business unless the individual concerned had the personal support and patronage of the ruler. The factory owner, A.F. Turchaninov, was granted only *personal* nobility by Elizabeth but had to wait until 1787, when he was 70 years old, to achieve *hereditary* nobility and be registered in the Nizhnii Novgorod nobility.

It was rather easier for wealthy merchants to acquire nobility through their children and grandchildren, either by the military service of their male heirs or through marriage of, mainly, their female heirs. The factory owner, P.I. Osokin, petitioned unsuccessfully for ennoblement in the 1750s, but his son achieved nobility through military service, retiring with the rank of *podpolkovnik* (lieutenant-colonel, rank 7). L.I. Dolgov, originally a Kaluga merchant, became an eminent citizen in Moscow and then President of the Moscow Town Magistracy in the late eighteenth century; three of his daughters married nobles and both his sons entered the guards. Marriages between daughters of low-ranking nobles and merchant sons were much rarer (as, of course, it resulted in the loss of the noble surname) but did take place. Nataliia Mezentseva, for example, daughter of a *podporuchik* (second lieutenant, rank 12), married the Moscow third-guild merchant, T.I. Vlasov.

Administrative service provided a path to ennoblement for a small number of commoners, although some were already wealthy individuals. The merchant and *gost'*, Il'ia Isaev, became President of the Riga Magistracy in 1727 and Vice-President of the Commerce College in 1731. By 1741 he had acquired the rank of *statskii sovetnik* (state councillor, rank 5) and hereditary nobility. His son obtained personal nobility through civil service (President of the Chief Magistracy); his daughter married an admiral. Both of Isaev's grandsons entered military service and one of them rose to become a brigadier. S.S. Kop'ev, the son of a clerk, became a translator in the diplomatic corps and owned 74 serfs by 1754. His son was born before Kop'ev had acquired hereditary nobility (and therefore was strictly speaking still a commoner) but had reached the rank of *nadvornyi sovetnik* (court councillor, rank 7) by 1762 when he retired to live off his father's estates which he had inherited.

It was always harder, however, for commoners to rise through the administration than for children of noble birth. Attempts were made after the inauguration of the Table of Ranks (see Chapter 3) to reserve certain posts in the administration for people of noble birth. In 1724 Peter I reserved the post of secretary for nobles; in 1739 a decree forbade the appointment of *voevody* (military governors) in Siberian towns from non-nobles. These restrictions were lifted after 1762, when Peter III allowed non-noble clerical staff who had served for eight years as *kanseliaristy* (clerks) to acquire officer rank and become nobles. Commoners had to serve for a longer period in each grade before promotion, which not only gave a privileged position to the nobility but at the same time ensured the state some much-needed continuity of personnel at lower clerical grades. Clerical staff of modest noble origin could rise rapidly. F.S. Golubtsev, for example, inherited only 14 male serfs, started as a copyist in 1721 and rose in his career to a *statskii sovetnik* (state councillor, rank 5); his grandson, F.A. Golubtsev, became the Minister of Finance, a Senator and a member of the State Council.

A few exceptional peasants achieved noble status. The Demidovs were originally state peasants, and Old Believers, from Tula province who rose to become one of the wealthiest iron-manufacturing families in the empire. Nikita Demidov was granted hereditary nobility by Peter I in 1720. In 1795, N.N. Demidov had an income of 596,000 roubles. The merchant Savva Iakovlev, born a peasant in 1712 in Ostashkov, supplied meat to royal palaces and the army and became a tax farmer. In 1758 he became a hereditary noble, and by the end of the eighteenth century was owner of one of the biggest ironworks in Russia and a millionaire. Fedor Panteleev, an economic peasant, became a first-guild merchant and factory owner, was awarded the order of St Vladimir 4th class in 1808 and was ennobled in 1820.

There was also some evidence that impoverished nobles could lose their noble status. In the early eighteenth century some nobles became *odnodvortsy*. In 1714 a decree noted that because of constant partitioning of estates some nobles were 'brought to such poverty that they find themselves with the *odnodvortsy*'. The census of 1743 listed separately those members of the *odnodvortsy* who had at one time been nobles. In the second half of the eighteenth century the process was reversed as noble status became more attractive and it was the *odnodvortsy* who asserted their noble status rather than the other way round. Nevertheless, as late as 1804 a law referred to 'not a few' people who had become *odnodvortsy* from the nobility.[2] The status of impoverished nobles, and in particular the families of low-ranking Muscovite servitors, could fluctuate from generation to generation. A.I. Pashkov and his son, O.A. Pashkov, were *deti boiarskie* (military servitors; originally impoverished lesser gentry or younger sons who had not attained boiar rank) in the seventeenth century, but the son of O.A. Pashkov was listed as a non-privileged *tiaglo* (taxed) person at the first census in 1719. His son, A.F. Pashkov, became a copyist and rose through the civil service to reacquire noble status. Problems were created for nobles by the uncertain status of the Muscovite servitors and then by the status of personal, as opposed to hereditary, nobles (that is, nobles who had not reached rank 6 in the armed forces or rank 8 in the civil administration; personal nobles could own land but not serfs). Children of personal nobles were not themselves noble (although it was common for such children to claim this status); they could fall into the category of *raznochintsy* from which they could rise or fall depending on talent or luck.

2. T. Esper 'The Odnodvortsy and the Russian Nobility', *Slavonic and East European Review* 45 (1967), pp. 128–9.

THE PARISH CLERGY — A CLOSED ESTATE?

By 1860, according to the historian Gregory Freeze, no other social estate in Russia 'was as rigidly hereditary and socially separate as the parish clergy'.[3] Freeze traces this process back to the eighteenth century in which the parish (or white) clergy became, in his words, a 'closed hereditary estate'. This was caused partly by restrictions on entry into the estate and partly by isolating the clergy culturally through their separate, and exclusive, education in seminaries (see Chapter 6). The clergy themselves were desperate to preserve clerical posts for their own sons (priests had to marry before being ordained) to prevent them from being conscripted. In effect, many posts became hereditary. Most children of priests married within the clerical estate.

The government was reluctant to lose members of the poll-tax paying groups to what it regarded as the unproductive clerical estate, which it felt was already too large. In 1744, the Senate forbade the ordination of poll-tax payers. The process was completed when in 1774 the Synod ordered bishops to dismiss clergy who were on the poll-tax register and forbade such appointments in the future, an order which was confirmed by the Senate in 1776. By this date, however, it was rare for anyone but the sons of the clergy to become priests, in contrast to the early eighteenth century when peasants, artisans and even a few members of 'privileged' estates were ordained. The nobleman I.I. Suvorov became an archpriest in the Kremlin in the early eighteenth century but this was an exception. Members of the Russian nobility (unlike younger sons in England and France) would not contemplate joining the lowly clerical estate (although they did enter monasteries and convents). The situation was rather different in the Ukraine. Petr Ivanovich Poletika, who claimed Polish noble descent, was the son of a doctor and commented, 'Medical knowledge or trade, and the priesthood, were never considered in Malorossia [the Ukraine] reprehensible in terms of noble virtue.'[4]

Entry into the clerical estate became less common as the century progressed, not only because of state policy but also because the career seemed less attractive by this time. Freeze estimated that in 1744–66 only 3–4 per cent of the clergy in the provinces of Vladimir and Pereslavl' came from poll-tax groups, and that this proportion had dropped to less than one per cent in Russia as a whole by the 1780s. In Siberia, however, the shortage of clergy meant that in the 1750s it was common to receive candidates for ordination from other social groups (12 per cent of candidates in 1750, 22 per cent in 1754 and 11 per cent in 1755). In remote areas peasants selected candidates from within their own community and families of priests could revert to becoming peasants. Rare cases of peasants becoming clergy persisted into the nineteenth century. A case came before the

3. Gregory L. Freeze, *The Russian Levites. Parish Clergy in the Eighteenth Century* (Cambridge, Mass., 1977), p. vii.
4. 'Vospominaniia Petra Ivanovicha Poletiki', *Russkii arkhiv*, (1885), no. 11, p. 307.

31

Kiev diocese of a serf who 'having been freed by his landlord Rzhevskii from serfdom and confirmed in this manumission by the Governor's Council in Kiev, was permitted to enter the clerical estate in 1820'.[5]

The clerical estate became very restricted in terms of *entry* in the course of the eighteenth century but was never closed in terms of *exit*. The estate consistently lost people, including both some of its least and best educated members, either by deliberate state 'culling' or by the choice of its ablest seminarists. Sons of clergy who failed to complete their education or to find a clerical position could find themselves 'culled' from time to time to provide recruits for the army (see Chapter 3), or fall into the category of state peasants. In 1748, a list was drawn up by the Metropolitan Antonii of Tobol'sk of 38 illiterate sons of clergy who could be added to the poll-tax paying population. Children of the clergy also joined the urban community; in Serpukhov (Kolomna province), at the first census in 1719, 19 children of clergy were registered in the urban community.[6] In Olonets province (in the north) in the period 1782–95, 7 sons of clergy joined the merchantry, 23 became artisans and 118 became peasants.

Educated clergy could also be lured away from the clerical estate to perform administrative service. This happened in the late seventeenth century, despite a decree of 1687 forbidding clergy to take administrative posts. By the beginning of the eighteenth century 30 per cent of the clerks of the Pomestnyi prikaz (the service estates office) came from a clerical background. The need for lower officials was particularly acute after the provincial reforms of 1775 (see Chapter 5). In 1779, 1,564 sons of clerics entered the civil administration, including 495 seminarists (that is, clerics who had just or not yet completed their education); in the period 1783–84, 35,000 sons of clerics left the estate, including 1,455 seminarists. Mikhail Speranskii was the son of a priest who rose to the highest position in the state in the reign of Alexander I. Sons of clergy also became teachers in the national schools established after 1786 (see Chapter 6) and, by so doing, formally left the clerical estate (Catherine specifically forbade priests to become teachers but, in practice, the educated sons of clergy provided the only possible source of teachers). In the reign of Alexander I, the Synod was instructed to release seminarists as teachers for the new secular schools. This path was attractive to many young men. Metropolitan Platon wrote in 1804: 'The rapid and high rewards of secular life are tempting them . . . A seminarist can get 200 roubles and officer's rank as a teacher in the village schools.' As a historian of church schools points out, the clergy provided a useful 'brainpower reserve' for the Russian state.[7]

5. Gregory L. Freeze, *The Parish Clergy in Nineteenth Century Russia. Crisis, Reform, Counter-Reform* (Princeton, 1983), p. 147.
6. N.V. Kozlova, 'Sotsial'no-ekonomicheskoe razvitie Kolomny v 20-40-kh godakh XVIII v', *Russkii gorod* 4 (Moscow, 1981), p. 127.
7. Christopher Bennett Becker, 'The Church School in Tsarist Social and Educational Policy from Peter to the Great Reforms', unpublished PhD thesis, Harvard, 1964, pp. 88, 69–70.

THE URBAN COMMUNITY — AN UNSTABLE ESTATE?

A combination of high urban mortality rates and economic uncertainty meant that the urban community needed constant replenishment from other estates. In contrast to noble status, which was acquired by only those commoners with exceptional wealth or long service records, the urban community was keen to recruit members of any other social estate. Many of the inhabitants of the towns were not legally members of the urban community even though they could practise urban occupations or trade (the social composition of towns is examined in Chapter 7). It was in the interests of the town that as many as possible of these productive people were registered into the urban categories so that they could contribute to the tax burden. The Tula Magistracy, for example, at the time of the first census (1719) wanted to register 143 people who traded in the town and owned shops or inns, including members of the clerical estate, monastic peasants, postdrivers, serfs and military servitors.

Peter I allowed retired soldiers and sailors to register into his newly established craft guilds (*tsekhi*). In the 1720s, of the 1,455 people about whom there is information who registered in the craft guilds in St Petersburg (which, however, as a 'new' town is perhaps not typical of the whole empire), 838 were originally peasants, 269 were townsmen from other towns, 188 were foreigners, 14 were monastic servants, 9 were soldiers or *strel'tsy* (originally 'musketeers', armed militiamen in infantry regiments in Moscow) and 5 were 'idlers' (*guliaki*). Monastic and church servants were formally allowed to join the craft guilds in 1745 and state peasants were given permission to register in craft guilds in the Siberian town of Irkutsk in 1759. In Tiumen', in Western Siberia, in the late eighteenth century, of the 53 members of the third merchant guild, only one claimed to originate from the peasantry – 12 came from the craft guilds, 9 were postdrivers, 4 were artisans, 3 from the *posad* (the urban community), 6 were *starozhily* (long-term residents in a settlement, who could in fact be peasants), 1 was a Voronezh merchant and 2 were already members of the merchantry. But in 1789–91 it was claimed that most of the members of the craft guilds were ex-peasants – 234 out of 289 males.

Much of the replenishment for the urban community came from the peasantry. Peasants required permission of the commune to leave and after 1762 serfs required written permission from their owners. In 1722 peasants were allowed to register in a *posad* provided they had capital amounting to at least 500 roubles (a very large amount and, indeed, more than was required for registration in the first guild), but they remained liable for peasant, and seigneurial dues, as well as urban taxes (the double taxation was only cancelled at the very end of the century). This did not deter peasants. In 1723–24, 27 serfs, 36 court peasants, 30 monastic peasants and 7 state peasants registered in the *posad* of Astrakhan'. In 1778 and the beginning of 1779 as many as 6,500 peasants applied to register into the urban community of Petrozavodsk (in Karelia) although only 895 were accepted. It has been estimated that in the first 60 years of the eighteenth century 1,416 households of court peasants from villages near Moscow registered as members of the urban community – of which 560 registered in Moscow and 63 in St Petersburg.

In the third census (1762) it was estimated that 3,755 merchants were of peasant origin, which only accounted for 1.6 per cent of merchants, although they were more significant in certain towns, particularly Moscow, St Petersburg and Siberian towns. Between the third census, in 1762, and the fourth census, in 1782, *c.* 2,200 new households (4,200 males) were registered in Moscow, of whom about 40 per cent, or approximately 1,700 were peasants. Eighty per cent of peasant newcomers registered in the merchantry in 1782, although two-thirds of these were registered in the third guild (the lowest guild, for which the least declared capital was required). By the fifth census, in 1795, there had been a new influx of peasantry, and an increase in registration as artisans, that is, a lower status than merchants (although former court peasants were more likely to register as merchants). Registration of peasants in smaller towns was less significant but still took place. Between 1782 and 1795 353 court peasants registered as merchants in the district towns of Moscow province. As many as 2,310 male peasants registered in the urban community of Nizhnii Novgorod between 1764 and 1782. The fact, however, that townspeople continued to be in conflict with trading peasants (see Chapter 7) suggests that relatively few such peasants in fact entered the urban estate. The majority continued to undercut merchant prices and trade within the towns without paying urban taxes. This reality of this was recognized in the urban legislation of 1824 when trading peasants were divided into six categories and obliged to purchase trading permits despite remaining peasants. And not all peasants who wished to join the *posad* were welcomed. In 1792, the town duma of Kostroma refused to register three houseserfs as artisans on the ground that they were too old (they were aged 37, 52 and 65) and would therefore not be able to contribute to urban dues. The case reached the Senate, which decreed that the town had to register the two younger peasants.

Enterprising peasants could rise within the town hierarchy or through trade. A.P. Berezin, born a peasant in 1725, became a first-guild merchant in St Petersburg in 1760, married the daughter of a merchant, and was elected as Town Head.[8] The Deviatov family, who were monastic peasants in 1685, rose through their trading activities so that by the 1760s their heirs were listed amongst the Borovsk, Moscow and St Petersburg merchants and industrialists. By the late eighteenth century Deviatovs were entering military service, a route to nobility. The serf, Nikolai Nikolaevich Shipov, who became wealthy through extensive trading activities, acquired his freedom in an unusual way. His owner had refused an offer of the enormous sum of 160,000 roubles for his freedom in the early 1820s (he claimed that this was because the landowner had allowed another serf to buy his freedom in 1815, who had then gone on

8. 'S.-Peterburgskii gorodskoi golova v proshlom veke. Zhizn' A.P. Berezina', *Russkii arkhiv*, (1879), no. 2, pp. 226–34.

to become such a wealthy Moscow merchant that the owner regretted letting him go!). In the 1840s Shipov deliberately let himself be captured in the Caucasus so that he would gain his freedom as a released captive.[9]

Movement from the nobility to the merchantry was rare although it did happen in Estonia and Livonia. There were exceptions; a decree in 1736 noted that a young nobleman had been inscribed into the Moscow merchantry, probably in an attempt to evade service. In theory, after the Charter to the Towns in 1785, nobles (and clergy and officials) who owned houses in the towns could register in the town 'society' as 'real citizens', but the evidence suggests that this took place only rarely (and, at any event, would not result in the loss of noble status). A report from Prince A. Prozorovskii from Moscow province in 1790 noted that 'several nobles had registered in the merchantry' in accordance with the regulations of the Charter to the Towns. He noted that two nobles had registered as eminent citizens, one had joined the first guild, four had joined the second guild and one had registered in the third guild.[10] The Senate looked at the case and instructed the nobles to resign from all urban categories. This decision was overturned in the guild reform of 1824, which specified that nobles trading in towns had to register in the first guild and pay the appropriate dues (they were later allowed to register in the guild of their choice).

Examples given above of the ennoblement of merchants and other towns-people through military or civil service or through the possession of vast wealth should not disguise the fact that the period under review was one of great economic uncertainty and many more merchant families lost their fortunes or became artisans than rose to the nobility. In addition, townspeople could be assigned to industrial enterprises or mines (merchants were exempted from this in 1785). In the reign of Peter I, craftsmen from towns were conscripted to work in the construction of St Petersburg and forcibly removed from their homes. In 1710, for example, Peter ordered 4,720 craftsmen from various districts to be settled permanently in St Petersburg. Some of these forced conscripts maintained their original legal status; others became hired labourers or simply army or navy recruits, on the grounds that they were employed in armouries and naval shipyards.

THE 'OUTSIDERS' IN THE ESTATE STRUCTURE

The trend in eighteenth-century Russia was towards the simplification of social grouping and the assimilation of various anomalous categories into mainstream social estates. The poll tax in particular (Chapter 3), and also Catherine II's policies towards the non-Russian borderlands, served to eliminate some groups

9. 'Istoriia moei zhizni. Razskaz byvshago krepostnago krest'ianina Nikolaia Nikol. Shipova, 1802–1862 g', *Russkaia starina* 31 (1881), pp. 147, 221–40.
10. RGADA, fond 16, delo 582, chast' 1, f. 19v., report from Prince A. Prozorovskii to the Senate from Moscow province, 1790.

and to merge others into the state peasantry. Nevertheless, several social groups remained outside the four main estates of the nobles, clergy, townspeople and peasants. To an extent the weakening of the unique features of some groups (*odnodvortsy*, descendants of various categories of military servitors, semi-'free' peasants, slaves, Cossacks) was complemented by the development and creation of other groups in the eighteenth and early nineteenth century.

One way of dealing with these awkward groups was to classify them broadly as *raznochintsy* – 'people of other ranks' – whose definition and composition was itself a matter of great uncertainty and inconsistency (see Chapter 1) but usually included non-noble officials and clerical staff, and at various times also included teachers in state schools, retired servitors and soldiers, children of personal nobility and orphans whose social origin was unknown. In this respect the category of *raznochintsy* could be said to constitute a problem for Russia in that its members never fitted into the estate structure; on the other hand it could equally be regarded as part of the solution, as a means of 'mopping up' awkward groups. Members of this 'free-floating' group could change status by occupation. In 1744 the Pskov Ratusha (an organ of urban administration, founded in 1699, but made subordinate to the *voevody*, or military governors, by this date) petitioned the Chief Magistracy for permission to register local '*raznochintsy*' who were married to the daughters or widows of merchants into the urban community in order to increase the tax-paying population of the town. Other *raznochintsy* attained personal or hereditary nobility through service in the civil administration. At the same time, membership of this group was constantly renewed by people who had left the social category of their fathers, such as children of clergy, townspeople working in a clerical capacity or as teachers, or children of old military servitors.

The upper echelons of the civil administration in central government and in the provinces were largely the preserve of the nobility; commoners who rose through service to attain noble rank left their previous social estate and became themselves personal or hereditary nobles (see above). But the large numbers of junior clerical staff are hard to classify as a social group. In contemporary documents these people could be referred to in general terms as *raznochintsy* or as *prikaznye liudi* (staff of a *prikaz*, or office). It was more common, however, for clerical staff to be classified according to their social background, irrespective of their present occupation. In Iaroslavl' in the second half of the seventeenth century clerks came from an urban background and from sons of clergy. In 1684, 14 of the 24 clerks in the distant Viatka *voevoda* office were children of townspeople. In the 1750s, two brothers working as clerks in Smolensk province were '*pomeshchik* people', that is, fugitive serfs. One of the brothers had worked for over 19 years in an office and had become registered as a *prikaz* (office) servant. A list of 119 junior officials in 27 institutions in St Petersburg province in 1789 included 14 from a *prikaznyi* (office) background, 13 court servitors but also 17 sons of clergy, 10 sons of merchants, 6 sons of artisans and 44 sons of 'guild masters' (presumably skilled artisans), 15 sons of nobles, 4 soldiers' children, 4 state peasants, one peasant (unspecified) and 5 foreigners.[11]

Workers in mines, foundaries and other industrial enterprises are also difficult to categorize as a social group. They mainly comprised peasants who had either been temporarily or permanently assigned to an enterprise or who worked there temporarily to meet their financial obligations. These workers either retained their status as state peasants or serfs or acquired a new, not dissimilar status, as 'assigned' (later termed 'possessional') serfs attached to the factory. But the workforce could also comprise representatives of other social groups who in effect abandoned their original social estate and became a separate group of freely hired workers, and whose children also became workers. These people included peasant fugitives, army deserters, convicts, prisoners of war, soldiers' children, postdrivers, impoverished artisans, prostitutes, orphans and native peoples. The 129 apprentices in the works of Ia.K. Riumin in 1717 included sons of townspeople (46), soldiers (21), clergy (17), court peasants (2), state peasants (1) and postdrivers (14) as well as the son of a boiar and a noble. To speak of a proletarian consciousness in this period is an attempt to apply later concepts to a largely pre-industrial society. Nevertheless, the eighteenth century saw the emergence of a small but distinct group of hired industrial workers who did not fit any other social category. Another distinct category of workers were the pilots and barge-haulers who dragged boats up the Volga. The dispossessed and desperate who undertook this backbreaking and poorly rewarded toil (haulers could receive as little as 3 copecks a day in the late seventeenth century at a time when it has been estimated that 2.3 to 2.4 copecks a day was needed for food alone – a figure which rose to 13 copecks a day by the end of the century) cut across the lower social groups and included fugitive serfs, state peasants, impoverished townspeople and army deserters. In the period mid-July to mid-November 1722, out of 11,119 boat workers, 8,593 were peasants, 229 were 'urban landless', 1,943 were artisans, 22 were registered in the clerical estate and, surprisingly, one was noble.

The estate structure was further complicated by the ambivalent status of retired soldiers and children of soldiers. Recruits to the armed forces formally left their social estate and became legally 'free', but this was a status which only complicated their relationship with other social groups if they were retired from the army on grounds of ill health or age. Although, as has been seen above, some former soldiers became townsmen and minor officials, and others were employed in guard duties and garrison service, for the majority this 'freedom' meant poverty and rootlessness, especially if coupled with physical disabilities. Those who had been peasants were unwanted in their home village as they were 'freed' from fiscal and labour dues and so became a burden

11. RGADA, fond 16, delo 533, chast' 2, ff. 139–241, report from Governor-General Ia.A. Brius from St Petersburg province, 1789.

on fellow peasants. In the main, former soldiers remained in the towns, where they became day labourers. The wives of soldiers (*soldatki*) were also in principle 'free'. In practice, many peasant wives remained behind in the village, albeit now in straitened circumstances (their fate is discussed further in Chapter 9). The exceptions who chose to accompany their husbands either performed menial labour in the camps or towns where the troops were billeted or became involved in prostitution.

Children born to soldiers before conscription retained their father's original social estate, but those born while their father was in service became a separate social category termed 'soldiers' children'. Boys were expected to become soldiers; the fate of girls is unclear (although Paul I established a section of the Imperial Military Orphanage for girls in 1798). Many soldiers' children were able to evade military service by concealing their origins, particularly if they were living with relatives, with the result that the number of soldiers' children was insufficient to replenish army ranks. The military authorities tried to retain as many soldiers' children as possible; in 1811, an announcement in the *St Petersburg Gazette* stated that a soldier's widow, Praskov'ia Paltusova, had been unsuccessful in her appeal to the War College for her nine-year-old son, Ivan, to be registered as an artisan rather than being taken as a recruit. In practice, however, many soldiers' children, especially illegitimate ones, returned to the social status of their parents, or became workers in arms factories.

The most dramatic attempt to create a new social group in this period was the establishment of military colonies by Alexander I. The colonies comprised soldiers who, when not on campaign, would assist in agricultural pursuits, and peasants (usually appanage or state peasants) who would farm the land and provide for the soldiers' family in wartime. The state provided land, buildings, agricultural equipment and livestock, and also hospitals and schools, and even installed English-style latrines in an attempt to create not only a prosperous but also a new type of civilized, healthy and clean-living citizen. Particular attention was paid to the education of children of colonists who, it was presumed, would form the basis of a new army; such children were termed 'cantonists' – in effect, a new and separate social group. Children born of soldiers or settlers in the colony were at the disposal of the military, although one son was allowed to remain to assist his father. In effect, the status of both soldiers and peasants was changed in the colonies in order to create a new social category which fused their functions – the 'colonist'. Alexander's plan was partly practical (the cost of maintaining the army was more than half the state budget) but clearly was motivated also by an almost utopian desire to create a new class of useful citizens.

Whole villages were razed and replaced by specially designed houses arranged symmetrically; peasants and nobles who lived on the land designated for colonies were moved elsewhere. By the end of Alexander's reign about three-quarters of a million people (soldiers, peasants and their families) were living in military colonies. In practice, although the colonies achieved some economic success they failed to develop as a new social group. All sections of society were opposed to such a development – the army generals feared that agricultural occupations would destroy the military spirit of the army; at least some of the nobility feared that Alexander was trying to create a sinister new caste which would be answerable only to the tsar, or that he was trying surreptitiously to create a new class of free peasants (the peasant-colonists were given land by the state); the higher levels of the bureaucracy feared the creation of a 'state within a state' subject to its own laws; most of all, the colonists themselves, peasants and soldiers, hated the colonies and the military discipline imposed upon them. As the traveller, Robert Lyall, commented:

> The peasants' habits were broken into . . . an inmate forced upon him, who is often a troublesome, and always an expensive guest; his sons all obliged to continue in the colony, and to submit to a strict military discipline; his daughters obliged to marry, if at all, within the narrow limits of the military colonies; and he himself obliged to relinquish the natural costume, for shorn beard, cropped head, and military dress, and to submit to the tyranny of an inquisitorial police. The iron hand of despotism could alone have induced the Russian peasant to submit to an institution so destructive to his domestic comforts, so revolting to his prejudices, and so contrary to his interests.[12]

There were several serious uprisings which were put down brutally by the army, the most serious being in Chuguev in 1819, although the colonies were not officially abandoned until after defeat in the Crimean War.

HETEROGENEITY WITHIN SOCIAL ESTATES

All the Russian social groups were divided by differences in income and status – as, of course, were social groups elsewhere in Europe.

The heterogeneous nobility

Great inequalities of wealth existed within the nobility. The number of serfs owned was crucial in determining both wealth and social status, as one English visitor noted: 'the Wealth of a great Man in Russia, is not computed by the extent of the Land he possesses, or by the Quantity of Grain he can bring to Market, but by the number of his Slaves [that is, serfs]'.[13] In 1696–98, approximately 500 of the *c.* 15,000 nobles owned over 100 peasant households each, (which comprised approximately 45 per cent of all serfs in noble ownership). In the 1720s it was estimated that 59.5 per cent of nobles owned 1–20 male serfs, 31.8 per cent of nobles owned 21–100 male serfs, 7.9 per cent of nobles owned 101–500 serfs, 0.8 per cent owned 501–1,000 serfs and 0.3 per cent owned over 1,000 serfs (that is, 17.3 per cent of male serfs). By the 1760s, it has been estimated that 32 per cent of nobles owned fewer than

---

12. Robert Lyall, *An Account of the Organization, Administration, and Present State of the Military Colonies in Russia* (London, 1824), pp. 36–7.
13. A.G. Cross (ed.), *An English Lady at the Court of Catherine the Great* (Cambridge, 1989), p. 57.

10 serfs, and 75 per cent owned fewer than 60 serfs. In 1797, 83.5 per cent of nobles owned fewer than 100 serfs, 12.1 per cent owned 101–500 serfs and 1.5 per cent owned over 1,000 serfs (that is, 35 per cent of the serf population). Noble incomes varied with the productivity of their land and the price of grain, but it has been estimated in the second half of the eighteenth century that ownership of 60 serfs could result in an income of only 180 roubles a year. The American historian, J. Hassell, estimated that a single man needed an income of at least 100 roubles a year to live comfortably in St Petersburg, a sum which had risen to 300 roubles by 1800.

The Sheremet'ev family was the richest family in Russia in this period. Count P.B. Sheremet'ev allegedly spent 16,000 roubles on his estate in Kuskovo alone in the year 1786. Count N.P. Sheremet'ev owned 185,610 male and female serfs and 990,793 *desiatiny* of land in the late eighteenth century. In 1798 he had an income of 632,200 roubles, but an expenditure of 692,000 roubles. The other great families in the eighteenth century included the Vorontsovs, the Golitsyns, Iusupovs, Orlovs and Stroganovs. Wealthy families in the Ukraine included the Kochubeis, Apostols and Razumovskiis. The Radziwiłłs were the largest magnate family in Belorussia. In 1790 it has been estimated that Karol Radziwiłł owned over 32,000 farms and some 300,000 peasants (although a significant proportion of these were mortgaged). The wealthiest families in Poland included the Potockis, the Oginskis, the Czartoryskis and the Zamoyskis.

In contrast, in 1771 the Senate received a report concerning over 200 sons of nobles who wanted to enter service but could not because of poverty; some of them even lacked suitable clothes and shoes. In 1774, a widowed noblewoman petitioned Governor-General Jacob Sievers for her three sons to be educated in the Novgorod garrison school for soldiers' children because she could not afford to employ a tutor or send them to a private school. P.I. Poletika (who claimed ancient Polish noble ancestry), born in 1778, depended entirely on his salary as a young lieutenant and shared two rooms with four friends:

> My breakfast consisted of two-copeck rolls and a glass of milk, my dinner and that of my companions consisted of Russian cabbage soup with beef and buckwheat kasha . . . My belongings consisted of a bed, two chairs, a table and a plain wooden chest.[14]

His situation did not improve when he left active service. He worked as a translator in the College of Foreign Affairs, but 'received no salary for a year'. Only when he became a collegiate assessor with a salary of 500 roubles a year within the College did he become financially secure. It was noted above that over 70 per cent of the Russian nobility owned fewer than 60 serfs. In the Ukraine, holdings of most nobles were even smaller than in Russia or in the Baltic provinces: a report in the late eighteenth century noted that there were 'more nobles and fewer serfs in the Hetmanate than in any other region of the

14. 'Vospominaniia Petra Ivanovicha Poletiki', p. 317.

empire'.[15] In Belorussia most nobles owned between two and 150 farms, but some were landless or only owned one or two peasants. About 60 per cent of the Polish nobility did not own their own land and were economically dependent on other nobles. By 1800, it has been estimated that the nobility had mortgaged 1,365,000 male serfs (that is, about 15 per cent of the peasant population) to underwrite their debts. But noble debt is as much a reflection of the cultural norms of the time as it is of economic desperation. Debtors included some of the most wealthy nobles: in 1800 Count N.P. Sheremet'ev owed 2,018,839 roubles and Prince I.P. Iusupov owed 100,000 roubles in 1798. Debts did, however, mean that it was difficult for nobles, whatever their wealth, to acquire ready sums to invest in their land.

A particular problem faced by the nobility was that, as lands had been originally acquired in return for service, the original interest of the recipient had been in the *income* from the land (which meant, in effect, the number of serfs on the land), not its location. Many nobles thus owned scattered estates and 'strips' of land interspersed with the land of others. As A. Bolotov, a minor nobleman, recorded:

> In this village I had only 3 households . . . 2 in the Bolotov hamlet, and 6 in Tulein . . . only 11 households in all. But even in the other hamlets there were also trifles and very small scraps . . . But added to this was the aggravating fact that all these small households – which did not amount to anything – not only contained little land, but that everywhere the land lay in holdings separated by the strips of the other . . . landlords. Thus it was impossible to embark on anything individual . . . so the natural consequence resulting from all this was that our incomes . . . were extremely small and amounted to almost nothing.[16]

The situation was exacerbated by the practice of multiple inheritance, which not only diminished the size of holdings but could make them more dispersed. The Penza nobility complained in 1767 that multiple inheritance had led to a situation where a noble could own 'five peasants in one place, four in another, and perhaps a single soul with a *chetvert'* of land somewhere else . . . and these divisions have been carried to such an extent that it is rare to find a village where there are not five or ten landlords'. In the same year the nobles of Kerensk complained that their plots were so small that they would soon be as badly off as the *odnodvortsy*.[17]

The divided urban community?

Within the legally defined urban community there were distinctions of status and wealth. In the second half of the seventeenth century the wealthiest

15. Zenon E. Kohut, 'Problems in Studying the Post-Khmelnytsky Ukrainian Elite (1650s to 1830s)', in Ivan L. Rudnytsky (ed.), *Rethinking Ukrainian History* (Edmonton, 1981), p. 113.
16. Quoted in Robert David Givens, *Servitors or Seigneurs: The Nobility and the Eighteenth Century Russian State*, unpublished PhD thesis, Berkeley 1975, pp. 213–14.
17. Wilson R. Augustine, 'Notes toward a Portrait of the Eighteenth-Century Russian Nobility', *Canadian-American Slavic Studies* 4, 3 (1970), pp. 397, 400.

merchants were termed the *gosti* and *gostinnaia sotnia*, while the rest of the urban community (termed the *posad* in this period) was split into three groups according to wealth – the 'best', the 'middle' and the 'younger', or poorer, *posad* members. In the course of the eighteenth century the composition of the urban community was redefined (see Chapter 1), culminating in the Charter to the Towns in 1785 which categorized the 'town society' into six groups according to occupation and income: 'real citizens' who owned property in the town; merchants registered in three guilds; artisans; foreign nationals and merchants from other towns; eminent citizens (including people with over 50,000 roubles of declared capital, bankers and shipowners); members of the *posad*.

The categorization of the urban community in 1785 was ambiguous. In particular the composition of the 'real citizens' who, as house owners, could potentially include non-urban social groups such as nobles, clergy and officials was unclear. More fundamental was the fact that in practice these six categories were inappropriate for the social composition of most Russian towns and assumed a diversity of wealth and occupation which in practice rarely existed. In 1786, A.R. Vorontsov reported to the Senate from St Petersburg province that representatives of eminent citizens, foreigners and merchants from other towns could only be found in the city of St Petersburg itself.[18] In Khar'kov (in the eastern Ukraine), which was quite an important economic centre, no one qualified to register as an eminent citizen and there were no foreigners or merchants from other towns.[19]

In most small towns the townspeople could only register as merchants of the lower guilds and artisans. Declared capital of 1,000 roubles was required for membership of the third guild, 5,000 for the second and 10,000 for the first guild.[20] In 1786, N. Saltykov reported that merchants only had sufficient capital to register in all three guilds in the city of St Petersburg itself, while in the district towns merchants were registered in the second and third guilds in Shlissel'burg and Novoladoga, and in the third guild only in Oranienbaum, Sofia, Luga and Gdov. Even when registrations in all three guilds took place these were heavily weighted towards the lower guilds. In 1764 the town of Ostashkov in the upper Volga had 77 merchants in the first, 56 in the second, and 141 in the third. When Catherine II increased the capital qualification for registering in the guilds in 1785 the membership of the upper guilds declined further. In 1796, there were no first-guild members and only 6 second-guild members in Ostashkov, while 384 were registered in the third guild.[21] In Nizhnii Novgorod there were 9 first-guild, 70 second-guild and 259 third-guild

18. SPgFIRI, fond 36, delo 477, f. 644, report by A.R. Vorontsov to the Senate, 1786.
19. D.I. Bagaley, D.P. Miller, *Istoriia goroda Khar'kova za 250 let ego sushchestvovaniia (s 1655-go po 1905-y god)* (Khar'kov, 1905), vol. I, p. 110.
20. RGADA, fond 16 (Vnutrennee upravlenie), delo 530, ff. 166-66v, report by General N. Saltykov to the Senate, 1786.
21. A.V. Demkin, 'Kupechestva Kaluzhskogo i Tverskogo namestnichestva v kontse XVIII v (izmeneniia v chislennosti)', in *Gorod i gorozhane Rossii v XVIII – pervoi polovine XIX v. Sbornik statei* (Moscow, 1991), p. 107.

members in 1786; by 1794 these figures were 5 first-guild, 26 second-guild and 493 third-guild members.

This is not to suggest that the urban community was homogeneous or that there were no tensions arising from differences of wealth. Institutions of urban self-government were, on the whole, dominated by the richest townspeople, sometimes to the disadvantage of poorer groups (see Chapter 4). At the bottom of the social scale of the towns were people who hired themselves out for daily work. Even more unfortunate were people who had, in effect, fallen into debt slavery through the system of *kabala* (see Chapter 3). However, the most serious problem faced by urban society was not in itself the lack of wealthy members to fill all six categories but the persistent economic instability of trade and manufacturing which led to wide fluctuations in the numbers able to register in merchant guilds. The wealthiest seventeenth-century merchant families – the *gosti* and *gostinaia sotnia* – had regularly risen and fallen. Of the 27 families registered as *gosti* in Moscow in 1705, only 5 had appeared in lists in 1687. Some families had simply died out, others had declined financially and a few had risen to join the ranks of the nobility. Matters did not improve as a result of legislation in the eighteenth century. The life of Ivan Tolchenov illustrates this vulnerability well. He had been a prosperous merchant in Dmitrov in the 1770s and the 1780s, but expenses for his son's wedding, losses at cards and poor trade meant that by 1796 he was being pursued by creditors and in 1797 he was forced to flee from them to Moscow and commence a new career managing a card factory. The study of the Moscow merchantry by the Russian historian Aksenov also illustrated the fluctuating fortunes of many families – only 26 out of the 382 families in the first guild in 1748 had managed to retain this status in the last two decades of the century. Constant replenishment was required from merchants from other towns, other categories of town inhabitants and peasants to maintain numbers.

The stratification of the peasantry?

Most foreign visitors found the institution of serfdom to be degrading and barbaric. But this did not mean that they found the serfs to be impoverished. Martha Wilmot, from an Anglo-Irish family, commented in the early nineteenth century:

> . . . those who imagine the Russ peasantry sunk in sloth & misery imagine a strange falsehood. Wou'd to God our Paddys . . . were half as well clothed or fed the year round as are the Russians . . . If they are *Slaves* 'tis likewise the Master's interest to treat them kindly. His population constitutes his riches, & he who neglects or oppresses his subjects becomes their victim & sinks himself.[22]

22. *The Russian Journals of Martha and Catherine Wilmot 1803–1808*, ed. by the Marchioness of Londonderry and H.M. Hyde (London, 1934), pp. 146–7.

Robert Lyall commented shrewdly that '. . . it is chiefly the vassals of the *poor* and of the *extremely poor* nobles, whose case calls for our sympathy and our commiserations'.[23] At least Russian peasants (serfs and state peasants) did not suffer for the most part the vulnerability of the landless labourer in other parts of Europe. On the other hand, peasants were, of course, subject to a run of bad harvests or epidemics which could dramatically change their fortunes. Such disasters could affect large areas or be confined to particular regions. The historian Arcadius Kahan has catalogued natural disasters in Russia – he listed ten major famines in the first half of the seventeenth century (including four years of crop failures in Moscow and Smolensk provinces from 1721 to 1724 and a famine from 1732 to 1736 which affected all Russia), six in the second half of the seventeenth century, eight in the second half of the eighteenth century, and five in the first quarter of the nineteenth century. In 1650–52 'People ate sawdust'; in 1739 'People, cattle, wild animals and birds froze to death on the roads'; in 1822 'People ate pine cones, oil-cake. Many died'.

A small number of peasants became very wealthy through commercial activities. A. Lomakin, a monastic peasant, moved to Moscow at the age of 20 to work for a merchant; 21 years later, in 1741, he had set up his own workshop producing silver fibre and employed three workers of his own. In the industrial village of Ivanovo in 1817, the factory run by Grachev had 900 looms and 103 printing stands, that of Iamanovskii had 1,000 looms and 110 printing stands (and in the region of 1,500 workers), and that of Garelin had 1,020 looms and 85 printing stands (and 1,407 workers). They were all serfs or former serfs of Count Sheremet'ev who was the *de jure* owner. Some serfs seemed to be in possession of large sums of money. In 1816 in the village of Baki (Lieven estate, Kostroma province) members of the family paid sums of up to 2,000 roubles to purchase substitutes for the recruit levy.[24] Nikolai Shipov was the son of a rich serf in Nizhnii Novgorod province – his father was fined the enormous sum of 7,000 roubles in 1820 when he let a peasant escape whom he was supposed to be guarding. In 1823, his father paid his master 1,000 roubles to avoid serving another term as an elected peasant official.[25]

Even within villages differences of status and wealth existed, stemming from the household size – in particular the number of healthy sons – or from good or bad housekeeping or simply luck. In 1800, N.P. Sheremet'ev wrote that 'In many of my estates inequality has existed for a long time relating to the possession of peasant land, so that some have excess land, others suffer extreme shortage.'[26] On the Andreevskoe village (Vorontsov family) in November 1819 the percentage of peasant households which could not pay their *obrok* (quitrent)

23. Robert Lyall, *The Characteristics of the Russians, and a detailed History of Moscow* (London, 1823), p. cxxxvii.
24. BL, Add. MS 47427, ff. 11v, 19v, Lieven papers, recruit book of the village of Baki, 1814.
25. 'Istoriia moei zhizni', pp. 146, 148.
26. L.S. Prokof'eva, *Krest'ianskaia obshchina v Rossii vo vtoroi polovine XVIII pervoi polovine XIX veka (na materialakh votchin Sheremetevykh)* (Leningrad, 1981), p. 111.

ranged from under 5 per cent in some villages to over 30 per cent in others (the average was 13.7 per cent of households). Landowners believed that large households were most likely to be prosperous, and able to pay dues, and discouraged household sub-division as a result. Small households were also particularly vulnerable to the recruit levy. Within the peasant household certain members – orphans, illegitimate children, widows – could be more vulnerable than the immediate family members of the head of household. Orphaned and illegitimate boys were more likely to be selected by the head of household as recruits than his own sons.

The normal indicator of the economic standing of the peasantry in this period was the number of horses owned. Peasants used one or two horses for ploughing and also required horses for fulfilling labour obligations such as carting goods. It has been estimated that a peasant family of four needed a minimum of two horses for economic sufficiency. In the village of Bogoslovskoe (Penza province) in 1773 the richest household of S. Andreev owned 16 horses, 6 cows, 8 pigs and 40 sheep and farmed 20 *desiatiny* of land, but 19 households did not possess a horse and had only one cow.[27] On the Lieven estate in Baki (Kostroma province) there was an attempt in the early nineteenth century to equalize recruit obligations according to the means of the household. Households were obliged to contribute according to their wealth to a fund which was to be used to purchase substitute recruits on behalf of all the peasants. This exposed great inequalities of wealth even within one estate – in 1816, 9 families paid 2,000 roubles, 18 families paid 1,000 roubles, 3 families paid 500 roubles, one family paid 250 roubles and the rest paid under 100 roubles, with one family paying as little as 10 roubles.[28] The scheme was later dropped, quite possibly because of objections from wealthy peasants.

There was a sense in which equality of opportunity was sought by peasants. They believed that there should be some equalization of land-holding between them which could be achieved through periodic redistribution. There were complaints from state peasants of north Russia and Siberia in the mid-eighteenth century concerning inequality of land-holding between peasants. In Turinsk volost' (Siberia) and Olonets, Archangel and Vologda provinces (north Russia) some redistribution of lands did in fact take place in the second half of the eighteenth century, although it was not done consistently or quickly; some land in Olonets province was only redistributed in the 1870s. But the issue of redistribution of lands merely exposed the divisions in wealth between the peasantry as change was only in the interests of the poorer peasants. Resistance mostly took the form of simple non-compliance. Alexander I issued no less than nine decrees ordering the repartition and equalization of land in north Russia; as late as 1870 it was rare to find partitioning communes in Olonets province. The process of repartition of state peasant land also progressed slowly in the Ukraine and New Russia in the early nineteenth century. A

27. I.A. Bulygin, *Polozhenie krest'ian i tovarnoe proizvodstvo v Rossii. Vtoraia polovina XVIII veka* (Moscow, 1966), pp. 170, 173.
28. BL, Add. MS 47427, ff. 132–4.

general redistribution of court land took place in the first half of Alexander I's reign. Within serf villages pressure could be put on the peasant commune by all, or some, of the peasants for a redistribution of land and/or *tiaglo* obligations. Landowners, in whose interests it was that all peasants could contribute to labour and money dues, could also force a redistribution of land between villages on their estates to equalize burdens. A land survey in 1794–95 showed that lands on the Pistsovo estate (Golitsyn family) were unevenly distributed – 19 villages had excess land amounting to 430 *desiatiny* while 16 villages had shortages of land of 473 *desiatiny*. In 1796 the commune formed a commission of representatives from the villages which led within two months to a new distribution.

It is difficult to be certain whether the differentiation or levelling process was the more dominant in this period. Soviet historians have tended to stress an increase in stratification of the peasantry from the late eighteenth century through to the emancipation of 1861. E.I. Indova found that in the Vorontsov holdings near St Petersburg the proportion of rich peasants rose slightly in the period 1812–32 (from 17.7 per cent to 19 per cent), middling peasants fell (from 32.9 per cent to 14.4 per cent), while the proportion of poor peasants rose more markedly (20.4 to 26.6 per cent of poor peasants, 8.4 to 14.7 per cent of 'very poor' peasants and 20.6 to 25.3 per cent of landless peasants) in the same period. Economic differences could lead to confrontation between peasants, as has been described above in the case of Baki and the recruit levy. Better-endowed peasants could successfully resist redistribution of lands within the village, and rich peasants could dominate the commune and influence its decisions (see Chapter 4). But stratification should not be exaggerated. Few peasants were very wealthy and as peasant wealth was normally calculated according to the *household*, and larger households had more financial obligations, the difference of wealth between *individual* peasants was probably less than the statistics on ownership of livestock seem to indicate. Furthermore, the low level of agricultural development, and the limited development of transport and the internal market (see Chapter 7), meant that there was a natural limit to the amount of land a peasant could farm productively, while extra land and dues could prove as harmful to peasant households as insufficient land. The study by Hoch of Petrovskoe village (Tambov province) in the early nineteenth century suggested that although economic differentiation existed, equalizing tendencies were also very strong (and that figures concerning peasant wealth could be incomplete or misleading). He found that, in practice, household size and wealth were in constant flux, owing to biological or random factors, and that it was impossible to see evidence of any permanent stratification.

In the western borderlands of the empire the condition of the peasants was rather different. In the Baltic provinces peasant communities included more landless peasants, who lived in peasant households as hired labour or in simple huts on the outskirts of the villages. Agriculture was more developed in the Baltic provinces, but peasants were still subject to economic disaster and were generally held to be worse off than Russian peasants. Peasant children died of starvation; in 1808 court proceedings described how mothers in Estonia gave their last piece of bread to their children with the result that they starved to death themselves. The serfs in this part of the empire were emancipated during the reign of Alexander I: in Estonia in 1816, Courland in 1817 and Livonia in 1819. But, at least in the short term, this failed to bring the expected prosperity to the countryside as peasants were freed without land and were forced to make unfavourable contracts with their former lords. According to the Decembrist Pavel Pestel', as a result the Baltic peasants found themselves in an even worse economic position than before. Hired labour continued to be the norm; in Sangaste (in the more agriculturally developed southern region of Estonia) hired labour was used on almost 90 per cent of farms in 1816 and 1850, in Türi, in the less developed north, it was 40 per cent in 1816 and 33 per cent in 1850. It has been estimated that between 1816 and 1850 social divisions in Estonia intensified and the number of poor landless farmhands and cotters increased. In Finland free peasants owned most of the land. In 1757, while under Swedish rule, the Swedish nobles had given up their fiefs in Finland and the land had been redistributed to the peasants. Here too, however, there were underclasses of poor tenant farmers and landless labourers.

The eighteenth century witnessed the impoverishment of the *odnodvortsy* as a whole as much of their land was sold to, or seized by, nobles (see Chapter 5). Within the *odnodvortsy* there were also divisions of wealth. In Belgorod province (in the south) in the 1760s many *odnodvortsy* held less than one *chetvert'* (0.54 of a hectare) of land; some were also landless and worked as farm labourers, or were poorer than state peasants. In the village of Selevskoe (Voronezh province) in 1767 444 male *odnodvortsy* owned only 600 *desiatiny* of land, which was too little for subsistence by contemporary norms. In the period 1761–65 some 527,000 *odnodvortsy* owned 17,675 peasants, which meant that there was only one peasant for every 30 *odnodvortsy*.

The armed forces: army, navy, irregulars

All armed forces maintain a sharp division between officers and rank-and-file soldiers and sailors, and all forces have prestigious academies and regiments (in the Russian case the Preobrazhenskii, Semenovksii and Izmailovskii guards' regiments) which create distinctions within the officer corps. Divisions within the Russian armed forces were, however, made more complex by three factors: first, the presence of foreigners and non-Russian subjects within the officer corps; second, the relatively late development of a Russian navy; third, the existence of irregular forces within the army.

Foreign officers (and some ordinary soldiers) were hired by the tsars (Michael and then Alexis) in the mid-seventeenth century to assist in the creation of the 'new model' infantry and cavalry regiments, which copied the structure and tactics of western and northern European regiments. This caused resentment amongst Russian noble servitors who were paid at a lower rate than foreigners and who felt that their own promotion was blocked by their presence. In 1649, 2,000 Russian cavalrymen opposed the appointment of a Dutchman as their commander, on the grounds that he was 'unbaptized' and lacked their practical experience. The new infantry regiments assembled by Peter I at the beginning of his reign to fight the Swedes were all commanded by foreigners. Foreigners continued to be paid more than Russian officers. In 1711, for example, a foreign colonel was paid 600 roubles, while a Russian colonel received 300 roubles; foreign lieutenant-colonels and majors earned 360 and 300 roubles respectively, while their Russian counterparts only received 150 and 140 roubles. In the course of Peter's reign, partly as a result of the establishment of military schools but also because of the need for manpower in wartime, Russians came to dominate the officer ranks. Pay for foreigners and Russians was formally equalized in 1720, although individual foreigners continued to be rewarded generously for their services. The presence of foreigners in the Russian army remained a source of resentment and tension. The seeming preference shown for officers of a German background by the empress Anna and then by Peter III was partly responsible for the unpopularity of the former and the overthrow of the latter. A disproportionate number of non-Russian nobles from within the Russian empire, in particular Baltic Germans, became officers. In 1812, the resentment and dislike of the 'Germans' at the headquarters of Barclay de Tolly (whose family was originally of Scottish descent but had settled in Livonia in the seventeenth century) allegedly led General Ermolov to ask Alexander I to 'promote' him to a German since the Germans were receiving all the rewards![29] The medical profession within the army remained dominated by German doctors until the nineteenth century.

Foreigners were also recruited by the tsars as naval officers and, in the early stages of naval development in the reign of Peter I, as ordinary seamen and shipwrights. This also caused resentment and tensions within the navy. Paul Jones (of Scottish birth but an American citizen when he was recruited by Catherine II in 1788) encountered resentment and antagonism not only from the Russian officers but also from the British officers in the pay of the Russian fleet, who remembered his exploits against them during the American War of Independence. But a further division arose as service in the navy was always regarded as less prestigious than that in the army. In 1774 Admiral Blunkett commented on:

> ... the general dislike the officers have to Sea Service ... which proceeds partly from their ignorance of their profession, & partly from the smallness of their pay which makes the Russian Navy by no means an eligible profession.[30]

In 1814, an anonymous British surgeon noted:

> The difference of the *esprit de corps* between the army and navy is obvious. The former know and feel the value, not only of their late services, but of

29. Michael Josselson, *The Commander. A Life of Barclay de Tolly* (Oxford, 1980), p. 117.
30. Robert R. Rea, 'John Blunkett and the Russian Navy in 1774', *Mariner's Mirror* 41 (1955), p. 247.

their usual weight in the country: the latter appear to labour under a feeling of inferiority, as if aware they were only a lower link in the chain of national power . . . The 'Guards', I soon found, were everything on board; the comforts of the seamen, the rules of the service, and all previous arrangements, being – nothing.[31]

Little was done to establish a tradition of recruiting sailors; they were conscripted from the provinces bordering the Baltic but ranks were often filled arbitrarily by ordinary soldiers who had no experience of the sea. The oarsmen in the galley fleets (in the Baltic and the Black Sea) were usually convicted criminals.

The composition of the Russian armed forces was further complicated by the presence of irregular troops. Tatar and Bashkir tribesmen fought as cavalry within the Muscovite army from the sixteenth and seventeenth centuries. Even in the eighteenth century non-Christians were levied on a separate basis from other 'non-privileged' members of society and could be required to provide particular services as an irregular cavalry force on the frontiers. *Odnodvortsy* provided a special land militia (for example, 3,731 were conscripted in 1771 for this purpose). Cossacks served on the frontiers and within the Imperial army as a cavalry force. In the late 1780s it was estimated that the total number of irregular forces, including Cossacks, numbered 73,651 men. By the late eighteenth century most of these irregular forces had been integrated into the Imperial army but they still retained their separate identity. Such troops had an unenviable reputation for indiscipline and savagery, which contrasted with the behaviour of the regular troops. As one commentator remarked during the Seven Years' War:

> The establishment of the Russian army, seems to make it in some measure necessary to retain the Cossacks and Calmucks, and in Campaigns against the Poles, Turks and Tartars, they are perhaps an indispensible evil; but in wars with other European nations, they may certainly be said to be more hurtful than useful to an army . . . [The Cossacks] ride well, manage their pikes dextrously, and are remarkable for their fidelity: but they plunder all the inhabitants who are not their declared friends, and treat them with inhumanity . . . [The Kalmyks] are much more cruel than the Cossacks, and have the same dread of fire.[32]

During the Napoleonic invasion of 1812 separate provincial militias were created, in addition to the regular army, whose initial purpose was to defend their territory from enemy raids. The number of men in the militias exceeded 200,000 in 1812, but these troops became rapidly assimilated into the regular army and were in practice deployed outside Russia's frontiers in 1813 and 1814.

---

31. *A Voyage to St Petersburg in 1814, with remarks on the Imperial Russian Navy* (London, 1822), p. 8.
32. J.G. Tielke, *An Account of some of the most remarkable events of the War between the Prussians, the Austrians, and Russians, from 1756 to 1763*, vol. 2 (London, 1787), pp. 14, 16, 35.

Cossack communities themselves were also sharply divided by wealth and status. By the mid-eighteenth century many of the poorer Cossacks had become indistinguishable from state peasants and had become bound in some way to the land of wealthier Cossacks or the Church. In particular, the category of Cossacks termed *pospolity* had fewer rights than Cossacks proper and performed labour services in place of military duties. They were themselves divided into those who had sufficient land and livestock to farm and those who owned nothing more than their hut, or *khata*, and the *polususedki* who did not even own their own hut but lived on the land of others. In 1767, some Cossacks complained to the Legislative Commission that:

> Many Cossacks, because of the above mentioned purchases and seizures of Cossack lands by all sorts of landlords, captains, and officers, and other Cossacks, because of great pressure and fear, leave their Cossack lands to the landlords, unwillingly become labourers (*pidsusidky*) or go abroad or to other places.[33]

It was tension *within* the Cossack communities arising from resentments felt by the poorer Cossacks towards richer Cossacks which in part led to Cossack disorders and revolts in the 1770s (see Chapter 5). The distinctions within the Cossack community became more marked from the second half of the reign of Catherine II, and particularly following the defeat of the Pugachev revolt, as the wealthier, more influential, Cossacks became part of the Russian nobility whilst their poorer brethren formally lost their Cossack status and became either state peasants or were forced to register as members of the urban community. In the Don Cossack region by the end of the century only about 4 per cent of the population registered in the Russian nobility and this elite maintained their exclusiveness by inter-marriage. In 1821–22 the elite Don Cossack nobility owned approximately 27 per cent of the land of the Don Cossack arable territory. This was at a time of population increase when the average holdings of ordinary Cossacks were shrinking to below the level required to sustain their minimum material needs.

SUMMARY: DEVELOPMENTS 1650–1825

The structure of society underwent significant change during the period 1650–1825 but this development was uneven and varied. The Table of Ranks in 1722 in principle opened the way for talented commoners to attain noble status through service to the state. In practice, the easiest path to ennoblement throughout this period was by service in the civil administration. A small number of wealthy merchants and industrialists, and a few entrepreneurs of peasant stock, were directly ennobled by the tsar but more attained this end over several generations through the military service of their male heirs and

---

33. Quoted in Z.E. Kohut, *Russian Centralism and Ukrainian Autonomy: Imperial Absorption of the Hetmanate* (Cambridge, Mass., 1988), p. 145.

the marriages of their daughters. The development of the clerical estate contrasted strongly with that of the urban estate – while the clergy became almost a closed caste by the end of the eighteenth century (at least as far as entry to the estate was concerned) the urban community remained porous and relied on constant replenishment from other social estates, particularly the peasantry. Attempts by Russia's rulers – in particular by Peter I in 1721 and Catherine II in 1785 – to redefine and recategorize urban society did not stabilize the composition of this estate. The Russian social structure remained complex; social groups outside the main *sosloviia* were maintained, enlarged and created, including *raznochintsy*, industrial workers, soldiers' children and military colonists. All social groups were heterogeneous in terms of wealth and status, but the urban community was probably most vulnerable to economic dislocation and to fluctuations of fortune in this period.

nice use of quotes to support general points; note contrast to Wirtzchefter's lame prose...

CHAPTER 3

Rights and obligations

Foreign travellers commented on the bondage of the serfs as an essential feature of Russia. Yet the more astute visitor also noted that other social estates, including the 'privileged' nobility, could be equally bound by obligations. As Martha Wilmot observed:

> This Nation imbibes intrigue, ideas of courting favour, avoiding disgrace and the extremes of power & dependence with the air they breathe. 'tis natural & it must be so from existing things. They [the nobles] hold a middle post between the exercise of nearly unlimited power over their Slaves, & the Consciousness of almost total dependence on a higher power.[1]

'Privilege' and 'non-privilege' became a defining feature of Russian social groups but the relationship between rights and obligations was a complex one. It became a sign of privilege to be relieved of certain obligations and burdens. At the same time, some obligations became themselves a form of privilege, while others remained simply a burden. Thus military service at officer rank, particularly in the guards, became exclusively a noble occupation after 1722. After the abolition of compulsory service in 1762, military service and some areas of civil service came to be seen as a privilege, rather than an obligation, for the nobles. In contrast, certain obligations, such as payment of the poll tax and quartering troops, categorized certain social groups as 'non-privileged' and this partly explains why the *odnodvortsy*, merchants and clergy struggled to free themselves from these obligations. Among peasants, the fact that state peasants paid money dues (*obrok*) to the state and not labour dues (*barshchina*) to a noble landowner indicated that their status was superior to that of serfs. In this way, obligations and rights both united and divided Russian society – united it in that, at least formally until 1762 and informally thereafter, *all* members of the empire were obliged to perform a function for the state, but divided it in that the form of this obligation became an indication of 'separateness' and came to define different social estates.

1. *The Russian Journals of Martha and Catherine Wilmot 1803–1808*, ed. by the Marchioness of Londonderry and H.M. Hyde (London, 1934), p. 299.

52

RIGHTS AND OBLIGATIONS OF THE 'PRIVILEGED':
NOBLES, CLERGY, MERCHANTS

The Russian nobility – a service nobility?

Service to the state was firmly linked with nobility in Muscovite Russia. The boiar aristocracy in the seventeenth century had exerted their influence on the state through the Boiar Duma, that is, an *administrative* organ, but in practice most of them (83 per cent between 1613 and 1689) had started their career in military service. Many of them also performed military-administrative functions within the state. For example, Prince A.N. Trubetskoi served as a military governor of Tobol'sk and Astrakhan' in the 1640s, headed the Kazan' and Siberian chancelleries and commanded forces against the Poles and Swedes in campaigns in the 1650s and 1660s. Landed estates (*pomest'ia*) were granted from the time of Ivan III (ruled 1462–1505) to the lesser nobility to make military service possible for them. The restrictions on the mobility, and, ultimate enserfment, of the peasantry by the mid-seventeenth century had taken place largely to ensure that these often absentee landowners could. be guaranteed an income from their often small and scattered estates.

By the second half of the seventeenth century the type of military service which could be provided by these nobles (in effect a horde of poorly armed cavalrymen) was becoming irrelevant to the military needs of the state, which now required more infantry to form a modern standing army. Furthermore, poor communications and inadequate records had made it easy in practice for nobles to evade their military obligations. Peter I attempted to compel the nobles to perform military service during the Great Northern War (1700–21). In 1710 all sons of the nobility were obliged to present themselves for inspection. This order was repeated in 1720 (suggesting that the first order was not fully obeyed) when young nobles between the ages of 10 and 30 were instructed to appear in St Petersburg with the threat that non-appearance would brand them as military deserters: 'they will be knouted, nostrils slit and dispatched on permanent hard labour'.[2]

It was only after the Great Northern War ended that Peter introduced a more systematic structure for military service. The Table of Ranks of 1722 divided all posts in the armed forces, the civil administration and the court into 14 ranks (covering 262 posts at this date). Service was to be for life, posts in government service were not hereditary and promotion was to be by merit. Clothing, carriages and livery were according to rank. Over the next two centuries all further posts were categorized within these 14 ranks (including, for example, teachers in the late eighteenth century); the Table of Ranks was finally abolished in October 1917.

The Table of Ranks has been regarded as a uniquely Russian institution, as an attempt by Peter to create a service meritocracy and to diminish the significance of lineage, and has been held responsible for the militarization of

2. Mikhail Iablochkov, *Istoriia dvorianskago sosloviia v Rossii* (St Petersburg, 1876), p. 355.

The Table of Ranks

Class	Civil	Military	Naval
1	chancellor	general-field marshal	general-admiral
2	real privy councillor[1]	general	admiral
3	privy councillor	lieutenant-general	vice-admiral
4	real state councillor[2]	major-general	counter-admiral
5	state councillor	brigadier/general-quartermaster	captain-commander
6	collegiate councillor[3]	colonel[5]/senior-quartermaster	captain (1st class)
7	*nadvornyi* councillor	lieutenant-colonel	captain (2nd class)
8	collegiate assessor	major	captain-lieutenant
9	titular councillor[4]	captain	lieutenant
10	collegiate secretary	lieutenant[6]	–
11	–	–	–
12	provincial secretary	second-lieutenant[7]	midshipman
13	protocolist/translator	ensign[8]	–
14	collegiate registrar	–	–

[1] *deistvitel'nyi tainyi sovetnik*
[2] *deistvitel'nyi statskii sovetnik*
[3] *kollezhskii sovetnik*
[4] *tituliarnyi sovetnik*
[5] *polkovnik*
[6] *poruchik*
[7] *podporuchik*
[8] *praporshchik*

Russian society and for the obsession with 'rank' and service in society, indeed, for the whole mentality of the nobility. In fact, the Table of Ranks was not unique; most European countries had tables of precedence, and Russia's own complex precedence rules had been abolished in 1682. Even so, the Table of Ranks stated in its first point that princes and royal sons-in-law retained precedence over other nobles. Furthermore, the Table was modelled on practice in other countries, in particular the Prussian regulations of 1705 and 1713. Peter was not attempting to destroy the power of the old nobility or to create a new elite based purely on service. His immediate entourage always included representatives from Russia's oldest families and his Senate was dominated by them. Indeed, in an earlier draft of the Table of Ranks Peter had proposed that high-born nobles should be given a privileged entry to the civil service but was persuaded against this by Prince A.D. Menshikov, himself a commoner who had risen through merit. In practice, members of the old nobility were best able to take advantage of the new opportunities in education and foreign training in Peter's reign and to rise swiftly through the ranks.

In fact, the Table of Ranks contained an anomaly in that *hereditary* nobility was granted to an individual who attained rank 6 in the army and rank 8 in the civil administration. On the other hand, service did allow talented low-born individuals to rise through the ranks and obtain personal nobility (for the holder of the rank and not his descendants; personal nobles could own land but not serfs) and ultimately hereditary nobility. Where the Table was of particular significance was in the deliberate precedence given to military over civil and court ranks (in the seventeenth century court ranks took precedence over military ranks, which was common practice in Europe at the time). Furthermore, by linking the military and civil ladders of promotion, Peter hindered the development of a separate civil branch of service. In practice, posts were interchangeable between military and civil service, specific administrative training was often lacking and military attitudes towards order and obedience permeated the civil administration as a result. Officials in the civil administration usually chose to take the equivalent *military* ranks and wore the uniform of their counterparts in the armed forces. Naval ranks were created in parallel with military ranks but the navy never had the same prestige as the army. Nearly one hundred years later an anonymous British surgeon commented:

> . . . the latter [naval officers] appear to labour under a feeling of inferiority, as if aware they were only a lower link in the chain of national power [compared with the army] . . . young men of a certain rank in life would not submit to this drudgery . . .[3]

As military service was already an accepted element in Russia, it is hard to claim that the Table of Ranks in itself created a new attitude of mind. But the importance of 'rank' as a indicator of status remained within Russian society, partly because hereditary and foreign titles never became a clearly defined alternative status symbol. Furthermore, the whole experience of Peter's reign created not just an atmosphere but also the reality of compulsion and of state control which affected, and oppressed, the nobility no less than other members of society. Nobles were not only made aware that service was expected of them but the means had been established to ensure that their service was actually performed and that it was more clearly regulated, and hence efficient. In 1722, the Herald Master's Office was established with the primary purpose of maintaining the educational and service records of all the male members of the nobility. The government enforced this service with great brutality. In 1723 an order was received by the commissar of Uglich (Iaroslavl' province) that nobles should present themselves for inspection:

> . . . and if these nobles are not at their homes, take their children, retainers and peasants and bring them to Uglich by the date mentioned above. And if you in disobedience do not send these nobles, you yourself will be taken to the court and tortured . . .[4]

There is no doubt that far more nobles did serve the state under Peter than under his predecessors and that it became hard to evade service. At the same

3. *A Voyage to St Petersburg in 1814, with remarks on the Imperial Russian Navy* (London, 1822), pp. 8, 15–16.
4. Quoted in Robert David Givens, 'Servitors or Seigneurs: The Nobility and the Eighteenth Century Russian State', unpublished PhD thesis, Berkeley, 1975, p. 66.

time, however, <u>new opportunities opened</u> up for nobles in his reign. Schools were established specifically for nobles (see Chapter 6), and service in the armed forces and, to a lesser extent, in the civil administration provided rewards in much-needed salaries and status. In the next four decades the Russian nobility <u>strove not to abolish service in itself</u> but to abolish its <u>more burdensome features</u> and its compulsory nature and to confirm other noble privileges. Indeed, by the second half of the eighteenth century, service to the state was perceived as <u>more of a privilege and honour</u> than a burden which distinguished the nobility from the 'non-privileged' members of society.

In the three decades after Peter's death in 1725 <u>conditions of service eased for the nobility</u>. In 1736 (in the reign of Anna), service was reduced from life to 25 years and one son, or an only son, was allowed to remain on the estate. Nobles could petition to leave service and it became the custom to register young nobles for service at an early age in order to complete the 25 years' service early (A.I. Bibikov, for example, was enrolled in a guards' regiment at the age of 2 and was <u>an officer by the age of 9</u>!). It became the norm for nobles to serve for less time than commoners before promotion from the lower military ranks. This practice was formally permitted in the civil administration only in 1790 but was <u>the custom before</u>. This was not only an advantage for young nobles but <u>contradicted</u> the Table of Ranks by showing that length of service rather than <u>merit</u> had become the accepted pattern for promotion, at least until Mikhail Speranskii introduced examinations in 1809. Nevertheless, <u>the element of compulsion, and brutality, also remained</u>. In 1732 over 200 minor nobles were held under guard in Sevsk (Belgorod province, in the south) because they had not been able to collect the taxes due from their serfs.

In 1762, Peter III <u>freed the nobility from compulsory service</u>. The noble could now choose to serve or not and was no longer subject to inspections. Andrei Bolotov, a minor nobleman, recorded his <u>feelings of joy</u> at his new freedom and promptly retired to his estates; other officers left the army and took up civil posts near their estates. <u>Most nobles, however, continued</u> to <u>serve voluntarily</u>. They needed salaries to supplement the income from their estates and rank continued to confer prestige and status in society. <u>Rank still determined the public appearance of nobles</u>. In 1775, for example, regulations were passed concerning the carriages and number of horses which different ranks could use – six for the top two ranks, four for ranks 3,4 and 5, a pair for ranks 6,7 and 8. 'If a Man does not serve to obtain a rank, he may possess Millions but he <u>will not have it in his power to put 4 Horses to his Carriage</u>', commented Martha Wilmot in the early nineteenth century.[5] Nobles who served were <u>regarded differently from those who did not</u>. The Charter to the Nobility of 1785 classified nobles into <u>six groups</u>, with separate groups for nobles who had acquired their noble status through military and civil service. Nobles who had not reached the lowest rank could attend the noble assemblies established by Catherine II after 1775, but could not vote or be elected to

5. *The Russian Journals*, p. 299.

posts reserved for the nobility in provincial administration created at this date (see Chapter 5). When Alexander I confirmed the Charter to the Nobles at his accession he also expressed the view that a distinction should be drawn between nobles who served and those who did not.

The Charter to the Nobility in 1785 defined the legal rights and privileges of the nobility for the first time. It confirmed the freedom from compulsory service (although the state could call on nobles in an emergency), ownership of serf villages, freedom from personal taxation and billeting, the freedom to travel and to enter service abroad. Nobles could not be deprived of their life, property and rank without a trial by their peers and nobles were no longer subject to corporal punishment. The Charter served to distinguish the privileges of the nobility from other sectors of Russian society and put the Russian nobility on the same footing as other European nobilities. Yet the vulnerability of the Russian nobility to tsarist authority remained. When Paul I came to the throne he in effect ignored the Charter, demanded compulsory service from the nobility, curbed the powers of the noble assemblies and reintroduced corporal punishment. Although Alexander I reconfirmed the Charter on his accession, the weakness of the nobles and their humiliating inability to uphold the privileges which they had been granted in the Charter had already been exposed.

The Orthodox clergy – a privileged estate?

The clergy, both the 'black' (monastic and episcopal) and 'white' (non-monastic and parish) were a privileged estate to the extent that they were not subject to the poll tax (although church peasants did have to pay the poll tax). Until the secularization of church land in 1764 the Church was a major land owner with its own peasants (1,700,430 males in 1719). The largest landowners were monasteries, but cathedrals and even parish churches owned land and peasants. In Vologda (north-east of Moscow) in 1678 around 6.2 per cent of the population were slaves belonging to servitors or clergy. After 1764 clergy were not allowed to own peasants, although some had house servants.

On the other hand, members of the clerical estate were subject to burdens and obligations which equated their status with that of the 'non-privileged' groups of society. In practice, neither the monastic nor the parish clergy were able to refuse to perform the obligations imposed upon them or to resist extensive government control over their functions. During the reign of Peter I the parish clergy were taxed on bathhouses, forced to quarter troops, and obliged to perform administrative and police duties. Peter instructed the clergy to read out government decrees in church and to publicize new tax regulations. The clergy were supposed to report peasants who evaded registration for the poll tax. Most significantly, clergy were instructed to break the sanctity of the confessional and report 'an unfulfilled but still intended criminal act, especially [one] of treason or rebellion against the Sovereign or the State, or an evil design against the honour or health of the Sovereign and the family of His

Majesty . . .'.[6] A priest who disobeyed Peter's regulations could be tried in the civil courts, subjected to corporal punishment, sent to the galleys or even executed. Most of these obligations were abrogated by 1760 but the clergy were still obliged to report the existence of Old Believers after this date. Monks were also instructed to perform a useful service to the state under Peter. In 1724, monasteries were divided by the state into three categories – some were to care for the sick, aged and infirm, some were to bring up orphans and some were to provide elementary education.

Members of the clerical estate who had not yet been ordained or received a post within the Church, that is, the sons of clerics, were particularly vulnerable to treatment as 'unprivileged'. In Peter's reign, monks who were considered as 'surplus' (Peter determined the size of monastic communities) were conscripted and in 1721 a special levy of the lower clergy was carried out. The Russian government throughout the eighteenth century attempted to reduce the size of the clerical estate, which it considered to be over-large and a potential threat to law and order. Levies throughout the eighteenth century certainly yielded large numbers of recruits from the clerical estate – over 7,000 in 1736 and almost 9,000 in 1769. In 1784, the government conscripted all excess clergy and all uneducated clerical children over the age of fifteen, raising over 32,000 men, although not all these became soldiers and many became minor officials or joined the urban community. In Siberia, there were constant complaints about the shortage of clergy in the eighteenth century, partly as a result of frequent levies of 'excess clergy'. On the other hand, this policy acted as an incentive for the sons of clerics to acquire an education so that they could find a post (although in some levies seminarists were not spared). The threat of conscription of 'idle-living clergy' in the late eighteenth century so scared the parents of Afanasii Sil'vestrov (his father was a sacristan) that they promptly requested, and received, a position for their son from the Bishop.[7]

The merchants – a privileged social group?

Within the urban community the wealthy merchants claimed special privileges in return for services to the state. In the second half of the seventeenth century the elite merchants were termed the *gosti* and the *gostinaia sotnia*. Both groups carried out administrative and fiscal duties for the tsar and in return were granted special privileges. The *gosti* were exempted from taxation and other duties, and had the right to trade abroad and, up to 1660, the right to own land. The *gostinaia sotnia* was also exempted from some taxes as a result of administrative services to the tsar. These groups declined in number and power in the early eighteenth century. Nevertheless, Russia's rulers deliberately tried to foster the growth of an urban elite by treating them separately from other categories of the urban population and by granting them special

6. James Cracraft, *The Church Reform of Peter the Great* (London, 1971), p. 238.
7. A.B. Smirnov, compiled, 'Zhizn' Afanasiia Sil'vestrova, sel'skago sviashchenika, v inochestve Zakhariia', *Russkaia starina* (1889), no. 2, pp. 370–1.

privileges. Peter I allowed merchants to purchase exemption from recruit-ment for 100 roubles. After the tax reform of 1775 merchants were freed from conscription and from the poll tax, a psychological gesture which established them as members of the 'privileged' classes (they had to pay a recruit tax and a tax on their declared capital instead of on their person like peasants and artisans). This concession did not, however, lessen the financial burden on merchants. The tax on declared capital increased from 1 per cent in 1775 to 1.25 per cent in 1797 and had risen to 5.225 per cent by 1818. Townspeople who served the state as *burgomistry* or *ratmany* (members of the urban courts established in 1775) were rewarded in 1785 by being released from the obligation to billet troops.

The Charter to the Towns of 1785 defined a separate, elite category of 'eminent citizens' within the towns, comprising those with capital of over 50,000 roubles, bankers, ship-owners, wholesale traders, townsmen who had served in the urban administration, artists and academics. The Charter freed first- and second-guild merchants and eminent citizens from corporal punish-ment and established the social privileges of each guild of merchants. It stipu-lated regulations (similar to those for nobles) on carriages: eminent citizens could drive in a carriage and four, first-guild merchants with a carriage and pair, second-guild merchants with a light carriage and pair, third-guild mem-bers with only one horse. The Charter also specified the occupation of each category of citizen, so helping to define and distinguish the wealthier mer-chants from the rest. Only first-guild merchants were allowed to trade abroad, second-guild merchants were allowed to carry out internal trade throughout the empire and third-guild merchants were restricted to trading in the vicinity of the town in which they were registered. Merchants could no longer be conscripted to work in the Salt Office and various other government offices.

In the eighteenth century wealthy merchants, and in particular owners of industrial enterprises, claimed the right to own land and serfs; this was re-sisted by the nobles, who regarded both forms of ownership as their monopoly. In 1721, in Cheboksary, on the Volga, five elite merchants owned 43 houseserfs. In 1737, Iaroslavl' merchants who owned peasants sent them in their place as recruits. During the reign of Peter I, merchants were given the right to purchase serfs to work in their factories and mines. The government assigned whole villages of state peasants to merchants, mostly to owners of mining and metallurgical plants in the Urals. In 1734 the number of assigned peasants was determined by law; individuals were entitled to between 100 and 150 families for every blast furnace under operation. The traveller, P.S. Pallas, described a saltpetre works near Astrakhan' which had been given in 1751 to a merchant, Fedor Kobiakov '. . . the Government granted him permission to purchase a village, not containing more than seven hundred inhabitants, one half of which he was empowered to remove thence and employ in his saltpetre-work'.[8] By the mid-eighteenth century merchant factory owners were

---

8. P.S. Pallas, *Travels through the Southern Provinces of the Russian Empire, in the Years 1793 and 1794* (London, 1802), vol. I, pp. 167–8.

in conflict with noble competitors over their rights to purchase villages of assigned peasants to work in the factories. The government by this date favoured the nobles and placed restrictions on the ownership of serfs by merchant factory owners. In 1752, merchants were restricted to the maximum purchase of 42 workers for each mill and in 1758 merchants were instructed to sell their serfs or see them confiscated. In 1762, in the reign of Peter III, merchants were finally forbidden to buy peasants with or without land (although they could still employ hired labour of course).

The *nakazy* (instructions) which deputies submitted to the Legislative Commission (a consultative body established by Catherine II at the beginning of her reign) give a picture of the situation relating to the ownership of serfs by merchants in 1767 and the tensions it involved. Merchants asked for permission to own serfs as workers and domestic servants. Noble *nakazy*, on the other hand, were concerned to preserve their monopoly of ownership of serfs and economic privileges vis-à-vis the merchants. The Charter to the Nobles of 1785 confirmed *de facto* their monopoly on the ownership of serfs. Paul I restored the right of merchants to purchase serfs for their industrial enterprises, but this was overturned by Alexander I in 1806.

Nobles had triumphed over merchants but in practice the ownership of land and serfs by merchants did not cease in the second half of the century although it decreased. If merchants were no longer able to purchase land they could still lease it from peasants or nobles. The nobleman A.T. Bolotov made mention in his memoirs of a large and wealthy village which came into the possession of a merchant in 1792. After 1801 all subjects, with the exception of serfs, were allowed to purchase uninhabited land; in 1817 non-noble landowners were allowed to mortgage their landed property. In 1820, four serfs on one of the Iusupov estates agreed to lease 7,675 *desiatiny* of pasture land to a merchant from Kursk. Furthermore, merchants continued to own house serfs despite the fact that this was illegal. Khristofor Stepanovich Aladzhalov, an Armenian merchant in Rostov-on-Don, noted in his memoirs that 'In the year 1813, 5 November, I bought a Russian girl for 260 roubles.'[9]

OBLIGATIONS AND RIGHTS OF THE 'NON-PRIVILEGED':
PEASANTS, ARTISANS, SLAVES

Members of the 'non-privileged' social groups were as conscious of their status in relation to their obligations and rights as members of the 'privileged' groups. State peasants and serfs shared many of the same obligations to the state. Yet peasants considered the status of state peasants to be superior to, and more privileged than, that of serfs. When serfs revolted or petitioned against their noble landlords they frequently demanded state peasant status for themselves. Postdrivers (*iamshchiki*) also regarded their status as separate from and superior to that of state peasants as they paid no poll tax or *obrok*. In the same

9. A. Dzhivelegov, compiled, 'Cherty provintsial'noi zhizni na rubezhe XIX veka', *Golos minuvshago* (1913), no. 7, p. 189.

way, townspeople (felt) that they should not be subjected to obligations which were identical to those of peasants. Consciousness of their superior status to that of peasants was also central to the demands and complaints made by the *odnodvortsy*.

The poll tax and other fiscal obligations

State peasants and serfs were equally liable to taxation. The word *tiaglo* came to designate both the taxes levied on individual peasants and the tax capacity of peasant households. In the early seventeenth century tax registers recorded the 'tax-paying ability' of peasants primarily in relation to the amount, and quality, of land held but also took into account other income-generating factors such as fisheries, flour mills and vegetable gardens. By the mid-seventeenth century the inadequacy of these registers, and the need of the state for more income, forced the government to abandon the system and replace it by an attempt to levy sums on the peasant household. New surveys of both land and population took place in the late seventeenth century but taxes continued to be levied on the household until the introduction of the poll tax under Peter I, which taxed each individual male (irrespective of age). The poll tax remained the basic form of taxation for the non-privileged classes until 1886. This, in principle, vastly simplified tax assessment, although the obligations of peasants remained based on a complex mixture of individual responsibility, size of household and general income-generating capacity of the household. As the peasant community had a collective responsibility for the collection and payment of the poll tax this meant in practice that the poll tax was allocated by the village commune according to means rather than by the number of male peasants per household.

The poll tax was the same for state peasants and serfs. It was initially set at 80 copecks, fell to 74 copecks in 1724 and 70 copecks in 1725 and then stayed at this level until the 1790s (it was slightly lower for a few years in the mid-century as a result of poor harvests). In 1794 the rate was increased to 1 rouble and in 1797 to 1 rouble 26 copecks; by 1812 it had risen to 3 assignat (paper) roubles, a rate which remained until 1839. The real value of the tax fell over the years (and in any event was far less than the sums paid by peasants for the purchase of recruits and other obligations) but this did not prevent the accumulation of massive arrears: over 20 million roubles by 1793. *Odnodvortsy* were made subject to the poll tax in 1723, which, in effect, reduced their status to that of state peasants. They resisted this tax as they believed that, like nobles, their service to the state took the form of military obligations. In 1782 it was reported from Smolensk province that *odnodvortsy* refused to pay poll tax and regarded themselves as noble because they had performed military service. In 1786 the government decreed that peasants owned by the *odnodvortsy* should pay the same poll tax as their masters.

Townspeople initially paid a poll tax of 80 copecks. By 1725 this had risen to 1 rouble 25 copecks, which increased to 2 roubles in 1769, fell back to

1 rouble 20 copecks in 1775, rose again to 5 roubles in 1797 and reached 8 roubles in 1810. The poll tax, therefore, was levied at a consistently higher rate on townspeople than on peasants. Weber described the taxation on townspeople in the reign of Peter I as 'an heavy Burthen upon them'.[10] The poll tax and other fiscal dues were allocated to the whole urban community rather than to the individual, so that townspeople could pay anything from a share of one-half or one-quarter of the full poll tax to several times its value, depending on financial circumstances. Townspeople also paid for the maintenance of urban institutions and prisons, and were obliged, like peasants, to supply horses, or equivalent sums, for imperial journeys. When, after 1775, the richest town inhabitants, the merchants, were taxed separately from the other urban inhabitants this put a greater burden on the poorer inhabitants to meet the poll tax demands. Special taxes could be levied on the urban population: in the desperate year of the Napoleonic invasion of 1812 all towns had to make an additional contribution. On the other hand, towns could be excused obligations; in 1776 the merchants of Saratov were freed for ten years from all obligations following the devastation of Saratov by fire and by the Pugachev revolt. Arrears of urban taxes rose as fast as they did in the countryside; in the four years before 1727, Moscow collected only 71,411 of the 242,899 roubles in tax which was due.

All state peasants and some serfs paid quitrent or *obrok*, but state peasants paid it directly to the treasury while the serfs paid it to their landowner. Part of the *obrok* could be paid in kind, although this practice declined during the eighteenth century. Peasant communities were collectively responsible for the payment and for arrears. But the amount paid by state peasants was smaller than that paid by most serfs. Peter I set the *obrok* at 40 copecks per male peasant for state peasants and it remained at that level until 1761, when it was increased to 1 rouble. By 1783 the *obrok* for state peasants stood at 3 roubles. In 1798 the government made an attempt to relate *obrok* payments to the ability of the state peasants to pay by dividing the provinces of the empire into four categories according to their wealth, with payments ranging from 3.5 to 5 roubles per male peasant. By 1812 these rates were set at between 7.5 and 10 paper roubles, but inflation meant that in terms of silver roubles this was the equivalent of between 1 rouble 87 copecks and 2.50 roubles. Nevertheless, the *obrok* payments of state peasants rose more than the poll tax in this period. It has been estimated that while the state's income from the poll tax (from all peasants) increased from 4,005,634 roubles in 1726 to 10,369,351 roubles in 1796, its income from *obrok* from state peasants increased far more rapidly (church peasants were included from 1764) from 694,979 roubles to 14,256,285 roubles in the same period. *Obrok* payments were frequently in arrears. In the period 1744–64 the state peasants in a village in Viatka province had arrears of some 19,000 roubles. *Odnodvortsy* were also obliged to pay *obrok*, although it was set at a slightly lower rate than for state peasants.

10. Friedrich Christian Weber, *The Present State of Russia* (London, 1968), vol. I, p. 65.

The *obrok* payments of serfs (and church peasants until the secularization of church land) were set by the landowner. The calculation of the *obrok* (and other dues) was normally made according to the broad tax-paying capacity, or *tiaglo*, of the serf or family, and could therefore vary within villages as well as from estate to estate, although there were estates where the *obrok* was levied according to the number of male inhabitants, that is, in the same way as the poll tax. The *tiaglo* unit was normally a unit of one man and one woman (termed a *venets*), and covered men aged between 15 and 65 and women between the ages of 15 and 50, but this too could vary. On the Iusupov estates each *tiaglo* unit comprised two men and two women until 1780 when it became one man and one woman. The average *obrok* payment for serfs rose from 1–2 roubles in the 1760s to 4 roubles in the 1780s. In the village of Nastas'ino (Iusupov estate) serfs paid an average of 2 roubles 50 copecks in 1787, 8 roubles in 1806 and 24 roubles in 1820. Serfs who left the countryside and made their fortunes elsewhere could be obliged to pay far more; four serfs from the village of Andreevskoe (Vorontsov estate) who lived in St Petersburg paid an *obrok* of 70 roubles in 1808. Arrears were massive; on the Musin-Pushkin estates in Iaroslavl' province in 1822, 60 per cent of the expected *obrok* of 88,009 roubles was in arrears.

The barshchina/obrok *debate*

Serfs (and church peasants until 1764) could be obliged to perform labour (*barshchina*) in addition to, or as a substitute for, *obrok*. Serfs regarded this as more onerous than *obrok*; in 1805 serfs on the estates of V.G. Orlov petitioned successfully to pay *obrok* rather than perform *barshchina*. *Barshchina* obligations were usually determined according to the *tiaglo* unit (although it was sometimes based purely on the number of peasants in a household) and peasants normally had to supply a horse and work half a *desiatina* (about half a hectare) of land on three fields. Typically, this meant half the time of the peasant or three days (or half a household worked the landowner's fields while the other half worked their own fields, the so-called 'brother for brother' practice). But there were cases where peasants were obliged to work four or even five days a week on noble land. In 1797, Paul recommended (but did not decree) that peasants should work no more than three days a week on the estate (and not on Sundays). This was resented as unwarranted interference by many nobles, although some took the opportunity to raise their *barshchina* to three days a week! The decree was cited in the code of laws in 1832 as the authority for the obligation of landowners to demand no more than three days' labour. In 1818, a decree forbade *barshchina* on church holidays, but this could be ignored in practice. (Labour service was demanded of serfs elsewhere in Europe but in general was most onerous in the east; in Lower Austria an obligation of 104 days a year was set in 1772, in Transylvania the level was set at four days a week in 1714 and in Galicia there were no limits to the number of days which could be demanded from serfs.)

The second half of the eighteenth century saw a rise in grain prices, and a depreciation in the value of the rouble, which some historians in the West and in Russia have seen as the cause of decline of *obrok* and increase of *barshchina* on serf estates. Soviet historians saw this as an indication of a crisis of the serf economy as landowners were forced to exploit the labour of their serfs more directly as a substitute for investment in their lands. But it could also be seen as a pragmatic reaction by nobles to the increasing value of grain, and therefore, labour. In Tula province a *chetvert'* of rye sold for 1 rouble 9 copecks in 1760 and for 2 roubles 84 copecks in 1790. Grain prices remained high until the 1820s. It is true that *barshchina* was more common on small estates where nobles lived directly on the produce of their land, and where, for the most part, there was a greater density of inhabitants, but *barshchina* was also more common where the quality of the soil was high and where communications were good, so allowing the easy transportation and export of grain. *Obrok* was most common in the central non-black-soil zone and in areas where serfs could be involved in non-agricultural pursuits. In fact, most large estate owners demanded both *barshchina* and *obrok* from their serfs, depending on factors such as population density, quality of land and location. The Menshikov estates in the first quarter of the eighteenth century demanded either *obrok* or a combination of *obrok* and *barshchina*; only one estate used *barshchina* alone.[11] In Moscow province in the 1760s the extent of *barshchina* varied from district to district but a mixed system of *barshchina* and *obrok* operated in 27 districts.[12]

Non-fiscal obligations

Peasants, townsmen and *odnodvortsy* were obliged to build and repair roads and bridges (as were peasants elsewhere in Europe, including in countries where serfdom did not exist). Peasants and *odnodvortsy* also had to perform carting and ferry duties, which could be onerous, especially at harvest time. In 1798 peasants in Olonets province had to provide 276 horses for the use of Paul I's retinue. Court peasants could be obliged to carry out building and repair work on royal palaces. Peasants and townspeople could also be obliged to undertake construction work for the army or the state. Weber reported at the end of Peter's reign that it was said that over 300,000 peasants died during the construction of Taganrog and even more died in St Petersburg and Kronstadt, constituting in his words 'the bottomless Pit in which innumerable Russian Subjects perish and are destroyed'.[13] Troops were also billeted on peasant villages and peasants had to provide fodder and horses for the army. Townspeople could also be conscripted as customs officials and assigned to factories.

11. S.M. Troitskii, 'Raionirovanie form feodal'noi renty v krupnoi votchine Rossii v pervoi chetverti XVIIIv (po arkhivu kniazia A.D. Menshikova)', *Ezhegodnik po agrarnoi istorii Vostochnoi Evropy 1968* (Leningrad, 1972), pp. 122–4.
12. M.F. Prokhorov, *Krest'ianskoe dvizhenie v tsentral'noi Rossii v tret'ei chetverti XVIIIv (po materialam Moskovskoi gubernii)* (Moscow, 1993), p. 23.
13. Weber, *The Present State of Russia*, I, p. 56.

The recruit levy

The most onerous, and feared, obligation was the recruit levy. Martha Wilmot commented that:

> The Man who goes as a Soldier is considered as *Dead* to his family . . . To be rejected is a great triumph . . . Happy he who is lame, deaf, blind or maim'd, (& by the by they often cut off a joint of a finger or cut a limb as the time for recruiting approaches & that 'tis known who is to be chosen) . . . [14]

State peasants (including postdrivers after 1732), court peasants, church peasants, serfs and townspeople were conscripted. In the period 1705–1825 there were 90 levies, which conscripted in the region of 4 million men. In 1705, Peter set the rate at one recruit per 20 households (in other words, this was another *household* obligation). The rate increased to one per 10 households in 1710 and then between 1713 and 1725 varied between one per 40 and one per 250 households. In 1775 Catherine II established the recruit unit at 500 males; the normal 'take' was one man per unit but in the Napoleonic Wars this was exceeded and in 1812 20 men per unit were conscripted. *Odnodvortsy* were also recruited; in one such case 190 *odnodvortsy* were recruited in the period 1747–62.[15] Most recruits became soldiers. Sailors were recruited from the provinces bordering the Baltic Sea; on other occasions ordinary soldiers were reclassified as sailors. In 1714, for example, 500 sailors were conscripted from coastal towns, and in 1715 1,500 soldiers were made into sailors. Special levies took place in coastal provinces in 1805, 1806, 1809, 1811 and 1812. Military service for ordinary soldiers was for life; in 1793 this was reduced to 25 years but this in effect meant life for all but the most fortunate. Peasants also had to pay for the uniform and travel expenses to the depot of the recruit. In November 1804 the serfs in the village of Baki (Kostroma, Lieven estates) paid 140 roubles for food, drink and medicine for recruits.[16] (The role of the peasant commune and urban institutions of self-government in selecting recruits is discussed in Chapter 4.)

The age limit for recruits varied during this time; in 1730 the lowest age acceptable was 15 but this rose gradually to reach 19 in 1808 (although in 1813 the limit was dropped to 12). At the other end of the scale the limit was raised from 30 in 1730 to 40 in 1812. In practice, both ends of the age limits were ignored. In 1788, five of the seven recruits from Nikol'skoe village (on an Orlov estate) were aged between 40 and 45 years old. Older peasants, of course, might be of little economic value to the village, which might explain why in 1810 the Moscow office of V.G. Orlov confirmed the decision taken by the peasant commune of the village of Alisteevo to 'give as recruits in advance from those families of older years' in the 'interest' of the estate.[17] The

14. *The Russian Journals*, pp. 155–6.
15. F.I. Lappo, 'Revizskie skazki kak istochnik po istorii russkogo krest'ianstva (po materialam 3-i revizii)', *Ezhegodnik po agrarnoi istorii Vostochnoi Evropy 1960* (Kiev, 1962), p. 241.
16. BL, Add. MS 47422, f. 183v, Lieven papers, miscellaneous estate papers.
17. V.A. Aleksandrov, *Sel'skaia obshchina v Rossii (XVII – nachalo XIX v)* (Moscow, 1976), p. 279.

recruits from the village of Baki in the early nineteenth century included a 58-year-old.[18] Some recruits were also under the age limit. Four of the recruits conscripted from the state peasants on Tiumen' volost' (in Siberia) between 1782 and 1788 were aged 15 or 16.

In Peter's reign recruits were supposed to be no shorter than 2 *arshiny* and 4 *vershki* (1.60m) but this limit was lowered at times of particular need. Doctors were supposed to pronounce the recruits fit, but the precise definition of fitness was only achieved in Alexander's reign. Men had to have no obvious medical defect and to have front teeth (in order to bite cartridges!). In practice, the authorities might be persuaded to take those who were not fully fit. In the story *A Bitter Fate* (published in 1789), by Mikhail Chulkov, the peasant 'hero', Durnosopov, was at first rejected by the recruiting board as being too short and too thin but the next day:

> . . . on his crown was set some 'hush money', but how much I cannot say exactly; to each of his legs a paper rouble was bound, all of which, in a single night, brought him up to the proper height and thickness of calves. They shaved his forehead, and Durnosopov was acknowledged a model recruit . . .[19]

Many recruits were married and had small children. The census of the same village of Baki in 1799, for example, included a *soldatka* (soldier's wife) aged 43, with three children aged at this date 14, 17 and 20.[20] On the Manuilovskoe estate (Gagarin family) in the period 1820–55, over 60 per cent of the recruits were married and over half of these had small children. Of the 26 recruits selected by Tiumen' (state) peasant volost' (in Siberia) between 1782 and 1788 eight were married. Half of the 198 recruits to the Azov infantry regiment in 1795 about whom information is available were married; in 1811, over half of the 547 recruits to the regiment were married.

Slaves and serfs – people without rights?

In the second half of the seventeenth century there was a separate category of slaves in the Russian empire, whose status was lower than that of serfs. The historian Richard Hellie has estimated that as much as 10 per cent of the population in 1649 were slaves. Most Russian slaves were in 'debt servitude' or *kabala* and were serving to pay off the interest for a monetary loan. In 1646 Ivashko Vasil'ev claimed that the scribe Savva Zverev had taken him home, made him drunk and taken him into *kabala*.[21] The usual period of *kabala* was five years but as it was difficult to pay off the debt in effect the servitude was for life. In the first quarter of the seventeenth century, slaves had on occasion owned other slaves but this was prohibited in the 1630s. By the 1680s those

---

18. BL, Add. MS 47427, f. 22, Lieven papers, recruit book of Baki villlage, 1814.
19. Harold B. Segel, *The Literature of Eighteenth Century Russia* (New York, 1967), vol. II, p. 71.
20. BL, Add. MS 47421, f. 224v., Lieven papers, census returns for the village of Baki for 1799.
21. V. Snegirov, *Moskovskie slobody. Ocherki po istorii Moskovskogo posada XIV–XVIII v* (Moscow, 1965), p. 132.

who were entitled to own slaves included members of the middle and upper service classes, servicemen of various ranks and scribes (*pod'iachie*), but the elite of the merchantry and clergy also owned slaves at this time. Kotoshikhin recorded in 1666 that:

> The boiars, counsellor members of the upper service class and favourites keep in their household slaves of the male and female sex, a hundred, two hundred, three hundred, five hundred, and a thousand, as many as they are able, depending on their rank and property. . . . In the same manner, people of other ranks keep slaves in their houses, as many as they are able to feed, hereditary and limited service contract slaves.[22]

Peasants also owned slaves in the second half of the seventeenth century. For example, some of the peasants of B.I. Morozov owned slaves: one of them, Antrop Leont'ev, owned Tatar slaves; his sons owned eight house slaves, two Polish prisoners of war as slaves and one Tatar captive.

The Code of 1649 paid a great deal of attention to slavery. It detailed the rate at which debts were to be paid off by those who were in debt servitude (*kabala*), specified the nature of 'debt contracts' and the conditions of labour for children of slaves during such contracts, and prohibited anyone under the age of 15 from selling themselves into slavery. The Code also enacted that slave owners had the obligation to feed their slaves. Slaves were allowed to appear in legal processes and to be put under oath. In 1669 the so-called February Statute established at least the minimum level of state protection of the lives of slaves by decreeing the compensation to be paid for killings of and by slaves without intent; deliberate murder of slaves was to be punished by the execution of the murderers. The Code of 1649 specified the sum of 3 roubles as the price of a slave, which had risen in 1691 to 4 roubles for a boy and 6 roubles for a widow. Slavery was essentially a feature of seventeenth-century Russia and earlier, although it continued for the first quarter of the eighteenth century. In Kazan' in 1720, 74 cases of *kabala* were recorded, involving 113 people (69 men, 25 women and 19 children) who were working to pay off debts – most of these were peasants. To give just two examples – S. Sokolov and his wife had to work for six years to pay off a debt of 30 roubles and a widow worked with her children to pay off the debts of her dead husband. Debts in Kazan' varied from 3 roubles to 35 roubles. It was, however, easier and more productive for the government to deal with a broad category of peasants, who were liable for conscription and could be registered for the poll tax, than to allow the continuation of a system of slavery which only benefited the slave-owners.

Slaves as a separate social category in effect came to an end after slaves were made subject to the poll tax in 1723. Nevertheless, debt servitude continued after this date. In 1736, the state decreed that debt slaves should be paid 24 roubles a year, half of which had to go towards paying off the debt, so

---

22. Quoted in R. Hellie, *Slavery in Russia 1450–1725* (Chicago and London, 1982), p. 492.

acknowledging that the practice persisted. In 1783, a debt slave was tied to a Second-Major Khanykov for 35 years. Ivan Men'shii, a state peasant, wrote in his memoirs that he was obliged as a youth to work for a merchant:

> . . . I was given to him as a worker for a short time, that is, for five years, and I fell into so-called *kabala*. I got clothing and shoes from him, but for the whole five years money, because of [our] poverty, had been given in advance, and that money was in all twenty-five roubles or white assignats. . . .[23]

Ivan Men'shii was later conscripted in 1813 when he was 18 years old, so this episode must have taken place in the early *nineteenth* century.

Serfs were not slaves; a serf was always recognized as a legal person, unlike a slave who was regarded as a chattel of his owner. Nevertheless, serfs had fewer rights than state peasants. They were under the jurisdiction of their lord for all but the most serious crimes (unlike state peasants who were tried by state courts and after 1775 had their separate courts of first and second instance). By the late eighteenth century state peasants could make contracts, but this right was not extended to serfs. The lord controlled the movements of his serfs, could force them to marry, could sell and mortgage them, and determined the fiscal and labour obligations to be exacted. Serfs petitioned against owners who they felt had infringed their 'rights' in some way, usually by imposing *barshchina*, claiming exclusive use of lands believed by peasants to be communal or, in the peasants' estimation, changing their status. However, such actions almost always met with violent reaction, either by the owner or by local garrison troops. In 1760, Elizabeth gave nobles permission to exile unruly serfs to Siberia to aid settlement of this area (although it should be noted that urban communities and state peasant villages were also given this right). This right was only abolished in the reign of Alexander I. Landowners could also arbitrarily resettle their serfs within their estates. Between 1774 and 1775 A.S. Suvorov resettled 226 serfs who were in arrears. After 1775 nobles could send disobedient serfs to the newly established houses of correction. In 1785 the St Petersburg house of correction included serfs who had been sent there by their owners.[24] The memoirs of the ex-serf N. Shipov recall that in the early nineteenth century his father, an elected serf representative, was threatened by his owner with dispatch to the house of correction or settlement in Siberia if the village failed to pay the *obrok* in full.[25]

Laws which attempted to restrict the owner's rights over the sale of serfs were in practice disregarded. The Code of 1649 had forbidden the sale of peasants without land but the practice continued (although the prohibition was repeated in 1808). Peter I passed two laws banning sales of individual

23. 'Vospominaniia Ivana Men'shago 1806–1849', *Russkaia starina* (1874), no. 2, p. 47.
24. RGADA, fond 16, delo 526, f. 320, report by P. Konovitsyn from St Petersburg province, 1785.
25. 'Istoriia moei zhizni. Razskaz byvshago krepostnago krest'ianina Nikolaia Nikol. Shipova, 1802–1862 g.', *Russkaia starina* 31 (1881), p. 146.

serfs, as opposed to whole families, but families continued to be broken up. In 1771, Catherine II forbade the public auction of serfs, but in the 1780s 40 female serfs were seen on sale in a market in Tula. The ban was repeated in 1808 but public sales continued to take place until the 1830s.

The *St Petersburg Gazette* included advertisements in the eighteenth century for the sale of individual and serf families (such advertisements were banned by Alexander I). The most vulnerable serfs were household serfs, particularly young men who could be purchased as recruits. The extent of human suffering endured as a result of these terse adverts in the *Gazette* for 1793 can only be guessed:

For sale an 8-year-old boy very agile and good at domestic service . . .

. . . for sale as surplus a 22-year-old man, trained in women's dressmaking, who is suitable also as a recruit . . .

. . . two boys for sale, one 17 and the other 14 years old, both good behaviour, and the latter trained as a barber. Their price 500 roubles.

. . . for sale a peasant stove-repairer, suitable as a recruit, with his wife and two daughters . . .

For sale a 35-year-old village *baba* [married peasant women] of good behaviour . . .

For 600 roubles for sale two boys, of whom one is 17 and the other 15 years old . . .

. . . for sale a man of good behaviour, who is trained in millinery and who can be used as a yardman and coachman. Also for sale an almost new carriage wheel.

For sale a peasant of 21 years from the country with his wife of the same age and young son . . .

. . . for sale 27-year-old *baba* with her 10-year-old son . . .

. . . for sale two unmarried girls aged 17 and 39 years . . .

Very little control was exercised over punishments meted out to serfs. Nobles did not have the right to execute a serf, but they could choose a punishment which would almost certainly result in death. Hundreds, or even thousands of blows could be inflicted, leading to the maiming or death of serfs; other nobles kept instruments for punishment, including spiked collars and stocks. Houseserfs were particularly vulnerable to the whims and tempers of their masters, and often their mistresses. One noblewomen is said to have whipped 80 female houseserfs for not collecting wild strawberries when she asked. Serfs were more subject to arbitrary behaviour on small estates where they came into personal contact with their owners. Some of the largest landowners, whose estates were left in the hands of their stewards, regulated punishments for particular offences. Punishments were laid down for serfs on

P.A. Rumiantsev's estates in the 1750s and ranged from fines for drunkenness, laziness and non-attendance at church to whipping for theft. But punishments were frequent and almost universal even in the early nineteenth century. A study of the village of Petrovskoe (Tambov province) found that in a two-year period from 1826 to 1828, 79 per cent of the adult males were flogged, 24 per cent more than once. The state could intervene in extreme cases. Countess Dar'ia Saltykova was believed to have killed over one hundred serfs in the late 1750s and early 1760s. She was investigated in 1762 and six years later sentenced to lose her noble status, be pilloried for one hour in Moscow and then confined in a convent for the rest of her life.

In practice the relationships between nobles and serfs was more complex than one of simple exploitation of the latter by the former. Good landowners made provision for serfs in time of famine and so gave them a certain protection against calamity (it was, of course, in the interests of the landowner that his serfs should survive and be capable of contributing labour and cash to him and the state). There were also examples of bonds of affection between nobles and their serfs, but these were not relationships between equals. Even the most benevolent nobles regarded their serfs as little more than children – amusing and affectionate at times, but essentially lazy and ignorant – and believed it was their right and duty to correct and punish them. Martha Wilmot commented shrewdly in the early nineteenth century that:

> A mixture of familiarity and Pride appears to me to be a striking characteristic of this country. . . . I have been more than once puzzled to find out which was the Mistress and which the *femme de Chambre* . . . the russian custom of caressing one moment the Slaves they beat the next. . . .[26]

'Ownership' of land and people by 'non-privileged' groups

It was noted above that Russian nobles claimed as their privilege the monopoly on the ownership of land with serfs. But the 'non-privileged' estates had the 'right' both to purchase and to lease unpopulated land. The concept, however, of 'ownership' of land has to be seen within the understanding of the time. Sale of land, as opposed to lease, implied something more permanent, but to peasants 'ownership' of land meant having the right to use the land and not permanent possession of it. In 1801 state peasants, merchants and artisans were given the right to buy non-populated land. In 1823 the state peasant commune acquired the right to purchase such lands as a legal entity. *Odnodvortsy* also owned their own serfs and sold them to other *odnodvortsy*. In 1762 17,675 male peasants were listed as the possession of *odnodvortsy*; by 1782 this had risen to 21,531. On 22 January 1762 the *St Petersburg Gazette* referred to a houseserf of the retired First-Major Kyrill Mikhailov 'who he had bought on 4 December 1753 . . . from the *odnodvorets* Petr Cheremisinov'.

26. *The Russian Journals*, pp. 48, 297.

In practice, peasants leased, mortgaged and bought land. In 1765 the government noted that these activities by 'black-ploughing' state peasants in north Russia had led to sharp differences of wealth between these peasants and forbade further sales of land the following year. The *nakazy* from 'black-ploughing' peasants to the Legislative Commission in 1767 asked for their rights to sell and lease land to be restored to them. Court peasants also sold and leased land, either individually or collectively, including in the north, south, central and Volga areas. In Iamburg district in 1732, for example, 25 court peasants leased land collectively but five of the peasants contributed most; by 1749 only seven peasants in the village were still paying to lease land. Stable peasants bought and sold land to each other, although this was prohibited in 1763. Postdrivers were given permission to sell land to other postdrivers in 1766. Monastic peasants, including landless peasants, who lived on the land of the Pafnut'ev-Borovsk monastery (near the town of Borovsk) leased land from the monastery and from noble landowners in the early years of the eighteenth century. Townspeople also owned or leased land, partly in consequence of the fact that many people who were legally defined as townspeople were in fact occupied in agricultural pursuits. Between 1615 and 1670 it has been estimated that 223 transactions (purchases or leases) concerning land took place in the district of Ustiug, involving 76 families from the urban community.[27]

Serfs could also buy land in the name of their owner; A.S. Suvorov wrote of his peasants 'I permit the whole commune to buy land and waste ground'.[28] Peasants could not buy property in towns but there were whole streets in St Petersburg and Moscow in which houses had been bought by the serfs of the Sheremet'evs and Orlovs in the names of their masters. The Sheremet'evs allowed their peasants in the industrial village of Ivanovo to sell and lease their houses to each other. In the period 1763–75, eight transfers of land took place between serfs on the Vasil'evskoe estate (Sheremet'ev family) – for example, A. Makhov and A. Soshnikov 'ceded' a field to V. Manenkov for 10 years for 10 roubles.[29] The price of land rose, so that in 1810 a serf on the Manuilovskoe estate (Gagarin family) complained that where he used to pay 15–20 roubles for a *desiatina* he now had to pay 60 roubles.[30] In 1827 serfs on one of the Iusupov estates leased 2,156 *desiatiny* of land at a cost of 5–5.5 roubles per *desiatina*. The wealthy serf Ivan Kutomanov, for example, leased 280 *desiatiny* and Mikhail Stronin leased 253 *desiatiny* of this land.[31] These noble families, of

27. Iu.A. Tikhonov, 'Zemlevladenie posadskikh liudei v Ustiuzhskom uezde XVII v', *Ezhegodnik po agrarnoi istorii Vostochnoi Evropy 1964* (Kishinev, 1966), pp. 270–9.
28. V.I. Semevskii, *Krest'iane v tsarstvovanie Imperatritsy Ekateriny II* (St Petersburg, 1901), vol. I, p. 125.
29. M.F. Prokhorov, *Krest'ianskoe dvizhenie v tsentral'noi Rossii v tret'ei chetverti XVIIIv (po materialam Moskovskoi gubernii)* (Moscow, 1993), p. 11.
30. V.A. Fedorov, *Pomeshchich'i krest'iane tsentral'no-promyshlennogo raiona Rossii kontsa XVII – pervoi poloviny XIX v* (Moscow, 1974), pp. 33–4.
31. I.D. Koval'chenko, *Russkoe krepostnoe krest'ianstvo v pervoi polovine XIX v* (Moscow, 1967), pp. 104, 123.

course, were some of the biggest and wealthiest landowners in Russia at the time, and practice on their estates cannot be assumed to be typical of Russia as a whole. Nevertheless, in 1807, 369 peasants collectively 'bought', that is, leased, 669 *desiatiny* of land for 8 years for 2,440 roubles from the Iaroslavl' nobleman, Chernosvitov.[32] Furthermore, serfs bought inhabited land and other serfs in the name of their owner. In 1794 two villages on the Sheremet'ev estates, Ivanovo and Stromikhin, included 528 male and 659 female peasants who had been 'bought and [were] living with their owners'. V.G. Orlov allowed his serfs to purchase peasants 'to serve them'; the purchasers did not have to pay *obrok* for these peasants but they were subject to poll tax and the recruit levy. Most serfs in fact bought peasants as 'substitutes' for the recruit levy. In 1799 and 1804 the peasants Ivan and Fedor Shvalev purchased, in the name of their owner, N.I. Saltykov, 303 *desiatiny* of land and 38 male peasants for 8,720 roubles.

THE STATUS OF NON-RUSSIANS WITHIN THE EMPIRE

The privileged western borderlands?

The western borderlands were given the important privilege of exemption from general conscription (they paid a special tax instead). In the early nineteenth century the inhabitants of Courland, Georgia and Bessarabia were given the same privilege. Service in the administration or the army opened up career prospects for the non-Russian nobility, who often occupied high positions out of all proportion to their numbers. This was particularly true of the Baltic German nobility although Ukrainians, particularly after 1785, and Poles, after 1815, also took advantage of the new opportunities which opened up for them in the Russian state. Merchants and artisans in Smolensk province had the right to own peasants without land, a privilege granted to them by the Polish king and confirmed again by the tsar in 1777.

Peasants in the western borderlands enjoyed certain advantages over their Russian counterparts. Landowners in the Baltic provinces were slightly constrained in their exploitation of serf labour by a system of regulations which defined the obligations of the peasants. After 1765, peasants in Livonia were guaranteed the ownership of movable property (although their labour obligations were left largely to the discretion of the landowner). Similar inventories of peasant obligations existed in Belorussia and Lithuania before their annexation by the Russian state. These inventories were only formally abolished in 1840, when Russian law was introduced into the western provinces and Polish law was supplanted. In Belorussia there existed a category of *vol'nye liudi* (free peasants), numbering over 14,000 in 1795 in Grodno province alone, who leased land but paid *obrok* on it. By 1858, however, the number of *vol'nye liudi* had dropped to 1,000. There was also a small number of peasants who owned

32. Fedorov, *Pomeshchich'i krest'iane*, p. 35.

land outright although these became *vol'nye liudi* in the course of the eighteenth century. It has been estimated that about one per cent of the land in western Belorussia and Lithuania was held by non-privileged classes in the late eighteenth century. The sale of peasants without land had been illegal in Belorussia before its incorporation into the Russian empire. Although this custom was upheld by the Senate, in practice landowners here, as in the Ukraine and the Baltic provinces where the same law had applied, copied their Russian counterparts and disregarded the law. In Finland, peasants were personally free and peasants and nobles signed contracts which specified payments in cash and kind and labour obligations.

The Russian government to some extent reduced the autonomy of borderlands by the introduction of fiscal uniformity in the late eighteenth century. In the process, some of the privileges of the peoples of borderlands were abolished as they became, *de facto*, the same as Russian state peasants. An indication of the merging of the Cossacks with the state peasantry, and the consequent ending of privileges, was their obligation to pay the poll tax in 1783 (although Don Cossacks were exempt). In the second half of the eighteenth century, the *obrok* payments by state peasants in the Ukraine were made the same as those paid by state peasants in Russia. Church peasants in the Ukraine (where church land had not been secularized) were set the same level of poll tax and *obrok* as state peasants. The poll tax was introduced into Belorussia at the same rate as in Russia almost immediately after the incorporation of the territory into the empire in 1772. At first, Belorussian peasants had in addition to pay a special tax for the right of Belorussian noblemen to distil and sell spirits, but this burden was partly relieved when the state reduced both taxes in 1773. In 1783 the spirits' tax was abolished and the poll tax restored to the level paid in Russia. The poll tax was introduced in the Polish-Lithuanian lands acquired after the second and third partitions. In Livonia and Estonia, peasants paid a special tax on land, based on lists from the late seventeenth century, until the poll tax was introduced into these provinces in 1783. In Old Finland (the southern region acquired in 1721 and 1743), peasants and townspeople paid a personal tax on all persons (male and female) over the age of 15.

Intervention by the government in relationships between the landowner and the peasantry was often to the advantage of the former. Catherine II's decree of 1783 added to the existing restrictions on the movement of Ukrainian peasants and, in effect, completed their enserfment. But Catherine did not intervene to alter relationships between landowner and peasant in the Baltic provinces or in Old Finland. In the Crimea, where peasants had been legally free, she did not introduce serfdom. In 1796, in the reign of Paul I, serfdom was extended to New Russia. In Georgia, the Russian presence from the early nineteenth century led to an equalization of burdens on the Georgian peasantry, while the lesser nobles were freed from their own vassal dependence on the Georgian princely families. Alexander I, however, made no attempt to introduce serfdom into the Grand Duchy of Finland, Bessarabia or the Congress Kingdom of Poland (where serfdom had been abolished in 1807).

Indeed, Alexander supported the initiatives in the Baltic provinces which led to the emancipation, without land, of the peasants in the period 1816–19 (in the case of Courland the nobles took no such initiatives but serfdom was abolished here as well in 1817).

Jews in the lands of partitioned Poland were made subject to the poll tax, which was set at separate rates for them (initially 1 rouble, at a time when peasants paid 80 copecks and merchants paid 1 rouble 20 copecks). In 1783 the poll tax was set at the same rate as for Russians. But in 1794, these Jews had a double tax imposed on them (4 roubles poll tax or 2 per cent of their declared capital for Jews registered as merchants, as opposed to one per cent for Russian merchants). The double tax for Jews was never formally abolished by decree and it persisted until at least 1812. Jews were not made liable for conscription but they had to pay a special tax for this exemption, which was set at 360 silver roubles, or 500 paper roubles, per recruit in 1794 (unlike Old Believers who were conscripted). In the early nineteenth century laws were passed which forbade Jews to own peasants, but in 1820 it was reported that 46 Jews in Grodno province owned 19,438 serfs. Jews in other parts of the empire acquired in the early nineteenth century fared slightly better. In Bessarabia, Jews were allowed to participate in the spirits trade and to hold leases. Jews in the Congress Kingdom in theory enjoyed equal civil rights with Poles after the introduction of the Napoleonic civil code into the Duchy of Warsaw. In practice, there was discriminatory legislation against Jews, and they paid an exemption in lieu of military service, although they were not as restricted in movement or occupation as in Russia.

The non-privileged Tatars and tribesmen

In contrast to policies pursued in the western borderlands, and to some extent in the south, the relationship between the Russian state and the non-Christian, often nomadic, peoples of Siberia and the south was one of mutual non-comprehension at best and savage exploitation at worst. Indeed, Russian penetration led to the drastic decline of native populations (see Chapter 1). Tribes were obliged to pay a tribute, or *iasak*, to the Russian state, which was extracted from them by force if not paid willingly. Natives could also be obliged to carry out labour services and to provide horses for Russian officials. They could be conscripted into special border units, called 'native Cossack regiments', or levied for the regular Russian army. It has been estimated that between 1735 and 1740 3,236 Bashkirs were forcibly conscripted as soldiers and sailors. Kalmyks were conscripted in the 1770s to form a protective cordon from Astrakhan' to the river Ural. Fiscal obligations varied. In Astrakhan' native (*aulnye*) Tatars paid no taxes but were obliged to transport military goods. Armenians and 'outside' (*slobodskie*) Tatars paid a lump sum in lieu of poll tax; the Senate resisted the attempt to impose the poll tax on the population of the town as it believed it would lead to the exodus of the trading population.

In 1795, 61 per cent of the population of Astrakhan' and the North Caucasus provinces were not subject to personal taxes.

In the reign of Catherine II there was an attempt to gain the loyalty of the Muslim population, in particular the Crimean Tatars and the Kazakhs, by a combination of incentives to leave the Muslim faith and concessions and privileges to the Muslim elites. Conversion to Christianity was rewarded by a three-year exemption from taxes, while Muslim Tatars were forbidden to own Christian serfs. Muslim leaders were given the right to own estates, provided there were no Orthodox peasants on the land. Kazakh nobles could be recognized as part of the Russian nobility, with the same privileges, in the early nineteenth century if they performed military service for the tsar.

Tribal people were particularly likely to be taken into slavery and this continued into the eighteenth and early nineteenth centuries. In 1654 two Cossacks sold a native woman for 15 roubles in the Siberian town of Tara. In 1693, two priests and a deacon owned natives in Berezov. In the early eighteenth century John Bell commented on the Iakuts, who 'often sell their children to the Russians, who are very fond of them'.[33] In 1712 a *voevoda* (military governor in a province) reported that:

> Those [natives] who are poorest and have no means of livelihood are handed over to Cossacks for winter labour in lieu of iasak [tribute]. . . . And their wives and children have been taken from many of them – so many have been taken that there is hardly a Cossack in Iakutsk who does not have natives as slaves.[34]

In the early nineteenth century Maria Guthrie saw Circassian women for sale at a market in the Crimea, 'brought in vast numbers every year by their own parents, and sold at from 2 to 4,000 Turkish piastres each, in proportion to their charms'.[35]

SUMMARY: DEVELOPMENTS 1650–1825

Throughout the period 1650–1825 the population of the Russian empire ful-filled obligations to the state. These obligations varied according to social estate and, to some extent, race. Nobles served in the armed forces or the civil administration, clergy tended not only to the religious needs of the popu-lation but also helped preserve civil order through their 'police' functions, townspeople and peasants paid taxes, billeted troops and performed labour services. Two major changes, however, occurred in this period. One was the

---

33. J.L. Stevenson (ed.), *A Journey from St Petersburg to Pekin 1719–22 by John Bell of Antermony* (Edinburgh, 1965), p. 73.
34. J. Forsyth, *A History of the Peoples of Siberia. Russia's North Asian Colony 1581–1990* (Cambridge, 1992), p. 69.
35. Maria Guthrie, *A Tour Performed in the Years 1795–6, through the Taurida, or Crimea* (London, 1802), p. 152.

introduction of the poll tax in Peter I's reign, which served to eliminate or merge social categories (slaves, *odnodvortsy* and various small categories of peasants). The social groups which had to pay the poll tax were seen to be 'unprivileged tax-paying people' which led to unsuccessful attempts by the *odnodvortsy*, and successful attempts by the merchants, to be relieved from this humiliating tax in recognition of their separate and superior status. Nobles, ordinary soldiers and clergy were exempted because they were 'service people' who performed other services for the state. In the late eighteenth century the extension of the poll tax to peasants in the western and southern border-lands served to weaken their separate status; the extension of the poll tax to Cossacks in 1783 in effect reduced their status to that of state peasants. The other important development concerned the nature of the service of the nobil-ity, which underwent substantial and traumatic change in the course of the eighteenth century. The Table of Ranks in 1722 was far-reaching in its effects although it never created a service meritocracy. In the course of the eighteenth century the Russian nobility eased its service obligations, culminating in the freedom from compulsory service in 1762. After this date, service, particu-larly in the army, came to be seen as a privilege rather than a burden for the nobility and was viewed almost as a mark of nobility in itself as well as an important source of income and status. The rights of the nobility were enshrined in the Charter to the Nobles in 1785. These rights remained weak, but the status, privileges and opportunities given to the Russian nobility in 1785 (coupled with the new posts reserved for them in the provinces after 1775) were sufficiently attractive to persuade many non-Russian nobles in the empire to seek membership of the Russian *dvorianstvo*. The logical corollary to the freedom of the nobles from compulsory service, that is, the ending of the serfdom which had been institutionalized at the very beginning of this period to give the nobles the economic means to carry out their military service, did not take place until 1861.

why doesn't she explicate the reservations contained in the 1762 emancipation of the nobility from compulsory state service?

CHAPTER 4

Social institutions

Institutions representing separate social estates – the peasant commune, urban organs of self-government, noble assemblies – are of particular significance in Russia in this period because of the absence of broader representative bodies. (No European state had a democratically elected parliament in this period, of course, and it was only after the French Revolution that on the continent of Europe national assemblies began to replace the traditional bodies which represented particular social estates.) In Russia, an assembly of the land (*zemskii sobor*) had been active from the mid-sixteenth to the mid-seventeenth century. The assembly first met in the reign of Ivan IV (ruled 1533–84), and comprised members of the Boiar Duma (itself an advisory council, not an elected body, which represented the interests of the boiar elite), the office-holding military servicemen and elected administrators of the Moscow urban community. The function of the assembly was vague, but in 1566 it voted for the continuation of the war with Poland-Lithuania. During the chaos of the Time of Troubles (1605–13) the assembly grew in importance, electing first Boris Godunov (1598) and then Michael Romanov (1613) as tsar. The assembly of 1613 included representatives not only from servicemen (overwhelmingly from the lesser service gentry) and townspeople but also from state peasants from north Russia, Cossacks and the clergy. It continued to play an important role in government in the first half of the seventeenth century, voting taxes and being consulted on foreign policy. In 1648–49 the assembly participated actively in the compilation of the *Ulozhenie*, or Code of Laws. This particular assembly comprised mainly the middle and lesser gentry and townspeople. Although the assembly was convened again in the 1650s for consultation on foreign policy, its power waned during the rest of the reign of Alexis (ruled 1645–76). It is thought that the last proper assembly met in 1653, although several consultations took place between the tsar and particular interest groups until the accession of Peter I.

Catherine II convened a special Legislative Commission in 1767 to discuss her Great Instruction (or *Nakaz*) and make proposals for compiling a new code of laws. There were 564 deputies at the first session of the Commission, 28 of whom had been appointed from the highest central government institutions (the Senate, the Synod and the colleges, that is, the central government departments established by Peter I), and 536 of whom were elected deputies from the gentry, the townspeople, state peasants, Cossacks and non-Russians. The social composition of the assembly (irrespective of which social estate the deputy was actually chosen to represent) was: 205 nobles, 167 merchants, 42 *odnodvortsy*, 29 state peasants, 44 Cossacks, 7 industrialists, 19 chancellery clerks and 54 tribesmen. The clergy were represented by a member of the Synod. The Legislative Commission was never intended to be a parliament in the modern understanding of the word. It was primarily a consultative body, a means by which the new ruler could understand the desires, needs and complaints of her subjects through the instructions they brought from their constituents and from the nature of the discussion on administrative and social matters. The deputies for their part often regarded their participation as yet another onerous burden imposed by the state.

Lack of national representative bodies did not mean that the population of the empire played no role in the administration of its own affairs. In this chapter, the fiscal, economic, administrative and judicial roles of peasant communes, urban institutions and, from the late eighteenth century, noble assemblies are examined. The attempt by the government to instil a sense of corporate pride in at least urban and noble institutions (but not in the peasant commune), and the attitude towards service by the participants, are central themes. Consideration is also given to the separate institutions of the Baltic provinces and the Ukraine and those of other non-Russians and to the representative institutions of Finland and the Congress Kingdom of Poland.

THE PEASANT COMMUNE (*MIR*)

In the period under study most peasants were subject to a form of communal organization, the *mir* (sometimes referred to as the *sel'skoe obshchestvo*, or rural commune, and later called the *obshchina* by the Russian nineteenth-century intelligentsia and also by Soviet historians). The commune became the standard form of peasant organization not only for seigneurial serfs, but also for court, monastic and state peasants. The *odnodvortsy* communities in the south also adopted a communal form of organization, although not necessarily the land-partitioning functions which are associated with the communes elsewhere.

The debate about the peasant commune

The origins of the peasant commune are uncertain and have led to fierce historical controversy, as the historian Blum has put it 'despite – or perhaps more accurately, because of – the sparseness of information about the earlier centuries of Russian communal development'.[1] The mid-nineteenth century witnessed a heated debate in Russia between the Slavophiles, who held that the

---

1. Jerome Blum, *Lord and Peasant in Russia from the Ninth to the Nineteenth Century* (Princeton, 1961), p. 508.

Russian commune was of ancient origin, and the Westernizers, who argued that it was a recent innovation created by the state to facilitate the collection of the taxes. To an extent, this debate tells us more about the intellectual climate and issues of mid-nineteenth century Russia than it does about the origin and features of the peasant commune (particularly because it downplays the significance of similar communal types of organization for peasants in earlier times elsewhere in Europe). But the debate went to the heart of the state-assigned function of the commune. Should it be regarded as a genuine egalitarian, land-sharing body (contrasted by the Slavophiles and others with the selfish individualism of the West) or was it simply a convenient tool of the state, imposed from above on an unwilling peasantry? It seems from the fragmentary material which exists that some form of communal organization existed in pre-Muscovite Russia, but that the role of the commune in the redistribution of land (the commune is often referred to as the 'land-partitioning commune') and distribution tax burdens only became common in the eighteenth century. On noble estates, this process was given an impetus by the new forms of tax assessment introduced by the poll tax in the reign of Peter I. On state lands (state peasant and court peasants, *odnodvortsy*), the assumption of the function of land redistribution and equalization of holdings took place rather later in the century, but again the motivation was largely a fiscal one.

The development suggests that the Westernizer line was correct in that the commune was established from above (by the landowner or the state) for primarily fiscal reasons. The commune was convenient (in that some form of communal organization already existed in most villages), practical (as peasants knew best how land should be distributed and the economic capabilities of individual households) and cheap (as the peasants paid for their own organization and elected officials). The imposition of a 'mutual responsibility' for dues, in that the community was collectively responsible for taxes and other obligations (and collectively responsible for any shortfall) enhanced the role of the commune in redistributing burdens. In practice, the commune could treat less desirable and more vulnerable members with a callousness that was almost inevitable given the fragile economic climate in which most peasants lived. The weakest went not so much to the wall as to the recruiting station. On the other hand, the communes did not act purely to fulfil the instructions of the state or the noble landowner. For example, the initiative for land redistribution sometimes came from state peasants themselves, as was the case in some villages in Siberia and amongst Cossack communitites on the Don. On serf estates the commune perfomed a wide variety of functions within the community, some of which purely concerned peasant interests and had little to do with the noble owner, and some of which went beyond purely economic matters. Indeed, a study of the communes below demonstrates that the interest of the peasants and the nobles could come into conflict as their economic (and sometimes moral) interests were not always the same.

Furthermore, we have to be wary of making generalizations about the functioning of the communes. The Soviet period saw the publication of a large number of impressive publications on peasant communes (including those of serfs, court, monastic and state peasants) which have drawn on extensive archival material. These studies have demonstrated that although the communes shared some important common characteristics they could differ according to their particular needs and according to the individuals concerned. The nature of surviving archival material also means that we know far more about the operation of communes on large noble estates (where correspondence between the commune and the central offices has been retained) than we will ever know about the small estates which were the norm (in the 1760s, 75 per cent of nobles owned less than 60 serfs) and where records were less likely to be kept. Nor do we know how communes functioned in villages which were divided between several noble owners, although we know that in these cases more than one commune could be set up within the village. Regional variations are also crucial, in relation to the definition of the commune and to its functions. In the north and north-west villages could combine to form one large commune. The role of the commune in land redistribution also varied according to region. Practice evolved differently among state peasants in north Russia and in Siberia, where there was abundance of land and few noble landowners, than in areas in central Russia where land was at a premium; particular pressures existed in the southern borderlands (among state peasant, serf, Cossack and *odnodvorsty* settlements); in the western borderlands different traditions of land tenure existed. Even within geographical areas, factors such as the size of the estate, the quality and uniformity of the land, the density of population, the extent of waterways and communications and predominance of *barshchina* or *obrok* forms of dues could also affect the functions of the commune.

The commune assembly and elected officials

The main organ of the peasant community was the commune assembly (*skhod*). This usually took the form of a communal meeting in the village (despite the variations noted above the great majority of communes represented one village) at which all male peasants could speak but where normally only the heads of household (or *pervostateinye*, 'first-rate' peasants) had the right to vote. If the head of household could not appear in person his vote could be given by a proxy, who could be his wife. In Molodoi Tud (Sheremet'ev estate) the commune assembly was described in 1790 as only representing a small number of 'first-ranking and middle-ranking peasants'.[2] In Siberian villages it was not uncommon to find members of other social estates, including merchants, artisans and Siberian Cossacks, represented in the communes, some of them even acting as heads. In 1799, for example, state peasant communes in the Kolyvan'-Voskresensk region were headed by, among others, a

2. L.S. Prokof'eva, *Krest'ianskaia obshchina v Rossii vo vtoroi polovine XVIII pervoi polovine XIX veka* (Leningrad, 1981), p. 134.

merchant, Lev Bolotov, and an artisan, Trofim Shestoboev. Each commune set its own age qualifications for attendance and voting. Most decisions were reached by a simple majority of votes but a two-thirds majority was required to resolve some important issues.

The size of the assembly varied according to the size of the village and local custom. Most serf commune assemblies ranged between 20 and 70 participants, but several village communes within one estate could combine on occasions and be far larger. State peasant communes also varied in size depending on the size of village, and whether more than one village or area was represented. The frequency with which assemblies met could also vary, even within one village; in the serf village of Nikol'skoe (Orlov estate) the assembly met between 16 and 32 times a year in the years 1771, 1780, 1785 and 1786 but only between four and eight times a year between 1806 and 1810. The assembly met more frequently during the winter months, November to April, than during the busier times of the year. Noble landowners could dispense with large and unwieldy meetings altogether by summoning a number of chief elders of the village to hear their instructions. The assemblies were not always conducted with decorum, drink being a vital ingredient. Reports on state peasant assemblies in the early nineteenth century included the following comments: 'As a general rule noise, screams, curses, threats and at times brawling'; 'without vodka, the skhod was no skhod'; 'one must admit resolutions were sold for vodka'.[3]

Large estates could have elaborate chains of responsibility from individual villages to managers or stewards, to administrative estate offices, to central offices in St Petersburg and Moscow. Some estate managers were able to control the assembly and make it subordinate to their wishes, but many estate managers became embroiled in disputes with the peasants. The records of the village of Baki (Lieven estates, Kostroma province) in the early nineteenth century documented frequent conflicts between the commune assembly and estate managers, with petitions being sent to the Lieven office in St Petersburg from both sides. The estate managers were accused by the peasants of bribery, assault and financial irregularities, especially concerning the recruit levy. The rights and wrongs of such accusations cannot be fully determined, but it is perhaps significant that the attack on one estate manager arose after his attempt to equalize the recruit burden by levying sums on each family according to its resources; this roused the ire of the wealthiest peasants, who then became his fiercest opponents.[4] Although nobles could intervene to cancel a decision of the commune, replace its officials, or even disband it altogether, such actions were rare and the commune was given considerable autonomy. In general, large landowners communicated from a distance with the commune and gave it written instructions, some of which were very detailed; smaller landowners would be more likely to intervene directly.

3. George Bolotenko, 'Administration of the State Peasants in Russia before the Reforms of 1838', unpublished PhD thesis, University of Toronto, 1979, p. 219.
4. BL, Add. MS 47429, ff. 53–55; Lieven papers, estate papers, 1813–16; Add. MS 47430, ff. 10–11v, 117–19, 136–136v, Lieven papers, estate papers, 1817–19.

The assembly had to elect a variety of peasant officials – *burmistry* (serf managers; usually appointed by the landowner but with the approval of the commune), *starosty* or *starshiny* (village elders or heads), *tseloval'niki* (sworn men, mainly responsible for treasury), *sotskie* and *desiatskie* ('one hundred-men' and 'ten-men', responsible for law and order in an area of one hundred or ten households), *vybornye* ('elected men', responsible mainly for fiscal matters), *zemskie* (assistants) and clerks, depending on local custom and the size of the village (regulations for the elected officials in state peasant assemblies were laid down in 1790). Peasant officials could be elected for a year, but some occupied the posts for life. Salaries of elected officials varied. In the late eighteenth century A.M. Golitsyn gave peasant elders 25 roubles a year. Some elected officials earned more than this, but in the state peasant communes of Siberia elders could earn as little as 10 roubles a year. Embezzlement of funds and other corrupt practices were common, partly because only limited checks could be made on financial and other records from within a community with few literate members. In 1758, the serfs of Molodoi Tud accused the clerk, Konovalov, of taking bribes and of disorder and drunkenness. On the other hand, commune officials could be punished – fined, beaten or even dispatched as recruits – if they failed to fulfil their owners' instructions and, in particular, if they failed to collect the *obrok* dues in full. The election process was often corrupt as votes could be bought. A report from Vladimir province (east of Moscow) on state peasant communes in the early nineteenth century noted that:

> . . . peasant assemblies often begin with feasts: some treat [fellow] peasants so that they will be elected; others to be freed of office; in such a case, [one finds] in the first group, peasants of unreliable character, and in the second . . . [those] interested in . . . their own well-being.[5]

The type of peasant who held office, and their attitude towards this service, varied. In some cases, peasant officials were simply appointed by their masters. The writer Alexander Herzen (born 1812) described the consequence when his father quarrelled with his brothers, with whom he shared ownership of the estate:

> The elder brother would appoint a village elder, the younger ones would remove him in a month, upon some nonsensical pretext, and appoint another whom their senior would not recognise. With all this, of course, backbiting, slander, spies and favourites were naturally plentiful, and under it all the poor peasants, who found neither justice nor defence, were harassed on all sides, and oppressed with the double burden of work and the disorganisation caused by the capricious demands of their owners.[6]

N.N. Shipov, a wealthy peasant, recalled in the early nineteenth century that his father 'as a wealthy and respected man was frequently *burmistr*', an obligation which he resented, partly because it distracted him from his extensive trading

---

5. Bolotenko, *Administration of the State Peasants*, p. 219.
6. *My Past and Thoughts. The Memoirs of Alexander Herzen*, trans. by Constance Garnett, intro. by Isaiah Berlin (London, 1968), vol. I, p. 14.

activities but also because it led to conflicts with neighbouring peasants over *obrok* payments.[7] State peasant officials were supposed to be married with children and not have a police record.

Service could be a burden, but it could also be an opportunity for wealthy peasants to assert themselves and ensure that allocations of obligations or land would be to their advantage. Elders on serf estates determined which peasants performed *barshchina* and serf and state peasant elders could ensure that household division favoured particular individuals and controlled the all-important recruit levy. In the serf village of Baki the commune was dominated in the early nineteenth century by the wealthy Voronin family who, in consequence, gained special exemptions from the recruit levy and then successfully resisted an attempt by a new estate manager to equalize recruit burdens within the peasant community. It has been argued that the communal structure enabled the older, wealthy, peasants, or patriarchs, to control the younger generation of male peasants with the constant threat of corporal punishment or the recruit levy if they failed to obey their decisions. It was not uncommon for rich peasants to refuse to run for office themselves but to back other, poorer peasants, who would serve their interests or use their influence to make sure that the estate clerks acted for them (in Baki, the clerk married into the Voronin family and became wealthy himself). In 1778, some wealthy court peasants in the vicinity of Moscow paid poorer peasants a small sum to take the posts of tax collectors (*sborshchiki*) for them.[8]

The functions of the commune

The commune impinged on all economic aspects of the peasant household, as well as some which were not strictly economic. Its main function was to ensure that the community fulfilled its *tiaglo* (fiscal and labour obligations) in full. In the process, the commune determined the contribution to be made by households to the poll tax and to the *obrok* payments and other local and central dues. The poll tax in principle was a levy on the individual (see Chapter 3) but as the tax was levied collectively on the commune, this became a communal obligation, and in practice the communes levied the tax differentially according to the ability of households to pay. Because the commune was collectively responsible for the total sum due, it was in its interests that all members should have the capacity to pay these dues. This led in turn to the commune redistributing land to ensure that its members had the same capacity to meet their financial obligations. This 'equalizing' tendency became more common during the eighteenth century.

Repartitions took place on all types of peasant land. A study of monastic properties in central Russia in the first half of the eighteenth century found

7. 'Istoriia moei zhizni. Razskaz byvshago krepostnago krest'ianina Nikolaia Nikol. Shipova, 1802–1862 g', *Russkaia starina* 31 (1881), pp. 145–6.
8. S.I. Volkov, *Krest'iane dvortsovykh vladenii podmoskov'ia v seredine XVIII v (30–70e gody)* (Moscow, 1959), p. 188.

considerable local variety, with redivisions varying from very infrequent (24 years in one case) to only two or three years. The majority were divided between every 10 and 20 years but some properties were repartitioned up to four times in the period 1714–59.[9] The government never forced *odnodvortsy* communities to move towards land-equalizing communes, although it encouraged voluntary developments in this direction, most of which took place between the 1830s and the 1850s (many *odnodvortsy* settlements, particularly the better-endowed ones, never took this route). Sometimes initiatives for redistribution came from peasants themselves but on other occasions the commune had to handle disputes when only a few peasants in the village sought redistribution. In practice, the low productivity of Russian agriculture in this period, the poor state of communications and the limited access to the market made it difficult for most peasants to make sufficient additional profit out of larger land holding to offset the greater tax burden they would meet. This partly accounts for the limited resistance shown by both state peasants and serfs to loss of some of their lands by redistribution by the commune – equalization, in this respect, was simply practical. Peasant communities acted in their own best economic interests when it came to repartition. Depending on local circumstances, some villages repartitioned frequently, others hardly at all, and still others found other solutions to land shortage such as leasing or buying land from other villages (see Chapter 3, pp. 71–2). The flexibility of the peasant commune in this respect demonstrates that it responded to the particular needs of the community which it served and of which its members were an integral part.

The communes determined the share of the *obrok* payment owed by each household. Serf communes on estates which used only *barshchina* lacked this function (although they determined the *barshchina* obligations per household) and this possibly accounts for their weaker authority in such villages. The commune could come into conflict with the landowners over *obrok* payments. A.B. Kurakin was in dispute with his serfs over the level of *obrok* for over two decades. In 1796 he tried to double the *obrok* payments on his estate; the commune resolved to increase it by only one and a half times. This was accepted at the time by Kurakin, although the level was later raised in 1803 and 1805. In 1807, Kurakin tried to increase the level dramatically and threatened to sell some peasants if he did not receive payments in full; the following year a new agreement was made for a lower level. This conflict illustrates the nature of the relationship between noble landowners and commune. The landowner could demand more and threaten his serfs, but the commune could put up sufficient resistance at least to delay or modify such plans. Such a relationship does not accord with the view of the commune as a passive instrument of noble or state exploitation.

One of the most important functions of the commune was to oversee the selection of recruits. In practice, both landlords and the commune used the

9. L.N. Vdovina, *Krest'ianskaia obshchina i monastyr' v tsentral'noi Rossii v pervoi polovine XVIII v* (Moscow, 1988), p. 69.

levy as a convenient opportunity to rid themselves of their least useful members. Landowners rarely interfered with, although they normally sanctioned, the selection of such recruits made by the commune. In this context 'least useful' meant, on the one hand, idle or troublesome peasants and, on the other hand, the poorest peasants, who could make only a small, or no, contribution to the poll tax. In 1788 the commune assembly of Molodoi Tud estate resolved to 'dispatch as recruits 71 men for negligence in ploughing, for not paying dues, suspicious [characters] and *bobyli* [landless peasants]'. The same assembly in 1779 threatened one peasant that if he did not volunteer as a recruit (he was a fugitive) his house would be destroyed, his grain scattered and his cattle driven off.[10] In 1819 three peasants were conscripted from Baki on the grounds of 'dissolute and drunken behaviour and failure to pay taxes'.[11] The estate manager on one of the Iusupov estates was instructed in 1825 to dispatch peasants as recruits without drawing lots if they had 'no aptitude for farming or other work' or if they could not be cured of 'drunkenness and debauchery'.[12]

The interests of the commune and the landowner were not necessarily identical; the landowner was happy to rid himself of disreputable peasants but lacked the same concern about poor households. The commune was concerned with dispatching the poorest peasants who could not contribute to the collective taxes paid by the peasants. This essential difference in interest could lead to conflicts between serfs and their landowners. Indeed, more enlightened nobles sometimes intervened to prevent the commune from dispatching weaker members, and insisted that the principle of recruiting from larger households prevailed. V.I. Suvorov, for example, criticized his *burmistr* for conscripting a married peasant and ordered that in future no married males, heads of households or sole males in the household were to be conscripted. Other landowners insisted that peasants with useful skills (artisans etc.) were exempt from conscription. But for the most part, peasant elders determined whose bad behaviour merited such a punishment and, for the most part, dispatched such peasants without interference from the landowner.

The communes fixed the timetable of work in the fields, although much of this was already determined by tradition and rarely led to disputes, determined the use of common woods and pasture land and divided empty land between peasants. Peasants needed the permission of the commune and a passport to settle elsewhere, as this could affect the tax capacity of the whole community. The communes also took action, usually following instruction from landowners, to prevent fires, control epidemics and to stop illegal production of spirits. However, the attempts of some more enlightened landowners to deal with destitution by the establishment of grain stores or by the introduction of almshouses for the poor were not necessarily welcomed by the communes, which were reluctant to contribute financially. Such contributions were

10. Prokof'eva, *Krest'ianskaia obshchina v Rossii*, pp. 152, 155.
11. BL, Add. MS 47431, f. 67v. Lieven papers, estate papers, 1819–25.
12. K.V. Sivkov, *Ocherki po istorii krepostnogo khoziaistva i krest'ianskogo dvizheniia v Rossii v pervoi polovine XIX veka po materialam arkhiva stepnykh votchin Iusupovykh* (Moscow, 1951), p. 39.

particularly resented by richer peasants who, as seen above, often dominated the communes. The communes did make provision for orphans and for other vulnerable members of society – the illegitimate, the elderly, the infirm, abandoned soldiers' wives, etc. – if family support were lacking for some reason. In the village of Nikol'skoe in the early nineteenth century, orphans were placed in the care of neighbours but the commune undertook to provide an allowance for their subsistence.

The commune intervened in quarrels between peasants and between parents and children. G.V. Gruzinskii instructed the commune on his Nizhnii Novgorod estate in 1785 that peasants could be punished by 'the will' of their fathers, but if the parents were themselves 'debauched' then children could undergo corporal punishment at the assembly inflicted by relatives and 'first-ranking' peasants. The commune was mainly concerned if disputes, or poor behaviour, should lead to any radical change in the composition of the household with implications for its *tiaglo* burden. The commune could also judge and punish peasants for petty crime (thefts of goods under the value of 5 roubles were not considered a criminal offence). Typically, such cases were resolved by the elected officials but put before the whole assembly if agreement could not be reached. In 1752 a commune on one of the Sheremet'ev estates investigated the case of a peasant, Isakov, accused of stealing honey; the evidence consisting of a shirt with honey on it was produced, and the peasant was beaten with rods. In 1817 F.V. Samarin instructed the commune to deal with adulterous peasants by administering corporal punishment or public humiliation. Communes punished peasants for adultery or expelled licentious soldiers' wives from the village. The communes also investigated cases of sorcery. In 1763, Ivan Chetverinkov, a peasant from Ust'-Nitsyn settlement (Siberia) accused another peasant of theft and telling fortunes (see also Chapter 10). The commune could employ other means in addition to corporal punishment to shame peasants, such as tarring them or forcing them to wear horse collars. Some landowners issued instructions for the commune to punish drunks. While landowners for the most part thought in terms of peasant discipline and good order, the commune was all too conscious that persistent drunkenness could prevent a peasant from fulfilling his tax obligations, for which the whole community would suffer. It was, therefore, prepared to confiscate land from drunken peasants and give it to more reliable members, even if this meant that the peasant concerned would be destitute; he could always, of course, be selected as a recruit.

URBAN INSTITUTIONS OF SELF-GOVERNMENT

In the early seventeenth century, the military governor (*voevoda*) exercised authority over both town and countryside in his province. Towns elected land elders (*zemskie starosty*) from within the urban community, whose main function was the allocation of state dues. Land elders were assisted by elected *tseloval'niki* (sworn men) and by elders responsible for taxation units within the town, that is suburbs, parishes or streets. The task of these elected officials was simply to serve as the fiscal agents of the state, and service was, not unnaturally, unpopular and often reserved for those who, for physical or other reasons, were unable to take part in active service (military servitors were excluded from participating in elections or standing for office). Power lay with the military governor, so the towns and their elected representatives exercised little autonomy. During the eighteenth century the tsars perceived the frailty of Russia's urban institutions as both a cause and a symptom of backwardness and attempted to stimulate corporate pride and economic activity through the establishment of institutions of urban self-government.

ush

The reforms of Peter I

Peter I's legislation of 1699 and 1721–22 established a new structure of urban administration. In 1699, towns were instructed to select their own administrators, called *burmistry*, to manage the administrative and fiscal affairs of the urban community. The posts were unsalaried, and Peter's motivation was purely economic and practical, namely to improve the economic life of the towns – and, in consequence, the tax-paying capacities of their inhabitants – and to streamline the process of tax collecting. In 1721–23 magistracies were established, comprising one president, between one and four *burgomistry* depending on the size of the town, and a number of *ratmany* as assistants, all of whom were to be selected by the townspeople. Magistracies were given responsibility for a wide range of administrative, fiscal, economic and welfare functions applying to the urban community as well as judicial powers for minor offences. In 1727, the magistracies were made subordinate to the military governor and stripped of most of their judicial powers but in 1740 their previous functions and powers were restored, at least in principle, although they were never able to achieve total independence from the governors and military governors.

How did urban institutions function after Peter's reforms? The institution which brought most of the legally defined townspeople together was the *posad* assembly (*mirskoi posadskii skhod*). This was presided over by a *posad* elder, or *starosta*, who was responsible to the *posad*, or urban community, and not to the magistracy. Much of the structure and many of the functions and procedures of the *posad* assembly mirror those of the peasant commune. Attendance at the assembly was, in theory, compulsory for members of the legally defined urban community, although in practice absenteeism was rife and attendance figures fluctuated. Attendance at the assembly of Dmitrov (a town near Moscow) ranged from 7 to 50 members in the 1720s and 1730s but the assembly in Serpukhov (south of Moscow) was attended by 212 members on one occasion in the 1740s. The number of eligible voters varied from town to town and even within towns on certain occasions. Electors sometimes included all members of the urban community and at other times just the wealthy and middle-ranked members.

We have little evidence about the activity of the *posad* assembly. We know that it conducted elections of members of the magistracy and other town officials; the elections at Kashira (north of Moscow) in 1744 apparently took place with 'great noise and shouts'.[13] The assembly could inform the magistracy of the needs of the town, but its main function seems to have been to receive instructions from the magistracy and distribute tax obligations amongst its members, in the same way as the peasant commune. The assembly, like the commune, had a collective responsibility for the *tiaglo* obligations of the urban community and a shared responsibility for any deficit. It also selected townsmen as recruits. Like the peasant commune, the *posad* assembly chose the most vulnerable members of the urban community. In 1732, for example, all the poorest merchants fled from the *posad* of Dmitrov on hearing the news that a levy was to take place. The levy was used by the urban community to rid itself of undesirable members and in 1760 the assembly acquired the right (as did landowners and state peasants) to exile harmful members of society to Siberia as settlers or dispatch them as recruits. It could also discipline its members – like peasants, townspeople could be subjected to corporal punishment in front of their peers. The assembly also had some limited rights to raise taxes to meet town requirements, although it seems that this right was rarely exercised in practice.

Little is known about the people who were elected by the assembly as members of the magistracies or about their attitude towards this unpaid service. Officials petitioned to be freed from service and the *nakazy* from townspeople to the Legislative Commission of 1767 asked for the period of service to be fixed, and limited, which suggests that service was still seen as an onerous burden. In Moscow, one councillor elected as a representative from 'merchants from other towns' successfully appealed to be relieved of his post as he had already served as the town head of Gzhatsk (east of the Urals), and others requested relief from duties because of illness or other reasons. Nevertheless, as one historian has put it, 'the power to tax is the power to destroy, and the wealthy merchants considered it a wise precaution, if not an absolute necessity, to control the magistracy office'.[14] The genealogical study of the Moscow merchants by the Russian historian Aksenov found that the wealthiest and most prominent families dominated posts in the magistracy. In the 1740s in Solikamsk (in the Urals), Aleksei Turchaninov, a salt industrialist, was accused of trying to influence the election of his candidate, which suggests that there were some advantages to be had from this.

The reforms of Catherine II

Significant changes in urban organization came about in the reign of Catherine II. The tax reform of 1775 broke the unity of the urban community by relieving

13. A.A. Kizevetter, *Posadskaia obshchina v Rossii XVIII stoletiia* (Moscow, 1903; reprint Newtonville, 1978), p. 691.
14. J. Michael Hittle, *The Service City. State and Townsmen in Russia, 1600–1800* (Cambridge, Mass., London, 1979), p. 134.

the richest members, the merchants, from the poll tax and taxing them on declared capital instead, thus, at a stroke, ending the collective tax responsibility of the urban community and the overriding fiscal role of urban institutions. The Charter to the Towns of 1785 (promulgated on the same day as the Charter to the Nobility) attempted to establish an urban corporate identity through urban institutions. The Charter established a general town duma (*obshchaia gorodskaia duma*), elected every three years from the 'town society' and made up of representatives of each of the six categories of urban dwellers (see Chapter 1). The general town duma could discuss town requirements and make representations to the governor, but its main function was to elect a town head and a six-councillor duma (*shestiglasnaia duma*), which comprised one member of each of these six categories. This executive duma was given a wide responsibility to protect the town, maintain order, encourage trade and augment incomes, extend welfare institutions, maintain public buildings and trading areas, and to settle disputes between craft guilds. Poorly drafted legislation meant there was considerable overlapping of functions, particularly between the six-councillor dumas and the town magistracies, which had been redefined in 1775 as courts of first instance for townspeople but which never relinquished the administrative functions they had previously held within the town.

The resulting urban institutions were dismissed by the historian M.T. Florinsky, in a view shared by many western and Russian historians: the 'corporate organization, foreign to Russian historical tradition, remained largely a dead letter'.[15] Nevertheless, my study of St Petersburg province (that is, of the small district towns as well as the city of St Petersburg) has offered a slightly different picture of these institutions. Some problems were certainly directly created by careless legislation. If the Charter had been followed to the letter the composition of the general town duma would have been perverse. While merchants, the wealthiest and most productive members of the town society, could only elect a maximum of three representatives (one for each merchant guild), the less well-off artisans could send one member for each craft guild (or *tsekh*) which existed in the town, and the poorest group, ordinary *posad* members, could, theoretically, outnumber merchants in larger towns by electing one member per *chast'*, or administrative section of the town. In principle, each category of the elite, wealthy groups of so-called eminent citizens (of which there were seven) and every foreign nationality could be represented. This could have led to a very uneven representation of urban society, but this was never a real issue as few towns had representatives of all these six groups anyway (see Chapter 2). In reality, most Russian towns only had representatives of the lower merchant guilds, artisans and *posad* members.

In fact, the practice in the city of St Petersburg showed that membership of the general town duma in the years 1788, 1789 and 1791 fluctuated widely – total membership ranging from 4 to 72 and, within this, merchant guild representation ranging from 1 to 11 members, craft guilds from 1 to 48,

15. M.T. Florinsky, *Russia: A History and an Interpretation* (New York, 1959), vol. I, p. 553.

foreigners from 1 to 8, real citizens from 1 to 10 etc.[16] Definite conclusions about practice throughout the country cannot be drawn. In Siberia, by way of comparison, the general town duma in Omsk in 1790 included soldiers and a priest as well as townspeople, and that of Tara in 1789 included one representative each from the clergy, soldiers, officials, Cossacks and coachmen and two deputies each from merchants, craft guilds (artisans), the *posad* and state peasants.[17] Six-councillor dumas in the district towns outside St Petersburg functioned with fewer than six members, reflecting the lack of representatives from all these groups. In practice, the composition of these dumas reflected the social composition of the urban community more accurately and sensibly than the Charter had done.

In principle, the Charter had allowed nobles to participate in urban instititons, as they could be classified as 'real citizens' if they owned property in the town. In Moscow, in the 1780s, the elected representative of the 'real citizens' in the six-councillor duma, elected from the general town duma, was noble, a *tituliarnyi sovetnik*, a councillor (9th rank). He requested to be relieved from his duty on the grounds that he was not occupied in trade and therefore did not meet the criteria set out by the Charter for membership of the six-councillor duma. This request exposed an anomaly within the Charter (the requirement concerning occupation did not apply to the general town duma) and was upheld by the provincial office. His replacement successfully argued the same case; the third candidate was a first-guild merchant who took up his post. In 1794 the councillor from the 'real citizens' in Tiumen' (Siberia) six-councillor duma was the son of a merchant.

Despite poor drafting of legislation and the unrealistic division of town society into six categories, the urban institutions in the St Petersburg province were in practice far from being moribund and urban society did show some willingness to participate in self-government. The attendance records of the members of the six-councillor dumas in district towns, as well as in the capital, were very high with almost no absenteeism. This is surprising, given the frequently expressed view that townspeople found such service unattractive and to be avoided if at all possible. But the St Petersburg city six-councillor duma met over 100 times a year; the Sofia duma (a small district town in the St Petersburg province) met 256 times in 1791 and 317 times in 1794. The business conducted by these dumas was dominated by economic matters, including grain supplies, salt and spirit monopolies, prices, petitions for contracts, taverns, expenditures and incomes. They also took responsibility for issuing passports (the Sofia six-councillor duma received 66 petitions for passports in 1791 and 93 petitions in 1794), discussed welfare institutions and handled disputes over bills of exchange. This suggests that the urban institutions

16. This material is drawn from TsGIA-SPg, fond 788, opis' 3, delo 1, journal of the St Petersburg general town duma for 1788; ibid., delo 3, journal for 1789; ibid., delo 8, journal for 1791.
17. V.V. Rabtsevich, 'Sotsial'nyi sostav organov gorodskogo samoupravleniia zapadnoi Sibiri v 80-kh gg. XVIII – pervoi chetverty XIX v' in *Istoriia gorodov Sibiri dosovetskogo perioda (XVII – nachalo XXv)*, ed. by O.N. Vilkov (Novosibirsk, 1977), p. 85.

performed a more active function than has previously been assumed by historians, although it has to be said that even within this one province the range and extent of activities varied considerably from town to town (in the town of Novoladoga, for example, all these functions were performed by the general town duma and there is no evidence that a six-councillor duma was set up at all).

The vitality of urban self-government cannot be proven for the whole country, and St Petersburg province, containing as it did the capital city, is not necessarily typical, although we know that urban institutions were established elsewhere and did function. Unfortunately, such is the dearth of memoir material that it is impossible to determine accurately how townsmen viewed service in these institutions. A study of western Siberian towns found that a small number of rich merchants dominated posts. In the period 1822–24, 14 merchant families occupied 53 posts in the town of Tiumen', and the position of town head was generally held by members of the Alasin and Prasolov families. It was also estimated that only 4 out of 37 merchants had failed to serve in Tobol'sk in the period 1819–21. In Tobol'sk, the post of town head was consistently taken by the richest merchants in the period 1786–1824. The pattern in Moscow also suggests that the wealthiest families dominated urban posts. The town head in Moscow at the end of the eighteenth century always came from the wealthiest families, such as D.D. Meshchaninov and S.D. Sitnikov. Meshchaninov came originally from peasant stock, although he rose to the first guild; possibly his assumption of office (he was town head from 1782 to 1786) was a symbol of his new status and respectability. It also seems that holding an official post was one of the required steps in furthering a career. M.P. Gubin was a second-guild merchant when he was town head of Moscow in the period 1789–92; by 1790 he was an eminent citizen and by 1801 a *kommertsii sovetnik* (an honorary title which did not confer rank) and a first-guild merchant. V.Ia. Zhigarev served as assessor in the conscience court when he was a second-guild merchant and then became town head when he became an eminent citizen (in 1801 he became a *nadvornyi sovetnik*, councillor, rank 7, that is, a hereditary noble). At the very least, these posts were considered to be of sufficient importance to attract wealthy merchants. This could well have alienated the poorer and less influential members of the urban community but direct evidence for this supposition is lacking.

The fact that further legislation was passed after the death of Catherine II concerning urban institutions and society suggests that the problems of the towns had not been resolved by the Charter of 1785. Paul I abolished the elected institutions of St Petersburg and, although Alexander I restored them, a study in 1815 found that the city lacked proper tax records, that a few powerful merchants controlled elections and forced poor townspeople to serve (which hardly suggests that a sense of corporate spirit had been generated) and that the whole structure was in need of a radical overhaul. To counter the misuse of elections in the capital, it was decreed in 1825 that no one was allowed to refuse to serve, but a complete reorganization of city administration only took place in 1846. On the other hand, in the desperate year 1812, the town dumas responded to the national crisis by collecting and donating considerable additional sums to help the war effort. In Kaluga province (which lay near the invasion route) the contributions of the dumas in roubles were as follows: Kaluga, 205,000; Kozel'sk, 10,035; Meshchovsk, 12,433; Mosal'sk, 4,271; Zhidrinsk, 3,430; Likhvin, 1,862; Peremyshl', 1,750; Tarusa, 440; Maloiaroslavets, 350 (a town later almost destroyed by the proximity of the battle); Medyn', 81.

NOBLE ASSEMBLIES

The peasant commune and the urban administration (at least until 1785) had to ensure that state obligations were fulfilled, including the collection of the poll tax and other fiscal dues and the recruit levy and other services. The collective responsibility for these obligations borne by the peasants and townspeople imposed some form of collective identity and shared interests on these communities. Such factors were not relevant for the Russian nobility. They were not subject to the poll tax or the other obligations of the 'non-privileged' social groups and, at least until 1762, their service obligations were exacted and recorded centrally by the state and not by the nobles themselves. Russian nobles had no political forum in which they could assert their interests or affect government policy. In the second half of the eighteenth century, however, Catherine II attempted to stimulate some form of corporate identity amongst the nobles through the establishment of institutions, namely the noble assemblies.

The establishment of noble assemblies

Assemblies were first established in 1766 to elect noble representatives for the Legislative Commission; marshals of the nobility were elected to preside over the assemblies. The role of the assemblies in conducting elections was confirmed and extended after the provincial reforms of 1775, when nobles had to elect not only posts in the new provincial institutions but also to select district and provincial marshals of the nobility, who were supposed to represent the needs and protect the interest of their constituents. As a result of the Charter to the Nobles of 1785 the assemblies (now called the *sobranie dvorianstva*) acquired a more formal existence at both district and provincial level. Although their primary function was still to conduct elections, assemblies were now given the responsibility for maintaining their own treasury, archive, building and secretary and for keeping the official register of the nobility in their district or province. The assembly had to record and retain the names and noble origins of the local nobility (in the six categories as laid down by the Charter) in a special book and was given the authority to deliberate and decide on claims of nobility (in other words, this had now become a provincial and no longer a central responsibility).

Catherine was quite possibly motivated by the desire to 'westernize' the nobles by developing a greater sense of the dignity of the noble estate, which she believed could partly be achieved through the creation of vigorous and respected corporate organizations. Governor-General Jacob Sievers told the Pskov assembly in 1777 that its purpose was 'to unite you in one society of well born extraction and dignity; in order to reward you with unexpected gifts, kindnesses, powers, advantages and privileges'.[18] The assemblies were supposed to act as a forum for nobles to express their shared concerns and to stimulate collective activity on behalf of the wider community. To a limited extent this was achieved. The assembly in Olonets province (in the north) undertook in 1777 to build and support a school at the cost of 5 copecks for every male peasant they owned; in Vladimir province (east of Moscow) the following year nobles donated 20 copecks for every male peasant.[19] The noble assembly in Tambov (south-east of Moscow) founded a school at its own expense in 1801.[20] The noble assemblies in the provinces of Moscow, Tula, Kaluga, Kursk, Iaroslavl' and Penza made a donation to their provincial boards of social welfare (*prikazy obshchestvennogo prizreniia*) which had been given responsibility for welfare institutions, including schools, after 1775. In 1812, the noble assemblies throughout Russia, like the town dumas, donated food-stuffs, cash and arms to assist the war effort.

There were also, however, practical reasons for the establishment of such institutions at a provincial level. After the ending of compulsory service in 1762, more nobles were able to live on their estates in the country and it was in the interest of the state that this manpower resource should be tapped. After the Statute of Provincial Reform of 1775, the noble assemblies played an important, and cost-free, role in conducting elections for posts in local admin-istration (the peasant commune and the urban institutions, of course, also elected officials as a primary function). Catherine hoped that a more developed pro-vincial society would be stimulated which would raise the economic and the cultural level of the provinces, and therefore of the empire as a whole. This required the active participation of the provincial nobility and the assemblies, being situated in the main provincial towns, were intended to provide a social, cultural and institutional centre for nobles. Certainly, the elections and the social whirl which accompanied them gave poorer provincial nobles an opportunity to mingle with their wealthier and more distinguished neigh-bours. Andrei Bolotov, a minor noble, commented enthusiastically in his memoirs on the excitement of the elections in Kaluga in 1784, where banquets, dances and town illuminations were arranged to entertain the visiting nobles, and lesser nobles like himself could mix with their wealthier neighbours at the assembly.

18. Robert David Givens, 'Servitors or Seigneurs: The Nobility and the Eighteenth Century Russian State', unpublished PhD theis, Berkeley, 1975, p. 381.
19. RGADA, fond 16, delo 636, f. 29v, report from R. Vorontsov from Vladimir and Tambov provinces, 1778.
20. I.I. Dubasov, 'Iz Tambovskikh letopisei', *Istoricheskii vestnik* (1880), no. 9, p. 144.

The operation of the noble assemblies

The problem was, however, that the vitality of the assemblies depended on the popularity of the new elected posts. In practice, the elective posts in the provinces did not prove as attractive, or easy to fill, as Catherine had envisaged (see Chapter 5). The low status of provincial posts meant that provincial assemblies also lacked status and importance in the eyes of the nobility. A further, and more fundamental, problem was the lack of provincial nobles to fill these posts, either because they could not meet the income or service qualifications (after 1785, the rank of commissioned officer and an income of 100 roubles were required in order to vote or to be elected) or because they simply did not exist in sufficient numbers in the provinces (see Chapter 7). The irony was that the poorest provincial nobles had been effectively excluded from active participation in the assemblies. But it was often the poorest, and least educated, nobles who remained on their estates, and therefore both needed these posts and were available to fill them, while more privileged and enterprising nobles sought more prestigious and better-paid posts in the armed forces or the central administration.

These factors soon affected the provincial nobles' perception of the value and significance of the assemblies. The evidence suggests that the first elections after 1775 were genuinely popular with wealthy as well as poorer nobles, but that this enthusiasm could not be maintained, let alone developed, in later years. According to the report of Governor-General A.P. Mel'gunov (which may have painted a deliberately rosy picture) the first elections in Iaroslavl' in 1777 were conducted successfully: the elected officials being 'honourable and beloved by their assemblies', the judges honoured to have been elected and assemblies displaying 'happiness' and 'rapture' at the proceedings. Yet he reported that at the second elections only 401 of the 769 nobles in the province attended the assembly, and that many of those who did not attend were the poorest nobles, owning between one and six peasants (who possibly could not afford to travel to the elections).[21] Attendance at the Iaroslavl' assemblies decreased with time – 705 nobles attended in 1777, 402 in 1780 and 301 in 1783. In practice, assemblies lacked independence and authority and could not be protected against the arbitrary power of provincial governors (who were, of course, appointed by the government and not elected by the nobility). In Penza province in 1792 the assembly met in the governor's house (despite the fact that governors had been forbidden to attend assemblies in 1788) and a clerk apparently whispered the preferences of the governor to the assembled nobles, who concurred with his preferences.[22]

In Paul's reign (1796–1801) the elective powers of the nobles and other functions of the assemblies were curtailed. Provincial noble assemblies were

21. RGADA, fond 16, delo 1012, chast' 1, ff. 45–6, 83, report from Governor-General A.P. Mel'gunov from Iaroslavl', Vologda and Kostoma provinces, 1777–84.
22. *Zapiski kniazia I.M. Dolgorukova: Povest' o rozhdenii moem, proiskhozhdenii i vsei zhizni. 1764–1800* (Petrograd, 1916), p. 249.

abolished, leaving just the district assemblies. The powers of the assemblies were restored in theory when Alexander I came to the throne, but in practice the authority of the governor over the assembly and its proceedings grew with time. In 1802 G.R. Derzhavin found that in Kaluga the governor:

> attended the noble elections in person, interfered in them, and in the event of submission of petitions against a partial ballot not only failed to put a stop to the disorder but threatened that if others were elected then they would not stay long in their posts.[23]

In the early nineteenth century, the marshals of the nobility were required to implement government decrees on such matters as the establishment of grain stores, measures against the spread of plague and the local military establishment which, although not matters of indifference to the local nobility, meant that the marshals were becoming more agents of the state than spokesmen for provincial nobles.

Nor did the assemblies always conduct themselves with dignity. In Podol'sk (near Moscow) in 1808, the disorders were such at election time that the police had to intervene to arrest some nobles, and the provincial marshal and the vice-governor were removed from their posts. The Vil'na assembly (in Lithuania) degenerated into disorder and fights in 1809; in two weeks it had only managed to elect the district marshals.[24] The electoral process also exposed the conflicts between the wealthy and poor provincial nobles and showed that the assemblies did not represent the interests of all the local nobles. In Kiev in 1800 the assembly was suddenly closed after three weeks. When it reopened only the wealthiest nobles were allowed to vote, so that the candidates of the president of the civil chamber were elected to posts.[25] It became traditional for the wealthier nobles to entertain their poorer brethren before the elections, and at the same time to press their candidates upon them.

Service as marshals of the nobility and as noble deputies to maintain the register of nobles often proved no more popular than elected posts in provincial administration (or posts in urban or peasant institutions for that matter). Elected deputies often simply failed to appear at the assemblies. In Tambov province marshals attempted to find reasons to justify retirement from their post – the Borisoglebsk district had three marshals in as many years.[26] The government hoped that the marshals would be representatives of the most enlightened and educated nobles, but the generally low cultural and educational level of most provincial nobles meant that the reality could be very different. One noble deputy in Tambov province, a certain Malyshov, was accused of transporting fugitive peasants to other provinces, of selling someone else's grain in place of his own and of incest. In 1802 the provincial

23. S.A. Korf, *Dvorianstvo i ego soslovnoe upravlenie za stoletie 1762–1855 godov* (St Petersburg, 1908), p. 339.
24. N.F. Dubrovin, 'Russkaia zhizn' v nachale XIX v', *Russkaia starina* 97 (1899), pp. 556, 559–60.
25. I.A. Linnichenko, 'Iz vremen imperatora Pavla I', *Istoricheskii vestnik* (1896), no. 8, p. 493.
26. Dubasov, 'Iz Tambovskikh letopisei', p. 141.

oh no! marshal of Riazan' served for twelve years, despite being described as 'in a true sense a robber and a debauchee' who took bribes and committed illegalities.[27] Nevertheless, representatives of the nobles could gain the respect of their peers. V.S. Khvostov, for example, recorded the esteem in which he believed he was held as Marshal of the Nobility in Gdov (north of Pskov in western Russia) at the end of the eighteenth century – 'I gained the love and respect of the Gdov nobility through endeavours within my powers for their benefit, my defence [of them] from oppression and my strict supervision of the rules for the recruit levy'.[28] Perhaps more significantly, the award of rank 5 for provincial marshals of the nobility in 1818 served to raise their status.

THE WESTERN BORDERLANDS

As the Russian empire expanded it took over territories – the Ukraine, the Baltic provinces, Finland, part of Poland-Lithuania – where representative and urban institutions already existed. Russian policy towards these territories varied according to the perception of the role which their institutions could play in ensuring stability and prosperity and on the particular policies of individual tsars.

The Hetmanate (the Left-Bank Ukraine) had its own army, administrative and judicial system and separate system of taxation. The structural organization of the Hetmanate arose from the military structure of the Zaporozhian army. At the apex was the hetman, who was the chief military commander as well as the chief executive. He was assisted in an advisory capacity by the Council of Officers, which comprised the hetman, his central staff, the regimental commanders of the ten regiments of Cossacks, company commanders and representatives from the Ukrainian gentry (until the eighteenth century sometimes also town mayors and members of the clergy) and in the management of central administration by the General Staff. Each of the ten Cossack regiments comprised both a military division and a territorial administrative unit, headed by a colonel (elected by the Cossacks until the eighteenth century and thereafter normally appointed). Cossack communities had enjoyed not only exemption from taxation and some rights of land ownership but also virtual autonomy and self-government. The institutions of direct Cossack democracy, namely the Cossack regimental council, had virtually disappeared by the beginning of the eighteenth century. The Cossacks still retained the right, however, to elect their own captains, or company commanders, and to be tried by their peers. By the accession of Catherine II Ukrainian autonomy appeared to be an anomaly and to serve no practical purpose. The Hetmanate was abolished in 1764. In 1781 the area was divided into three provinces as the new local government institutions were introduced and, at a stroke, Ukrainian instititions of self-government were abolished. Within a further ten years the

27. Dubrovin, 'Russkaia zhizn', p. 551.
28. 'Zapiski Vasiliia Semenovicha Khvostova', *Russkii arkhiv* (1870), no. 3, p. 588.

traditional Cossack military organization was replaced by regular Imperial army regiments.

The Baltic provinces were far more successful than the Ukraine in retaining their organs of self-government in the eighteenth century. This success arose from a variety of causes, including more strongly developed and well-organized institutions, the loyal service of the Baltic German nobles in the tsar's army and civil service, the loyalty and wealth of the German Riga merchantry who dominated urban administration, the ability of Baltic Germans to argue the merits of their local autonomy at St Petersburg, and the admiration for Baltic institutions shared by Peter I and Catherine II. The diets (*Landtage*) of Estonia, Livonia, Courland and the island of Osel dated from the sixteenth century. They comprised representatives from the landowning nobility, and became the foremost administrative, and fiscal, organs in the provinces. The diets, and the organs of administration which were associated with them (the Chancery of the Nobility or *Ritterschaftskanzlei* in Estonia, the Council of the Diet or *Landratskollegium* in Livonia), allowed the nobility to dominate the judiciary and the economy, and, by extension, the peasantry. In the same way the wealthy, mainly German, merchants dominated the urban institutions of Riga and other towns in the provinces. Successive tsars from the time of Peter I confirmed the rights and privileges of the corporate bodies of the nobility and the wealthy merchants. This did not mean that the Baltic provinces were not subject at various times to tsarist interference and diminution of their autonomy. Peter made the Baltic population subject to the Justice College in St Petersburg, Catherine II introduced both the Russian provincial institutions of 1775 and the urban institutions of 1785 (this was later rescinded by Paul but re-established by Alexander) and Alexander I restructured the administrative boundaries of the provinces and interfered in their diets. However, the provinces retained their distinct representative and urban institutions, as well as control over education at all levels.

When Russia acquired the Grand Duchy of Finland in 1809 (reunited with Old Finland in 1812) Alexander recognized the 'constitution' of Finland, which meant recognition of the Finnish diet, and gave the Finns a certain amount of autonomy (exercised through the Government Council, renamed the Senate in 1816), including authority over its administration, the judiciary, the armed forces, the postal services and the economy. In the Congress Kingdom of Poland (acquired in 1815) Alexander introduced a new constitution. These 'constitutions', however, were very different. The Finish constitution was essentially an *ancien régime* constitution, a form of government which had been determined when Finland was part of Sweden. In this respect, Alexander did no more than recognize the rights and privileges of Finland, and the *status quo*, in the same way that he had confirmed the rights of the Baltic provinces. The Polish constitution, on the other hand, was essentially a modern, post-French Revolutionary, written, constitution, which guaranteed the basic rights of freedom of religion and the press, the sanctity of property and freedom from arbitrary arrest. The constitution also established a separate Polish army and the use of Polish in all official business. The autonomy of the Kingdom, however, was severely limited by the fact that it was bound in perpetuity to the Russian empire in the person of the tsar, who was king of Poland, and, more directly, the Kingdom was put under the authority of the tsar's chosen viceroy.

An integral part of the Polish and Finnish constitutions was the existence of elected diets, retained in Finland's case and re-established in the Congress Kingdom of Poland. The Finnish diet, which was based on the representation of Finland at the Swedish diet before 1809, comprised four estates – the nobility, the clergy, the townspeople and the peasants (who were not serfs of course). The Finnish diet, however, was only a consultative body and had no legislative powers. The deputies were forbidden in 1809 to discuss a project which attempted to define the Finnish constitution and were instructed that what was expected of the diet was not 'decrees but only its opinion'.[29] Furthermore, there was no written agreement in 1809 about the frequency of the diets and the next one was not convoked until 1863. It was only in the late nineteenth century, during the period of Russification, that the Finnish diet came to be seen as a guardian of the national interest, and only then that the significance of the confirmation by Alexander I of the Finnish 'constitution' of 1809 was discussed in terms of Finnish liberty. The Polish diet, or *Sejm*, in contrast, had been given considerable legislative and administrative powers and a commitment to convene it every two years and to hold its sessions in public. The Polish franchise was restricted by social estate, profession and property but nevertheless between 106,000 and 116,000 citizens became eligible to vote (only 80,000 people out of a far larger population were eligible to vote in Restoration France). In practice, however, constant clashes between Alexander and the Polish diets meant that the diet was never able to function as a responsible legislative body and was prorogued and dissolved at will by the tsar. It ceased to be convoked after the Polish revolt of 1830–31. Diets and, at a local level, dietines, had been a central part of the political make up of the Polish-Lithuanian state in the seventeenth and eighteenth centuries and the Poles, of course, had experienced earlier constitutions, of which the constitution of 3 May 1791, and not that of 1815, was regarded as the true expression of the will of the Polish nation.

In the lands acquired by the partitions of Poland the Jewish *kahal* (an assembly of the prominent Jewish elders) was retained by the government (although it had been abolished in Austria and Prussia in the late eighteenth century) and exercised extensive administrative, cultural, social and economic control (including the collection of taxes), over the Jewish community. In 1800, I.G. Friesel, governor of Vil'na, reported that:

> Having established their own administrative institutions, called Synagogues, Kahals, or associations, the Jews completely separated themselves from the

29. K. Ordin, *Pokorenie Finliandii. Opyt opisaniia po neizdannym istochnikam* (St Petersburg, 1889), vol. II, supplements, pp. 86, 88.

people and government of the land. As a result, they were exempt from the operation of the statutes which governed the peoples of the several estates, and even if special laws were enacted, these remained unenforced and value-less, because the ecclesiastical and temporal leaders of the Jews invariably resisted them and were clever enough to find means to evade them.[30]

The general view of Russian commentators and foreign travellers was that the *kahal* only represented an elite, oligarchic, group of the Jews and did little of value for ordinary Jews. The *kahal* was abolished in 1821 in the Congress Kingdom of Poland and in 1844 in the rest of the Russian empire.

SUMMARY: DEVELOPMENTS 1650–1825

Although the origins of the Russian peasant commune are obscure it is clear that this form of social organization became the norm in the course of the eighteenth century for serfs and state peasants throughout Russia and in other parts of the empire as well. The government in part determined the functions of the peasant commune by imposing collective responsibility on the peasant community for fiscal and other obligations. But the commune had a far wider, and independent, role in the social and economic life of the peasant com-munity and was never merely the agent of the state or the landowner. The government intervened more actively to attempt to create institutions of self-government for the urban community (in particular in the reigns of Peter I and Catherine II) and corporate bodies for the provincial nobility (in the reign of Catherine II). Although urban dumas and noble assemblies performed some of their intended functions, and continued to operate without major structural alteration in the early nineteenth century, it proved difficult to inject vigour into the new institutions, and more difficult still to create a sense of shared corporate mentality and pride, which Peter, and to a greater extent, Catherine, had hoped for. Establishment of institutions could not overcome the essential economic instability of the towns or the poverty and low cultural level of many of the nobles who lived in the provinces.

---

30. Isaac Levitats, *The Jewish Community in Russia, 1772–1844* (New York, 1970), p. 29.

CHAPTER 5

Law and order

Violence was endemic in Russian life. This chapter examines government attempts to deal with lawlessness and disorder, in particular through the extension of civil administration in the provinces and reforms of the judicial system in the late eighteenth century. The fundamental problem facing the Russian empire was the lack of resources – both financial and in manpower – to administer its vast lands.

SOCIAL CONFLICT

Violent confrontations in the countryside

Violent conflict between masters and serfs was always a threat, and often a reality, particularly on small estates where the noblemen were in close personal contact with their serfs. The traveller Edward Clarke commented in the early nineteenth century that some nobles treated their serfs so badly that they 'dare not venture near their own villages, for fear of the vengeance they have merited by their crimes'.[1] It was not uncommon for serfs to vent their anger through arson and murder of their masters. Houseserfs were most likely to carry out these attacks. The Soviet historian Prokhorov estimated that 112 murders and 49 attempted murders of nobles by their serfs took place in the period 1751–73, and found evidence of 32 cases of arson in the period 1775–1800 in Moscow province alone.[2]

More protracted disobedience and revolts also took place. In 1713 it was reported that serfs in Nizhnii Novgorod, Rostov and Verei were not fulfilling obligations for their master. Prokhorov estimated that there were 216 revolts involving more than 10 serfs in the period 1751–73, although such statistics have to be treated with caution as they include everything from brief outbursts to protracted disputes. Revolts stemmed from a variety of causes, including

1. Edward Daniel Clarke, *Travels in Various Countries of Europe, Asia and Africa*, vol. I *Russia, Tartary and Turkey* (London, 1810), p. 94.
2. M.F. Prokhorov, *Krest'ianskoe dvizhenie v tsentral'noi Rosii v tret'ei chetverti XVIII v (po materialam Moskovskoi gubernii)* (Moscow, 1993), pp. 50, 53.

harsh punishments, increased *obrok* payments, the change from *obrok* to *barshchina*, the introduction of new work practices or the threat of resettlement. Disturbances were particularly intense when estates changed hands or when triggered by rumours of impending freedom, as happened in the reign of Peter III, during the Pugachev revolt and in the year 1797 in the reign of Paul I. Such violence was not unique to Russia of course, and was prevalent in particular in frontier areas or at times of political uncertainty. In the Western Ukraine under Polish rule there were serious revolts in 1734–7, 1750 and 1768. In France, it took three years for troops to crush the revolt by peasants in Languedoc; the eruption of rural violence in the 'Great Fear' of 1789 came at a time of revolutionary unrest and disturbances.

It was not only serfs who resorted to violence. It has been estimated that there were 8 revolts by monastic peasants in the 1730s, 17 in the 1740s and 32 in the 1750s. Indeed, the number of disturbances on church and monastic property was one factor in introducing the secularization of church property in 1764, an act which succeeded at least in reducing disturbances by these peasants. Clashes between state peasants and government officers were less frequent than on serf estates, but disturbances usually arose over the amount of financial and other obligations required from them, and also from the state's attempts to equalize land-holdings amongst state peasants in north Russia and Siberia. In 1816, state peasants in Pskov province staged a collective protest declaring 'Let them chop off our heads, let them whip us with the knout, but we will not apportion our land'.[3] Peasants also clashed with peasants from neighbouring villages, usually over disputed land. In 1716, monastic peasants from the village of Timoshevo claimed that they were set upon while clearing some land by about 70 serfs 'with axes, scythes and cudgels' who also claimed the land. A fight between the villages of Bolashkovo and Krasnyi Kholm in 1740 left 7 dead and 27 seriously wounded.[4]

Conflicts also took place between peasants and soldiers who were billeted upon them. A.S. Pishchevich recalled in his memoirs of the 1790s that he took care when quartering troops in villages to meet first with the peasants and establish general rules of conduct for both sides. He was probably an exception in this respect, and his motivation was less humanitarian than an awareness of the disorders which frequently occurred; in his words, as a result of his action 'the peasants were frightened to harm the soldiers and the soldiers were frightened to touch the peasants'.[5] Soldiers were often dispersed in small groups and billeted in villages at up to 100 versts (106.7 kilometres) from their military headquarters. This meant that it was almost impossible to check on their behaviour or that of their hosts. Frequently, conflict arose between

3. N.M. Druzhinin, *Gosudarstvennye krest'iane i reforma P.D. Kiseleva* (Moscow-Leningrad, 1946), vol. I, p. 103.
4. L.N. Vdovina, *Krest'ianskaia obshchina i monastyr' v tsentral'noi Rossii v pervoi polovine XVIII v* (Moscow, 1988), pp. 196–97.
5. A.S. Pishchevich, *Zhizn' A.S. Pishchevicha, im samim opisannaia 1764–1805* (Moscow, 1885), pp. 203–4.

peasants and soldiers over the most basic issue of food rations. In times of poor harvests, in particular, peasants could refuse to feed their uninvited guests and soldiers often responded by stealing food. More barracks were built in the second half of the eighteenth century but the Russian army remained too large to be housed entirely in barracks (as did most European armies until the very end of this period); indeed, it was partly the problem of billeting troops which led to the establishment of military colonies in the reign of Alexander I.

Violent confrontations also took place between *odnodvortsy* and nobles. *Odnodvorets* land lay in the borderlands where the forces of law and order were weak and where the ownership and boundaries of land were often uncertain. In these conditions, the *odnodvortsy* were often powerless to prevent encroachment on their land by the more powerful, and often armed, local nobles. A typical complaint by *odnodvortsy* deputies from Efremov (south of Moscow) to the Legislative Commission in 1767 was that:

> The nobles cause us no little poverty and ruin and, coming to the home-stead, they commit theft and robbery, and take the hay from the fields, and take the hay and hayfields themselves, and hunt in our woods, take horses and other animals, and hunt our cattle in the fields, and their cattle take our grain; and that without any payment or permission.[6]

In 1775 the nobleman Shpikulov attacked the *odnodvorets* village of Gribanovka (Tambov province), stealing cattle and grain and destroying houses. He then stole some of the land and treated the *odnodvortsy* like his own serfs, obliging them the following year to supply him with carts. This case, however, was investigated and Shpikulov was arrested and held for two weeks.[7]

Poorer nobles could suffer in the same way as *odnodvortsy* at the hands of more powerful neighbours. The nobles of Peremyshl'-Vorotynsk complained in 1767 that 'the strongest lord takes the best land, clears the woods for plowfields, and seizes more than his share of the common and arable land'.[8] Powerful nobles could descend on lands with armed serfs and seize whatever they wished but often the threat of legal action over land disputes was effect-ive as poor nobles knew that they could not afford to start legal proceedings. Casual violence was often a feature of the lifestyle of young, arrogant and bored nobles. The young Vinskii, a minor Ukrainian nobleman, described the violence of his lifestyle in the country when he and his friends were 'always idle, often drunk, not stopped from pranks, we soon became the terror of the whole town' and where on one occasion 'My people, having heard about a fight, burst into the monastery and there began real carnage', with the result that Vinskii nearly lost his life.[9]

6. V.I. Semevskii, 'Kazennye krest'iane pri Ekaterine II, 1762–1796 gg. Ocherk iz istoricheskago izsledovaniia', *Russkaia starina* 24 (1879), p. 48.
7. I.I. Dubasov, 'Iz Tambovskikh letopisei', *Istoricheskii vestnik* (1880), no. 9, pp. 134–5.
8. Wilson R. Augustine, 'Notes Toward a Portrait of the Eighteenth-Century Russian Nobility', *Canadian–American Slavic Studies* 4 (1970), p. 400.
9. G.S. Vinskii, *Moe vremia. Zapiski G.S. Vinskago*, intro. by I.M. de Madariaga (Newtonville, 1976), pp. 52–3.

Violent confrontations in towns

Major riots took place in Moscow and other towns in the 1640s, which were so dangerous that they led to the summoning of the Assembly of the Land (*zemskii sobor*) and the compilation of the Law Code of 1649. In June 1648 the mob in Moscow, angry about high food prices and increased taxation, had burnt down and looted houses and property belonging to boiars in Moscow and murdered several leading government officials with the utmost savagery. The fate of Nazar Chistoi demonstrated the wild fury of the mob as they:

> . . . knock him on the head with an axe [saying] this is for the Salt [tax]. Then, the Man being halfe dead, they haled him down the stayres by the heeles, dragg him like a dogg over the whole Court, and having stripped him, they flung him starck nacked upon the dunghill . . . [where] they put him qu[ite] to death.[10]

The only other riot which approached the same scale took place in Moscow in 1771, at the height of a devastating plague. When Archbishop Amvrosii dared to remove an icon which was venerated as having special powers to protect from plague, the panic-stricken mob rioted, resulting in the deaths of over one hundred rioters. Amvrosii himself was beaten to death in a wild frenzy.

These riots took place in exceptional circumstances. Violence and disorder were, however, endemic in Russian towns (as they were, of course, elsewhere in Europe: urban riots against the imposition of new taxes or increased bread prices were frequent throughout Europe and 12,000 soldiers and militia were used in London to put down the Gordon Riots in 1780, resulting in the loss of nearly 300 lives). At the end of the seventeenth century the town of Kadom (Tambov province) experienced six hours of fighting 'to the death' between townspeople and Muscovite servitors. Weber noted in the early eighteenth century that Easter was the most dangerous time, 'when all the Rabble are drunk and mad' and estimated that as many as 60 persons were murdered in Moscow during this period.[11] Violence between citizens was also common. In 1767, the merchants of Syzran' criticized the wealthy merchant Ia.S. Petrov because 'having held one of the merchants, Fedor Zabirzin, for a long time, [he] whipped him painfully no one knows for what . . .'.[12]

A particular problem encountered in Moscow and St Petersburg (as in other major European towns) was the number of beggars on the streets. Friedrich Weber commented that in Moscow in the early eighteenth century there were 'such Numbers of Beggars and Rogues, and . . . so many Excesses and Disorders, that after Sun-set no body ventures abroad without sufficient Company'.[13] In 1718, a decree instructed that any able-bodied people found roaming the streets were to be beaten with rods and returned to their village; if caught

10. Philip Longworth, *Alexis. Tsar of All the Russias* (London, 1984), p. 42.
11. Friedrich Christian Weber, *The Present State of Russia* (London, 1968), vol. I, p. 128.
12. M.D. Kurmacheva, *Gorod Urala i Povolzh'ia v krest'ianskoi voine 1773–1775 gg* (Moscow, 1991), p. 47.
13. Weber, *The Present State of Russia*, I, p. 128.

again they were to be knouted and the men given hard labour and women and children sent to factories. In 1744, at a time of famine, the St Petersburg police registered 5,372 beggars in the city.

Soldiers in garrisons were also involved in revolts and disturbances. Serving men in Siberia in the second half of the seventeenth century frequently rioted in the towns, set on *voevody* (military governors) or fought with other garrisons. Riots of soldiers took place in Tomsk in 1649–50 and in 1695–96 military servitors tried to take the town of Irkutsk. The *strel'tsy* were always a volatile and violent group. Established in Moscow in 1550, in the reign of Ivan IV, the *strel'tsy* were originally militiamen drawn from the non-servile population in order to protect the person of the tsar. The *strel'tsy* developed into a military caste, whose status became hereditary, but by the second half of the seventeenth century their military effectiveness had become questionable. When not on active campaign, they were often idle in garrisons, where they could provoke disorders within the towns. *Strel'tsy* participated in or instigated several major revolts in the second half of the seventeenth century (most notably in 1648, 1662, 1682 and 1698–99), and became a focus for popular discontent. In 1682, a three-day riot by *strel'tsy* in Moscow caused the deaths of 18 notables and several dozen ordinary townspeople. The revolt in 1698–99 gave Peter I the pretext to destroy the regiments; it was followed by mass executions along with lesser punishments and widespread torture. It was said that in consequence mass graves outside the city contained over one thousand bodies. The Russian armed forces which emerged from Peter's reforms were more easily controlled and disciplined. Nevertheless, soldiers and sailors could be involved in minor acts of disorder. In 1812, riots lasting two days broke out among Cossack militiamen in Chembar, Insar and Saransk (Penza province) who ran amok after refusing to follow orders and seizing liquor. In 1818, an instruction by Baron Rozen referred to lower ranks frequenting taverns and inns so that 'they are encountered on the streets in an indecent condition'.[14]

Violent confrontation in industry

The harsh conditions in many industrial enterprises and the reliance on forced labour (assigned peasants) led to many disturbances. Conditions in the cloth factory owned by A. Driablov in Kazan' led to unrest involving crowds of up to one thousand workers from 1737 to 1742. Whipping, arresting and exiling workers failed to curb the disorders, which were finally put down by troops. The 1760s were marked by violent confrontations in ironworks and other manufactories. A.I. Bibikov spent nine months in the Urals during which he 'pacified' five state enterprises; this entailed punishing 196 workers, of whom 18 were knouted, 49 were whipped three times, 49 whipped twice, 44 whipped once and 36 beaten with rods. There were disturbances throughout the 1760s

---

14. M.K. Sokolovskii (comp.), 'Russkaia voennaia starina', *Russkii arkhiv* (1906), no. 8, p. 617.

in the iron works in Voronezh province owned by P.I. Repnin, during which 19 skilled workers (who complained that their salaries had been reduced or simply not paid) were whipped for their 'contrariness and mischief'; in 1766 11 workers were knouted and exiled to Nerchinsk for daring to petition against Repnin.

The government reacted to the events in the 1760s by passing regulations on employment conditions in state-owned ironworks which, amongst other things, gave the assigned peasants a greater degree of control over the organization of their work and established procedures for complaints. The Repnin works were also taken over by the treasury. The slightly improved conditions reduced the number of disorders for a decade but the Ural works erupted again during the Pugachev revolt as many workers joined the rebels (a further 74 works were attacked and plundered and 56 occupied during the revolt). The government learned from the revolt; in its wake wages were doubled in state-owned manufactories and the power of the foremen to punish workers was restricted. The improved conditions led to calm for two decades but disturbances broke out again in the early nineteenth century. In 1806, most assigned peasants in the Urals were freed.

Although the government addressed at least some of the complaints of assigned peasants, it could not force private industrialists to do the same and the evidence suggests that conditions in privately owned factories failed to improve. In 1818, workers at the Osokin factory in Kazan' petitioned against their owner:

> Osokin has redoubled his cruelties against us and has caused violent death of many by beatings . . . We have endured boundless deprivation and brutal treatment for more than 23 years . . . In winter we work in frozen quarters, and since many of us lack warm clothing, not only is it impossible to work in such bitter frost, but there is no place even to warm our hands.[15]

Troops had to be brought in to crush Osokin's disobedient workers in 1820. Eleven workers were exiled to the Irkutsk woollen mill, and 10 workers who refused to sign a pledge of obedience were flogged, one of whom died in the process.

Violent confrontations with nomadic peoples

awk ?

Relations between Russians and the mainly nomadic tribespeople in Siberia and in the south and south-eastern borderlands were marked by violence and brutality in the seventeenth century as settlement took place. Russian officials, soldiers and merchants mercilessly exploited native peoples, often extracting goods and money by force and seizing native women. The native people reacted with sporadic violence. In 1665, Tungus killed a tribute collector and

15. M.I. Tugan-Baranovsky, *The Russian Factory in the Nineteenth Century* (Homewood, 1970), pp. 117–19.

50 men on the river Okhota; in 1680 the son of the *voevoda* (military governor) of Iakutsk and 39 men were killed while transporting furs; in 1683, Iukagirs killed a *desiatnik* (corporal) and 15 Cossacks. There could also be clashes over land ownership between Russian peasants and tribespeople. At the end of the seventeenth century, Mordvins complained in Tambov province about Russian peasants occupying some of their unploughed land and killing, wounding and robbing them.

On the other hand, Russians living on or close to the frontiers in the first half of the eighteenth century feared raids by non-Russian tribesmen. The peasants of Tambov province lived in fear of Kuban' Tatar raids in the 1730s; in 1738 there were rumours that 20,000 Karakalpaks were about to descend on the district of Shatsk.[16] In the first half of 1708 'Bashkirs and Tatars, ravaging, burnt eight villages, also churches, four chapels, 33 small settlements' in the vicinity of the town of Kungar in the Urals, killing 716 people and leaving 2,122 missing.[17] There were Tatar risings in 1708, 1735 and 1739 and six Bashkir risings between 1646 and 1755. The Russian conquest of Bashkiria was marked by savagery on both sides, with whole villages and livestock destroyed, the population killed or taken into captivity and the land laid waste. During the 'pacification' of Bashkiria in 1735–40, 696 villages were destroyed, 3,236 Bashkirs were dispatched to the armed forces and 8,383 women and children dispersed as serfs. By the second half of the eighteenth century, tribespeople had been 'pacified', dispersed or assimilated (although tribespeople in the Urals participated in the Pugachev revolt; see below).

A LAWLESS SOCIETY?

In principle, the movement of the population of the Russian empire was restricted and controlled. Not only were serfs tied to their master's estate, but state peasants and townspeople had to seek permission to leave their place of residence. In 1674, for example, the town of Iaroslavl' successfully petitioned for the return of townspeople from Moscow.[18] These restrictions were enforced in the reign of Peter I. In 1714 towns became obliged to keep a register of all arrivals and departures; in 1719 no one was allowed to move from one town or village to another without a special passport. Regulations on passports increased with the second and third censuses in 1742 and 1762; in 1768 the acceptance of the passport system was recognized by the imposition of tax on the issue of passports. The establishment of regular censuses discouraged population movement as adjustments to the total tax burden of the village or the town based on the size of the male population were only made at census

16. I. Dubasov, 'Shatskaia provintsiia v 30-kh godakh proshlago veka', *Istoricheskii vestnik* (1896), no. 8, pp. 466–7.
17. A.A. Preobrazhenskii, 'Epizod klassovoi bor'by v Ural'skom gorode nachala XVIII v', in *Goroda feodal'noi Rossii* (Moscow, 1966), p. 412.
18. David Hugh Miller, 'City and State in Muscovite Society: Iaroslavl' 1649–1699', unpublished PhD thesis, Princeton 1974, p. 223.

time. Townsmen were not allowed to move unless they had paid all their taxes, thus excluding many of the poorer members of the urban community who constantly lived in arrears. In 1805, artisans were given the right to register in other towns without the permission of the fiscal chamber (the highest financial organ in the province), but this decision was reversed in 1820. Even merchants had to guarantee to pay all their dues for the year in advance before they could receive permission to move. However, the population control did not work in practice. Indeed, it could be argued that the rigidity of the system created outcasts and outlaws who plagued all members of society.

Fugitives

Mass flight – of individuals, families and whole villages – was the most effective means for serfs to resist intolerable burdens. In the period 1719–27 some 199,000 serfs fled from their masters; from 1727 to 1742 it has been estimated that a further 327,046 male peasants fled. Between 1782 and 1791 in the region of 35,000 serfs fled from Kiev and Chernigov provinces in the Ukraine alone, which constituted approximately 5 per cent of all peasants in the region. Serfs fled to escape burdens or punishments but also to seek a better life for themselves by settling in Siberia or the frontiers as state peasants.

In practice, it proved impossible to prevent flight. The *St Petersburg Gazette* contained frequent notifications and physical descriptions of fugitive serfs with the request for them to be apprehended:

This tenth day of August [1771] at ten o'clock in the morning there fled a houseserf . . . Lazar Ekimov, who is of middle height, pointed face, swarthy, hair dark brown, no front teeth, on his right hand his little finger is missing, on his right leg the mark of a wound on the shin, wearing new clothes of white cloth; whoever apprehends him, or informs collegiate secretary Pankrat Tarabanovskii, in his house on Nevskii prospekt, will be given a proper reward.

On the 24th March last [1793] there fled from collegiate assessor cavalryman Andrei Andreevich Beer a serf Ivan Ivanov, who is not more than 13 years old. He is not tall, round-faced, hair cut short. When he fled he had on him dark clothing with a sheepskin fur overcoat with tassles, a round hat, and boots . . . If this Ivanov appears anywhere, and if he is calling himself by another name, do not apprehend him but inform the nearest government office.

But it was not only serfs who fled. It has been estimated that 37,464 male court peasants fled in the period 1724–30 (about 9 per cent of the total number of court peasants). In 1743 over 10,000 *odnodvortsy* fled to avoid service in the land militia, although most of them were tracked down. Serfs or state peasants assigned to industrial enterprises also fled to escape the appalling conditions of work (or to work on their lands; some peasant desertion was seasonal). In the late 1740s over 800 workers fled from the state cloth factory in Moscow, of whom nearly 600 were never caught. As townspeople were just as bound to their place of residence as peasants, those who left without permission could also become fugitives. The *St Petersburg Gazette* appealed in July 1793 for the apprehension of a 16-year-old artisan, Ivan Alekseev, who was accused of fleeing from St Petersburg with 130 roubles and the keys to a shop.

Deserters

Army deserters added to the numbers of people who were not fixed to their place of residence. The level of desertion could be very high, particularly during the reign of Peter I. In 1708, two parties of recruits lost 988 from a total of 11,733 men. This was despite the harsh punishments which were inflicted on deserters who were apprehended. In 1705, it was decreed that one in three deserters, drawn by lot, was to be hanged and the other two knouted and dispatched for hard labour to Siberia. The issuing of further decrees imposing harsh penalties indicated that intimidation did not have the desired effect. In both 1710 and 1732 it was estimated that some 20,000 men were lost through desertion. Soldiers could also demonstrate an extraordinary capacity to withstand terrible punishments for desertion and to reoffend. The soldier F. Moskalev was punished three times for desertion; twice in 1786, when he ran the gauntlet, receiving first 1,000 and then 6,000 blows, and again in 1787, when he received 8,000 blows. Many deserters (and peasants) fled over the frontiers to Poland and then to Prussia and many were recaptured fairly easily, but sufficient numbers remained in the countryside to pose a threat to law and order.

To put this in context, all European armies suffered very high desertion rates and the Russian army was probably more successful than most in holding on to its troops. In the period 1713–40 the army of Frederick William I of Prussia lost over 30,000 men; it was estimated that in the American War of Independence the British lost 1,200 men in battle, but over 42,000 deserted. The Russian military authorities also attempted to improve the efficiency and medical care of recruiting stations as the greatest number of desertions took place before the recruits ever reached their regiments. There is some evidence to suggest that matters had improved by the early nineteenth century. Robert Wilson, who served with the Russian army during the Napoleonic Wars, commented in 1817 that 'Bodies of recruits, of which three-fifths used to perish [or disappear] in the journey, now arrive with no more than common casualties.'[19] In the period 1819–21, desertion rates in the Second Army rose from 1.3 to 1.6 per cent of the total number of troops; less than for other European armies, but still a large number of people considering the overall size of the Russian army (estimated at 480,000 in 1811).

19. Robert Thomas Wilson, *A Sketch of the Military and Political Power of Russia in the Year 1817* (London, 1817), p. 122.

Robber gangs

The prevalence of robber gangs, comprising mainly fugitives and deserters, made travel dangerous for everyone. The Senate ordered in 1735 that all the trees along one of the roads leading from St Petersburg were to be chopped down so that bandits could not shelter in them. A report from near Kaluga in 1745 commented that 'thieves and robbers . . . also deserters and recruits and other people have increased'.[20] A report in 1752 noted that 'in Serpukhov district [Moscow province] many thieves and robbers have appeared . . . they destroy nobles' homes'.[21] In 1767, the nobles from Riazhsk (Voronezh province) called for the execution of all criminals, bandits, robbers and people who concealed fugitives and outlaws. At the end of the eighteenth century, a robber gang, nineteen-strong, terrorized the inhabitants of Kirsanov district (Tambov province), descending not only on travellers but also attacking people in their homes.[22] In Simbirsk, in the early nineteenth century, robber gangs included a Cossack, I.G. Mel'nikov, who 'was terrifying for all travellers . . . they said that he had cast a spell on guns so that it was impossible to kill or wound him with a bullet'.[23]

Rebels

Spontaneous violence was endemic at a local level but this period also witnessed major revolts, of which the most prominent were those of Stenka Razin (1667–71), Kondratiy Bulavin (1707–08) and Emel'ian Pugachev (1773–75). The revolts involved impoverished Cossacks, many of whom resented the encroachments into their traditional lifestyle by government officials and richer Cossacks alike (see Chapter 2), peasants and tribespeople. Mordvins, Mari and some Bashkirs, Tatars and Kalmyks joined the Razin revolt, Mordvins participated in the Bulavin revolt and Bashkirs, Tatars, Kazakhs and Kalmyks joined Pugachev (at least 1,000 Bashkirs joined Pugachev's forces). Impoverished workers and townspeople also came over to the rebel side. Volga boat haulers participated in the Razin and Bulavin revolts and Pugachev's revolt attracted discontented factory workers from the Ural factories, whose desperation has been described above. Old Believers (see Chapter 10) also participated to a small extent in the Razin revolt and to a greater degree in the Bulavin revolt and even more in the Pugachev rebellion.

The violence of both rebel supporters and of the troops dispatched to suppress them was intense. Razin's rebel army conducted a 'reign of terror: they would hang people up by their feet, stick holes through their ribs, and

20. P. Alefirenko, *Krest'ianskoe dvizhenie i krest'inskii vopros v Rossii v 30–50-kh godakh XVIII veka* (Moscow, 1958), p. 118.
21. Prokhorov, *Krest'ianskoe dvizhenie*, pp. 44–5.
22. I.I. Dubasov, 'Tambovskii krai v kontse XVIII i nachale XIX stoletiia', *Istoricheskii vestnik* (1884), no. 10, p. 113.
23. 'Istoriia moei zhizni. Razskaz byvshago krepostnago krest'ianina Nikolaia Nikol. Shipova, 1802–1862 g.', *Russkaia starina* 31 (1881), pp. 138–9.

hang them up on iron hooks'.[24] The main focuses for the anger of the mob were high-ranking boiars and government officials. In Astrakhan', which Razin seized in 1669, the governor was tortured and thrown to his death from the belfry, his sons were swung from a pendulum crashing into the city walls, the *voevoda*'s secretary was hung by the ribs on fleshhooks and tortured to death and 'foreigners as well as Russians of all walks of life, were piteously killed and tortured to death, being hung up by their feet and ribs'. On the other hand, the description of the actions of Prince Ia.N. Odoevskii when he retook Astrakhan' demonstrates that vicious and cruel actions were practised to the same degree by government forces:

> He had many quartered or burned alive, whilst he ordered many others to have their tongues cut out or to be buried alive. This was the fate of the guilty and the innocent alike. Finally, when there were only a few people left, he had the whole town destroyed and ordered the houses to be rebuilt outside the town. When these were half finished they had to be taken down again and transferred back to the castle. This had to be done by the men, their wives and children, who had to pull the carts themselves as there were no horses. It even happened that many pregnant women fell as a result of the heavy work and died in child-birth like animals.[25]

The Bulavin revolt partly arose from the brutal actions of Prince Iu.V. Dolgorukii. According to Bulavin, when his forces were seeking out fugitive peasants on the Don they:

> . . . set fire to many Cossack villages and knouted many long settled Cossacks, cut off lips and noses and hanged babies from trees, and also took maidens of the female sex to themselves for carnal acts in bed.[26]

When Bulavin was betrayed by his own Cossacks, his body was suspended by its feet over the river Kalancha, where his rebel army had been defeated. His head was cut off and preserved in alcohol; his headless body was later quartered and his limbs mounted on stakes in the centre of Cherkassk, his rebel stronghold, in the square where 200 rebels were also hanged. It has been estimated that some 7,000 Cossacks died during or in the aftermath of the Bulavin revolt. The Pugachev revolt was also partly motivated by bitterness over the brutal suppression of a revolt by Iaik Cossacks in 1772. The sacking of Kazan' under Pugachev led to an orgy of killing, looting and drunkenness; in one day 162 were killed, 129 wounded, 468 went 'missing' and 2,063 of the 2,873 houses in the city were destroyed by fire. While something in the region of 3,000 people lost their lives at the hands of the rebels, about 10,000 rebels were also killed during the Pugachev revolt.

24. S. Konovalov, 'Ludwig Fabritius's Account of the Razin Rebellion', *Oxford Slavonic Papers* 6 (1955), p. 76.
25. Ibid., p. 92.
26. E.V. Anisimov, *The Reforms of Peter the Great* (New York and London, 1992), p. 83.

These major revolts led to serious disorders in the countryside and towns. The urban poor participated in the Razin revolt, but peasants also looted and burned noble estates in the provinces of Penza, Tambov, Nizhnii Novgorod and Riazan'. Serfs rose during the Bulavin revolt not only in southern lands between the Dnieper and Volga rivers but also in provinces in central Russia and as far north as Kostroma and as far west as Smolensk. G.I. Volkonskii reported from Tambov province that there was 'much destruction, plunder and killing', although only one Tambov landowner is known to have lost his life. In the final stages of the Pugachev revolt (the so-called 'Pugachevshchina without Pugachev') the countryside was set alight along the Volga and in the provinces of Penza and Nizhnii Novgorod. The number of murders (if not the savagery) far exceeded anything experienced in the Razin or Bulavin revolts. Disturbances broke out at some distance from the area of revolt as rumours of Pugachev's activities spread. According to one estimate, there were 22 outbreaks of peasant revolt in Moscow province during this period. It was estimated by General P.I. Panin that in all 1,572 nobles, 1,037 government officials and 237 clergy lost their lives at the hands of the rebels. 'Everyone was gripped with fear . . . Death hung continually over the heads of the landowners', commented an eyewitness.[27] Of the 1,572 nobles killed (796 men, 474 women and 302 children), 665 were hanged, 635 were bludgeoned or tortured to death, 121 were shot, 72 were stabbed, 64 beheaded and 15 drowned.

THE CIVIL ADMINISTRATION

The Russian provinces were grossly under-administered. The government lacked sufficient trained staff to run its administrative and fiscal agencies and to staff its courts. As late as 1763, Russia employed 16,500 officials in central and local administration (ranging from high-ranking noble administrators to lowly clerks and secretaries), while Prussia, with less than one per cent of Russia's land area, employed some 14,000 people in a far more structured and coherent civil service in the same period. In the late eighteenth century a major attempt was made to rectify the inadequacies of local administration, partly spurred on by the weaknesses which had been exposed during the Pugachev revolt. It should be noted, however, that most of Russian society continued to live outside and below the law, according to traditional customs and dependent on local centres of power, as did much of the rural population of Europe at the time. But in Russia the situation was exacerbated by two factors. Firstly, serfdom meant that nobles acted as judges and tax collectors for the state for their serfs, with the result that the largest social group was in effect isolated from the jurisdiction of the state. Secondly, peasants – serfs and state peasants – were governed by *customary* law and not the law of the land on the matters which concerned them most, that is, inheritance and property law (discussed more fully in Chapter 9).

27. Paul Avrich, *Russian Rebels* (London, 1973), pp. 158, 233–4.

Legislation on provincial administration

Catherine II implemented major reforms in the structure of local administration, courts and the police. In 1775 she promulgated the Statute on Provincial Administration; as the preface to this law acknowledged 'there is both an insufficiency of administration and a shortage of people capable of administering'. The statute divided Russia into provinces and sub-divided provinces into districts of roughly the same population size. It established a new and elaborate structure of provincial fiscal and judicial organs. In addition, special institutions were established (houses of correction and workhouses) which were supposed to deal with the problem of beggars and destitute able-bodied people in towns (the welfare institutions set up in 1775 are discussed in Chapter 6). This reform was followed in 1782 by the Police Code, which created a new agency, a police board, in all towns, with responsibility for maintaining order and ensuring that proper standards of moral behaviour were observed. The new structure of administration was introduced not only into Russian provinces but also into the western and southern borderlands and resulted in the loss of institutional autonomy of these regions.

The legislation was in places confusing and contradictory and made unrealistic assumptions about the practicalities of implementation. The court structure, for example, which established separate lower courts of instance for nobles, townspeople and state peasants was over-complex. It ignored social groups outside these main estates, like *raznochintsy*, (except in Moscow and St Petersburg, where special courts were established) and was unclear about procedures when members of different social estates were involved in litigation. This issue was only resolved in 1786, when it was decreed that the case should be heard in the court which corresponded to the social estate of the defendant, but even after this date practice did not accord with the law. In 1788 the Ekaterinoslav Upper Land Court (a court for nobles), for example, heard a case involving two merchants. Members of the clergy and soldiers were tried in separate courts; serfs, of course, were outside the jurisdiction of the courts.

Furthermore, although the new judicial structure was imposed on the borderlands, Russian law was not. The Baltic provinces applied customary Livonian and German law, the provinces acquired from Poland-Lithuania (and the Congress Kingdom after 1815) used the Lithuanian Statute, the Ukraine employed local codes which were themselves a mixture of the Lithuanian Statute and common law with elements of Magdeburg Law applying in some towns, Old Finland (and the Duchy of Finland after 1809) applied Swedish law and Bessarabia used Rumanian law. Nomadic tribes in Siberia were allowed in practice to handle minor cases outside the Russian courts according to tradition, Bashkirs settled minor disputes according to Islamic law and Kalmyk courts operated according to a mixture of Mongol and customary laws. (A unified legal system, of course, does not apply in the United Kingdom today either.) Local laws could lead to confusion. In 1824, the Senate overruled a case concerning trade in Poltava on the grounds that it had been decided according to the Lithuanian Statute and not Magdeburg Law. It instructed the local municipal courts to apply the Magdeburg Law, which proved difficult as the courts did not have copies of the Law.

A noble civil service?

The legislation of 1775 attempted to improve the quality of administration, partly through raising the status of local officials and local administration (by the construction of new impressive buildings, design of town and provincial crests, etc.) but most of all by providing adequate salaries to attract the provincial nobles to take these new, middle-ranking, elected posts. Governor-General Jacob Sievers saw the Statute as the means to put to good use provincial nobles 'who have been loafing since 1762 [freedom from compulsory service] and who have all but lost interest in the public good and in their duty to their country'.[28] One estimate is that 27,000 posts were created in the provinces by the end of the reign of Catherine II, of which 10,608 were elected posts (4,053 reserved for the nobility).

If the government hoped by these means to create a new 'noble civil service', equivalent in status to military service, then it failed. Firstly, the elected posts for the nobles were not as well paid as appointed posts or military posts, and the property and service qualifications which were introduced severely restricted the number of nobles who could stand for election. Secondly, military service always remained more glamorous than civil service and posts in the central administration were more prestigious than those in the provinces. Thirdly, there were simply not enough resident nobles to fill these new posts, especially in the distant provinces, and consequently levels of absenteeism were high. On the other hand, it seems unlikely that the intentions of the government were so ambitious. No provisions for training for the civil service were introduced until the nineteenth century and no attempt was made to try to create the sort of *esprit de corps* or civil service ethos which so marked the Prussian civil service.

Elected posts had lower salaries than appointed posts and, unlike military posts, no pensions. They failed to attract the wealthy provincial nobles and so the status of such posts declined in time. In 1775, in most provinces elected nobles earned 360 roubles a year as assessors in the upper land court (a court of second instance for the nobility), 300 roubles as judge of the district court (a court of first instance for the nobility) and 200–250 roubles as assessors in other courts and institutions. Salaries in junior posts were only comparable with lowly jobs as tutors or teachers. G.S. Vinskii, who was exiled to Orenburg, was employed as a tutor at a salary of 300 roubles a year, while teachers in the major national schools, established in 1786, earned 400 roubles a year in the higher class and 200 roubles in the lower class. In comparison the

28. Robert E. Jones, *Provincial Development in Russia. Catherine II and Jacob Sievers* (New Brunswick, 1984), p. 116.

lowest grade of army officer (*praporshchiki* or ensigns, 13th rank, or *podporuchiki*, second-lieutenants, 12th rank) could earn more than this, depending on the regiment in which they served. In 1786 ensigns earned 145–356 roubles and second-lieutenants 165–396 roubles in the dragoon regiment; a second-major earned 387–454 roubles. After 1785, nobles who had not reached the rank of a commissioned officer or who had an income of under 100 roubles, that is, *many* provincial nobles, were not able to stand for elected posts. There were even vacancies in the more highly paid appointed posts. In 1808 it was reported from Pskov province that the post of president of the criminal chamber had been vacant for a long time.[29]

To young nobles the glamorous image of army life contrasted favourably with the stultifying atmosphere of office work. N. Tolubeev was forced to enter the provincial service in the late eighteenth century for health reasons but was filled with envy at the sight of his neighbour's sons in their uniform 'with lace on their collars. . . . I lamented for a long time that I could not follow them'.[30] V.I. Altuf'ev served in the Fiscal Chamber (which dealt with treasury and tax business) in Tambov province but persistently attempted to join a regiment, finally succeeding in finding a place in a grenadier regiment. D.B. Mertvago joined the army at the age of 19 as a sergeant; after two months' service he took leave for a year and then entered state service. By the age of 22 he was a procurator, a post which was intended to ensure that correct legal practice was followed in the courts. Senior posts in the provinces were filled by nobles who had already served for many years in the army, leading the American historian Givens to describe provincial service as a 'pension system'. He found that 85 per cent of the presidents of the criminal and civil chambers (the highest provincial courts of appeal) in 1788 were appointed directly from military service.[31] Administrative posts in the provinces were viewed as the inferior branch of service, most suitable for a retirement post or for those lacking in sufficient funds and influence to secure a more prestigious post elsewhere. An American traveller in Siberia in the 1780s commented on:

> . . . two old discharged officers (colonels) who at their own request have quitted the Service, and constituted Judges and Justices of the Law.[32]

An improved civil administration?

The corruption of local officials in the seventeenth century has been well attested. The townspeople of Shuia (a town north-east of Moscow) made a

29. N.F. Dubrovin, 'Russkaia zhizn' v nachale XIX v', *Russkaia starina* 98 (1899), p. 492.
30. N. Tolubeev, *Zapiski N. Tolubeeva (1780–1809)* (St Petersburg, 1899), p. 34.
31. Robert D. Givens, 'Eighteenth-Century Nobiliary Career Patterns and Provincial Government' in Walter McKenzie Pintner, Don Karl Rowley (eds), *Russian Officialdom: The Bureaucratization of Russian Society from the Seventeenth to the Twentieth Century* (London and New York, 1980), p. 122.
32. S.D. Watrous (ed.), *John Ledyard's Journey through Russia and Siberia 1787–1788* (Madison, Milwaukee, London, 1966), p. 146.

not untypical complaint in 1665 about the *voevoda* (military governor), Ivan Borkov:

> And when he was governor he began to oppress us, your orphans, the townspeople, and to impose big fees and fines for no reason and to cause us losses. He beats us . . . without investigation and without guilt, and he put [us] in jail for his greed; and taking us out of jail, he beats us half to death with cudgels without charges and without guilt. And in the same year 172 [1663/64] he, the governor, beat the customs officer, Volod'ka Selivanov, half to death after having locked him up in his house, and he caused great disruption to the collection of customs duties.[33]

Bribery, present-giving and corruption were endemic within local administration – as they were of course, elsewhere in Europe; at least in Russia, unlike in France, offices could not be bought. In the second half of the seventeenth century it was still assumed that officials would maintain themselves through 'feeding' (*kormlenie*), that is, through the imposition of fees in cash and kind for various duties, a system which was obviously open to abuse. In 1674, it was said of V.K. Kusynin, a clerk (*pod'iachi*), that he took 'double and more' of 'food' (*korm*) than he should. In 1669 a complaint was made against a clerk who, despite being given gifts, 'did not do the job'.[34]

Matters did not improve in the first half of the eighteenth century. In 1706, a *burmistr* (elected representative in the town magistracy – at that time an administrative organ and not a court) from Iaroslavl' was found guilty of stealing over 40,000 roubles from official town accounts.[35] A.P. Zhukov, a *voevoda* in Penza province in the 1740s, was notorious for bribe-taking and for his 'cruel punishments' of beating people 'with rods mercilessly'.[36] Andrei Bolotov recorded in his memoirs his view of the *voevoda*, Kolomnin, in the 1760s who was such a bribe-taker that even on his deathbed he held out his hand for a bribe before signing a receipt![37]

To what extent did the reforms of the late eighteenth century improve matters? When government inspectors were sent to the provinces in the late 1780s they found that most of the new institutions had been set up, although less comprehensively in the remotest provinces. In distant Kolyvan' province, for example, 'because of the shortage of merchants and artisans' members of the magistracies were elected from 'nobles or learned people or from officials or from *raznochintsy*'.[38] More institutions had been set up and more officials,

---

33. V.A. Kivelson, *Autocracy in the Provinces. The Muscovite Gentry and Political Culture in the Seventeenth Century* (Stanford, 1996), pp. 137–8.

34. N.F. Demidova, *Sluzhilaia biurokratiia v Rossii XVIIv i ee rol' v formirovanii absoliutizma* (Moscow, 1987), p. 144.

35. Miller, *City and State*, p. 351.

36. E.I. Zaozerskaia, 'Pomeshchik Zhukov i ego khoziaistvo', in *Dvorianstvo i krepostnoi stroi Rossii XVI–XVIII vv* (Moscow, 1975), p. 215.

37. *Zhizn' i prikliucheniia Andreia Bolotova* (Moscow-Leningrad, 1931; reprint Cambridge, 1973), vol. II, p. 365.

38. RGADA, fond 259, kniga 4222, f. 739, Journal of the First Department of the Senate.

of all levels, were in place, but in the short term this did not have a great impact on the behaviour of officials or on the general cultural standards of the civil administration. An account relating to Tambov province in the late eighteenth century listed the following incidents involving relatively highly ranked officials: an *ispravnik* (land commissar, rank 9, elected noble official) descended on a village which had not paid its dues, accompanied by soldiers who tortured and beat the village head and other peasants; a *gorodnichii* (rank 8, town provost with responsibilities for law and order) beat up a priest, stole and ruined merchants' goods, and arbitrarily punished citizens; a noble assessor and registrar in the lower land court took bribes.[39] P.S. Baturin gave a vivid description in his memoirs of the failings of his highly paid colleagues in the Kaluga Criminal Chamber, the highest court of appeal for criminal cases in the province, in the late eighteenth century. The president was a German, knew little Russian and was dependent on the secretary; the procurator spoke without any grammatical rules and the councillor was 'proud, base, self-interested and extravagant, conceited and lacking in understanding'.[40]

Respect for administration was not enhanced by the treatment of the minor clerical staff by their superiors. Johann-Georg Korb described the treatment meted out to clerks in the central government offices in the reign of Peter I, when one clerk was given:

> . . . a kind of cudgelling – as being the prime offender . . . The clerks, after the manner of outrageous criminals, were chained with iron to their places, and fettered, to teach them how to write night and day.[41]

Most training of clerks was done on the job. Timofei Kalashnikov started work as a copyist in 1772 at the tender age of 10 and was taught to read by a clerk. When he was 16, and a clerk, he was wrongly accused of starting a fire in the offices and summarily punished: 'the *voevoda* himself, with the help of his assistant and the procurator whipped me with a birch, saying, "Be more careful in the future".'[42]

The legislation of 1775 vastly increased the demand for clerical staff but did not address the problems of recruitment or training. Salaries remained low; copyists could earn as little as 10–30 roubles a year and secretaries and clerks earned in the region of 50 roubles a year. Salaries were only paid three times a year, and sometimes payments were delayed. Junior office staff were often drunk and disorderly in taverns, and became involved in brawls and violent disorder. The records of the St Petersburg Criminal Chamber for the first six months of 1788 included reference to eleven cases of junior officials being brought before the court because of drunkenness or other forms of disorderly

39. I. Dubasov, 'K istorii otzhivshago chinovnichestva', *Russkii arkhiv* (1878), no. 1, pp. 30–9.
40. P.S. Baturin, 'Zapiski', *Golos minuvshago* (1918), nos 1–3, pp. 68–9.
41. [Johann-Georg Korb], *Diary of an Austrian Secretary of Legation at the Court of Czar Peter the Great*, trans. by the Count MacDonnell (London, 1863), vol. I, p. 110.
42. 'Zhizn' neznamenitago Timofeia Petrovicha Kalashnikova prostym slogom opisannaia s 1762 po 1794 god', *Russkii arkhiv* (1904), no. 10, p. 172.

behaviour. Furthermore, it was not possible to find sufficient numbers of qualified people to fill these junior posts. In Iaroslavl' and Vologda provinces in 1784 the lack of clerical staff meant that economic (state) and court peasants took their places instead; Vologda province in 1786 needed secretaries in all the courts of second instance.[43] In this situation governors could not afford to be overscrupulous. In 1797 the Governor of distant Viatka, S. Zinov'ev, reported to the Procurator General, Prince A.B. Kurakin, that he had dismissed several officials for bribery the previous year and now asked if they could be reinstated as he was so short of suitably trained personnel.[44] V.N. Gettun recorded in his memoirs in the late eighteenth century that he was bound by the leg to his desk by his superior so that he could not leave his post – a treatment not dissimilar to that meted out to the Petrine clerks.[45]

The Police Code increased the number of police officials in towns but in some ways the role envisaged for them was rather limited. They could deal summarily with petty crime, such as thefts of under 20 roubles (too petty to be worthy of the attention of the courts) and minor problems of disorder, such as begging and drunkenness. In this respect, this was less a police force in the modern understanding of the term, and more a supplementary agency to the judicial process at the most basic level. Indeed, one could say that the police acted in the towns in a not dissimilar way to peasant communes, which also dealt summarily with minor offences. At the same time, however, the police were given ambitious and wide-ranging responsibilities for the maintenance of buildings, paving of streets, prevention of fires, sanitation and erection of lamp-posts. The police were also given a moral role in the towns, being responsible for ensuring that bathhouses were properly segregated according to sex!

It is difficult to assess how effectively the police force operated after the reforms of 1775 and 1782. The number of officials with police duties, and government expenditure on their salaries, increased after 1782 (even in France, where the police force had been centralized, there were fewer than 4,000 police officers for a country with a population of some 26 million in the 1780s). There is evidence that the urban environment improved in the late eighteenth century. In particular the purchase of firefighting equipment reduced the hazard of fire, and better paving and lighting in towns, as well as increased numbers of nightwatchmen, made the streets safer. Lights, however, were expensive, and a proposal to establish lights in Archangel in 1767 was rejected because the provincial chancellery and town magistracy feared that they would cause fires.[46] In practice the police lacked the means to enforce order and, as

43. RGADA, fond 16, delo 1012, chast' 1, f. 228v, report by Governor-General A.P. Mel'gunov from Iaroslavl' and Voloda provinces, 1784; SPgFIRI, fond 36, delo 478, f. 69, report by A.R. Vorontsov from Vologda province, 1786.

44. J. Hassel, 'The Vicissitudes of Russian Administrative Reform 1762–1801', unpublished PhD thesis. Cornell, 1967, pp. 172–73.

45. V.N. Gettun, 'Zapiski G.N. Gettuna 1771–1815', *Istoricheskii vestnik* 1 (1880), p. 29.

46. A.O. Podvysotskii (comp.), 'Popytka osveshcheniia ulits v Arkhangel'sk v 1767–1768 gg', *Russkaia starina* 26 (1879), pp. 101–2.

elsewhere in Europe, had to rely on local garrison troops in cases of riots and other disorders.

Beggars, as has been seen above, posed a potential threat to good order. After 1775, able-bodied beggars and vagrants were to be set to work in newly established workhouses in provincial capitals. These institutions were supposed to 'put a stop to their opportunities for depraved idleness', but they also had a humanitarian aim, namely to provide work for the destitute. At the same time, more clearly punitive houses of correction were to be established for disobedient or idle children and serfs, indecent women and those living a dissolute life. According to one set of figures, in St Petersburg in 1785 there were 617 occupants of the workhouse and 446 in the house of correction; figures from a different source for the following year gave 546 people employed in the workhouse. But the fine distinction between the purposes of the two institutions as laid down in 1775 was lost in practice. A decree of 1781, and the Police Code of the following year, instructed that those convicted of minor thefts (under 20 roubles) were to be sent to the workhouses, so establishing that these institutions had a corrective as well as a humanitarian purpose. In 1785, it was reported that some of the inmates in the St Petersburg house of correction had been sent there by '*pomeshchiki*'.

When the country experienced the greatest threat to law and order towards the end of this period, namely the Napoleonic invasion of 1812, the forces of law and order proved barely adequate. In the town of Kaluga, for example, which lay close to Napoleon's invasion route, the Civil Governor ordered the police and the town duma to maintain calm and order by controlling the movement of population into and out of each ward of the town, maintaining supplies, ensuring that goods and valuables did not fall into enemy hands, and reporting on marauders and prisoners of war. In practice, it proved impossible to control the population (who fled from the town and villages), to prevent disturbances on noble estates, and to curb theft and disorders committed by the Russian army and the local militia. There were also shortfalls in the amount of grain which the province was supposed to supply to the army. On the other hand, it was possible to remove physically the staff and papers of local government institutions from the town, to maintain a check on foreign residents in the province, to transport prisoners of war and to establish a temporary, albeit inadequate, hospital. To put this rather patchy performance into perspective, however, probably no provincial administration in Europe at the time could have dealt more effectively with such extreme circumstances.

LAW AND JUSTICE

Legal codes and training

The Law Code of 1649, which codified criminal and civil laws and established judicial procedures, remained the fundamental source of Russian law until 1835. Parts of it were superseded on an ad hoc basis by further law codes, such as Peter I's Code of Military Law of 1716, and by laws and decrees passed by the tsar or Senate. There were further attempts to codify the laws in this period but none was successful. The Legislative Commission of 1767 had been convened for this purpose, but it had made no progress when it was prorogued in 1768. Alexander I set up a commission in 1801 to codify the laws, which resulted in a hastily composed and entirely inadequate law code of 1812, largely based on Napoleon's Civil Code, which was never put into practice. Full codification of the laws did not take place until 1832, in the reign of Nicholas I, when the laws passed since 1649 were published in a 'Complete Collection of the Laws of the Russian Empire'. In practice, cases were resolved by using whatever laws came to hand or were deemed most appropriate. These could include the Code of 1649, the Code of Military Law (penalties for rape, for example, were based on the Military Law as well as the Code of 1649), Catherine's *Great Instruction* of 1766 (although this was a statement of principles and had <u>no legal validity</u>) and decrees passed by the Senate at various times. On the other hand, private and seigneurial justice existed elsewhere in Europe and systematic codification of the laws was not the norm in other countries in pre-Napoleonic Europe.

A fundamental problem was the lack of legal training in Russia. The provisions in the 1775 statute on provincial administration underlined the assumption that legal training was not a prerequisite by instructing that judges in the district court (a first instance court for nobles) were to be elected by the nobles. The qualifications required to be elected were a period of service (to have reached the lowest rank of officer) and wealth (an income of at least 100 roubles), but not education or training. In practice, most judicial institutions were headed by nobles who came directly from a military background. Russian judicial procedure was primarily concerned with the enforcement of regulations, for which a basic education and a military background would be adequate. Clerical staff found the witnesses (which was not always an easy task), and prepared the evidence in a series of proofs, which mainly comprised confessions. This evidence was signed by both parties and presented to the court, accompanied by the relevant laws which the clerical staff deemed most appropriate. <u>Trials were secret and closed</u>. This procedure meant that judges and assessors relied on the work of junior clerical staff and there was little scope for discretion or interpretation of the law.

Gradual improvements began in Catherine's reign. The first professorship of law at Moscow University was established in her reign; the first *Russian* professor of jurisprudence, S.A. Desnitskii, who was trained at Glasgow University, was appointed to Moscow University in 1773. Guides to Russian laws started to be published, the first being Chulkov's *Judicial Dictionary* of 1788. Training only became widespread in the nineteenth century. It has to be said that Russian suspicion of legal training and specialization was not entirely unjustified, given the corruption found amongst trained judges elsewhere in Europe at the time. English justices of the peace, of course, were not trained and Catherine II, who had avidly read Blackstone's *Commentaries* in French translation before 1775 was supposed to have been impressed by this feature of the English judicial system.

Could justice be obtained?

There were many complaints about slow, arbitrary and corrupt practices in the *nakazy* of deputies to the Legislative Commission in 1767. The noble deputies to the Legislative Commission complained about the length of court procedures and the extent and complexity of the appeals system, particularly concerning land disputes. The *nakaz* from the nobles of Riazhsk (Tambov province) complained that:

> For fifteen years . . . not a single lawsuit has been decided, except those in which the parties have settled out of court . . . while the officials of the chancery are given to great drunkenness, scandalous living, and disorderly conduct of business . . . [and] are found in a state of uninterrupted drunkenness even during the court proceedings themselves.[47]

The advantage lay with the rich and powerful; as elsewhere in Europe the ability to pay, or otherwise influence the course of justice, was crucial. One town delegate in 1767 complained that:

> . . . city officials were afraid to confiscate the wares of the serfs in trade as the law provided, lest the peasant's master regard the action as robbery and enter suit for recovery . . . Every merchant will prefer to suffer some damage than get involved in a law suit with a nobleman.[48]

Given the problems of recruiting able staff for senior and junior posts, described above, it would be unrealistic to expect the administration of justice to improve overnight. 'The judges present in civil and criminal courts blatantly haggled with the accused and justice was sold like an ordinary commercial object', was the comment of D.B. Mertvago, himself an employee of a court in distant Ufa province.[49] When Major-General Potapov arrived in Olonets province in 1782 he found 'severe disorder' in the conduct of criminal cases, records poorly and carelessly kept, income and expenditure inaccurately recorded, orders unfulfilled, outstanding cases, and cases not settled according to the law. The secretaries of the lower *raspravy* (courts of first instance for state peasants) left court books in disarray and had failed to perform their duties.[50] In 1788 the secretary of the St Petersburg district court (a first instance court for nobles) was accused of being drunk while reading the evidence for a murder case.[51]

47. Augustine, 'Notes Toward a Portrait', p. 382.
48. Jack Moore Lauber, 'The Merchant–Gentry Conflict in Eighteenth-Century Russia', unpublished PhD thesis, Iowa, 1967, p. 213.
49. 'Zapiski D.B. Mertvago', *Russkii arkhiv* (1867), nos 8 & 9, p. 186.
50. *Polnoe sobranie zakonov rossiiskoi imperiii*, no. 15360, vol. 21, pp. 423–30, 3 March 1782.
51. TsGIA-SPg, fond 1724 opis' 1, delo 30, f. 20v, Journal of the St Petersburg Criminal Chamber, 1788.

On the other hand, the reforms of 1775 did attempt to deal with one of the greatest problems within the judicial system, namely, the delays within the system, which could ruin litigants and generally played into the hands of those wealthy enough to afford to continue the proceedings. The Statute of 1775 established a new appeals mechanism: there were courts of three instances in the provinces from which appeal could be made to the Senate. In one respect this new structure was astonishingly successful in clearing the backlog of cases; in 1786 1,441 cases were outstanding in the St Petersburg courts, but this was from a total of 53,868 cases which came before the courts in that year. Most cases took four or five years to progress from the lowest to the highest provincial courts, which was relatively speedy. A backlog of unresolved cases, however, still remained. In the St Petersburg Civil Chamber in the 1780s there were cases which had been in the courts for over twenty years. In Kherson in 1810, there were 6,000 unresolved cases and over 600 prisoners awaiting trial.[52]

There is also evidence that at least some local officials took their responsibilities seriously. Baturin, whose criticisms of his colleagues in the fiscal chamber are noted above, studied the laws assiduously and he was deeply critical precisely because his own behaviour was so different. Mertvago, whose comment on bribery is cited above, devoted six months to legal studies so that he could fulfil his duties more competently. Even though it was acknowledged that bribery still existed in the courts, its presence was found to be shocking. 'Bribes are the incurable poison of the courts', wrote I.V. Lopukhin, President of the Moscow Criminal Chamber in 1800.[53] But bribery has to be seen within the context of the time. Bribes were endemic in the administrative and legal systems of all countries in Europe. In Russia, it only became an offence to offer a bribe, as opposed to accepting a bribe, in the reign of Peter I. Even in the early nineteenth century a distinction was drawn between the two offences. And there was a feeling that bribe-taking by impoverished clerks was almost acceptable; it was the well-paid officials and the powerful who needed to be curbed.

Finally, there is some evidence that from the late eighteenth century that new attitudes towards crime and punishment were beginning to emerge. Catherine II led the way with her *Great Instruction* of 1766, which voiced the enlightened views of Beccaria on crime and punishment (for example, condemning torture and cruel punishments, and preferring correction to retribution). I.V. Lopukhin, President of the Moscow Criminal Chamber, advocated the view at the beginning of the nineteenth century that cruel punishments were pointless and that it was better to leave many guilty persons unpunished than to condemn one innocent man. The Russian legal procedure allowed little opportunity for flexibility in the lower courts but when cases reached the highest place of appeal – the Senate, or even the tsar – they were often judged more leniently

---

52. Dubrovin, 'Russkaia zhizn'', 98, p. 488.
53. I.V. Lopukhin, *Zapiski nekotorykh obstoiatel'stv zhizni i sluzhby* (Moscow, 1860), p. 73.

and humanely. Catherine established so-called 'conscience' or equity courts in each province in 1775 which, among other things, were supposed to act as courts of arbitration (in principle, anyone held for more than three days without being charged could appeal for their case to be heard in this court). In practice, these courts never functioned as Catherine intended but they did serve a different, and useful, purpose in that, in several cases referred to them – including crimes committed by minors or lunatics and manslaughter charges – the court was able, unlike ordinary courts, to take account of mitigating circumstances and to pass appropriate sentences.

Torture and punishments

The Code of 1649 sanctioned the use of torture in judicial investigations. Torture was outlawed by Peter III in 1762, and this was reaffirmed by Catherine II at her accession (it was abolished in clerical courts in 1763 but not formally abandoned in military courts until 1782). In this respect Russia was in line with, and indeed slightly ahead of, other continental European countries – torture was abolished in Sweden in 1772, Austria and Poland in 1776 and France in 1780. In practice, torture did take place, to some degree, but when it was made known to the authorities it was not tolerated. As late as 1801 a case was investigated concerning an artisan accused of arson who was tortured in Kazan' before being sentenced to be knouted by the town magistracy.[54]

Those who were convicted by the courts were subjected to harsh punishments (although no harsher than those inflicted outside the judicial system on serfs or factory workers by their owners, or on soldiers and sailors by their officers, often for minor offences). The death penalty for all crimes except murder, rebellion and brigandage had been abolished in 1753, in the reign of Elizabeth (in England, by contrast there were almost 200 different crimes for which the death penalty could be given in 1800). In practice, people were still sentenced to death but almost always reprieved. The former *voevoda* of Kaluga, Miasoedov, was sentenced to death for bribery and embezzlement but was reprieved by a pardon from Catherine II.

The corporal punishment inflicted, however, often led to a more agonizing death than would have been the case with execution. The knout was the most feared instrument of punishment. Victims could die under a few well-directed blows on the ribs, but it was not uncommon for sentences of up to 500 blows to be carried out, followed by the branding and slitting of the nostrils of the victim. Other forms of corporal punishment included whipping, and beating with sticks and rods. After 1785, neither nobles nor merchants could be subjected to corporal punishment unless they were first stripped of their status. Clergy were freed from corporal punishment in 1763 but until 1801 priests could be defrocked first and then subjected to corporal punishment.

54. Dubrovin, 'Russkaia zhizn'', 99, pp. 242–3.

Soldiers and sailors were judged according to Peter I's Code of Military Law (itself based on practice elsewhere in Europe), which continued to be read out to them in the early nineteenth century and remained in force until 1839. The code established the harshest penalties for even minor offences; offences punishable by running the gauntlet were mentioned no less than 40 times in the statute. Running the gauntlet (during which the victim was forced to walk between ranks of his fellow soldiers while they beat him with switches or thongs) was used in other European armies of the day, but in Russia it seems to have been used for even quite minor offences and carried out with greater brutality than elsewhere (that is, by having up to 1,000 men in the line or by sentencing the victim to several 'passes'). There was some attempt later in the eighteenth century, under the influence of men like G.A. Potemkin, to regulate and to limit the extent of corporal punishment in the armed forces, but harsh punishments for the minor offences were reinstated in Paul's reign, and, in practice, officers had almost complete discretion over punishments. In 1806, Alexander I restricted the use of running the gauntlet and outlawed 'cruel punishments' – these did not include running the gauntlet as it was not considered cruel! In 1819, 25 of the 52 military colonists who ran the gauntlet died within 10 days. (In the British navy flogging continued until 1879, when it was 'suspended'; boys and naval cadets were to be caned until after the Second World War.)

William Richardson commented in the 1780s on Russian prisons that:

> . . . a poor wretch, without friends or money, confined in a Russian jail, runs some hazard of starving. I have sometimes visited those mansions of misery; and if famine, chains, nakedness, and filth, are shocking, the scenes I beheld were shocking.[55]

John Howard tersely described the cells in the prison in Tver' (between Moscow and St Petersburg) in the 1780s as 'so offensive, that a medical gentleman did not choose to look into more than one of them'.[56] For the most part, however, Russians were not sent to prison and the prisoners were mostly waiting to be tried, or were fugitive peasants who had been caught. Little provision was made for these prisoners by the state, and prisoners, some in chains, begging for alms were a common sight in Russian towns. Monasteries could be used as places of confinement and exile, in particular for nobles (often women) who were convicted of excessive ill-treatment of their serfs and for priests and others who had broken Church laws (as well as for the insane). Convicted prisoners could be exiled as settlers to Siberia, given forced labour in the mines and factories of the Urals or, as in European Mediterranean countries, dispatched to the galleys. However hard conditions were in Siberia, they were certainly no worse, at least for settlers, than those experienced by

55. William Richardson, *Anecdotes of the Russian Empire* (New York, 1968), p. 236.
56. John Howard, *The State of the Prisons in England and Wales, with Preliminary Observations, and an Account of some Foreign Prisons and Hospitals* (3rd edn, Warrington, 1784), p. 92.

British prisoners sent as indentured servant labour to America (around 30,000 convicts were sent to Maryland and Virginia between 1717 and 1776) or transported to Australia.

SUMMARY: DEVELOPMENTS 1650–1825

The Russian empire gave an appearance of almost total lawlessness throughout this period. Violence was endemic in both rural and urban life. Bands of robbers, desperate fugitives and deserters terrorized rich and poor alike. The civil administration was not large enough to control the population and not honest enough to command respect. The government was unable to address the fundamental causes of the number of fugitives and 'outcasts' in society as long as serfdom continued. But it did attempt to curb other forms of lawlessness in the late eighteenth century through the expansion of civil administration, and in particular through reform of the judicial system and the establishment of an urban police force. The results were patchy; it proved difficult to find willing and able nobles to take up the elected posts and to find the right calibre of men to fill posts across the spectrum, and corruption and bribery persisted. But there is some evidence that modest progress was being made: more dedicated men were entering the judiciary, the courts functioned more efficiently and there were more police officials to tackle disorders within towns. However, policing of the countryside remained largely outside the control of the state and, as far as it existed at all, it was conducted by landowners amongst their serfs or by peasant communities themselves.

nice comparisons with other countries

CHAPTER 6

Education and welfare

Three major themes will be explored in this chapter: first, the extent to which the perspectives and aims of the ruler (in particular, Peter I, Catherine II and Alexander I) governed the nature of educational and welfare provision; second, the respective roles played by the state and the Church in education and welfare; third, the extent to which education acted to define or isolate certain social groups (in particular, the nobility and the clergy). The educational provision in the Ukraine and the western borderlands of the empire is also examined.

Formal education existed in seventeenth-century Muscovy only in private Church schools. Foremost among these was the Kiev Academy, founded in 1632 when the Ukraine was still part of Poland-Lithuania. The Kiev Academy was a traditional west-European style academy, or grammar school, whose teachers preserved and exported Latin scholastic methods and Aristotelian ideas to Russia. In Moscow, a Slavonic-Greek-Latin Academy was opened formally in 1687, modelled on the Kiev Academy which provided the first teachers. The Moscow Academy attracted 70 pupils in its first year. In the late seventeenth century a fierce dispute broke out between factions within the Church hierarchy over the predominance of Greek or Latin, which finally led to the expulsion of the leaders of the Greek faction in 1694 and determined that Latin should dominate at the Moscow Academy. Children of nobles also studied at a school at the Chudov monastery, which had been founded by a Ukrainian, Epiphany Slavinetskii. Another graduate of the Kiev Academy, Dmitrii Rostovskii, established a school in Rostov at the turn of the eighteenth century in which Russian grammar, Greek and Latin were taught to some 200 pupils from all social backgrounds. Jesuits were present in Moscow from 1684 (although they were expelled between 1689 and 1698) and provided education not only for Catholics but also for Orthodox Russians. In 1700 there were 30 pupils of the Jesuits in Moscow, including the sons of the leading boiar families such as the Golitsyns, Naryshkins, Dolgorukiis and Golovkins.

Such elementary education as existed for the majority of the nobles or the merchant classes took place at home, as, indeed, it continued to do so well into the eighteenth century – the merchant, Ivan Tolchenov, noted in his memoirs in January 1779: 'Began to teach the alphabet to my son Petrushka'.[1] Children, as in other Christian countries, were taught to fear and respect the laws of God and the power of the ruler, with the assumption that frequent punishment would aid in saving their souls. Basic literacy was taught at home through alphabet primers based on major religious texts. Nevertheless, it was estimated in the mid-seventeenth century that although most Moscow merchants could sign their name, even this degree of literacy was rarely achieved by artisans, peasants or soldiers.

SEGREGATED EDUCATION

The nobility: military academies and elite institutions

Peter I saw education primarily as a means to train competent servants of the state. He assumed, as always, that the best way of imbuing the nobility with respect for learning was to threaten them. Nobles had to attend special 'reviews' at the ages of 12, 16 and 20 during which they were examined to ensure that they had acquired basic literacy and numeracy; those who failed at 16 could be conscripted into the navy as ordinary sailors. Failure to attend a review could result in the arrest and confiscation of property of the young noble and condemn his family to demotion or postings in remote towns. Reviews took place in 1704, 1706, every year from 1711 to 1714, 1716, 1718 and 1720, some of which Peter attended in person. By a decree of 1714, sons of nobles were obliged to undergo instruction in arithmetic and geometry and were not permitted to marry without obtaining a certificate! Lest it should be thought that this was an idle threat, it should be noted that five years earlier Peter had condemned the aristocrat V.P. Sheremet'ev to hard labour and dispatched his wife to a spinning mill because they had let their son marry before completing his education (the son was claiming exemption from study abroad because of his recent marriage; after Peter's response he promptly departed and his parents were pardoned).

Peter I wanted above all to raise the technical standards of the Russian armed forces and, in particular, to establish a Russian navy. In 1701, he founded the School of Mathematics and Navigation, staffed in the first instance by a Scot and Englishmen, namely Henry Farquharson, Stephen Gwyn and Richard Grice. By 1716 the School had produced in the region of 1,200 graduates, capable of displacing foreigners as officers in the new navy. Subjects taught included arithmetic, geometry, trigonometry, navigation, navigational astronomy and geography. At first the pupils were of mixed social origin – the 198 pupils in 1705 included 38 sons of nobles and 43 sons of clergy – but by 1716 the School had become a provider of technical education primarily for the nobility, although it was never exclusively noble and vacancies were filled by commoners (but not serfs) if there were no noble applicants. Flogging and

1. *Zhurnal ili zapiska zhizni i prikliuchenii Ivana Alekseevicha Tolchenova* (Moscow, 1974), p. 159.

other forms of corporal punishment were common (a soldier was present in each class to beat the boys) and it was perhaps not surprising that rates of truancy were high; in 1722, 127 pupils were listed as runaways. Some of the desperation felt by pupils could have arisen from the fact that promised state stipends often failed to materialize (the same fate befell teachers' salaries), and in 1714–15 pupils were to be found begging barefoot in the streets.[2] Further technical institutions were established in Peter's reign and Peter also sent young nobles abroad to acquire, in his view, 'useful' knowledge such as navigation, ship construction and mathematics. But most of these nobles were already adults (P.A. Tolstoi was 52!) and were acquiring advanced technical knowledge or education.

Peter's priorities were for a technical, secular, 'useful' education, but this did not mean that he abandoned, or rejected, all traditional elements of education or that he found no merit in the few educational establishments which existed at his accession. Indeed, it could be said that the tsars constantly faced the dilemma of whether to provide a practical education for specific service needs or a broader education to create a 'cultured' population which would in general raise the social and economic level of the country. Peter's specialized schools only provided higher technical training (most pupils entered the School of Mathematics between the ages of 15 and 18) and it was assumed that pupils had acquired basic literacy and numeracy skills before enrolling. These basic skills continued to be taught in the home.

The Moscow Slavonic-Greek-Latin Academy extended the subjects it taught but remained fundamentally the same and many of its teachers continued to be drawn from the Kiev Academy, which meant the retention of Latin, and not Greek, at the centre of the curriculum. Until the 1740s the Moscow Academy drew its pupils from the nobility but also from commoners (M.V. Lomonosov, the son of a peasant, was educated at the Academy and became the first Russian member of the Russian Academy of Sciences). Nor, at least until the last years of his reign, was Peter opposed to the education provided by the Jesuits in Moscow. In 1707, the Jesuits taught some 50 pupils who came from the most influential noble families. The Jesuits were valued for their instruction in foreign languages and graduates of their school often entered the diplomatic service. Capuchin (Franciscan) missions also established schools in Astrakhan' and St Petersburg. In 1719, the Jesuits were expelled from Russia but the Capuchin school in St Petersburg continued and in 1720 was teaching five pupils from the Russian nobility as well as three Catholics and two Lutherans. There was also a Lutheran Academy in Moscow, which in 1702 had 238 pupils, most of whom were Russians, and which followed the traditional syllabus of a European grammar school.

After Peter's death the Russian rulers extended the elite institutions of a military and non-military nature (partly modelled on elite institutions in Prussia,

2. W.F. Ryan, 'Navigation and the Modernisation of Petrine Russia: Teachers, Textbooks, Terminology', in Roger Bartlett, Janet M. Hartley (eds), *Russia in the Age of the Enlightenment* (London, 1990), pp. 78–9.

France and elsewhere in Europe). Although at first these did not cater solely for the nobility, in time they became more exclusive as more members of the nobility came to value education as a path to service opportunities and social advancement. In the process, nobles came to favour particular, elite, institutions above those which were open to commoners. The acquisition of education was becoming less of an obligation and more of a privilege reserved for the sons of the nobility.

In 1726 a gymnasium was founded in St Petersburg; it took 112 pupils in 1726, 58 in 1727, 26 in 1728 and 74 in 1729. Initially, most of the pupils were maintained by the state and came from a variety of social backgrounds, including a few serfs (such as the children of the household serfs of Kyrill Razumovskii). At first, noble and non-noble pupils continued to be taught together in the same classes and the predominantly German teaching staff also ensured that many of the pupils would be non-Russians. But from 1735, and more rigidly from the 1750s, segregation took place by social class. The Academy of Sciences was founded in 1726, opening in 1727. The first university in Russia was founded in Moscow in 1755, in the reign of Elizabeth, with two gymnasia associated with it, which provided its first intake of students. At first the pupils came from simple backgrounds, but then more nobles began to attend. A further gymnasium was established in Kazan', where noble and non-noble pupils were taught separately. At the beginning of Anna's reign, a special Russian Cadet Corps school for nobles was founded; by 1762 it had 600 pupils. The curriculum included not just arithmetic, geometry and military arts but also history, geography, foreign languages and law; in other words, this was a rejection of the narrow, technological education established by Peter. Between 1732 and 1762, 1,557 students graduated from the school. Although the elite military and naval schools were prestigious, the educational experience was not always rewarding. M.V. Danilov described conditions in the Moscow Artillery School, which he entered in 1737: teaching took place 'without any order' and one of the teachers was 'drunken and quarrelsome, he was under arrest for a third murder', and flogged his pupils with great cruelty.[3]

In the early years of the reign of Catherine II, the curricula of the Cadet Corps and the gymnasia were broadened to include Russian and foreign languages, philosophy, natural sciences, history and geography. S.R. Vorontsov commented in 1789 that graduates of the elite Cadet Corps 'could play a comedy well, write verses, in a word, they knew everything that an officer should know'.[4] Petr Poletika, a Ukrainian who entered the Cadet Corps at the tender age of six in the mid-1780s, found the experience less enlightening. He recalled that he was 'often and severely beaten with the birch' (despite the fact that corporal punishment was forbidden), and that although he learned two languages and basic arithmetic his 'moral education could not but have harmful consequences from the frequent and immoderate punishment'. He

3. 'Zapiski M.V. Danilova', *Russkii arkhiv* (1883), no. 3, p. 28.
4. Max Okenfuss, 'From School Class to Social Caste. The Divisiveness of Early-Modern Russian Education', *Jahrbücher für Geschichte Osteuropas* 33 (1985), p. 342.

also found all but one of his teachers, <u>all of whom were French</u>, to be 'ignorant people . . . brutal in their punishments'.[5] In the reign of Alexander I, a <u>new</u>, <u>elite lycée for 50 sons of the aristocracy</u> was set up in a wing of the palace at Tsarskoe selo in 1811. Pupils were instructed in <u>Russian, Latin, French and German</u> as well as mathematics, history and the fine arts and were supposed to form the basis of a better-educated civil service. <u>Alexander took a personal interest in the operation of the new institution</u> and even insisted that the pupils should be allowed to cultivate their own gardens.

By the 1760s, at least some of the aristocracy had come to perceive education as essential to mark them as 'civilized' and cultured persons, thereby distinguishing them from other members of society. The nature of the education given to the nobility in these elite establishments, based as it was on the study of western languages, literature and thought, has led historians such as Marc Raeff to talk about the 'alienation' of the educated nobleman. In his view, the education process contributed to this alienation in several ways. First, the nobleman became alienated from his place of birth, and at the same time from his family and the household serfs who were his childhood companions, by being forcibly transported to a cold, unwelcoming boarding school. Second, the <u>acquisition of the French language in particular</u>, and west European culture in general, separated the nobility not only from their own serfs but also from Russian commercial classes (who, if they had any knowledge of foreign languages, were more likely to know German). Third, the nobleman became imbued with 'western' values, knowledge and ideas which he could not translate into practice in his homeland, so leading to an alienation from the state which had provided the education and, to a large extent, determined the curriculum which was followed.

Some young Russian nobles in elite establishments <u>learned French better than Russian</u> and absorbed western ideas and philosophy, not only through the curriculum but also through conversations and discussions with fellow students. Many of the young army officers who joined secret revolutionary societies in the 1820s had been educated at these institutions (<u>147 of the 166</u> Decembrists – the army officers who staged an unsuccessful revolt in 1825 in the interregnum following Alexander's death – sentenced by the Supreme Criminal Court for whom information exists had <u>some form of formal institutional education</u>). Many had first been introduced to foreign writings and ideas at this stage. On the other hand, the number of nobles in elite boarding schools was <u>small</u>. The western orientation of Russian education reflected as much as created the cultural preferences of the Russian nobility in the second half of the eighteenth century. In the process, however, the average nobleman <u>only picked up a smattering of foreign languages and culture</u> which could make his 'alienation' from his homeland <u>seem comic to his fellow</u>, better-educated, nobles. Furthermore, the experience of the Russian nobility was <u>not unique in Europe</u> and <u>it is arguable it was no more 'alienating'</u> than, for *Nice!*

5. 'Vospominaniia Petra Ivanovicha Poletiki', *Russkii arkhiv* (1885), no. 11, p. 308.

example, the dispatch of young Englishmen to boarding schools or Germans to elite grammar schools which concentrated on study of classical languages.

The nobility: private schools, tutors and priests

Nobles who could not afford to send their children to the elite military schools established by Peter and his successors made use of private schools, or pensions, which until 1786 were not regulated or inspected. Some of these were prestigious – for example, the Nobles' Pension, which opened in Moscow in 1779 and had 400 students by 1790 – but many were run by foreigners and did little more than teach a few rudiments of foreign language, and accomplishments such as dancing and drawing. In 1780 it was estimated that there were 28 pensions in the St Petersburg area alone, teaching about 500 pupils, of whom only 200 were Russian. Notable private schools in St Petersburg included the two schools founded by freemasons which were first funded by, and then funded, the monthly periodical *Morning Light*, a largely masonic publication, and a school attached to St Isaac's cathedral, founded at Catherine's own expense in 1781. The latter had 486 pupils, mostly the sons of merchants, officers, clerks and officials, soldiers and servants, including a small number of girls. Catherine attempted to make the curricula of private schools conform with that of the new national schools after 1786 but, in practice, standardization could never be fully achieved.

Nobles were often reluctant to let their offspring mix with commoners in the state schools. In Tambov, governor G.R. Derzhavin (the poet) arranged that teachers in the national school should teach noble boys privately in his own home (although he initially had to use force to make boys attend). In 1777, the Tver' nobility set up a special school for 180 poor noble boys and this trend became more marked in the reign of Alexander I, with special noble schools established in Tula, Tambov and Khar'kov. Special emphasis was laid on the teaching of foreign languages at these schools, which was thought to be particularly appropriate for noblemen.

By the late eighteenth century it was becoming the custom to employ tutors to teach sons of noblemen in their homes (as, of course, happened elsewhere in Europe). These were often foreigners, but retired soldiers and priests were also hired. In particular, French tutors were valued as French became the language of the nobility. Some of these tutors were little more than adventurers. One told the traveller John Carr that 'In summer I be clerk to a butcher at Cronstadt, and in winter I teaches English to the Russian nobility's children.'[6] Prince Evgenii Obolenskii told the Commission which investigated the Decembrist Revolt that 'My tutors . . . were French governors who changed every year and sometimes twice a year and left no trace of their teaching . . . there were sixteen or eighteen of them.'[7] By the second half of the eighteenth

6. John Carr, *A Northern Summer; or Travels round the Baltic, through Denmark, Sweden, Russia, Prussia, and Parts of Germany, in the Year 1804* (London, 1805), p. 293.
7. M. Raeff, *The Decembrist Movement* (New Jersey, 1966), p. 47.

century the roguish French tutor and the half-educated Russian noble had become familiar themes in Russian satirical literature. The following words are put into the mouth of a foolish young nobleman who has just returned from Paris in Denis I. Fonvizin's play *The Brigadier* (published in 1769):

> . . . Don't you know how our French teachers are? Even though the greater part of them are illiterate, nevertheless they're the best people in the world for the upbringing of children. Do you know that I, I whom you see before you now – that I have lived here at the pension of a French coachman before my departure for Paris.[8]

The experiences described in memoirs by nobles demonstrate the ad hoc, haphazard and often incomplete nature of the education many experienced. In practice, tutors could be brutal, partly because they were largely unsupervised. A.A. Bolotov, a minor nobleman, was first taught to read by a Ukrainian teacher from religious texts at the age of six and then, three years later, became the victim of a brutal German, who 'not only whipped me mercilessly with a switch over all my body' but behaved 'like a wild beast', on one occasion inflicting 200 blows on him.[9] His third tutor did not use corporal punishment and taught him German, French, drawing and geography. He then spent one year in a private school in St Petersburg (where he became thin because of lack of food) and then, after a short spell with a new tutor in Vyborg, he joined the army at the age of 16. Children who moved around the country with fathers in service could undergo quite a cosmopolitan education within the Russian empire. S.A. Tuchkov (from an old noble family) learned the catechism at home from a priest and then was taught to read by a soldier for two years. He then followed his father to Vyborg, where he attended the school of a Lutheran pastor and learned German, before moving to Kiev, where he was taught first by a French tutor ('who knew not a word in Russian') and then by the rector – a monk – of the Kiev Academy. As a result, to his father's disgust, the young Tuchkov not only learned foreign languages, history and geography but also acquired some knowledge of subjects deemed unnecessary for service in the army, such as rhetoric, poetry and Latin (his father said that 'Latin was only needed for priests and doctors').[10]

The clergy: seminaries

Unlike western Europe, the Russian state had little competition from the Church in the provision of formal education. Parish priests did little more than provide basic religious instruction in the home for some children. Peter I instructed the Church to perform a useful service for the state by providing

8. H. Segel, *The Literature of Eighteenth-Century Russia* (New York, 1967), vol. II, p. 368.

9. *Zhizn' i prikliucheniia Andreia Bolotova* (Moscow-Leningrad, 1931; reprint Cambridge, 1973), vol. I, pp. 56, 63.

10. *Zapiski Sergei Alekseevicha Tuchkova 1766–1808*, ed. K.A. Voenskii (St Petersburg, 1908), pp. 2–7.

accommodation for cipher schools which would provide elementary education for the nobility (see below), but this was a short-lived experiment. Catherine II and Alexander I took the view that teachers in the national schools should be secular. Indeed, in Russia the pattern was that the state to a large extent determined that the parish clergy should be educated, rather than the parish clergy taking initiatives in the education of Russian youth. After the secularization of church lands in 1764, even the finances of seminaries were dependent on state support. The consequence of state policy towards the education of clergy, and the nature of the education that ensued, was that education served to isolate the clergy. As the elite nobles became divided from the rest of the population (including impoverished provincial nobles) by their acquisition of French, so the distinctiveness of the clergy lay in their knowledge, albeit often hazy, of Latin.

In the seventeenth century, as well as the Academy in Moscow, seminaries had been established on the initiative of local clergy in Novgorod, Chernigov and Rostov. In the period 1702–08 in the region of 200 pupils were taught at the Rostov school. But it was the state which decreed that this educational provision should be extended to the clergy. In 1721, Peter instructed that schools for the sons of clergy had to be established in every diocese; by 1727, 46 schools had been opened, teaching 3,056 pupils. Some of these schools had a precarious existence. The Suzdal' school (east of Moscow) had 109 pupils in the period 1723–26 but then closed. It reopened in 1736 with 78 pupils but closed again in 1744, when there were only 28 pupils enrolled. In 1737, (during the reign of Anna) these diocesan schools became regular Church seminaries. At first, in the reign of Peter, and to some extent also in the 1730s and 1740s, these diocesan schools taught pupils not just from the clergy but from other social groups. By the middle of the eighteenth century, however, they had become the preserve of the clergy alone. The number of pupils at diocesan schools continued to grow, from 4,673 in 1766 to 11,329 in 1783, to 20,393 in 1799 and 29,000 in 1808.

Peter I not only instructed the clergy to establish schools but also interfered with the curriculum. In his 'Spiritual Regulation' of 1721 he stated that diocesan schools should follow the curriculum of the Moscow and Kiev Academies, but, as he assumed at the time that these schools would also provide education for non-clerics, he added that there should be some 'useful instruction: for example, navigation in regulation boats, geometrical exercises, construction of regulation forts etc'![11] At first the diocesan schools only gave the most basic education, in particular because there was a shortage of teachers qualified to teach in Latin, and most children of priests continued to be educated at home. In the 1760s the curriculum of the seminaries was reformed. Russian became the language of instruction and foreign languages and secular subjects, such as history, geography and arithmetic, were introduced. Latin, however, remained the core of the curriculum, even though few of the pupils were able to master

11. James Cracraft, *The Church Reform of Peter the Great* (London, 1971), p. 267.

it and progress to the more advanced classes. In 1808, a more radical reform was introduced by Mikhail Speranskii, himself a product of seminary education. This modernized the curriculum, giving more emphasis to modern languages and natural sciences, and established a proper structure of clerical schools, so that basic instruction was provided in parish and district-level schools while advanced instruction was reserved for seminaries and academies. Tests were introduced for teachers before they took up appointments and the Church had its monopoly on the sale of wax candles restored so that capital could be accumulated to fund the schools properly. Reform of the syllabus and organization of the church schools had taken place once more at the initiative of the state, not of the Church.

Discipline and living conditions in the seminaries were as harsh as in state schools, and the trauma of leaving the family for an overcrowded and brutal boarding school was at least as severe as that experienced by many sons of Russian nobles. In 1723, 14 of the 52 pupils at the Kazan' episcopal school fled (of the others, 9 were sent home because they were too poor and 11 because they were too young, 2 were dismissed because they were too dull and 6 died, leaving only 5 pupils in the school). In 1750, the seminary in Riazan' (southeast of Moscow) lost almost a third of its pupils through flight. One pupil ran away from the Vladimir seminary 'because of the incomprehensibility of Latin science and because of the intolerable beatings'. Many pupils lacked proper financial support. A report on the seminary in Vladimir commented that 'many pupils . . . go out and beg food like common beggars'. Teachers could be lazy, drunken or brutal and teaching methods consisted mainly of rote memorization, with the result, according to Bishop Simon of Riazan', that 'Pupils often leave the seminary much duller than they entered.'[12] Overcrowding meant that in the Iaroslavl' district school in the early nineteenth century a 'pupil from one end of the classroom cannot hear and see what the teacher does and says at the other end'.[13] Some classes contained more than one hundred pupils.

Some improvements took place in the second half of the eighteenth century and early nineteenth century. Under Metropolitan Platon, reforms were carried out to the curriculum of the Moscow Slavonic-Greek-Latin Academy, including an increase in instruction in Russian, and more textbooks were acquired. His more benign regime meant that fewer pupils fled from the Academy in this period. Even so, Aleksandr Mikhailov, who arrived at the Academy in 1794, recorded his impression of 'darkness, heat, dampness, noise, cries and whistling in class . . . And the food – damp cabbage, onions and kvass, millet porridge'.[14] On the positive side, seminaries were able to produce people of

12. Gregory L. Freeze, *The Russian Levites. Parish Clergy in the Eighteenth Century* (Cambridge, Mass., 1977), pp. 99–100.
13. Gregory L. Freeze, *The Parish Clergy in Nineteenth-Century Russia: Crisis, Reform, Counter-Reform* (Princeton, 1983), p. 114.
14. 'Umstvennyi vzor na protekshiia leta moei zhizni ot kolybeli i do groba (1778–1825g): Iz rukopisnoi avtobiografii o Aleksandra Mikhailova', *Dushepoleznoe chteniia* (1896), no. 11, p. 367.

talent, including doctors, lawyers, academics and administrators. Indeed, the state at various times deliberately used educated seminarists as a resource to fill posts in central and local administration, to provide teachers for national schools and students for institutions of higher education (in 1795, the seminaries were instructed to provide 50 recruits a year for medical training, as they were the only schools which taught Latin). In diocesan schools as a whole, however, the problems of overcrowding, poverty, poor teachers and an over-ambitious curriculum were not overcome. As Speranksii commented:

> The seminaries were founded toward the end of furnishing Russia with a more enlightened clergy; but . . . our clergy has remained almost entirely in its former state of ignorance, while the seminaries have furnished the university with its best people and given the civil service not a few skilled administrators.[15]

Soldiers' sons: garrison schools and colonists

The sons of soldiers and sailors born after their fathers were conscripted were regarded as a distinct social group whose future lay only with the armed forces and were given a special and separate education and training in the garrison schools deemed appropriate to this end. Education was provided for them from the age of 7 (up to this age they lived with their relatives in the country) to 15, when they joined the army as regular soldiers. Garrison schools were also attended by boys whose fathers were not soldiers. The Astrakhan' garrison school in 1764 taught 324 soldiers' sons and 200 orphans of merchants and *raznochintsy*. The subjects studied by the different groups varied, as the children of *raznochintsy* learned crafts and those of merchant origin learned navigation, geography and languages of neighbouring countries. In the 1730s, there were 4,000 pupils in garrison schools; numbers rose to 12,000 in 1797 and to 16,000 by 1801.

Conditions in the garrison schools were probably even worse than in other schools. The schools were overcrowded, housed in poor buildings, lacked sufficient provisions and were staffed by poorly paid teachers. In these conditions sickness and mortality were high. Even Aleksei Arakcheev, who had been put in charge of military colonies by Alexander I and was known as a severe disciplinarian, commented in 1824 that:

> It is difficult to maintain children in a state institution at such a young age which still demands female care. Moreover, children separated from their parents or guardians, to whom they have been accustomed, miss them and when forced to study [they] fall ill, fill the hospital and spread mortality [which is] especially noticeable for this age-group.[16]

15. Christopher Bennett Becker, 'The Church School in Tsarist Social and Educational Policy from Peter to the Great Reforms', unpublished PhD thesis, Harvard 1964, pp. 70, 72.
16. E. Kimerling, 'Soldiers' Children, 1719–1856: A Study of Social Engineering in Imperial Russia', *Forschungen zur osteuropäischen Geschichte* 30 (1982), p. 108.

Paul I decreed that the unfortunate pupils had to listen to a reading of the military regulations each Sunday, especially the articles dealing with obedience and punishments. Nevertheless, the garrison schools continued to attract a number of children from merchant or petty official backgrounds.

Children of soldiers and peasants in military colonies, established in Alexander's reign, were known as 'military cantonists' and were also supposed to provide a pool of future soldiers. At the age of 8 they were to don uniform and receive basic instruction in literacy, numeracy and drill. In some ways, the cantonists can be seen as the ultimate products of tsarist education policy. The practical emphasis of Peter I reached its fulfilment in a form of education designed to create competent and obedient soldiers. The most ambitious aims of Catherine and Alexander to 'mould' society were also at stake; the new cantonists would form a cadre of soldier-peasants, devoted to the tsar and to the army, quite outside the existing social and judicial structure. In the process, Alexander continued the practice of borrowing the most modern educational theories from the West (the method of teaching basic skills was copied from the Lancastrian method in Britain – a form of rote learning, whereby older pupils, or monitors, passed the information to groups of pupils, who then questioned each other). Yet, the application of Alexander's ideas also suffered from the worst defects of educational systems of the period – insensitivity, brutality and a belief that military discipline was the only way to mould young minds.

THE NATIONAL EDUCATION SYSTEM

Peter attempted in a heavy-handed way to establish a network of elementary schools. Trained pupils from the Navigation School were sent to the provinces to establish elementary schools in monasteries or dioceses. Thirteen of these so-called 'cipher' schools were opened in 1716; 26 were still in existence in 1726, despite a decree of 1722 (see below). The cipher schools had been intended to provide compulsory education for the sons of nobles aged between 10 and 15 but, in practice, they were attended by boys from different social estates, and above all by the sons of clergy. The social composition of pupils in the schools in the first ten years of their existence was: clergy, 931 (plus a further 500 sons of clergy in the Novgorod cipher school); clerks, 374; soldiers and Cossacks, 402; nobles, 52; townspeople, 93; others, 199. Pupils in the cipher schools have left no accounts of their experiences but in these first ten years we know that 322 pupils fled from the schools, and a further 233 were discharged as incapable. In Tambov, in the early eighteenth century, pupils at the cipher school fled to the iron factories in the north, where passports were not essential.[17] That they should seek sanctuary in an environment which most peasants sought desperately to avoid suggests that life in the

17. I.I. Dubasov, 'Ocherki Tambovskago byta XVII i XVIII stoletii', *Istoricheskii vestnik* (1892), no. 9, p. 662.

schools was <u>unbearable</u>. In 1722, the Church was <u>absolved</u> from any further responsibility for the cipher schools with the result that they closed and pupils were transferred to garrison schools (see above). In 1721, town magistracies were instructed to open schools in every town but, as no funds were provided for this purpose, <u>the decree remained a dead letter</u>.

Catherine II created and funded the framework for a system of state schools in the empire which were, <u>at least in principle, open to all classes and both sexes</u>. In 1775, the Statute of Provincial Administration instructed that schools should be established in all provincial and district towns. In 1782, a special Commission was set up to devise a structure and curriculum for a state school system based on the best practice elsewhere in Europe (and in particular within the Austrian empire, where primary education had been made compulsory in 1774). This led to the <u>Statute on National Schools in 1786</u>, which established the new structure of schools: a major school in the main town of each province and a minor school in the main town of every district. Catherine, unlike Peter, did at least make sure that there was some financial provision for schools. Boards of general welfare had been established in all provinces in 1775, with an initial capital of 15,000 roubles, to open and oversee welfare institutions and schools (see below).

The minor schools provided the first two years of instruction and the curricula of each class in the minor and major schools (two classes in the fourth year of the major school) covered the following:

Subjects	Hours in each class					
	1	2	3	4i★	4ii★	Total
Religion	5	4	5	–	–	14
Russian	11	6	3	3	3	26
Arithmetic	9	6	3	–	–	18
Latin	2	3	4	3	3	15
Foreign language	3	6	6	3	3	21
Ethics	–	–	5	–	–	5
Geography	–	–	5	–	–	5
History	–	–	4	6	6	16
Science	–	–	–	5	5	10
Mathematics/physics	–	–	–	7	7	14
Drawing	6	6	6	6	6	30
Total	36	36	36	36	36	

★ 4i – fourth year, first class; 4ii – fourth year, second class

The curriculum was <u>largely based on Austrian practice</u>, with an emphasis on utilitarian subjects and a solid grounding in civic reponsibility and respect for the ruler and laws. A textbook, *On the Duties of Man and Citizen*, was specially written for use in schools to mould good citizens by <u>stressing civic</u>

and not religious values (it was withdrawn from schools in 1819 when the Archbishop of Tver', Filaret, and the Minister of Public Instruction, A.N. Golitsyn, thought it contained revolutionary ideas). Religion was taught in the first two classes, but the textbooks were provided by the Commission and not the Church, and instruction was to be given by secular teachers and not by priests. Ambitious plans were made to teach relevant local languages – Greek in the southern provinces, Arabic on the borders of Persia, Chinese in the far eastern provinces. French was not taught, probably on the grounds that nobles would learn it privately and the rest of society did not need it. Many schools lacked suitable textbooks, maps and equipment. Nevertheless, the Vologda major school (in the north) owned 147 books in Russian, French, German and Greek, two thermometers, 253 natural history specimens, an 'electric machine', a telescope, a microscope, a ship's compass, a theodolite and ten cases of scientific instruments.[18] In 1792, 52 pupils in Irkutsk major school (in eastern Siberia) were studying Mongolian, 27 studying Chinese and 6 studying Japanese; after 1794 the study of Mongolian and Chinese was abandoned but Japanese continued to be taught (along with French and German) until 1816.[19] In theory, corporal punishment was not allowed, although it probably took place (as it certainly did in elementary schools in other parts of Europe).

Catherine differed from Austrian practice in that she insisted that teachers should be secular and not priests. In practice, however, at least the first generation of teachers, and a large proportion of subsequent generations, were sons of clergy, some of whom were forcibly removed from the top classes of the seminaries where they were being educated. The recruitment of teachers from the clerical estate was made the more necessary because only one institution was established in St Petersburg for teacher training. Modest salaries for teachers in the lower classes (60–150 roubles in minor schools, but 150–500 roubles in the major schools), lack of pensions and slow advancement (it took eight years' service in the minor school to reach the 14th rank) meant that teaching was an unattractive career for members of other social estates. Not only were salaries in the lower classes often inadequate (a teacher from a minor school in St Petersburg, where prices were high, complained to the Commission that he did 'not have any money for basic needs, like shirts, boots and other minor necessities'),[20] but they were not always paid on time or in full. The Commission was petitioned by teachers begging to be relieved of their duties, claiming illnesses or their unbearable separation from widowed, elderly, mothers. As the Commission usually refused these requests, teachers found themselves trapped in jobs they had not sought under conditions which were less than ideal.

---

18. A. Voronov, *Fedor Ivanovich Iankovich de-Mirievo ili narodnaia uchilishcha v Rossii pri imperatritse Ekaterine II-y* (St Petersburg, 1858), pp. 62–3.
19. A.N. Kopylev, *Ocherki kul'turnoi zhizni Sibiri XVII-nachala XIX v* (Novosibirsk, 1974), p. 91.
20. RGIA, fond 730, opis' 1, ed. khr. 31, p. 25, material relating to teachers in St Petersburg province, 1783–1802.

It is hardly surprising in the circumstances that, in practice, not all teachers met the high standards of moral probity and knowledge envisaged in Catherine's design and could not, therefore, hope to implement in full her ambitious curriculum. Drunkennesss and disorderly behaviour by teachers was not uncommon. Ivan Vinogradov, a teacher in the St Petersburg major school, was accused on several occasions of drunken behaviour and was finally dispatched by the Commission to serve as a common soldier (rather like disreputable peasants selected by the peasant communes as recruits).[21] To put this in context, however, teachers, at least in elementary schools, elsewhere in Europe were poorly paid, often incompetent and brutal and frequently took to drink (in 1802–03 in Cleves in Prussia, where primary education was well developed, 43 out of 67 teachers who were inspected were found to be incompetent).

Education was free (textbooks were to be provided for poor pupils free of charge), voluntary (unlike in Austria where it was compulsory) and, in principle, open to all classes. The social composition of schools varied greatly according to the locality and it is difficult to generalize about the whole empire. In Perm' (east of the Urals) in 1787 the largest contingent of pupils (28 out of 100) were children of minor officials, but 16 pupils were from a noble background and 23 were soldiers' children.[22] An analysis of the social origin of pupils in major and minor schools in the provinces of Novgorod (in 1787), Kaluga (in 1788), Tver' (in 1786), Iaroslavl' (in 1788), St Petersburg (in 1786, minor schools only), Tambov (in 1788) and Tula (in 1788) showed that 713 pupils were from an artisan background, 344 were of merchant stock, 206 were children of nobles and officers, 291 were soldiers' children, 156 were children of clerks, 142 were peasants, 45 were children of priests and 228 were 'others' (factory workers, *raznochintsy*, foreigners, foundlings, etc.). Most of the children of nobles and officers were to be found in the major schools. All schools were located in towns. Yet the figures above seem to indicate that some peasants did, in fact, attend some state schools. In 1786 there were 26 peasants in the Tver' major school; in 1788, there were 40 peasants in the Kaluga major school. Whether these were trading peasants or household serfs is not clear.[23]

The numbers of schools and pupils rose (although many private schools already in existence were also absorbed into the system). By 1786, 165 national schools had opened, teaching 10,230 boys and 858 girls; by 1792 there were 302 schools teaching 16,322 boys and 1,178 girls. This was an achievement, in particular because attendance at school was voluntary. Nevertheless, the pattern of education provision was uneven; provision was good in St Petersburg, Moscow, Novgorod, Tver' and Iaroslavl' but in distant provinces there was

21. Ibid., pp. 79, 81.
22. Galina Smagina, 'Die Schulreform Katherinas II: Idee und Realisierung'; paper given at a conference in Zerbst 1996, publication forthcoming.
23. RGIA, fond 730, opis' 1, ed. khr. 71, report by Osip Kozodavlev to the Commission on National Schools from Novgorod (ff. 57–101), Tver' (ff. 116–17), Kaluga (ff. 299–305), Tula (ff. 312v–29), Tambov (ff. 335–43), Iaroslavl' (ff. 403–20); ed. khr. 41, ff. 239–48, list of the pupils in St Petersburg province.

often insufficient population to maintain schools effectively. In distant Viatka in 1797 it was reported that 'these inhabitants see little value in education, and do not wish to send their children to school', preferring them instead to learn a trade.[24] Even within a province, the numbers of pupils in schools could vary considerably from school to school and fluctuate wildly. In the period 1789–96 the numbers of pupils in the St Petersburg district minor schools ranged from 43 to 89 in Sofia, 148 to 162 to Kronstadt, 21 to 39 in Shlissel'burg, 20 to 39 in Luga, 32 to 50 in Rozhdestvo, 31 to 51 in Iamburg, 20 to 34 in Novoladoga, 26 to 72 in Peterhof and 9 to 35 in Krasnoe selo (the minor school in Iamburg was closed in 1797 and the Rozhdestvo school in 1799).

The fluctuation in numbers was due to a rather casual attitude taken by parents towards education. It was also a product of the limited value set on education by most parents, who were only interested in their children acquiring basic skills in literacy and numeracy and had little desire to see them progress from minor to major schools or to the higher classes in the main schools. Osip Kozodavlev reported to the Commission from his inspection of state schools in the late 1780s that:

> The numbers in the third and fourth classes were small. The second class pupils usually did not wish to go on to the third class, because the parents and the pupils themselves did not see the value in studying in the higher classes . . .[25]

In Archangel, only 52 of the 1,432 pupils finished the course in the major school in Catherine's reign; in Ekaterinoslav (in the southern Ukraine) the proportion was 61 out of 1,624 pupils.[26] In Perm', 74 of the 100 children enrolled in the major school in 1787 were aged 7–12 (51 were aged 7–10), which suggests that most were seeking elementary instruction (the other children were aged 4 (1), 5 (4), 6 (6), 13 (4), 14 (4), 15 (6), 20 (1)). As major schools were only opened in provincial centres they were relatively few in number anyway. In practice, many teachers had to abandon the ambitious curriculum, and the modern interactive teaching methods which were prescribed, in favour of more basic subjects and traditional rote learning.

Alexander I extended the work of Catherine II. In 1804, the structure of national schools was completed by the establishment, at the bottom, of parish schools in every village and, at the top, of six universities. These comprised the three existing universities at Moscow, Dorpat (largely German and refounded; originally founded in 1632) and Vil'na (largely Polish), and three new creations in St Petersburg, Khar'kov and Kazan'. The principle of open access to all free classes and all income levels applied in Alexander's state

24. N.I. Serbov, 'Shkola v tsarstvovanie Ekateriny II', in S.A. Kniaz'kov, N.I. Serbov, *Ocherk istorii narodnago obrazovaniia v Rossii do epokhi reform Aleksandra II* ed. S.V. Rozhdestvenskii (Moscow, 1910), p. 149.
25. RGIA, fond 730, opis' 1, ed. khr. 71, p. 30.
26. Voronov, *Fedor Ivanovich Iankovich de-Mirievo*, p. 73; I.M. Cherniavskii, *Materialy po istorii narodnogo obrazovaniia v Ekaterininoslavskom namestnichestve pri Ekaterine II i Pavla I 1784–1805* (Ekaterinoslavl', 1895), p. 25.

schools and was extended to cover university entrance and tuition. State scholarships were given to students at gymnasia (the former major schools) and
universities. St Petersburg gymnasium, for example, had 60 scholarships for
sons of soldiers and orphans, while the Khar'kov gymnasium had 40 free
places and the Tobol'sk gymnasium had 10 places. Fees were introduced in
St Petersburg schools in 1819 but children of poor parents and orphans
were exempt.

The parish schools were to provide basic instruction in reading, writing,
arithmetic and religion, and covered practical subjects including agriculture,
natural science and hygiene. The curricula of the upper classs of the minor
schools (now called district schools) covered religion, law, Russian, history,
geography, mathematics, physics, natural science, technology and drawing.
Latin and German were taught to pupils who were proceeding to the former
major schools (now called provincial schools or gymnasia), where the curriculum was expanded to include psychology, logic, ethics, aesthetics and political
economy. This 'encyclopedic' syllabus proved impossible to fulfil. In the last
few years of Alexander's reign the curricula of schools and universities underwent a radical change and became less secular and more traditional. In schools,
subjects now perceived to be 'harmful', such as philosophy, and practical
courses were replaced by a greater emphasis on history, religion and ancient
languages. Yet, even at this stage, Alexander was as reluctant as Catherine II
to involve the clergy more actively in teaching and instead looked to English
models of Lancastrian schools to impart basic literacy and numeracy at a
parish level. By 1825 the empire had a total of 1,411 schools (360 of which
were private), in which 69,629 pupils were being educated. Whilst this was
a considerable advance, given the paucity of provision at the beginning of
the eighteenth century, it should be noted that only a tiny proportion of the
population was affected. By way of comparison, in Austria, where a national
system of education was most developed, by 1781 it was estimated that 208,000
school-age children were attending schools in the Austrian and Bohemian
provinces; in Paris at the same date there were 334 elementary schools. In the
late eighteenth and early nineteenth centuries primary education became the
norm in France, Prussia, Denmark and Holland.

THE EDUCATION OF GIRLS

The education of the daughters of nobles for the most part took place in the
home and was limited to the acquisition of household skills. Erazm Stogov
(born 1797) commented that:

> Both my grandmothers were illiterate. When I asked why these noble women
> were illiterate, my father answered: 'Why do women need to be literate?
> Their affairs consist of pleasing their husbands, bearing, feeding and nursing
> their children, and looking after the home. For this literacy is not necessary.
> Women need literacy to write love letters. Besides, a literate girl cannot

find herself a fiancé – they all would avoid her. And neither I nor my father knew your mother was literate or she would not have been my wife.'[27]

In practice, only the most wealthy and sophisticated noble families employed governesses for girls. It was more common for mothers to teach their daughters their own skills, with possibly the assistance of the priest for basic religious instruction. A.A. Bolotov, a minor nobleman, bought a piano so that his daughters could be given music lessons and employed a dancing master, but although he considered the possibility of his daughters learning French, he decided that he could not afford a governess to teach them.

There were very few private schools for girls until the reign of Alexander I. The major exception was the Smolnyi Institute, founded in 1764 by Catherine II and based partly on the school of Saint-Cyr, founded in France for the daughters of impoverished nobility in 1686 by Mme de Maintenon. The school was to have two separate divisions for noble girls (at Smolnyi) and non-noble girls (at the Novodevichii Institute). The instruction was to last for twelve years, during which noble girls would learn religion, Russian, foreign languages, arithmetic, history, geography, law, drawing, dancing, music, sewing, heraldics and social manners; the curriculum for non-nobles was more practical. Unlike Saint-Cyr, where the staff were nuns, the teachers in Smolnyi were secular (as in the national schools established after 1786). Indeed, Catherine stressed that her aims were more practical; as the *St Petersburg Gazette* reported, 'They will be good Russian wives, caring mothers, and zealous homemakers.' The instructions for the founding of the school stressed the importance of exercise, hygiene and a simple diet.

It proved difficult at first to attract applicants but by 1794 440 noble girls and 410 commoners had completed the course; by the end of the 1790s, over one thousand pupils had attended the school. Smolnyi was inspected in 1783 by Jankovich de Mirievo (the key member of the Commission on Education) and found lacking in many respects, but particularly in that Russian was badly taught and that instruction in French was not understood by the pupils. As a result, more Russian teachers were employed and the curriculum restructured and simplified. Part of the problem was the recruitment of able teachers, despite the relatively good salaries (250–500 roubles a year). Russian teachers were recruited from the commoners who studied in the school as pupils. It is uncertain to what extent this improved standards but there is no doubt that the popularity of the school for the nobility grew. By 1791 there was no more room in the noble section for pupils and the non-noble section had become inundated with girls of noble origin. Five years later there were 368 noble girls enrolled in the school and only 135 commoners. Within the assumptions of the time about the purpose of female education, Smolnyi was accounted a success. As Prince I.M. Dolgorukov commented on Katerina Nikolaevna Apochinina (who married into the Naryshkin family), a Smolnyi graduate:

27. Carol S. Nash, 'The Education of Women in Russia', *1762–1796*, unpublished PhD thesis, New York University 1978, p. 14.

> She spoke French well, knew music, sang pleasantly, danced with grace, and played roles in the theatre well. In a word, this girl was completely prepared for the world . . .[28]

By the end of Alexander's reign 12 boarding schools specifically for the daughters of gentry had also been established under the auspices of Alexander's mother, the Dowager Empress Maria Fedorovna.

The state schools established by Catherine in the 1780s were open to girls. In practice, only a few girls attended these schools, but it is perhaps surprising that any did so at all. The number of female pupils in state schools rose from 44 (from a total of 518) in 1782 to 1,178 (out of 17,500) in 1792 and 2,007 (out of 24,064) in 1802. Unfortunately, these statistics do not provide a breakdown of the social background of the female pupils. In St Petersburg, there were 48 girls (and 286 boys) in the major school and 278 girls (and 1,417 boys) in the minor schools in the city in 1790; in 1795 there were 41 girls (310 boys) in the major school and 369 girls (1,900 boys) in the minor schools. In the minor schools in the district towns of the St Petersburg province girls could be found in 1790 in all the minor schools except in the town of Gdov in the following numbers: Sofia, 14 girls, 57 boys; Kronstadt, 34 girls, 156 boys; Shlissel'burg, 5 girls, 34 boys; Narva, 5 girls, 55 boys; Oranienbaum, 9 girls, 51 boys; Luga, 1 girl, 35 boys; Rozhdestvo, 2 girls, 24 boys; Iamburg, 16 girls, 35 boys; Novoladoga, 1 girl, 36 boys; Peterhof, 7 girls, 59 boys; Krasnoe selo, 2 girls, 26 boys; Tosno, 2 girls, 20 boys.[29] Perhaps the participation of girls in schools in or near the capital is not so surprising. But there were 6 girls enrolled in the major school in Perm' in 1787. And in the 1790s, the traveller John Parkinson was 'surprised to see four girls in the first class' of the school in Astrakhan'.[30] In Tobol'sk province in Siberia there were 2 girls in the major school in 1793 and 7 in 1799, as well as a small number of girls in minor schools.[31] In 1824 it was calculated that there were 338 girls in district schools and 3,420 in private schools. Albeit in a small way, the tsars had directly encouraged and facilitated the education of women within the empire.

EDUCATION IN THE BORDERLANDS

One of the features of the pattern of educational provision within the Russian empire was that education was more developed in the western borderlands, acquired from the seventeenth to the early nineteenth centuries, than in Russia proper.

In the seventeenth century, educational provision in the Ukraine was far more advanced than in neighbouring Muscovy. There was a system of parish,

28. J.L. Black, *Citizens for the Fatherland. Educators and Pedagogical Ideas in Eighteenth-Century Russia* (New York, 1979), p. 167.
29. RGIA, fond 730, opis' 1, ed. khr. 41, ff. 402–8, 620–22v, lists of teachers and pupils in the St Petersburg schools.
30. John Parkinson, *A Tour of Russia, Siberia and the Crimea 1792–1794* (London, 1971), p. 177.
31. Kopylev, *Ocherki kul'turnoi zhizni Sibiri*, p. 89.

secondary and higher schools. At parish level, the priest, or a student from the Kiev Academy, would provide basic instruction for Cossacks, townspeople and some peasants. At the higher, secondary, level, sons of nobles were also educated by priests. One estimate is that there were 866 schools in the ten regiments of the Hetmanate (Left-Bank Ukraine) in the 1740s. In the eighteenth century the curriculum of the Kiev Academy was broadened to include geometry (in 1707) and Greek, German and Hebrew (in the 1730s). It continued to provide Russia with educators, writers and theologians well into the eighteenth century. After 1786, the Academy bought the new books issued for the national schools and gradually introduced new subjects. Unlike diocesan schools in Russia, the Kiev Academy continued to educate sons of nobility, and not just the sons of clergy, while maintaining its Latin curriculum. In 1819 the Academy was renamed the Kiev Ecclesiastical Academy and became more narrowly focused on the education of priests.

Part of the process of the assimilation of the Hetmanate into Russia in the reign of Catherine II involved education. In the 1760s, Ukrainians were at last able to send their sons to the Cadet Corps, which served to assimilate them with young Russian nobles, and their daughters to the Smolnyi Institute. As opportunities opened up in Russian service for young Ukrainians, these institutions became more popular. Shafonskii claimed in 1786 that:

> . . . gentry with sufficient means keep foreigners as teachers, but the others send their children to schools in Moscow, St Petersburg and other places or to the various cadet corps, and some even send them abroad, so that already in the Little Russian [Ukrainian] schools it is practically only the sons of priests and other clerical children who study.[32]

Nevertheless, the general level of education, both at the parish level and at the Kiev Academy and other seminaries in the Ukraine remained higher than in Russia. Pupils from the Ukrainian seminaries were heavily recruited as teachers in national schools after 1786. Ukrainians, educated in seminaries, featured strongly amongst the student body of the newly founded Teachers' Seminary in St Petersburg, comprising 37 out of 211 entrants in 1782–86 and 16 out of 55 entrants in 1790–95. Latin-trained graduates of the Kiev Academy also provided many of the students of the medical faculties in Russian universities. It proved more difficult to establish Russian institutions on Ukrainian soil, however. After 1786, national schools of the Russian model were introduced into the Ukraine, but many Ukrainians were at first reluctant to attend schools which were regarded as an alien imposition and inferior to native schools. This might account for the fact that the Kiev major school attracted a particularly unusual number of female pupils: 35 girls and 99 boys in 1789 and 68 girls and 142 boys in 1790. In 1808, there were 20 girls in the Vitebsk gymnasium and 13 in the Mogilev school (both towns were in Belorussia).

32. David Saunders, *The Ukrainian Impact on Russian Culture 1750–1850* (Edmonton, 1985), pp. 41–2.

The educational experience of noble boys in the Ukraine and western borderlands remained somewhat different from that of Russian nobles, but could be equally brutal and inadequate. G.S. Vinskii was initially educated at a church school by the priest, where, according to his memoir, '. . . what and how I was taught I do not remember, except that he [the priest] frequently and painfully whipped me, especially on Saturdays . . . This stupid-barbaric habit was common in almost all parish schools . . .'. He was then taught by tutors at home, with various degrees of physical punishment, before being sent to a school in Chernigov at the age of 10, where the 'inspector frequently beat me for no reason', and then to the Kiev Academy, where he learned rhetoric, Latin and Polish and a little French and German but, according to him, no mathematics (so that he still had to count on his fingers) and then finally to a private school to learn French. His formal education ended at the age of 16, when he joined the army.[33] Despite Vinskii's criticisms, this education proved sufficient to find him employment as a tutor to a noble family (teaching arithmetic, amongst other subjects) after he had been exiled to Ufa.

Polish schools had been reorganized by the Polish Education Commission in 1783 and the structure of elementary, secondary schools and universities was maintained in Polish-Lithuanian lands in the empire after the second and third partitions of Poland and the creation of the Congress Kingdom of Poland in 1815. The language of instruction remained Polish and the University of Vil'na continued in existence, although some of the textbooks which were deemed too nationalistic were banned. Literacy rates in the Baltic provinces, Finland and the lands of partitioned Poland remained higher than in Russia. In 1816 there were 720 elementary schools in the Congress Kingdom of Poland, with 23,101 pupils; by 1821 this had risen to 1,222 schools and 37,623 pupils. Part of the difference was the role played by the churches and clergy (both Lutheran and Catholic) in education in the borderlands. In the Baltic provinces and Finland, Lutheran clergy had provided basic instruction for children in rural schools since the seventeenth century. In Estonia, for example, an elementary school system was in place from the 1680s and a teacher training institute was established in Tartu (Dorpat) in 1684. By 1786–87, there were nearly 600 rural elementary schools in Estonia and northern Livonia, and it has been estimated that two-thirds of the adult population of Livonia were literate. The Roman Catholic Church, religious orders and priests had traditionally played an important part in education in Lithuania.

When Alexander I set up a new structure of universities in 1802, Vil'na, founded as a Jesuit college, was one of the few institutions considered to be of the academic level of a university in the empire. In 1809, the empire acquired another non-Russian institution of higher education – the Åbo Akademi in Finland. The Polotsk Jesuit college taught 327 pupils in 1807, of whom 311 were sons of nobles, 12 were artisans and 4 were sons of uniate clergy (it was

---

33. G.S. Vinskii, *Moe vremia. Zapiski G.S. Vinskago*, intro. by I.M. de Madariaga (Newtonville, 1974), pp. 8–14.

closed in 1820 with the expulsion of the Jesuits from the Russian empire). Alexander's education statute was partly based on the structure and curricula of schools in the Vil'na educational district (which included the Lithuanian provinces of Vil'na and Grodno, the Belorussian provinces of Minsk, Mogilev and Vitebsk and the Ukrainian provinces of Kiev, Podolia and Volhynia, in all, about one quarter of the territory of European Russia).

WELFARE INSTITUTIONS

Tsarist policy towards welfare shared several of the characteristics of educational provision. As in the case of the schools, the question arose of the respective roles and responsibilities of the Church and the state towards the sick, aged and incurable. Again, as with education, initiatives were largely taken in practice by the government, which then determined the type of care which should be provided, for whom and, to an extent, how much it should cost. Indeed, welfare and education were often tackled in the same decrees, and put under the auspices of the same institutions, as will be seen below. Finally, welfare institutions, like schools, were essentially an urban phenomenon, designed in this instance to deal with beggars, the sick and the destitute who appeared on the streets. The difference, however, was that formal provision for welfare was not necessary in the countryside as the peasant communes and peasant families had their own strategies for dealing with vulnerable members of the community.

The first government initiatives on welfare came in the reign of Peter I. Peter instructed monasteries and churches to provide for the sick and the elderly (including discharged soldiers) by setting up special almshouses. In 1721, 4,411 men and women were cared for in 93 almshouses attached to religious institutions. In 1724, monasteries were divided into three categories and each category given a particular welfare responsibility. Peter ordered in 1712 (and again in 1714 and 1715, which suggests that his decrees were not implemented) that churches should set up special homes for illegitimate children. Peter did not, however, assume that welfare was purely the responsibility of the Church. In 1723, in contradiction of his earlier decrees, he instructed that illegitimate boys in public care aged 10 or over should be conscripted into the navy. On two occasions, in 1712 and then in 1719, he instructed that hospitals should be set up in every province under the military governor. The decree on urban government of 1721 ordered that the town magistracies should establish hospitals, houses of correction (to set the idle poor to work) and schools in every town. However, since no government funds were made available for these institutions, the practical results were negligible. Government initiatives were most active at times of plague, when cordons and quarantine measures were put in place, although they could never be enforced or fully effective. Such measures, typical of Europe at the time, could not prevent devastating consequences; a plague in the Astrakhan' region in 1692–93 was supposed to have killed in the region of 10,000 people (to put this in perspective, some 100,000 people are said to have died in the great plague in London in 1665). Draconian laws were also passed against beggars (see Chapter 5). Peter's immediate successors continued his policies. Further almshouses were founded in the reigns of Catherine I, Anna and Elizabeth. Elizabeth established a special invalid home for discharged soldiers in Kazan' in 1758.

As in education, the reign of Catherine II saw major new initiatives in welfare provision. In 1763, Ivan Betskoi, Catherine's adviser on education, set up a foundling home in Moscow (modelled on foundling homes which he had visited in Germany), in which he proposed to employ the latest educational methods. Foundling homes were also set up in St Petersburg and other towns but they failed to realize Betskoi's ambitions, mainly because of the alarmingly high death rate (which also occurred in the foundling homes of other European cities). In 1764, 424 of the 523 babies taken into the Moscow home died and the average mortality rate was in the region of 15–30 per cent per annum in the period up to 1796 (but reached 98 per cent in 1767 due to a smallpox epidemic). Furthermore, survival of foundling babies became dependent on a complex system of farming infants out to peasant wet-nurses, and then to peasant families until the age of 7 so that babies were sent back to the very primitive and hazardous society from which Betskoi had hoped to isolate them. It has been estimated that 26,055 of the 32,823 children sent to the country between 1768 and 1797 died and only 5,417 returned to the found- ling homes. In the 1760s, Catherine also established a Medical College and hospitals in Moscow and St Petersburg (including hospitals for venereal diseases) and instructed that pharmacies should be opened in every province. In the early years of her reign the assumption that the Church had a responsibility for maintaining the sick, the insane and discharged soldiers was retained. After 1764, when church land was secularized, the government allocated special sums for the welfare functions of churches and monasteries.

A major change in welfare provision came with the Statute on Provincial Administration of 1775. New boards of public welfare were set up in every province with reponsibility for hospitals, almshouses, asylums, orphanages, workhouses, houses of correction (see Chapter 5) and schools. Catherine, unlike Peter, made some financial provision for these institutions and the boards were given an initial capital of 15,000 roubles each. The boards were permitted to lend part of their capital to the local nobility and merchantry at interest, in order to increase their financial resources and further their activities but they were also encouraged to seek charitable donations from provincial society. In 1786, capital expenditure for the new schools was provided by the state, with the boards responsible for maintenance and salaries thereafter. In practice, the boards varied greatly in their ability to increase their revenue through donations or commercial activities. In 1802, the St Petersburg board had an income of 131,091 roubles 53 and a quarter copecks, but this was far in excess of other provinces. Amongst the wealthy boards were those of Moscow, with an income of 74,873 roubles 91 copecks, and Kiev, with 36,423 roubles 61 copecks, but the provinces of Archangel', Kostroma,

Novgorod, Orenburg, Orel, Perm', Poltava, Simbirsk, Tambov, Vitebsk, Vologda and Voronezh all had an income of under 10,000 roubles.

In the 1780s, inspectors were sent to the provinces to check how well the Statute had been implemented. Their findings were mixed. In Olonets province, in the north, senator A.R. Vorontsov found in 1786 that the board had not yet been set up and that the only welfare institution was the Petrozavodsk hospital.[34] In Kaluga province in 1785, in contrast, there were five almshouses, a workhouse and an orphanage.[35] In 1786 Vorontsov found that in St Petersburg (where it might be expected that implementation of the Statute would be most successful) there were 1,654 patients in the hospital (and a further 139 in the smallpox hospital, founded by Catherine, who had been inoculated in 1768), 69 inmates in the asylum, 516 orphans in the orphanage, 1,233 residents in the almshouse and 546 in the workhouse.[36]

It proved difficult, however, to persuade people to make use of and to support these new institutions. When a charitable home for orphans and poor children was set up in Iaroslavl' in 1786 it was impossible at first to find orphans to fill the places and instructions had to be sent to the district towns to provide suitable candidates (seven were eventually rounded up in time for the ceremonial opening on Catherine's birthday). Most orphans and illegitimate children were taken into the houses of relatives. Russian society was slow to respond to the financial needs of the welfare institutions. A small number of almshouses were set up on the initiative of individuals but organized charitable societies only flourished in the early nineteenth century when Alexander I and his mother, Maria Fedorovna, gave them their personal support. In 1816 these societies were consolidated into the Imperial Philanthropic Society, which was given an annual government subsidy of 150,000 roubles. By 1825 there were 21 officially sanctioned charitable societies, 5 prison societies and 7 mutual aid societies. Furthermore, in practice the distinction between the humanitarian workhouse, which was supposed to provide work for the destitute, and the house of correction, which was a punitive institution for the idle able-bodied, was lost and petty offenders were sent to the workhouses.

Some of the showcase hospitals in Moscow and St Petersburg were impressive. John Howard, the prison reformer, wrote of St Petersburg in the 1780s that, 'I visited several hospitals in this city with pleasure, the rooms, even of the insane, being as clean as those in Holland.'[37] The poor were to receive treatment in hospitals without charge; in 1784, the Catherine Hospital in Moscow reserved 80 beds for the poor and 70 beds for those who could pay. But it proved difficult to find suitably qualified staff in the provinces to establish hospitals. The numbers of medical professionals grew only slowly during

34. SPgFIRI, fond 36, delo 478, f. 126, report by A.R. Vorontsov from Olonets province, 1786.
35. *Topograficheskoe opisanie Kaluzhskago namestnichestva* (St Petersburg, 1785), pp. 16–17.
36. SPgFIRI, fond 36, delo 478, f. 23, report by A.R. Vorontsov from St Petersburg province, 1786.
37. John Howard, *The State of Prisons in England and Wales, with Preliminary Observations, and an Account of some Foreign Prisons and Hospitals* (Warrington, 1784), p. 88.

the eighteenth century, reaching in the region of 2,000 persons by 1803 (the majority of foreign, mainly German, origin). It was estimated that in 1782 the Russian empire had a ratio of doctors to inhabitants of 1:26,000, and that the number of doctors was fewer than the medical establishment in north-west France at the time.

A fundamental problem was that until well into the nineteenth century people had an understandable distrust of hospitals, as mortality rates were extremely high (even in St Petersburg in 1785, 302 of the 1,282 patients in hospital died).[38] The Tula hospital had only 50 patients in 1780 and the Petrozavodsk hospital, noted above, had only 25 patients in 1786.[39] It was not that medical care was not needed – the plague which affected Moscow and other towns in 1770–72 claimed in the region of 120,000 victims and in 1784, 10,000 people died of the plague in Kherson – but that the hospitals were not trusted to give it. In practice, the sick, even in the towns, were cared for at home. Furthermore, traditional and popular remedies were trusted in preference to the medical profession. Herbs were used extensively. It was reported in Tomsk, in Siberia, in 1739–41 that 'the peasants treat fever thus: they drink the dried leaves of St John's wort warm in a concoction from a hollowed tree trunk or a fish cavity'.[40] Such measures, which, at the very least, probably did no harm, were common throughout Europe, of course. The use of religious ceremonies and magic to ward off and counter disease is discussed in Chapter 10. It was mainly nobles who followed Catherine's example and inoculated themselves, and their serfs, against smallpox (about 20,000 people were inoculated); mass inoculation only took place in the nineteenth century. Despite the deficiencies of medical care, Russians had a reputation for longevity. In Iakutsk, in eastern Siberia, John Ledyard was told of a man who was claimed to be 110 years old and in perfect health and it was generally assumed that the rigours of the custom of bathing toughened Russians so that they were remarkably hardy and healthy.

SUMMARY: DEVELOPMENTS 1650–1825

Significant progress was made in this period in creating both education and welfare institutions. The role of Russia's rulers was crucial: Peter I established the principle that provision should be made in both areas, and in practice laid the foundations for at least specialized technical state schools and seminaries; Catherine II supplied the funds to make it possible to fulfil these obligations

38. RGADA, fond 16, delo 526, ff. 319–20, report by P. Konovitsyn from St Petersburg province, 1785–86.
39. RGADA, fond 16, opis 1, delo 980, f. 17, report by A. Vorontsov and A. Naryshkin from Tula and Kaluga provinces, 1785; SpgFIRI, fond 36, opis 1, delo 478, f. 126, report by A.R. Vorontsov from Olonets province, 1786.
40. N.A. Minenko, 'The Living Past. Daily Life and Holidays of the Siberian Village in the Eighteenth and First Half of the Nineteenth Century', in Marjorie Mandelstam Balzer, *Russian Traditional Culture, Religion, Gender and Customary Law* (Armonk, New York, London, 1992), p. 190.

and, in the process, greatly expanded central and provincial responsibility for both education and welfare; Alexander I extended educational provision at the university and district level and encouraged private initiatives and charitable societies. Of course, the majority of the inhabitants of the Russian empire never attended a school or entered a hospital or other welfare institution during this period. But acceptance of the value of education and of the responsibility of local government for welfare provision is a slow process and the achievements of Russia's rulers should not be underestimated. It has to be remembered that in Russia, unlike almost any other country in Europe, there was little in the way of Church or monastic traditions of education and the government had to create a school and welfare structure from almost nothing.

good int'l comparisons again

? ed?

CHAPTER 7

Occupations: agriculture, industry and crafts

This chapter looks at what people did for a living in the Russian empire. Although I will be discussing industrial developments and urban crafts, this chapter is primarily concerned with peasants. The vast majority of the population of the Russian empire were, of course, peasants, and were employed in agriculture. Agriculture was *peasant* agriculture; modest innovations instigated mainly by noble landowners or Russia's rulers are discussed below but had a minimal impact. Far more significant developments took place in Russian industry during this period, but the composition of the workforce remained largely peasant. Peasants also dominated craft production and frequently constituted the largest proportion of the inhabitants of towns (as opposed to the legally defined urban community).

AGRICULTURAL STAGNATION?

The land under cultivation grew during this period, not only through conquest but also by extension of settlement in the east and south, clearing forests and converting meadow and pastureland into ploughland. More black-earth land was cultivated, with the result that the overall productivity of land within the empire remained about the same. The empire suffered not from land shortage but from underdeveloped agricultural methods and from poor communications. Above all, agricultural output was affected by climatic conditions. Poor conditions in the first half of the eighteenth century – in particular crop failures for successive years in 1721–24 and 1732–36 – resulted in famine conditions. On the other hand, the seventeenth to the early nineteenth centuries saw the expansion of both the internal market and foreign trade. Grain markets emerged first along river arteries, in particular along the Volga and the Dvina rivers. In the first half of the eighteenth century, markets developed in the Baltic provinces and north-west (centred around the ports of Riga and St Petersburg), and the area south of Moscow incorporating the provinces of Moscow, Tula, Kaluga, Riazan', Voronezh and Orel. In the second half of the eighteenth century the market expanded, partly as a result of the abolition of internal tolls in 1753 and partly through canal construction and improvements to internal waterways, so that the Volga and Baltic markets merged to became one far larger network. The territorial gains in the reign of Catherine II opened up commercial markets to central Europe in the west and greatly expanded opportunities for the export of grain from the newly founded Black Sea port of Odessa. Grain exports from Odessa increased from about 400,000 *chetverti* a year from 1778 to 1790 to about one million *chetverti* a year by the end of the century.

only ested. 1794/5? cp - 174

The agricultural year

The labour of peasants (serfs and state peasants) changed little in the period under review. A typical pattern of the agricultural year for peasants in central Russia was as follows:

15 April–6 May	plough for the spring, sow peas
9–14 May	sow spring wheat
15–20 May	sow oats
21 May–9 June	sow barley
10–15 June	manure and plough fallow field
25 June–8 July	mow hay
8 July–9 August	harvest winter rye, sow winter crop
10–15 August	harvest winter wheat
15–20 August	harvest barley
20–23 August	harvest spring wheat
23 August	harvest peas
end August–beginning September	harvest buckwheat

The major crop in central Russia was rye, with oats as the leading spring crop; barley and wheat were also grown extensively. Wheat and buckwheat were export crops and their cultivation increased as the internal market developed in the eighteenth century. The same was true of the 'industrial' crops of hemp, flax and oil seeds, which were the most important crops after cereals. Flax was grown in particular in the Baltic provinces, Belorussia, the central industrial provinces and along the shores of the Black and Azov seas. Hemp was grown in particular in the western provinces of Smolensk, Mogilev and Chernigov and in the central agricultural zone. Peasants and townspeople alike grew vegetables, in particular cucumbers and cabbages. Peasants were reluctant to experiment with new crops – the introduction of potatoes led to disturbances in the 1760s known as *kartofel'nye bunty* (potato revolts) – but this was not simply due to stubbornness and ignorance. Given low productivity and the uncertainty of the weather, new crops were risky and peasants operating within a subsistence economy could afford to take few risks. Peasants kept horses, cattle, sheep, goats, chickens and geese. The production of livestock products, such as tallow, hides, butter and meat, also increased during this period. Horses were fed on hay, oats, rye-mash or straw in the winter or when ploughing;

the rest of the time they grazed in pastures. Cattle were used for milk and bullocks for pulling the heavy ploughs. Women usually cared for the domestic livestock while the men were in charge of the horses.

The peasants mostly used the *sokha*, a wooden plough with metal shares, which dug a shallow furrow and could be pulled by a single horse. It was an ineffective instrument, although cheap and easily made, but the use of heavier ploughs was restricted because they required more animals to pull them. The *kosulia*, a heavier plough which dug deeper and still used only one horse, was used to a limited extent in the north and the non-black-earth central provinces. In the Ukraine, New Russia, and land along the Middle Volga, peasants used the heavier wheeled plough, the *saban*, which was pulled by four horses or up to eight oxen (although the *sokha* was used as well). The main hand tools were the scythe for mowing hay and reaping, the sickle for reaping (although the scythe was used in the Ukraine and the Baltic provinces) and the flail for threshing. Little change took place in agricultural practice during this period. Peter I attempted to persuade the Russian peasants to make more use of the scythe. He sent about 100 peasants from the Baltic provinces to instruct Russian peasants in its use but with little effect. Amongst the other retarding features of Russian agriculture were the limited use of manure, the three-field system (so that one field remained fallow), the division of land into strips (with the loss to cultivation of land used to mark boundaries and to give access to the strips), communal tillage and periodic redistribution of strips (both of which discouraged innovation). On serf estates, the landowner's fields were ploughed first, but in general it was assumed that serfs would put more effort into their own plots and work them more effectively. On most estates serfs worked in teams, half working on the landowner's field and half working on their own fields. In the heavily forested north, peasants used slash and burn cultivation. These peasants lived mainly by hunting and fishing, as did the nomadic tribes of Siberia and the Far East. But the forests were exploited for fuel and for export products such as timber (especially for masts) and pitch.

The grain yield was normally in the region of twice or three times the seed sown (four to six times in the Baltic provinces), but, as the three-field system operated, one-third of the land lay idle all the time. Far higher yields were achieved in western and north-western Europe, particularly by the late eighteenth century. The yield was consistently highest, as one would expect, in the black-earth region. Some historians have argued that a decline in yields took place in the last quarter of the eighteenth century as the soil became exhausted but this cannot be proven conclusively. The study made by Hoch of a village of Petrovskoe in Tambov (in the black-earth region) in the first half of the nineteenth century found fluctuating but generally high yields, in the region of between four and seven times the seed sown, but this was in an area of reasonably good arable land. In general, however, yields in the first half of the nineteenth century had increased little, if at all, from the preceding two centuries and Russian yields remained lower than those of other European countries.

question of stagnation not explicitly answered

Houseserfs

Not all serfs worked on the land. The wealthiest families had hundreds of houseserfs in their town and country houses. Martha Wilmot, who was the daughter of a modest Anglo-Irish landowner (and therefore unfamiliar with the more extravagant lifestyle of the wealthier aristocrats in England) was shocked by what she saw:

> ... the number of servants is dreadful. Think 2, 3 and often 4 hundred servants to attend a small family. A Russian Lady scorns to use her own feet to go up stairs, and I do not Romance when I assure you that two powder'd footmen support her lily white elbows and nearly lift her from the ground, while a couple more follow with all manner of Shawls, Pelises, &c. &c. &c.[1]

Houseserfs could constitute a large proportion of the serfs on an estate. Nobles also formed troupes of musicians and actors. In the second half of the eighteenth century, S.M. Kamenskii had 400 houseserfs and maintained two serf orchestras. Count P.M. Skavronskii apparently loved music so much he ordered his houseserfs to communicate with each other in recitatives! Some exceptionally talented serfs eventually managed to purchase their freedom, but others remained dependent on their master's whim and could suddenly find themselves made into lackeys again.

Houseserfs were often skilled craftsmen or trained in domestic duties or as maids or manservants. They could be given a food allowance or small salaries. On one of the Iusupov estates in 1814, for example, there were 35 houseserfs, some of whom, including elderly peasants, were given a food allowance, while others received a small salary (14 received 5–20 roubles a year and one secretary received 100 roubles). The total expenditure on these household serfs was 299 roubles, 81 *chetverti* of rye and 10 *chetverti* of groats.[2] Serfs much preferred to work in the fields than to be dependent on the whims and caprices of a master in his house, and there was great resistence to serf children being removed from their homes and taken as servants into the master's house. Houseserfs were particularly vulnerable at the time of the recruit levy; they were more dispensable than other serfs and were often chosen as recruits or sold to other nobles to be used in their recruit quota.

Peasants in non-agricultural pursuits

Nobles could simply make their peasants into artisans to perform work on their estates. V.S. Khvostov carried out extensive building on his estate in the 1790s, having 'assigned twelve of my peasants as carpenters'.[3] Most peasant villages produced simply-made goods such as bast shoes for sale or wove

1. *The Russian Journals of Martha and Catherine Wilmot 1803–1808*, ed. by the Marchioness of Londonderry and H.M. Hyde (London, 1934), p. 56.
2. K.V. Sivkov, *Ocherki po istorii krepostnogo khoziaistva i krest'ianskogo dvizheniia v Rossii v pervoi polovine XIX veka* (Moscow, 1951), p. 141.
3. 'Zapiski Vasiliia Semenovicha Khvostova', *Russkii arkhiv* (1870), no. 3, p. 582.

cloth; others were predominantly or entirely devoted to non-agricultural pursuits. The court peasants of Moscow province were well known for their artisan and commercial activity. Certain villages in the province specialized in particular goods; sheepskin hats were made in the villages of Opalikha, Odintsovo, Evseevo and Dimino. Court peasants from Moscow province were said to own 163 shops in Moscow in 1702; in 1731 one court peasant, I. Volkov, owned 10 butcher's shops in the Arbat area of Moscow. In 1731, court peasants owned 245 butchers' shops in Moscow.[4] In the late 1760s it was noted that 'nearly half the district [of Kashin], and especially the villages of Kimry and Medveditskoe . . . consists of bootmakers and shoemakers' who 'for the most part live in Moscow during the winter and sometimes the summer too'.[5] Court peasants from this province also became involved in seasonal work in Moscow and other towns or industrial villages. The village of Ivanovo (a centre for Old Belief) and the surrounding area (Vladimir province) was an exceptional case and became entirely dominated by the textile industry. By 1825 there were about 125 large cotton-printing and weaving works in the village.

State peasants, and serfs on *obrok* estates, needed non-agricultural work to supplement their income and enable them to pay their fiscal dues. Peasant craftsmen existed in all villages but were particularly prevalent in regions where land was poor or where communications assisted trading activity. One area in which trade developed early was Nizhnii Novgorod province, where records exist of 455 trading peasants at the beginning of the eighteenth century. The records show that most of the transactions made by these peasants were for small sums (under 50 roubles) but 8 peasants had over 1,000 roubles in capital.[6] Peasants could organize themselves into associations, or artels, in which they worked together under a leader who determined the labour of individuals and shared out the profits. Artels were usually organized for particular types of work, such as fishing, masonry or barge hauling. The significance of trading peasants for the composition of Russian towns is discussed below.

Rural fairs acted as centres of trading activity throughout Europe. The number of rural fairs in Russia increased more than urban fairs during the second half of the eighteenth century; urban fairs grew from 244 in the 1750s to 864 in the 1790s while rural fairs increased in the same period from 383 to 3,180. By 1800, 1,615 of the 3,180 village fairs were held on seigneurial land, over 50 per cent of all fairs. Many of these fairs were small and of short duration, and sold foodstuffs and home-produced peasant goods. But some were major events which brought traders not only from other parts of the

---

4. E.I. Indova, 'Les activités commerciales de la paysannnerie dans les villages du tsar de la région de Moscou', *Cahiers du monde russe et soviétique* 5, 2 (1964), p. 226.
5. D. Morrison, *'Trading Peasants' and Urbanization in Eighteenth-Century Russia: the Central Industrial Region* (New York and London, 1987), pp. 124, 134.
6. V.R. Tarlovskaia, 'Torgovye krest'iane povolzh'ia v kontse XVII–nachale XVIII veka', *Istoriia SSR* (1983), no. 2, p. 151.

empire but also from abroad. The three major fairs in Russia took place at Makar'ev (near Nizhnii Novgorod), Irbit (in west Siberia), and Korenevo (Kursk). There were also major fairs in the Ukraine, Siberia, Iaroslavl' province, Orenburg, Riga and Kiakhta (on the Chinese border). The timing of the major fairs was such that it enabled traders to move from one to another. Fairs were one of the social occasions where rural and urban pastimes merged, in particular because they often took place on church holidays, between and after major agricultural activities, or when the weather was most clement (two-thirds of all fairs took place between May and September). Peasants also sold their wares within the towns at markets or bazaars. There was also a network of pedlars, or itinerant traders, linking towns and villages.

The landed gentry?

In the seventeenth century, estates had been given to serving nobles to enable them to carry out their military service. Peter I's reassertion of the obligation of all nobles to serve the state in the military or civilian administration meant that in the first half of the eighteenth century nobles rarely had contact with their estates (and sometimes their families). Brigadier Kropotov informed the Senate in 1727 that he had not visited his estate for 27 years. As Andrei Bolotov commented in 1750, 'all the nobility were then in military service, and in the country there lived only old men by themselves, who were no longer able to serve or who through illness and senility, or for some particular reason, were retired, but these were few'.[7] Absentee landords could, of course, show concern for their estates, but this essentially meant exploiting the lands to the full rather than introducing any innovations. In the 1740s and 1750s A.P. Zhukov, a moderately wealthy noble who owned two estates in Penza, gave detailed instructions to his stewards to ensure that his income from crops was as high as possible, including telling them to sell cabbages at Easter when they were more expensive![8]

The freedom of nobles from compulsory service in 1762 in the reign of Peter III allowed them, if they wished, to return to their estates. The extent to which this happened is a matter of debate; we know that some nobles eagerly took advantage of the law and resigned their commissions, but most needed both the income and the status which accompanied service. For the most part, it was the poorer nobles who stayed on their estates. Wealthy and influential nobles educated their sons in the capitals, were in service in the army or the capitals or, if they had retired, maintained at least one house in St Petersburg or Moscow and only visited their estates in the summer. In 1787, 550 of the 1,012 male nobles with estates in Penza province lived outside the province; 370 lived in estates in other provinces and 180 were absent in state service. In

7. *Zhizn' i prikliucheniia Andreia Bolotova* (Moscow-Leningrad, 1931; reprint Cambridge, 1973), vol. I, p. 129.
8. E.I. Zaozerskaia, 'Pomeshchik Zhukov i ego khoziaistvo', in *Dvorianstvo i krepostnoi stroi Rossii XVI–XVIII vv* (Moscow, 1975), pp. 221–6.

Vladimir in 1784 only 952 noble families were resident; 2,084 were absent. On the other hand, many nobles had spent their childhood in the country on their estates, and this meant that they were never totally divorced from their roots.

There is some evidence to suggest that at least some noble landowners took a serious interest in the improvement of agriculture, which could also increase income from their estates. In the second half of the eighteenth century, the Free Economic Society, founded by a group of 15 nobles in 1765, published a journal in which landlords contributed suggestions for the improvement of agriculture; Andrei Bolotov, for example, wrote an essay on the disadvantages of shared ownership of villages. Agricultural societies, of course, were common elsewhere in Europe at this time. The more enterprising landowners attempted to introduce new crops, such as millet, poppy seed and spelt and conducted experiments with new strains of oats and buckwheat. Some also tried to persuade their serfs to replace the *sokha* with the heavier *plug* plough or the sickle with the scythe, and encouraged the use of manure and rotation of crops. A.I. Polianskii, for example, introduced the *plug* and the practice of manuring on his estates in Penza province in the 1760s. There were limitations, however, to the improvements which could be made to estates, particularly if the land was underpopulated, poor or fragmented. The reliance on serf labour imposed its own limitations and peasants were adept at resisting innovation. Peasants supplied their own tools and horses and they worked according to their own customs and at their own pace. This made dramatic innovation impossible; for the most part, noble agriculture was peasant agriculture, and peasant agriculture was in essence subsistence economy. The reasons for the apparent shift from *obrok* to *barshchina* on serf estates is a matter of debate amongst historians (see Chapter 3) but, at the very least, it demonstrates a certain level of economic awareness by landowners that the price of grain was rising (and with it the value of serf labour).

INDUSTRIAL TAKE-OFF?

Peter I provided a great stimulus for Russian industry, driven as he was by the need to arm and supply his armies for the Great Northern War. In his reign state mines, foundries, arsenals and cloth factories were established to meet these military needs. He encouraged native entrepreneurs and skilled foreigners to develop these industries and assigned peasants to them as a captive workforce. Statistics on the growth in the number of enterprises are of limited use, partly because census takers tended to classify all types of manufacturing enterprises under the general heading of 'factory', irrespective of its size or function. Attempts by Soviet economic historians to interpret these statistics are also hampered by difficulties of definition, but give some indication of the general growth of manufacturing industry in Russia. One estimate is that manufactories grew from some 80 to 200 in 1725 to between 650 and 700 in the 1760s and reached about 2,000 by the end of the century. By 1825, it has been estimated that there were 5,261 manufactories with 210,600 workers (excluding all mines, metallurgical plants, distilleries and flour mills and also manufactories in the relatively economically developed Grand Duchy of Finland and the Congress Kingdom of Poland).

The development of industry

Iron production was the most successful eighteenth-century industry in the Russian empire. The Urals became the major centre of the iron industry from early in the century (growing from four enterprises in 1716 to around 50 in 1745 and over 100 by 1762), but there were also large foundries in Siberia and Karelia. By 1800 the Russian empire had become the greatest producer of pig-iron in the world (although thereafter the mining industry stagnated and was overtaken by the vast increase in British production). Precious metals were mined in the Urals and south-west and eastern Siberia; silver was mined in Nerchinsk (eastern Siberia) from 1704 and then in the Altai region. Output in precious metals grew only slowly over the eighteenth century and Russia continued to rely on the import of silver (she became self-sufficient in copper from the 1760s). Salt was produced in the greatest quantity in the northern Urals, especially in Perm' province, although it was also produced in the El'ton salt lake (east of the lower Volga), on the northern shore of the Caspian Sea, in part of the Ukraine, the Crimean sea lakes, parts of Siberia and the far north. Output of salt grew throughout the period but less rapidly than other commodities, partly because its price was kept artificially high to ensure tax revenues (salt was a government monopoly). Tula had been the centre for the armaments industry since the 1630s, but increased demand in the reign of Peter I led to an expansion of production here and the establishment of factories and armouries outside Tula, of which the armouries in St Petersburg and Moscow were the most important. The Admiralty dockyard in St Petersburg was established as early as 1696 to build naval and merchant ships; it grew to become the largest single industrial complex in Russia in the eighteenth century.

Moscow rapidly established itself as the centre of the textile industry, but regional centres also developed in the provinces of Vladimir, Khar'kov, Astrakhan' and Iaroslavl' and in Estonia and Livonia. The woollen industry developed rapidly so that Russia had become self-sufficient in army cloth by the time of the Seven Years' War (1756–62). By 1797 there were 83 wool cloth producers (owned by 40 nobles, 37 merchants, 2 townsmen, 1 peasant and 3 state enterprises), employing 25,930 workers and serfs. Linen mills grew in number from 10 in 1725 (with under 2,000 workers) to 318 in 1799 (with 29,303 workers). Moscow also became the centre for the silk-weaving industry, although Astrakhan' and St Petersburg were also important. The industry grew from 9 silk-weaving plants in 1725 (360 looms) to 23 in 1745 (1,086 looms) and 357 in 1797 (4,701 looms). The cotton industry only developed in the second half of the eighteenth century; it became particularly important in the early to mid-nineteenth century. Paper mills had operated from the seventeenth century. Production expanded during the eighteenth century but was given a particular boost by Catherine II's decree of 1783 which allowed individuals to set up their own printing presses. One estimate is that production rose a thousandfold over the eighteenth century. Bricks had been manufactured since the sixteenth century; the building of St Petersburg stimulated a demand which continued to increase throughout the period.

Communications

Road transport was poor throughout Europe but climatic conditions and the distances between settlements made communications in Russia particularly difficult. The major road between Moscow and St Petersburg had 24 post stages in the 1720s. The journey from Novgorod to St Petersburg (some 170 km), by one of the major roads in the empire, was reduced from five weeks to two weeks as a result of improvements carried out in the reign of Peter I (by comparison, the 350-km journey between Lisbon and Oporto took about a week). The roads between Moscow and Pskov and between Khar'kov and Smolensk were also improved in his reign. Nevertheless, ambassadors claimed in Peter's reign that it took them up to five weeks to travel between Moscow and St Petersburg (some 650 km). In 1768 a traveller covered the distance in 13 days. In 1786, major repairs were made to the bridges on the Moscow–St Petersburg road. Alexander I travelled the distance in 36 hours but most travellers could not hope to negotiate the post stages so swiftly. In 1817 work started on a hard-surface road but by 1825 it had been laid only between St Petersburg and Novgorod. In 1820 a stagecoach service was started between St Petersburg and Moscow and the journey was reduced to four and a half days in good weather conditions. In the reign of Catherine II, construction began on the military road between Vladikavkaz and Tbilisi and on a main road linking Moscow and St Petersburg with Tobol'sk and Irkutsk in Siberia.

On good roads in good conditions travellers could travel at a maximum speed of about 10–16 kilometres an hour. But most roads were not in good condition and passage on any roads became almost impossible in the autumn rains or the spring thaw. Even the improvements and repairs to the Moscow–St Petersburg road were insufficient. Parkinson commented in the 1790s on this road that 'in consequence of the late thaw, it was become one succession of ridges and holes'.[9] The road had been constructed of tree trunks covered with a layer of gravel, sand or dirt and the wood rotted or subsided into the marshy ground. Other major roads were normally bordered with birches and had drainage ditches but usually only one path in the middle, with side paths on either side covered with a layer of sand. Minor roads were narrow dirt tracks. Bridges were often in a poor state of repair and postdrivers normally crossed themselves before attempting to negotiate them! In the 1760s Catherine specified the dimensions of major and minor roads. In 1775, the construction

9. John Parkinson, *A Tour of Russia, Siberia and the Crimea 1792–1794* (London, 1971), p. 98.

and maintenance of roads was made the responsibility of the *ispravnik* (land captain) and the lower land courts (a police organ); in 1800 Paul established an Expedition on the Roads of the Empire to supervise the construction of roads and bridges. Travel was rather easier in the winter when sledges were used. Samuel Bentham took three days to travel from Ekaterinburg (east of the Urals) to Tobol'sk in January 1782 (a distance of some 500 km).

The poor roads made river transport the most effective way of moving goods over long distances. European governments invested heavily in canal building in the eighteenth and early nineteenth centuries (in England 165 new canals were built between 1758 and 1802) and Russia was no exception. Two major constructions took place in the early part of the century; the Vyshnii Volochek canal (completed at the end of Peter's reign) linked the upper Volga with the river Volkhov, through which boats sailed north to the Ladoga canal (completed in 1732), which led to the river Neva and the Baltic Sea via St Petersburg. The journey from Vyshnii Volochek to St Petersburg via this network took about two weeks in the spring (when the rivers were high) and three weeks to a month in the summer and autumn. Trade grew over the century. The number of people working in some capacity in river transport grew from some 60,000 to about 200,000 at the end of the century. Government tolls collected at the Vyshnii Volochek canal rose from 5,855 roubles in 1764 to 47,672 roubles in 1795. In the 1770s and 1780s the locks and dams of the Vyshnii Volochek system were rebuilt in stone and the traffic was more effectively organized. In 1769, 1,742 boats and barges travelled through the Vyshnii Volochek canal system. In 1787, 3,499 boats passed through the canal, manned by 68,980 crew; ten years later this had risen to 4,588 boats, manned by 91,760 men. The system was further improved by the opening of the Msta–Volkhov canal in 1804. In the early nineteenth century the river Dnieper became linked to the Western Dvina by the Berezina canal and the Volga became linked to the Neva by the Sias', Svir', Mariinskii and Tikhvin canals. Russia had acquired an extensive internal river network although factors such as low water levels, rapids and frozen water meant that transport could be slow and uncertain. Even in the early nineteenth century boats only travelled at the rate of 10 versts a day (just over 10 km) up the Volga and at a rate of 20 versts a day through the Vyshnii Volochek system after the improvements had been made. It took at least a year for goods to be moved by river from Astrakhan', on the Caspian Sea, to St Petersburg, on the Baltic.

The social background of entrepreneurs

Until the 1760s, most factory owners came from a merchant background; some, like the Demidovs, were originally state peasants. Merchants took the lead in establishing textile factories in the early eighteenth century and were able to retain dominance in this area until the end of the century. Merchant entrepreneurs also took the lead in establishing iron and copper works, and were particularly active in the period 1721–70. Metallurgical works in the

Urals and Siberia were dominated by seven prominent merchant families who between them established or purchased 72 works in the mid-eighteenth century – the Iakovlevs, Osokins, Tverdyshevs, Miasnikovs, Luginins, Gubins, Turchaninovs and Pokhodiashins. Silk factories remained almost exclusively in merchant ownership.

Nobles became more active in establishing manufactures on their estates in the second half of the eighteenth century, partly encouraged by the expanding market but also as a result of the freedom from compulsory service in 1762, which released some potential for industrial enterprise. In the same year, merchants were forbidden to buy peasants, with or without land, to work in their manufactories (restrictions on ownership had been in place since the 1740s). In the 1790s there were over 10,000 skilled workers ('masters') and 36,000 serfs (around 16,400 of whom were actively working) in noble-owned mines in Perm' and Orenburg provinces alone. The most successful noble entrepreneurial family was the Stroganovs, who owned extensive salt, copper and ironworks in the Urals. In the eighteenth century the Stroganov family and their heirs established 20 copper and ironworks. Other noble families acquired mining wealth by marrying the daughters of prominent merchant families, including the Tverdyshevs and Miasnikovs. In 1800 in Minsk province noble magnates owned 39 out of 88 industrial enterprises (not including distilleries and flour mills).[10] Nobles generated considerable income by setting up distilleries on their land. In 1753 there were 1,298 distilleries owned by nobles and in 1765 nobles were given a monopoly over distilleries. By the 1790s there were 28 major distilleries owned by nobles in the province of Penza alone. In the period 1802–04, 966 serfs and 170 other workers were employed in noble-owned distilleries in the province. By 1813–14, an official report on manufactories revealed that nobles owned 64 per cent of mines, 78 per cent of woollen cloth factories, 60 per cent of paper mills, 66 per cent of crystal and glass works and 80 per cent of potash works.

The industrial workforce

Peasants worked in industrial enterprises either on a temporary basis (serfs or state peasants earning money for *obrok* payments) or were assigned to a particular factory permanently. The poor conditions in industrial enterprises led to frequent disturbances and revolt (see Chapter 5). Colonel Mavrin reported to Catherine II in the mid-1770s (at the time of the Pugachev revolt) that:

> The workers are the prey of factory owners who are robbers and think of nothing but their own gain; they rob the peasants of all they possess, for workers are forced to leave their homes, and are sent four, and even seven, hundred versts away to work in factories.[11]

10. P.G. Kozlovskii, 'Razvitie proizvoditel'nykh sil v magnatskom pomest'e zapadnoi i tsentral'noi Belorussii vo vtoroi polovine VIIIv', *Istoriia SSR* (1972), no. 2, p. 65.
11. S.P. Turin, *From Peter the Great to Lenin: A History of the Russian Labour Movement with Special Reference to Trade Unionism* (London, 1968), p. 14.

The villages of assigned peasants could fall into decay as men were unable to tend their fields. In two Siberian villages of assigned peasants in 1771:

> . . . many of the plough-lands were deserted, and the houses were falling into ruin from age and neglect . . . Badly built houses, gloomy and impoverished inhabitants . . .[12]

The factory might be at a distance of as much as 700 versts (over 700 km), which meant that peasants could not return to their villages at harvest time (assigned peasants only began to receive payment for travelling time in 1769, at a rate of 3 copecks a day). Assigned peasants could be obliged to supply a manufactory with a certain amount of raw material. The assigned peasants in Karelia sent one male member of each household to the ironworks of Olonets for an average of over 200 days a year in addition to travelling time; those who could not supply their own horses worked more days than those who could.[13] Many works only operated seasonally. This was not in order to make life easier for the peasants who needed to tend their fields but because heavy frosts or very hot weather often meant that the manufactories lacked sufficient water to function.

Work in industry was universally unpopular with peasants. There were some regulations on hours worked in state-owned enterprises, but in practice many workers had a twelve-hour day and it was common to work a fourteen-hour day in cloth factories. Women worked in particular as spinners in the textile industry. Children as young as six were employed in the Demidov mines; other industries employed childen aged seven or eight. Children from the St Petersburg foundling home worked in the Aleksandrov ironworks in St Petersburg in the early nineteenth century – surely not what Betskoi had in mind when he envisaged the creation of a new class of 'useful' citizens from orphans in the 1760s (see Chapter 6). Corporal punishment was common for ordinary workers and absenteeism was punished by beatings. Demidov instructed in 1702: 'Subdue the disobedient and the lazy, depending on the offence, with rods and whips and fetters . . .'[14]

In the state manufactories in the Urals, assigned peasants with horses earned a modest 6 copecks a day in the winter and 10 copecks a day in the summer in 1724–68, which rose to 12 and 20 copecks in the period 1779–96. Peasants without horses earned as little as 4 copecks in the winter and 5 copecks in the summer in 1724–68, and 8 and 10 copecks in 1779–96. Wages, however, had been deliberately increased after the Pugachev revolt of 1773–75 which had spread to manufactories in the Urals. Indeed, an analysis undertaken in the 1870s of wage rates in the Urals in the 1840s by Le Play, a French mining engineer and sociologist, suggested that Russian workers were better off than freely hired labour elsewhere in Europe at the time (based partly on the fact that many Russian workers still drew some income from their land). Wage

12. James Mavor, *An Economic History of Russia* (London and Toronto, 1925), vol. I, pp. 475–6.
13. Ia.A. Balagurov, *Pripisnye krest'iane Karelii v XVII–XIX vv* (Petrozavodsk, 1962), p. 106.
14. E.I. Zaozerskaia, 'Pripisnye i krepostnye krest'iane na chastnykh zheleznykh zavodakh v pervoi chetverti XVIII v', *Istoricheskie zapiski* 12 (1941), p. 139.

rates could be lower and less reliable in privately owned enterprises. Serfs working in enterprises on their landowners' estates often performed this labour as a *barshchina* obligation, although some received payment in cash or kind.

Skilled or freely hired workers could command high salaries. Master workers in state enterprises earned an annual wage of 30 roubles in 1723–68, rising to between 32 and 40 roubles in the period 1783–96. Furthermore, state mines had a complex administrative structure and staff included secretaries, copyists and foremen as well as skilled craftsmen. In 1800, regulations for state textile factories specified that the director should earn 3,500 roubles, the foreman 500 roubles, and skilled workers between 400 and 1,000 roubles, depending on their occupations (a joiner and blacksmith 'masters' earned 400 roubles; a 'machine master' earned 1,000 roubles). These salaries were very high by the standards of the time. In contrast, the salaries of workers were as little as 10 roubles a year. In the seventeenth and first half of the eighteenth century, foreign specialists could be brought in at wages which were not only higher than those paid to Russians but were very high by European standards in order to lure skilled craftsmen away from their homelands. However, under Peter, foreigners often complained that they never received their promised pay and were sometimes not paid at all. These specialists included shipbuilders, arms manufacturers and mining engineers.

Training and welfare in industry

Russian manufactories contained 'apprentices', often the sons of workers who, it was assumed, would replenish their ranks. In 1717, the works owned by Ia.K. Riumin employed 129 apprentices, of whom 46 were townspeople, 21 soldiers' children, 17 church peasants and 14 the sons of postdrivers. In St Petersburg, there were 60 apprentices at a porcelain factory in 1804 and 120 apprentices in the Admiralty dockyards in 1806. Some mines and foundries in the Urals had schools attached to them (although Demidov opposed the establishment of schools as he believed that even young children could undertake some useful work without instruction). Schools which instructed pupils in basic literacy skills were attached to the Admiralty dockyards in St Petersburg. In 1732, the Admiralty schools taught 211 pupils in St Petersburg, 87 in Kronstadt and 47 at the Sestroretsk works. In 1826, a technical school was founded at the St Petersburg iron foundry.

The title of 'apprentice' could, however, mean little more than that these were children of workers who were performing certain duties, rather than being indicative of serious training. Pallas commented in the late eighteenth century from a china clay factory near Ekaterinburg that 'Each apprentice is expected to dig every day, in summer, ten puds [164 kg] of pure, white earth, which cannot always be done.'[15] An apprentice, Ioil Grigor'ev, petitioned in

15. *The Habitable Lands, described, or the present State of the People in all Parts of the Globe, from North to South* [a translation of P.S. Pallas, *Journey to Russia and Siberia*] trans. by John Trusler (London, 1788), vol. III, p. 72.

the 1740s that he had worked in the factory for 17 years and still only received 1 rouble 50 copecks a month, something which suggests that he was not being trained but simply employed at a low rate for, presumably, a fairly lowly task. One master beat an apprentice, Luka Nikiforov, to death in the Admiralty dockyards in 1741. Most children started work as apprentices at the age of about 15.

Basic medical care was provided for workers at some state enterprises. In the 1720s, hospitals were set up at the Admiralty dockyards and the Sestroretsk armaments factory. The government ordered the Kolyvan-Voskresensk works in 1747 to employ a physician and in 1752 to set up a hospital. The Mining Statute of 1806 prescribed a degree of medical care in all mines and iron-works, but in practice it was ignored by private owners and only applied in state-owned manufactories. State-owned enterprises also paid small pensions to widows and children of workers but this policy was not adopted by private owners. The contrast between state and private policies towards workers reflects not so much a humanitarian dispute as a difference in perceptions about who should shoulder the responsibility for welfare within the community. The government extended its regulations on the armed forces to state-run manufactories (which were largely concerned with the production of arms); the private industrialists regarded welfare as a state matter and not the responsibility of individual factory owners. Peasant workers and their families were, in any event, cared for within the peasant community. Welfare for freely hired labour only became a major issue in the second half of the nineteenth century.

URBAN OCCUPATIONS

Russian merchants and traders did not make a good impression on British travellers. Robert Lyall wrote in the 1820s that, 'Speciousness, craft, dishonesty, swindling, lying, and even perjury, form the grand lineaments of the character of all the guilds of the Russian merchants, and of the burgesses.'[16] This negative view, however, could be the product of the difference in popular perception of the merchant estate in Russia and Britain, which was particularly offensive to British travellers, who were rarely of noble origin themselves. Robert Ker Porter was shocked to find in the early years of the nineteenth century that:

> To us, who regard our merchants as the pillars of our country, it is surprising to see the prejudices of the Russian nobility against the mercantile profession. . . . However, notwithstanding this general prejudice, I have sometimes met with a few (but very rarely) of both sexes of the Russian *noblesse* at the houses of our merchants: but they have always been persons of an extraordinarily enlarged mind, rendered still more liberal by travelling, and probably a residence in England.[17]

16. Robert Lyall, *The Character of the Russians, and a Detailed History of Moscow* (London, 1823), p. cxxx.
17. Robert Ker Porter, *Travelling Sketches in Russia and Sweden during the Years 1805, 1806, 1807, 1808* (London, 1809), vol. II, p. 5.

If there were some contempt for the mercantile profession in Russia this did not prevent nobles or peasants from involvement in trade and industry, as has been seen above. Indeed, the greatest problem faced by the urban community in this period was the competition it faced from peasants and, to a lesser extent, nobles, and its greatest weakness was its failure to protect urban crafts and merchant industry from this penetration.

The non-urban element of town communities

One cause of the weakness of the urban community can be found in the social composition of towns in which the legally defined urban estate was greatly outnumbered by other social groups (who did not pay urban taxes). The population of Moscow in 1730 was 138,792, of whom only 23,707 were legally part of the urban estate. Of the rest, 35,959 were houseserfs, 32,475 were nobles and *raznochintsy*, 18,310 were peasants, 15,348 were officers and soldiers and 5,456 were clergy. In the period 1788–95 the population of Moscow had grown to some 175,000, of whom only 11,900 were merchants and 9,100 were artisans while 53,000 peasants, 17,600 officials and *raznochintsy*, 8,600 nobles, 7,000 military and 3,600 clergy also resided in the city. In St Petersburg (which, because of the presence of the court never had a typical social composition) in 1801 there were 14,310 registered merchants (both sexes) and 12,676 artisans, but 50,454 peasants as well as 39,058 members of lower military ranks and 35,002 *raznochintsy*. The number of posts in government offices increased dramatically in St Petersburg after the creation of the ministries in 1810–11, with the result that the number of *raznochintsy* rose from 35,000 to 67,000, comprising over 22 per cent of the population of the city.

Peasants made up the largest non-urban section of the population of Russian towns, but other social groups could be significant. In Kaluga in the mid-1720s townspeople comprised about 60 per cent (around 400) of the households, but the other residents included postdrivers (116 households), retired soldiers, minor officials and children of clergy (70 households altogether), clerks (40 households) and nobles (58 households).[18] In Turinsk (in western Siberia) in 1782 there were 38 merchants and 286 artisans registered as inhabitants of the towns, but also 347 state peasants, 20 economic (former church) peasants, 41 houseserfs, 20 assigned peasants, 265 postdrivers, 40 exiled settlers, 16 retired servitors and 4 foreigners. It has been estimated that the number of members of the armed forces (officers and men) in Russian towns grew in real terms although it dropped as a percentage of the town population in the eighteenth and early nineteenth century; one source for European Russia gave figures of 74,000 officers and men (15.4 per cent of the population) in 1737–44 and 175,800 in 1811 (6.7 per cent of the population). Russian towns were not exceptional in this respect, of course. Other European towns had garrisons

18. N.V. Kozlova, 'Sotsial'no-ekonomicheskoe razvitie Kolomny v 20–40-kh godakh XVIIIv', *Russkii gorod* 4 (1981), p. 124.

and included clergy, nobles and officials amongst their inhabitants. But in Russia the overwhelming presence of peasants coloured the nature of urban life and hindered the development of a separate urban culture.

A further complication was that not all the registered urban categories lived within the towns. As late as 1783 only 19.9 per cent of the merchants and 12.3 per cent of the artisans registered in Petrozavodsk actually resided in the town; the rest lived in the country. On the other hand, so-called 'agrarian' towns, where most or all of the population were involved in agrarian pursuits, existed throughout the period. In Nizhnii Novgorod province in 1797, only the towns of Nizhnii Novgorod, Balakhna, Gorbatov, Arzamas and Kniaginino registered a large number of merchants and artisans; the towns of Perevoz and Lukoianov comprised solely economic peasants (5,095 and 2,085 respectively). And not all members registered in the *posad* actually engaged in artisan or commercial activities. In 1761 it was reported from the town of Sapozhok (south-east of Riazan') that 'our 186 merchants are not registered by guilds' and 'do not have any markets, and do not trade in any goods, but are occupied with sowing and cultivating grain on the rented land of inhabitants of the town, and from this they earn their living'.[19] In 1767, state peasants from Olonets province (in the north) complained about townspeople who lived in villages and who 'did not practise any trade'.[20]

Urban life on the periphery of empire was further complicated by the different national and racial mix of the inhabitants. Commercial activity in the lands acquired after the partitions of Poland was largely, but not entirely, in the hands of Jews. In 1781 Jews had been allowed to register in the merchantry but in 1791, following a complaint against Jews who had registered in the Moscow merchantry, Jews were forbidden to enrol in the merchant estate in any town outside Belorussia and New Russia. This, in effect, restricted Jewish residence to a pale of settlement in the lands acquired after the partitions of Poland. The only town which could receive Jewish settlers was Odessa (in 1794 the Jews comprised 10 per cent of the population of Odessa and, with Greeks, became the merchant class of that city). In fact, many Jews in former Polish-Lithuanian lands were engaged in rural occupations. The Statute of 1804 recognized this and allowed Jews to register as either farmers, manufacturers, merchants or artisans. The government of Alexander I, however, continued to force the Jews away from the countryside and into urban settlements and urban social categories (partly to protect the peasants from what was perceived as the pernicious activities of Jews as inn-keepers and sellers of spirits). Towns in Georgia were dominated by the nobility, who owned most of the property, and Georgian artisans were, in effect, serfs of the local nobles. What commercial life there was in Georgian towns was usually in the hands of Armenians.

19. Wallace Daniel, 'The Merchantry and the Problem of Social Order in the Russian State: Catherine II's Commission on Commerce', *Slavonic and East European Review* 55, 2 (1977) p. 198.
20. Iu. R. Klokman, *Ocherki sotsial'no-ekonomicheskoi istorii gorodov severno-zapada Rossii v seredine XVIII v* (Moscow, 1960), pp. 75, 65.

Finally, a brief mention should be made of prostitutes in the towns. The number of these women is impossible to estimate but they were certainly of sufficient number for the government to legislate in the early eighteenth century that they should be dispatched, along with vagrants and beggars, to work in factories. John Carr was not unimpressed by those he saw in early nineteenth-century St Petersburg:

> ... they live in a quarter by themsleves, and I believe are not very numerous; some of them are Polish, of course handsome; some Germans, of course fascinating; and some, and the most of them, fair and frail wanderers from the upper parts of Finland, which ... is said to possess many pretty faces and good persons amongst the females.[21]

Urban crafts and craftsmen

Towns specialized in the production of certain goods. Iaroslavl' in 1759–66 listed 36 different artisan occupations but specialized in the manufacture of shoes and clothing. Moscow was also dominated by these trades (in 1826 there were 1,417 masters in shoes and clothing) but metal goods were also prominent (625 masters). Within towns a variety of crafts were pursued. In 1684–85 the following crafts, and numbers of practitioners, were found (or at least registered) in the town of Torzhok (Tver' province): bakers, 13; tavern-keeper (owner of simple eateries), 1; kvass maker, 1; spice-cake maker, 1; malt makers, 24; butchers, 6; blacksmiths, 16; metal pot maker, 1; carpenters, 11; wainwright and wheelmaker, 1; window-frame makers, 2; comb maker, 1; furriers, 2; sheepskin makers, 5; tawser, 1; tanners, 9; shoemakers, 19; glove makers, 11; saddlers, 2; dyers, 5; tailors, 4; hatmaker, 1; stocking makers, 2; net maker, 1; silversmiths, 4; icon-makers, 2; fishermen, 2.[22]

The main problem for the urban community was the fact that the peasants in the towns competed directly with them in the production and sale of the types of product listed above. The urban community attempted unsuccessfully to establish its exclusive right to trading activities. In the seventeenth century the main conflict was with peasants who were owned by boiars, the Church or monasteries on so-called 'white' property (belye mesta), which was not subject to tiaglo or urban taxes. Particular competition came from monastic serfs who acted as traders and competitors, often renting shops and establishing small markets where monastic produce could be sold. Townsmen also clashed with the possessors of belye mesta over the ownership and use of meadows and ploughlands on the outskirts of the towns. The Code of 1649, which was issued in the wake of urban rioting, abolished belye mesta suburbs and, at least on paper, restricted the rights of peasants to trade in the towns. As a result, much monastic property was confiscated.

21. John Carr, *A Northern Summer; or Travels round the Baltic, through Denmark, Sweden, Russia, Prussia, and Part of Germany, in the Year 1804* (London, 1805), p. 282.
22. M. Iu. Volkov, *Goroda verkhnego povolzh'ia i severno-zapada Rossii pervaia chetvert' XVIII v* (Moscow, 1994), p. 80.

Conflicts between the urban community and monasteries continued after this date as monasteries still owned considerable property in the towns. The second half of the seventeenth century saw, for example, constant clashes between the urban community and monasteries in the town of Iaroslavl', where the monasteries managed to reclaim some of their property in the 1650s and whose monastic peasants still came to the town to trade. The Spas monastery, for example, took over 53 new houses in the town and installed its own skilled peasants in them. Gradually, these peasants were obliged to register as townspeople – for example, Sereshka Salel'ev, a monastic peasant who had set up his own shop in Iaroslavl' was forced to pay urban dues in 1680. By the mid-1680s the town had imposed restrictions on further encroachment by the monasteries and in 1691 almost 90 per cent of shops in Iaroslavl' were owned by townspeople (including *gosti*, merchants, artisans and widows); monasteries and churches owned only 8.8 per cent.[23] Nevertheless, as late as 1710 *belye mesta* still accounted for over 25 per cent of the property in the town. Peter I's urban reform of 1721 resulted in the enrolment of many settled monastic peasants into the urban community, but it was only the secularization of church land in 1764 and the abolition of the category of church and monastic peasants which finally ended this conflict.

However, conflict between townspeople and trading peasants (state peasants or serfs who produced and sold goods to pay their *obrok* dues) continued throughout the eighteenth and early nineteenth centuries. Peasants could undercut the prices for goods without contributing taxes or other urban services. The elite of trading peasants owned their own peasants and hired workers, and could act in direct competition with merchants. Complaints about unfair competition from peasants dominated the merchant *nakazy* in 1767. Merchants in Pskov complained about the court, economic and seigneurial peasants who competed with merchants in the hemp and fishing trade, and merchants in Valdai complained that peasants dominated the grain and other trades.

The urban community attempted to deal with the competition from trading peasants by forcing them to register as townspeople and so contribute to urban taxes and other dues (described more fully in Chapter 2). Indeed, the towns needed this constant replenishment in order to sustain the numbers registered as merchants and artisans. But the assimilation of large numbers of peasants into the urban community did not ease the problem of peasant competition. The conflict between trading peasants and townspeople was not addressed in the Charter to the Towns in 1785. Merchants continued to complain about peasant competition. In Pskov in 1819 the artisans expressed the wish 'to allow artisans in Pskov to trade with the same rights which have been given to peasants'. In 1823 merchants in Moscow prepared a memorandum

---

23. David Hugh Miller, 'City and State in Muscovite Society: Iaroslavl', 1649–1699', unpublished PhD thesis, Princeton, 1974, pp. 208, 210–11, 278.

on the decline of trade in Russia, which laid the blame at the door of the trading peasants, who:

> ... through their great numbers possess completely many areas of urban industry and trade, which previously was engaged in by merchants and *posad* people.[24]

These complaints partly led to the guild reform of 1824 and new regulations concerning trading peasants when the existence of trading peasants was de facto recognized by dividing them into six ranks in a manner similar to the divisions between merchant guilds.

Urban guilds and apprenticeships

There is some evidence that a guild and apprentice structure existed in Muscovy in the seventeenth century. The historian E.M. Tal'man found evidence of 228 apprentices in Moscow in the period 1631–99. In terms of their social background, these apprentices comprised 161 townspeople, 24 serving people, 18 peasants, 8 monastic peasants and servants, 6 foreigners, 4 *gosti* and *gostinye sotni* (elite merchants), 4 state officials, and 3 'idlers'.[25] In 1680 there were 18 apprentices in the Gold and Silver Departments *(prikazy)*. But the apprentice system was less developed and rigid than in western Europe, and less developed in Russia outside Moscow. Some rules on the standards of craftsmanship existed in the seventeenth century in centres of craftsmanship like Novgorod and Pskov, and in the towns in the Ukraine and Belorussia where Magdeburg Law applied, but they were not as strict as those in the West. The Code of 1649 laid down some regulations for apprenticeships stating that they should usually be of five years' duration, but although most of the apprentices in the Royal Armoury in the 1680s worked for five years (after which they became journeymen), some remained apprentices for 15–20 years or longer. In the town of Tikhvin (located south of Lake Ladoga), periods of apprenticeship for blacksmiths fell in the second half of the seventeenth century from 12–14 years to 3 and a half years, but after this period some remained as 'perpetual journeymen' since they lacked the means to establish their own smithies.[26] Furthermore, apprentices could be tied to their master through the *kabala* system (see Chapter 3, pp. 66–8), whereby they had to serve a master for a number of years, or even for life, in order to pay off a family debt. Most apprentices started at the ages of 12 or 13 and the apprenticeship lasted until they were between 18 and 20 years old.

There were certain rules governing mutual responsibilities between master and apprentice in the seventeenth century. Masters were supposed to provide

---

24. P.G. Ryndziunskii, *Gorodskoe grazhdanstvo doreformennoi Rossii* (Moscow, 1958), pp. 85, 88.
25. E.M. Tal'man, 'Remeslennoe uchenichestvo Moskvy v XVII v', *Istoricheskie zapiski* 27 (1948), p. 95.
26. K.N. Serbina, 'K voprosu ob uchenichestve v remesle russkogo goroda XVII veka', *Istoricheskie zapiski* 18 (1946), pp. 152–3, 154.

food, clothing, footwear and usually, but not always, pay, and had a responsibility to teach their art fully to their apprentices. Apprentices were supposed to be obedient and behave with decorum, and could be punished for drunken or rowdy behaviour. The evidence suggests that these responsibilities were not always fulfilled. For example, in 1678 a widow, Fedora Vorontsova, complained that her son, Minka, had been apprenticed to a silversmith, Gavrilo Ivashnev, for five years but that 'Gavrilo, arriving drunk, beats and maims my son for no reason.'[27] Fedor Fedorov, an apprentice in the Silver Department petitioned to leave his master in 1679 on the grounds that he had not been paid for four years. On the other hand, masters complained about apprentices who had fled from their employ and tried to reclaim them; in 1682 a master tailor, Ivan Artem'ev complained that his apprentice had not only fled but had stolen from him.[28]

In the eighteenth century Peter I and then Catherine II tried to stimulate the development of craft guilds (*tsekhi*) in Russian towns as a means to improve the economic state of the towns and the quality of goods and, in a general sense, to attempt to bring Russian urban life more in line with what was seen as the more sophisticated practice in central and western Europe. In 1721 Peter ordered that craft guilds should be set up and regulated and that apprentices should serve for seven years, and journeymen for at least two years. These guilds, however, were never as exclusive as other European guilds (all artisans were encouraged and allowed to join Russian guilds) nor were they self-regulated to the same degree. In practice, members of social groups outside the towns could become members of the guilds; at various points in the century retired soldiers or their children, clergy and church servants and state peasants were permitted to register in guilds. Furthermore, the guilds were never able to establish a monopoly over crafts within the towns, where craftsmen frequently avoided registration, nor, most importantly, were they able to exclude peasant craftsman. Finally, guilds were never able to control the quality of goods which were produced.

Figures for the membership of Peter's craft guilds are hard to establish. One source gave a total of 6,885 people registered in 153 craft guilds between 1722 and 1726.[29] The largest number of craft masters worked in Moscow, which was rather an exception in the early eighteenth century, partly because it was also home to a number of foreign craftsmen. A separate foreign suburb of Moscow had been created by tsar Alexis in 1652 (the previous foreign suburb had been destroyed during the Time of Troubles in the early seventeenth century). This suburb became known as the *Nemetskaia sloboda* and was the home of foreign craftsmen and traders. Peter I spent time in his youth mixing with foreigners in the *Nemetskaia sloboda*, and this may have been one source of his desire to force Russian merchants to accord to his idea of a western-style

27. V. Snegirev, *Moskovskie slobody. Ocherki po istorii Moskovskogo posada XIV–XVIII* (Moscow, 1956), p. 109.
28. Tal'man, 'Remeslennoe uchinichestvo', pp. 82, 86.
29. K.A. Pazhitnov, 'Remeslennoe ustroistvo v Moskovskoi Rysi i reforma Petra', *Istoricheskie zapiski* 8 (1940), p. 171.

'burgher'. Foreign silversmiths and tailors were particularly sought by the noble elite in Moscow. In the 1720s Swedish prisoners of war also worked in a variety of trades including those of hairdresser, shoemaker, musician and saddler. In St Petersburg in 1722, 82 per cent of artisans were registered as masters, but only 14.6 per cent as apprentices and 3.4 per cent as journeymen (a category which never developed fully), suggesting that the type of training ladder which existed to preserve quality in the towns of western and central Europe was lacking in Russia.

Craft guilds declined after Peter's death. In 1761 the Commission on Commerce only found 5,145 craft masters in 33 towns. Most of the craft masters in 1761 were found in Moscow (1,363); 887 were found in Torzhok (near Tver') 786 in Simbirsk (in the Volga region) and 633 in Kaluga but most towns registered fewer than one hundred masters. Catherine II attempted to stimulate the development of guilds in her Charter to the Towns in 1785. In typical fashion, she assumed that passing detailed regulations on organizational structure, membership, activities and training would serve to stimulate craft activity. In principle, after 1785 only members of craft guilds could hire apprentices, and conditions for apprentices and journeymen were laid down for the first time in minute detail (the regulations for craft guilds constitute 117 points, the bulk of the Charter). Apprenticeships had to be for between 3 and 5 years; hours of work for apprentices were fixed from 6 a.m. to 6 p.m. (with half an hour for breakfast and an hour and a half for lunch, that is, a far shorter day than apprentices in central Europe were accustomed to at this date); masters could punish apprentices for idleness or drunkenness (in 1799 masters were allowed to send unruly apprentices to the house of correction for up to a month); apprentices had to be 'faithful and respectful' to their masters; apprentices could progress to journeymen after a test, and from there, after three years and a further examination, become masters. The exclusivity of the craft guilds was soon weakened by allowing masters to hire daily and seasonal labour and by permitting temporary membership of the guilds.

In practice, the guilds were no more successful after 1785 than under Peter in establishing a monopoly for their crafts. Even at the end of the century craft guilds were often only to be found in provincial capitals. In 1797 it was reported from Vyshnii Volochek that 'of craftsmen there were metalworkers, blacksmiths, coppersmiths, goldsmiths, cobblers and tailors but they do not form guilds'.[30] Under these circumstances, it is not surprising that a developed apprentice system failed to take root. Relations between masters and apprentices were not rigidly controlled, and masters could employ hired labour instead from a pool of poor artisans and peasants in the towns.

SUMMARY: DEVELOPMENTS 1650–1825

This was a period of contrasts in the development of agriculture, industry and crafts. Industry expanded dramatically from the early eighteenth century. But

30. F.Ia. Polianskii, *Gorodskoe remeslo i manufaktura v Rossii XVIIIv* (Moscow, 1960), p. 146.

it did so predominantly through either the forced labour of assigned peasants or the temporary labour of *obrok*-paying serfs and state peasants. A skilled workforce and freely hired labour were beginning to develop in this period but they remained small. In contrast, agriculture underwent few changes in practices during this time, although the land under cultivation continued to grow. From the second half of the eighteenth century there is some evidence that noble landowners began to show greater commercial awareness of the markets for agricultural produce and a few at least attempted to modernize their estates. Of more significance, however, was the participation of nobles in industrial development, either on a large scale by establishing iron works or other manufactories, or on a small scale by developing distilleries on their land. During the eighteenth century a shift took place in the ownership of industrial enterprises from the merchant estate to the nobility (although part of this was due to the ennoblement of several prominent merchant families). Merchant-industrialists proved too weak to resist competition from nobles; the same is true of the broader urban community which struggled throughout this period to contain competition in the production and sale of goods by peasants (who, if serfs or church peasants, were encouraged in their activities by their owners). A weak guild structure existed in at least some parts of Russia in the seventeenth century. Further attempts by Russia's rulers to stimulate the development of western-style craft guilds – in particular by Peter I in 1721 and Catherine II in 1785 – did not protect urban crafts and failed to solve the problem of peasant competition. The urban community failed on three fronts: it could not exclude peasants from the towns; it could not absorb these competitors fully into the urban community; it could not use the guilds to exclude peasant goods through the establishment of high quality standards. These problems remained unresolved in 1825.

[handwritten annotation:] weak windup? contradicts Anisimov + Pavlenko

CHAPTER 8

Lifestyle: housing, dress, diet and pastimes

This chapter looks at the way people lived, what they ate and drank, what they wore and the way they entertained themselves. Two broad themes are discussed. First, the extent to which this culture was *shared* is considered, that is, both the extent to which different social groups lived, dressed, dined and amused themselves in common and also the extent to which a distinction could be drawn between lifestyles in the town and in the country. The second theme concerns the extent to which the lifestyle of social groups *changed* during this period, with particular reference to the nobility and to the initiatives taken by Russian rulers to change social customs.

HOUSING

Houses of the nobility

In the seventeenth and early eighteenth century the homes of many nobles were not much larger or more luxurious than those of wealthier peasants. Andrei Bolotov, a minor noble, described his father's house in the early eighteenth century as a simple, dark building comprising three main rooms and two other rooms. In the main room the walls were unadorned and the ceiling uneven. Furniture consisted of benches around the walls, wooden chairs, and a long wooden table. A few wealthy nobles had built grander residences in the capitals before the eighteenth century, such as Prince V.V. Golitsyn who in the late seventeenth century built a two-storey, 53-roomed mansion in Moscow, described by de la Neuville as 'one of the most magnificent in Europe; it is covered with copper, furnished with very rich tapestries and highly curious pictures'. The interior was decorated in a mixture of Russian and western styles with icons as well as 'German prints', imported furniture, jugs, clocks and carpets.[1] In 1718 the Lopukhin home in the village of Iasenevo (Moscow district)

1. Lindsey A.J. Hughes, *Russia and the West, the Life of a Seventeenth-Century Westernizer, Prince Vasily Vasil'evich Golitsyn (1643–1714)* (Newtonville, 1984), pp. 94–5.

presented a contrast in styles between the old and new. It was built of wood and comprised seven rooms (five on the ground floor and two on an upper storey) and outhouses. Some of the windows were made of mica rather than glass but the house contained over 30 foreign paintings as well as icons and simple furniture.

In the second half of the eighteenth century splendid new mansions were built for the aristocracy. Between 1765 and 1787 Count Petr Sheremet'ev, one of the richest nobles in Russia, transformed what had been a modest hunting lodge at Kuskovo, in Moscow province, into a magnificent palace:

> Its wooden walls are stuccoed and painted to resemble veined white marble; lining the walls are paired pilasters, also stuccoed and painted to resemble green marble, alternating with niches holding large alabaster vases with gilded, papier-maché trim . . . The furnishings are French gilt, with French girandoles and a Russian chandelier. Next to it is the music room, with Chippendale furniture . . .[2]

Building on a grand scale also took place far away from the capitals, although such constructions often blended traditional Russian with western architecture. Even poorer nobles rebuilt and refashioned their residences. Bolotov, for example, modernized his house, as the rooms were 'poor, and dark, and nasty'.[3] Amongst other things, he enlarged the windows, created a garden (and wrote 80 articles on landscape gardening) and brought books into the house. Russian aristocrats adopted English landscape design for their gardens and parks in the second half of the eighteenth century. Parks included summer houses, small classical temples, elegant bridges, artificial lakes, fountains, belvederes and grottos. Hothouses and orangeries also became fashionable and wealthier nobles established their own botanical gardens. Prince Aleksei Kurakin had two hot-houses for growing pineapples in his estate in Orel province; he delighted his guests in winter with the tropical birds which flew around his orangery.

Western fashions also affected interiors, so that by the late eighteenth century many noble houses were 'fitted up in the style of London and Paris, and the new fashions make their appearance as soon as in those two capitals'.[4] Catherine II's own extensive collections of paintings, fine furniture, china, glassware and mirrors encouraged the nobility to acquire examples of decorative arts. At the same time, Russian craftsmen began to make furniture and porcelain in the European style. Yet specifically Russian features still remained in gentry houses, in particular the 'divan room' with comfortable sofas on which nobles reclined, and which are not found elsewhere in Europe. In addition, Russian great houses often lacked a library. And the splendour of

New Haven

2. Priscilla Roosevelt, *Life on the Russian Country Estate: A Social and Cultural History* (Yale, 1995), p. 59.
3. *Zhizn' i prikliucheniia Andreia Bolotova* (Moscow-Leningrad, 1931; reprint Cambridge, 1973), vol. I, p. 242.
4. William Coxe, *Travels into Poland, Russia, Sweden and Denmark* (Dublin, 1784), vol. II, pp. 102–3.

noble residences could be marred by another Russian feature, the lack of separate servants' quarters and the custom of servants, and sometimes guests, of sleeping on any surface they could find, so that 'while the walls of the elegant suite of apartments in the front, were covered with paintings, the floors of that in the back, were covered with human beings, like so many dogs'.[5]

The town

Most Russian towns were built of wood. This not only made them vulnerable to devastating fires (in the Moscow fire of 1712 over 3,000 houses and 500 shops were destroyed and one quarter of the city was left in ruins; the city was destroyed in the fire of 1812), but also made them look not unlike sprawling villages. Small towns were often dirty, usually unpaved (planks were laid across the main streets), and packed with small wooden houses and churches. The market stalls of towns, usually arranged in 'rows' or in one large building, differed little from fairs. Small towns were hardly distinguishable from villages, in particular because many towns were almost totally devoted to agriculture and conducted hardly any commercial business. As late as 1803 most of the houses in the provincial town of Tambov were still thatched. Even Moscow had something of the appearance of a large village. As Edward Clarke described the city at the beginning of the nineteenth century:

> . . . you behold nothing but a wide and scattered suburb, huts, gardens, pig-sties, brick walls, churches, dunghills, palaces, timber-yards, warehouses, and a refuse, as it were, of materials sufficient to stock an empire with miserable towns and miserable villages.[6]

Nevertheless, significant changes in the appearance of towns took place in the course of the eighteenth century. The most startling development, of course, was the construction of the capital, St Petersburg, founded in 1703. St Petersburg was the first 'planned' city, modelled on the modern cities of western Europe. Streets were broad, straight and paved with stone. Houses had to be built facing the street (instead of sideways on, the normal pattern in villages and small towns) and were to be constructed of stone or brick. St Petersburg impressed foreign travellers by its 'westernness', by the orderly layout of its streets and by its Italian- and French-designed stone buildings as well as by its wealth. Other new towns also developed rapidly, if less spectacularly than St Petersburg. Odessa was founded in 1795; by 1804 it had 15,000 residents and 506 stone houses.

During Catherine's reign attempts were made to improve the appearance of provincial towns by building government buildings in stone and by encouraging town planning, especially in the aftermath of fires. The aim was partly

5. Robert Lyall, *The Character of the Russians, and a Detailed History of Moscow* (London, 1823), p. lvi.
6. Edward Daniel Clarke, *Travels in Various Countries of Europe Asia and Africa*, vol. I *Russia Tartary and Turkey* (London, 1810), p. 47.

practical – streets and wooden houses, for example, were to be widely spaced to prevent the spread of fire – but also had the more ambitious purpose of giving the town a more 'European' appearance. The traditional concentric pattern was replaced by a design of radial or grid-like streets. The local government reforms of 1775 and the Charters to the Nobles and to the Towns of 1785 encouraged the growth of provincial offices and local institutions, which were often constructed around newly created squares. The new administration brought a certain number of noblemen into the provincial towns for employment and to attend elections. New private houses were encouraged by exemption from taxes on the building for five years or by interest-free loans, but their construction was also regulated; they had to be two storeys high and built of brick or stone. Improved sanitation was an integral part of late eighteenth-century town planning. Fountains, water pipes and drainage ditches were installed, factories, stables and cemeteries were moved to the outskirts of towns and decrees were passed against the dumping of waste in the streets.

The degree to which Catherine's plans were implemented varied enormously. Many towns witnessed little change, but major reconstruction did take place, particularly in towns which had been damaged by fire. The town of Tver' (between Moscow and St Petersburg) was hit by two major fires in 1763 and 1773. The destruction gave an opportunity for the energetic Governor, J. Sievers, to implement some of Catherine's planning ideas and reconstruct the town. By the 1780s, Tver' had over 200 brick houses, numerous new public buildings, newly laid-out streets, paved main streets and 19 stone or brick churches. Even in a backwater like Penza, P. Pallas was able to comment in the 1790s that:

> Since the establishment of the provincial government, many noble families have been induced to settle here, and to build strong, beautiful mansions, disposed in regular streets.[7]

Most urban dwellings were of one or two storeys. Traditionally, from the sixteenth and seventeenth centuries houses were 'three-windowed', that is, they comprised one storey with three rooms, and three windows, which faced the street. By the end of the eighteenth century the style which predominated comprised the best room, or ante-room, which fronted the street and a back room, or vestibule, which opened into the courtyard through which the house was entered (the 'izba-seni-izba' type house). Another common style was the so-called 'five-walled' house, which comprised the best room, hall, bedroom, kitchen and larder and which also presented a long facade with three windows onto the street. Additional rooms were built onto these basic models according to family requirements. As the eighteenth century progressed more two-storey houses were built, usually with a separate entrance to the second storey from the street so that the main householder could occupy the upper floor

---

7. P.S. Pallas, *Travels through the Southern Provinces of the Russian Empire, in the Years 1793 and 1794* (London, 1802), vol. I, p. 20.

separately from other family members. The interiors of town houses of the wealthier inhabitants changed in the course of the eighteenth century. Glass replaced mica in windows, tapestries and other coverings were hung on walls and wooden flooring replaced rough floors. In at least the main rooms, paintings and a greater variety of furniture appeared. The wealthiest merchants, especially in Moscow, St Petersburg and provincial centres, began to build larger houses in brick and stone.

The village

Russian villages could vary in size from a few houses to a complex of streets and side streets. Small villages were termed *derevnia* (plural *derevni*); larger settlements were known as a *selo* (plural *sela*). *Sela* acted as the centre for several *derevni*, and normally had a church with resident clergy and communal buildings. These might include shops, a mill, a tavern, a grain store and an administrative building, which could be an estate office on a seigneurial property or a government office in a state peasant village. The layout of villages varied according to topography and region, although most villages followed a linear formation, often on the banks of a river or a lake. In the eighteenth century it became more common to divide clusters of houses with streets and side streets, in the main to counter the devastating effects of fire (this was especially true when villages were rebuilt after fires).

The peasant hut (*izba*) varied according to region, but changed little in the period under study. In the north of Russia, where timber was abundant and extended families common, houses tended to be large. Because of the climate houses in this region were commonly built off the ground over cellars and had steep, pitched roofs so that snow could be cleared easily. The outbuildings – barn, haystack, threshing barn, drying room – and the yard were usually covered by one roof. A small log cabin (the *klet*) was often built in the yard and used for storage in the winter and as an additional bedroom for a young married couple in the household in the summer. Peasant huts in the north were often decorated with wooden carvings on the window frames, shutters and roofs. In southern Russia, the huts tended to be smaller and less decorated; only some of them had cellars and these tended to be less deep than cellars in the north. They usually had a hip roof (four slopes) and the courtyard was uncovered. Almost all huts had a *klet* and an anteroom (or *seni*), both of which were used for storage or as additional sleeping quarters in the summer. In the Ukraine (and parts of the former lands of Poland-Lithuania and the Baltic provinces), the peasant hut, or *khata*, differed in construction and appearance. In the northern Ukraine the *khata* was normally constructed of wood, but in the south, where wood was less plentiful, it was common to use wood for supports for clay, stone or chalk walls. The walls were plastered or whitewashed, and could have painted designs on them. It was also common for *khaty* to have an anteroom, or *seni*.

All peasants' huts contained a cooking area, where the stove was located, an

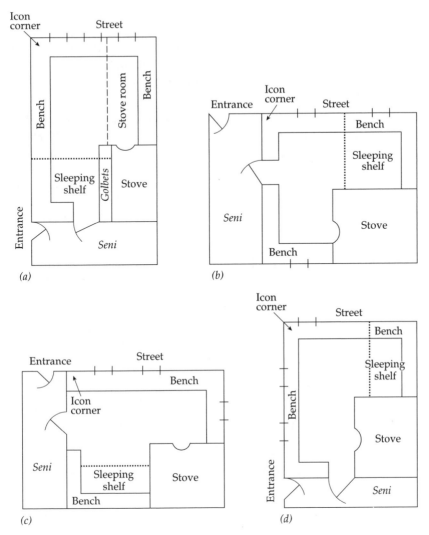

Basic plans of peasant houses in nineteenth-century Russia: (a) North and central Great Russian *izba*; (b) South-eastern Great Russian *izba*; (c) South-western Great Russian *izba*; (d) *Khata* of western Great Russia, Belorussia and the Ukraine

icon corner in which there were one or more images (always on a diagonal line from the stove), and a sleeping corner. The stove could occupy up to a quarter of the room. As well as being used for warmth and cooking, the stove also served as a sleeping area in cold weather. In the 1720s, Weber was shocked to note how peasants kept warm in their huts:

> They have extraordinary large Stoves, which take up one fourth Part of the Room. Such a Stove being well heated, and then shut up towards Evening, the whole Family go to lie promiscuously on the Top of it, and bake

themselves thoroughly. . . . At *Tweer* [Tver'] I met a whole Family of twenty Persons, Master and Mistress, Children married and unmarried, with the Servants, lying thus together on Heaps on the Stove, and the Shelves above; and upon my asking them, whether they lay easy, and had Room enough to sleep, they answered me, they rested perfectly well in such a warm Place, and wanted no Beds.[8]

The poorest huts had no chimney but only a hole in the wall for smoke to escape, with the result that the inside of the hut was often dark and blackened. Lighting was provided by a dish which hung from the ceiling, containing a burning splinter. Richer peasants had windows made of mica.

Huts traditionally contained 'male' and 'female' areas, sometimes marked with a wooden partition or curtain. The female area (or the *kut'*) contained the stove, cooking supplies and access to the cellar, if one existed. The male area, or 'clean' area, contained the icon. Benches lined the walls, which were used for sleeping in warm weather. A sleeping loft was often positioned above the stove. In the winter livestock could be kept in the hut, in the area below the sleeping loft termed the *polati*, or anteroom. Most peasant furniture was simple, comprising wooden benches and tables, but towards the end of this period some rich peasants acquired material goods more normally associated with the dwellings of merchants or nobles. In 1827, the exiled Decembrist V.M. Shakhovskoi noted in the house of a rich peasant in the Baikal area of Siberia 'furniture of beautiful wood, in the corner an English table-clock'.[9]

The cleanliness of the peasant hut could vary, and was partly a reflection of the wealth of the inhabitants. In the second half of the eighteenth century, for example, peasant huts were cleaner in relatively prosperous Iaroslavl' province than in impoverished Olonets province in the north. John Parkinson found the neatness in one peasant hut near Tobol'sk 'would have been no disgrace to Norway'.[10] All wooden houses, peasant or noble, were, however, plagued by cockroaches. Julius von Klaproth, writing in the early nineteenth century, commented that:

. . . the ceiling and the walls of the room are nearly covered with them, and unless the greatest precaution be used they are every moment falling into the victuals and drink. If a loaf of bread be left all night uncovered, you find it next morning perforated in such a manner by the tarakans [cockroaches] as to resemble a sponge.[11]

Foreign travellers often commented that the homes of non-Russians (peasants and artisans) particularly in the southern and western parts of the empire were cleaner than those of Russians. According to Clarke, peasants in the

8. Friedrich Christian Weber, *The Present State of Russia* (London, 1968), vol. I, pp. 118–19.
9. M.M. Gromyko, *Trudovye traditsii russkikh krest'ian Sibiri (XVIII – pervaia polovina XIX v)* (Novosibirsk, 1975), p. 254.
10. John Parkinson, *A Tour of Russia, Siberia and the Crimea 1792–1794* (London, 1971), p. 122.
11. Julius von Klaproth, *Travels in the Caucasus and Georgia, performed in the Years 1807 and 1808, by Command of the Russian Government*, trans. by F. Shoberl (London, 1814), p. 60.

Ukraine were so clean that, 'In their little kitchens, instead of the darkness and smoky hue of the Russians, even the mouths of their stoves were white' and there 'was no where any appearance of dirt or vermin'.[12] John Ledyard found the 'Tartars universally neater than the Russians, particularly in their houses'.[13] Klaproth found that amongst the Circassians the 'utmost cleanliness prevails in all their buildings, as well as in their dress and cookery'.[14]

Bathhouses

Bathing was the custom for all members of society, not only in Russia but also in Livonia and Finland, although quite possibly more practised by peasants than nobles. 'The Noblesse generally bathe . . . once a month and the common people twice a week on Wednesdays and Saturdays,' commented John Parkinson at the end of the eighteenth century.[15] Almost all peasant villages had a bathhouse, which contained a flueless dome under which a fire was built. When the stones became hot, the peasants poured water on them until the room filled with steam. Birch twigs were used to stimulate circulation and remove dirt. Public baths, and the vision, or even the idea, of both sexes shamelessly mingling together naked, was a source of fascination and disgust to foreign travellers. Olearius entered a bathhouse in Archangel in the seventeenth century and observed that men and women were separated, but only by planks, and that they entered and left by the same doors. In the 1790s Parkinson hovered outside the bathhouse and was amazed to see women naked at the public baths, although the sexes bathed separately. Mixed bathing was specifically prohibited, although the fact that this prohibition had to be repeated on several occasions in the mid-eighteenth century and that the Police Code of 1782 instructed the police to ensure that this was implemented suggests that these strictures were not always observed.

DRESS AND APPEARANCE

Gentry dress

When Olearius visited Russia in the 1630s he found the elite boiars dressed in long kaftans and robes, and tall fur hats. Decrees in 1675 and 1680 specifically banned foreign styles of dress, which in itself indicates that foreign dress was beginning to infiltrate, albeit to a small degree. But in the course of the eighteenth century the dress of Russian nobles became indistinguishable from that of nobles elsewhere in Europe. Peter I provided a major impetus for the westernization of Russian dress. He not only instructed that Russian dress

---

12. Clarke, *Travels in Various Countries*, vol. I, p. 216.
13. Stephen D. Watrous (ed.), *John Ledyard's Journey through Russia and Siberia 1787–1788* (Madison, Milwaukee, London, 1966), p. 145.
14. Klaproth, *Travels in the Caucasus and Georgia*, p. 323.
15. Parkinson, *A Tour of Russia*, p. 80.

should be replaced by western-style clothing and that beards must be shaved, but was prepared to enforce these decrees with whatever means proved necessary. Apart from being prepared to wield the razor and the scissors (to trim long Muscovite coats and sleeves) himself, Peter also penalized financially those who did not submit voluntarily, or quickly, to his demands. In 1705, those who wished to retain their beards had to pay dearly for the privilege – 60 roubles for nobles, 100 roubles for merchants in the first guild, 30 roubles for third-guild merchants, postdrivers and junior deacons. Bearded visitors to Moscow from other towns had to obtain a special permit, in the form of a disc, which had to be displayed at all times. Peter issued directives on the adoption of foreign dress codes, including short jackets and sleeves and western-style shoes for all except the clergy and the peasantry. In 1715 and 1718 Peter decreed that leather for shoes should henceforth be cut as in the west. As usual, Peter's decrees contained an element of threat: 'And whosoever violates this decree will be deprived of all his property and punished by being sent permanently to work on the galleys.'[16]

The initial assault on beards met with opposition from nobles and merchants (and their wives). Beards had traditionally been associated with Orthodox Christianity; priests in the west were clean-shaven and in popular mythology, and in particular in Old Believer thought, beardlessness was linked with evil western-oriented reforms of the Church and with heresy (see Chapter 10). In the provinces, more government intervention was required to prevent shops from selling traditional clothing. Nevertheless, among most of the nobility, and in particular at court, the new fashions were easily accepted. By the turn of the century, according to ever-sarcastic Catherine Wilmot, 'The dress too is a bad imitation of the French.'[17] At home, however, the Russian nobleman might still wear a comfortable soft gown (the *khalat*), provoking the comment from Ledyard at the end of the eighteenth century that in matters of dress 'Within Doors the Russian is an Asiatic & without an European.'[18] Travellers commented with disgust that lice and vermin were found on members of high society as well as on peasants.

Ladies took to western fashions as much as, and perhaps more readily than, men. Peter I's daughters were deliberately dressed in the latest French fashions. By mid-century, ladies at court were expected to dress lavishly according to contemporary western fashions; Elizabeth maintained a wardrobe of thousands of dresses. In Catherine II's reign, traditional Russian dress became popular for ladies at court on special occasions, but only as an exotic fashion item. Western hairstyles also became fashionable; by the late eighteenth century a French hairdresser, or a houseserf trained in the art, had become a social necessity. Make-up for women, however, remained 'oriental' in the, to western

16. L.N. Semenova, *Ocherki istorii byta i kul'turnoi zhizni Rossii pervaia polovina XVIII v* (Leningrad, 1982), p. 129.
17. *The Russian Journals of Martha and Catherine Wilmot 1803–1808*, ed. by the Marchioness of Londonderry and H.M. Hyde (London, 1934), p. 194.
18. *John Ledyard's Journey*, p. 197.

eyes, excessive use of rouge applied to the cheeks. Martha Wilmot complained in the early nineteenth century that the custom of kissing noble ladies on both cheeks required one to kiss 'thro' *thick* and *thin*'![19]

Urban dress

Peter's reforms of dress and beards also affected townspeople, but they accepted the westernization of their dress far less readily than did nobles. As late as 1743 a decree had to be passed instructing that everyone except the clergy and peasants had to dress in the western style and be clean shaven. In practice, western and traditional dress (long kaftans) continued to coexist in many Russian towns until the very end of the eighteenth century. Merchants, and in particular their wives, never adopted western fashions to the same extent as the nobility. Indeed, the differences between their dress and habits was one factor in hindering social contact between townspeople and nobles who had properties in the towns. Merchant wives in the early nineteenth century at Easter dressed in their finery:

> Headresses of pearls & veils of muslin embroider'd with gold & with silver, or silk embroider'd with ditto, their pelises of gold silk lined with the most expensive furs, their faces painted red & white altogether give them a very shewy & handsome appearance.[20]

There is a suggestion here that such exotic dress was somewhat oriental and marked the merchant classes as different and more alien than the 'westernized' nobles, who by this time looked and dressed like members of their class elsewhere in Europe. The conspicuous wealth of merchants' wives was also designed to distinguish wealthy merchants from poorer artisans and town dwellers whose dress remained simpler and closer to that of the peasants.

Peasant dress

Peasant dress and appearance remained more or less constant throughout this period. Peter's decrees on western dress and beards did not apply to the peasantry in the countryside (although bearded peasants who came to Moscow in Peter's reign had to pay a fine of one copeck when they passed the city gates). Peasant dress continued to depend on mainly local and home-spun material and was practical and suited to the climate and the agricultural occupations of the wearer. Male peasants, according to a description in the reign of Peter:

> . . . wear a coarse Coat reaching to the Knee, and in Summer-time they let the Shirt, which is but short, hang out over the Breeches, and gird it with a Girdle, into which they put a great Knife with a Sheath before, a Whip on one Side, and their Fur-Gloves and Hatchet behind. Their hair is cropt to

19. *The Russian Journals*, p. 60.
20. *The Russian Journals*, p. 86.

their Ears, and their Heads covered Winter and Summer with a Fur-Cap. Their Beards remain yet untouched . . . Their shoes are tied together with Bast . . . About their Neck they wear from the Time of their Baptism a Cross, and next to it their Purse, though they commonly keep the small Money, if it be not too much, a good while in their Mouth . . . and keep it under their Tongue.[21]

Peasants wore leggings of cloth which were held in place by ties, and woven bast shoes, made usually of lime bark. Some peasants could afford leather boots, and the early nineteenth century saw the production of high-top felt boots (*valenki*). There were regional variations to peasant dress (indeed, minor differences and adornments occurred between most villages). Shirts were traditionally fastened on the left side of the neck in Great Russia but in the middle in the Ukraine, with a stand-up collar. Trousers were tight fitting in Russia, Belorussia and the Right-Bank Ukraine, but were worn loose and baggy in the Left-Bank Ukraine and amongst Cossacks.

Female peasants also wore a long shirt, with long sleeves and a stand-up collar. This was considered sufficient attire for young girls, but married women always wore an overgarment. In north Russia this took the form of a type of shift, or pinafore, over the shirt. In the south of Russia this at first consisted of cloth hanging from a waistband but by the nineteenth century had become more of a traditional skirt. Outer garments were similar to those worn by men. Unmarried peasant girls normally wore their hair in a plait, sometimes tied with ribbons. Married women parted their hair in the middle, braided it in two plaits, and always wore a headdress, under which the plaits were attached. In the south of Russia this headdress was called a *kichka* and resembled two horns.

On festivals and Sundays peasants dressed in more elaborate and embroidered outfits. Martha Wilmot described the dress of peasants on the Belorussian estate of Princess Dashkova:

> . . . the fanciful Indian looking blue robe border'd with embroidery all round and button'd down the front, the large white Sleeves and the bracelets of colour'd beads, the necklaces and on some the Turban, on others the Gold embroider'd head dress form'd like a Crown clos'd on the top with the hair plaited or gaily tied with knots of ribband and hanging down the Back on the young girls of the Village.[22]

John Parkinson gave the superior and detached English view of Russian peasants in their best outfits on a holiday that he 'could [not] help comparing the goodness and neatness of their cloaths with the rags and tatters of the populace of Italy'.[23]

21. Weber, *The Present State of Russia*, vol. I, p. 120.
22. *The Russian Journals*, p. 39.
23. Parkinson, *A Tour of Russia*, p. 152.

DIET AND COOKING

Gentry food

Until the eighteenth century the main difference between the diet of the common people, whether in the country or the town, and the nobility was not what they ate but how much they ate. The greater contacts with the West and the appeal of western fashions in all things led to the importation of western cooking, and western chefs, at least into the households of the aristocracy. It was in the eighteenth century that a range of hors-d'oeuvres entered the diet of elite nobles, including cheese, which was hardly known in the peasant diet. The importation of foreign wines and spirits into noble households also increased in this period (see below). Furthermore, food at the noble table was sweetened with sugar, and not with honey, which led not only to new forms of dessert but also to the creation of a new meal – afternoon tea. Russians themselves were conscious of the contrast between the habits of the privileged and the common people.

Nevertheless, despite these refinements Martha Wilmot was not impressed by the fare offered in the house of Princess Dashkova, demonstrating a British, or rather Anglo-Irish, distrust of fancy cooking:

> . . . two Soups are always brought to Table and distributed by a servant, one compos'd of Herbs, I believe some odious essence of Rosemary or some such thing, ornamented and enrich'd by lumps of fat – the other is neither more nor less than offer'd *petit patées* of bad paste and much worse chop'd Veal, hard Eggs and Herbs. If you don't chuse any, you may let it alone and sit looking at those that do till they have done. You are then presented with a Fowl smother'd in butter and boil'd to rags, and the same ceremony goes forward. Next is offer'd vegetables of various kinds and so disguis'd that it requires some Wit to find them out. Next roast Meat, then Wild Boar Ham, and in short such a train of dishes after the same fashion as keeps one hours at the table.[24]

Many travellers found the dining habits of the nobility had only a thin veneer of civilization and that, in practice, Russian nobles displayed features which to the eyes of western Europeans marked them as 'uncivilized' or 'oriental'. The custom remained of reserving the best food and wine for the guests of honour at the top of the table. Visitors also found the vast number of dishes and the time taken over meals (the main meal could last several hours) to be excessive and decadent. Even the much-remarked-upon hospitality of Russians, of whatever class, could be seen as as a sign of Russia's questionable level of civilization.

In the country even a sophisticated nobleman could be as uncouth in his habits as the peasant. 'Visit a Russian, of whatever rank, at his country seat,

24. *The Russian Journals*, pp. 30–1.

and you will find him lounging about, uncombed, unwashed, unshaven, half-naked, eating raw turnips, and drinking *quass*,' commented Clarke in disgust.[25] In Gogol's *Dead Souls* (written 1842) the main character, Chichikov, dines in 'Russian' style on a remote estate:

> . . . the table was already spread with mushrooms, pies, fried eggs, curd tarts, potato cakes, pancakes, and pasties of all sort of different fillings, some with onions, some with poppy seeds, some with curds, some with smelts and goodness knows what else.

One character, Sobakevich, is forthright in his views on food:

> That scoundrel of a cook of theirs, the one who's been trained by a Frenchman, he'd buy a cat, skin it, and serve it up for a hare . . . All the scraps . . . they put into your soup . . . But I tell you straight I'd refuse to eat such filth . . . If I have pork, then put the whole pig on the table, if it's mutton, then fetch the whole sheep, if it's goose, the whole goose![26]

Urban food

The diet of all but the wealthiest townspeople depended very much on the food which was imported from the surrounding countryside and to that extent could not differ fundamentally from the peasant diet. Many townspeople also had their own kitchen gardens in which they grew vegetables and kept hens and other livestock. In the 1760s it was estimated that 20,000 head of cattle were kept by residents of St Petersburg! Fruit seems to have been generally available in markets in towns (and many towns had orchards within their boundaries); foreign travellers commented particularly on the quality of Russian apples, melons and water melons. Basic foodstuffs, and non-luxury goods, were not found expensive by travellers. The price of bread in Moscow was regulated from the seventeenth century, in an attempt to forestall urban unrest over high prices. Cabbages in St Petersburg in Catherine's reign cost as little as one copeck each. Nevertheless, possibly townspeople as a whole had a less healthy diet as it contained more sugar. Robert Lyall commented on the black teeth of Russians, 'chiefly among the merchants' wives'[27] (this, however, could result from the practice of some Russians, at least in the seventeenth century, of staining their teeth black to enhance their beauty). Poor artisans and temporary residents – postdrivers, migrant labourers, etc. – also ate in common eating houses where the food was probably very basic. Furthermore, the number of taverns in towns (see below) meant that heavy and frequent drinking was common.

There was probably more difference between the diet of wealthy merchants and poor artisans and day labourers than there was between the town and country. The better-off inhabitants of towns seemed to be more susceptible

25. Clarke, *Travels in Various Countries*, vol. I, p. 90.
26. Nikolai Gogol, *Dead Souls*, trans. by David Magarshack (London, 1961), pp. 66, 107.
27. Lyall, *The Character of the Russians*, p. cxix.

to scurvy than poorer sectors of society. In 1778, Dr Charles de Mertens commented that:

> I was surprised to find, during an abode of many years at Moscow, that many gentlemen merchants and strangers were attacked by a slow scurvy, having their gums soft, swollen and blueish, the breath strong, and many scorbutic spots on the legs, whilst it was rare to find among the lower people, either of town or country, a single person with these marks.

His explanation was diet; while the better-off ate large amounts of meat and fish, the common people 'exclusive of the daily use of the sour cabbage, which I consider the most powerful of all preservatives, they were indebted for their safety to the great quantity of raw greens, such as onions, leeks, radishes, turnips, peas in the pod and others, which they eat'.[28]

Peasant food

Travellers often noted that the peasants were well fed, although their diet was simple. 'A Russian consumes as much bread in a month as a Frenchman in a year' commented Parkinson in the 1790s.[29] Stephen Hoch's study of the diet of serfs in Petrovskoe (Tambov province) in the early nineteenth century found that they ate meat quite frequently and that their diet was reasonably nutritious and well balanced, so that:

> . . . the peasants of Petrovskoe were therefore better nourished than their French and Belgian counterparts at the turn of the nineteenth century and certainly had a better diet than most persons living in developing countries today.[30]

William Coxe's description of the peasant diet is from the late eighteenth century but it changed little in the period under study:

> The food of the peasants is black-rye-bread, sometimes white, eggs, salt-fish, bacon, mushrooms; their favourite dish is a kind of hodge-podge made of salt, or sometimes fresh meat, groats, rye-flour, highly seasoned with onions and garlic, which latter ingredients are much used by the Russians.[31]

Cucumbers, onions, and garlic were grown everywhere; indeed the use of these ingredients in cooking meant that 'you may know the Approach of any of them [i.e. the peasants] by the Scent, before you see them, especially in Lent'.[32] Soups were made mainly from cabbage (*shchi*) and beetroot, meat

28. Roger Bartlett, 'Britain, Russia and Scurvy in the Eighteenth Century', *Oxford Slavonic Papers* (1996), pp. 27–8.
29. Parkinson, *A Tour of Russia*, p. 133.
30. Steven L. Hoch, *Serfdom and Social Control in Russia. Petrovskoe, a Village in Tambov* (Chicago and London, 1986), p. 50.
31. Coxe, *Travels into Poland, Russia*, vol. I, p. 305.
32. J. Crull, *The Ancient and Present State of Muscovy, containing a Geographical, Historical and Political Account of all these Nations and Territories under the Jurisdiction of the Present Czar* vol. I (London, 1698), p. 163.

stock and vegetables (*borshch*). Peasants seemed to eat little dairy food; according to Richardson in the late eighteenth century, 'They make no cheese; and are not much acquainted with the uses of milk.'[33] Peasants also supplemented their diet with berries, mushrooms, nuts and honey. On special occasions, peasants prepared pies (*pirogi*), filled with fish, cream cheese, berries or cabbage, pancakes (*blini*), and puff pastries layered with cream. At fast time, most members of society refrained from meat, and fish became the only source of protein. Fasts as an expression of religious belief are discussed in Chapter 10. But as far as diet is concerned it should be noted that fasts could occur in over 30 weeks of the year and that peasants observed fasts more rigidly than other sectors of society.

The one major change introduced into peasant diet in the eighteenth century was the potato, brought back by Peter I from his visit to the West in 1697–98. It made slow progress as a crop until the end of the eighteenth century, and, indeed, led not only to passive resistance but also to violence (so-called 'potato revolts') when landlords attempted to force peasants to introduce the crop. The unpopularity of the potato stemmed partly from its condemnation by the Old Believers as the apple of Eve, but probably was due more to the low yields from the crops when potatoes were first introduced.

Dining habits and cooking

Russian society became differentiated during the course of the eighteenth century not only by what was eaten but also by when the meal took place. The working day of the peasant varied according to the season and according to region (in Archangel province in the north, for example, the peasant day in the summer started and ended earlier than in Tver' province, further south). But peasants typically rose at around 4 a.m. in the summer, ate a main meal between 10 a.m. and 12 noon and then ate again at 4 p.m. Workers in St Petersburg in the early eighteenth century had an equally long working day; in the summer workers started work at 4 a.m., ate breakfast between 9 a.m. and 10 a.m. and lunch between 1 p.m. and 3 p.m. and continued working until 9 p.m. Artisans and day labourers in towns on the whole retained meal times which were not dissimilar to those of the peasants. They rose early and had a large breakfast and an early lunch.

In the seventeenth century, and early eighteenth century, nobles shared this pattern. Nobles rose at about 5 a.m., ate their main meal at 12 noon and retired at about 10 p.m. By the late eighteenth century, however, nobles, not only in their urban residences but also on their country estates, rose much later and ate their main meal at about 3 p.m. In towns, the evening entertainment then began at about 7 p.m. with dinner parties; balls often started as late as 9 p.m. or 10 p.m. and a late supper could be taken at midnight. Wealthy and influential merchants who dined with nobles adopted a similar timetable.

33. William Richardson, *Anecdotes of the Russian Empire* (New York, 1968), p. 202.

The luxury, and social occasion, of afternoon tea was a meal reserved for members of the nobility and wealthy merchant families.

It is not entirely clear whether food was baked inside ovens or boiled or fried on top in this period. By the seventeenth century it was common to find flat-topped stoves (on which people also slept). During the eighteenth century, western-style ovens and ranges spread throughout society. An account from the end of the eighteenth century (by a shipwrecked Japanese in Kamchatka) suggests that by this period food was prepared differently according to social class:

> Simple people prepare their food morning and evening as follows: they put grain and other products into pots, place them before the hearth, close the pipe [which let the smoke out], as explained above, and it quickly cooks . . . The nobles have a different sort of fire in the kitchen. The base is made of stones, an iron grid is set above it on which they put frying pans and saucepans.[34]

Nevertheless, Martha Wilmot's description above of the preparation of food in Princess Dashkova's house suggests that meat could be boiled in peasant fashion for nobles as well. Cooking utensils included frying pans, flat-bottomed dishes and pots; new utensils, such as ceramic and metal casserole dishes came into Russia from the reign of Peter I. G.S. Vinskii, a minor Ukrainian nobleman, who was exiled to Ufa for fraud, had his sensibilities offended at his first meal in his new lodgings: 'What a meal, my God! Clay dishes, wooden spoons' (forks only became common for ordinary people in the eighteenth century).[35] As tea became more widely drunk in the second half of the eighteenth century, so the samovar became a common piece of kitchen equipment, not only amongst nobles and merchants but also for some artisans and peasants.

Drink

Mead, *kvas* and beer were drunk from Kievan times. *Kvas* was a lightly fermented beer, which could be brewed from malted rye, barley, wheat, pastry or bread, and flavoured with fruits, berries and herbs. Wine was imported from the late fifteenth century. In the seventeenth century, Spanish, French and German wines could be found at the table of boiars. Even in distant Siberia in the late eighteenth century, John Ledyard found 'French & Spanish wines here: but so mutilated that I was told of it before I knew it to be wine'.[36] Tea was probably introduced into Russia from the early seventeenth century, but the tea trade only became significant in the reign of Catherine II. At first, among Russians at least, tea was an expensive luxury drink reserved

34. R.E.F. Smith and David Christian, *Bread and Salt. A Social and Economic History of Food and Drink in Russia* (Cambridge, 1984), p. 19.
35. G.S. Vinskii, *Moe vremia. Zapiski G.S. Vinskago*, intro. by I.M. de Madariaga (Newtonville, 1974), p. 108.
36. *John Ledyard's Journey*, p. 157.

for the nobility alone but by the nineteenth century, as imports increased and prices dropped, its consumption spread to all sectors of the population. In Siberia, however, tea was the basic drink of many nomadic peoples and as early as the 1730s in the Baikal area 'the inhabitants rarely take kvass, but they all drink tea'.[37]

In the eighteenth century the number of gentry-owned distilleries grew dramatically (nobles were given a monopoly of distillery production in the mid-eighteenth century) and vodka became more available. Consumption of spirits grew in the course of the eighteenth century, something which can perhaps be regarded as a 'westernization' of the tastes of townspeople in particular, who now showed a preference for spirits over 'homely' beer or *kvas*. John Perry noted, in Peter I's reign, priests lying drunk 'about the Streets' and that 'it is far from being accounted any Scandal to be drunk, that the very Women, not only the meaner sort, but even Women of Distinction and Fashion, will make no Scruple to own, that they have been very drunk'.[38] 'Though great sobriety prevails in the houses of the Russian Nobles,' John Parkinson warned in the late eighteenth century, 'if you drink with a Russian Merchant it is hardly possible to get away without becoming intoxicated.'[39] By 1811 it has been estimated there were 11,153 taverns and eating places and 9,982 drinking stalls, or booths which could be temporary, in Great Russia and Siberia.

Excessive consumption of spirits was a particularly Russian phenomenon and normally more to be found amongst townspeople and peasants (although Old Believers did not drink spirits) than amongst the nobles, who consumed a greater variety of alcoholic beverages. Vodka had be drunk down in one shot, after blowing on the top of the glass or crossing the glass or the mouth to drive away the devil, who was waiting to enter the open mouth. In the Ukraine, in contrast, wine was also drunk in taverns and an account written in 1787 noted that Ukrainians 'drink slowly and in small amounts; they chat rather'.[40] Muslims in the empire, of course, did not drink alcohol.

Tobacco

Tobacco was banned in 1634 as satanic (it was thought to induce trances); sellers and buyers of tobacco were subject to the death penalty. Tobacco was sold again in 1646, as a state monopoly, but banned once more in the Code of 1649, with instructions for gruesome punishments for anyone caught in possession of tobacco:

> If musketeers [*strel'tsy*], and wanderers, and various people are brought in for arraignment with tobacco twice, or thrice: torture those people many times, beat them with the knout on the rack, or around the market places.

37. Gromyko, *Trudovye traditsii*, p. 273.
38. John Perry, *The State of Russia, under the Present Czar* (London, 1716), pp. 227–8.
39. Parkinson, *A Tour of Russia*, p. 50.
40. Smith and Christian, *Bread and Salt*, pp. 223–4.

For many arraignments slit the nostrils and cut off the noses of such people. After the torturings and punishment, exile them to distant towns, where the sovereign decrees, so that others looking on will learn not to do that.[41]

In 1697, at the beginning of Peter's reign, the ban was lifted (Peter smoked a pipe himself). The Board of Trade had urged the British government to support such a move as:

> The extent of those territories, the number of the people, and their passionate love of tobacco are such that a free use of it there, and the liberty to import it, would be of very great advantage to his Majesty [William III] and this kingdom . . . We also believe that the ministers of that Emperor [Peter I] may be made sensible of the great usefulness of tobacco to soldiers in the fatigues and hardships of war, especially in a cold country . . .[42]

In 1700, 1,450,000 pounds of tobacco were imported from Britain to Russia but by the end of the eighteenth century Russia had become an exporter of tobacco herself (tobacco was grown in the Ukraine).

PASTIMES AND ENTERTAINMENT

By the second half of the eighteenth century the scale and type of entertainment offered in large towns to both the common people and to the upper echelons of society indicated that some division was beginning to take place between a specifically urban culture and rural pastimes. This division, however, should not be assumed to be complete; many entertainments centred on fairs, which not only attracted peasants but could take place in the country as well as the town, and on major religious and national festivals which could attract peasants into towns from the surrounding countryside. Plays, folk dramas and puppet shows could be staged in villages as well as in towns. Furthermore, the composition of the urban population remained largely peasant, and to some extent, transient, throughout this period.

Popular pastimes

Chess was played by all members of (male) society. In Moscow, Coxe often saw 'tradesmen and common people playing it [chess] before the doors of their shops or houses'.[43] Chess and draughts were also played by non-Russians within the empire, including Kalmyks, the Armenians and the Crimean Tatars. Amongst outdoor entertainments, swings were favourites for all members of society, of both sexes and all age groups; large public swings were set up at

41. Richard Hellie (trans. and ed.), *The Muscovite Law Code (Ulozhenie) of 1649* vol. I (Irvine, 1958), p. 229.
42. *The Calendar of State Papers, Domestic Series, of the Reign of William III. 1 January–31 December 1697* (London, 1927), p. 296.
43. Coxe, *Travels into Poland, Russia*, vol. I, p. 415.

fairs and festivals. In winter, skating, sledging and sliding on ice hills were common pastimes for all. Parkinson was shocked at the speed at which participants descended the ice hills and at the 'practice of skating down these frightful descents, and that not infrequently with a child in their arms or on their head'.[44]

Matthew Guthrie has provided us with a unique record of games played by peasants in the late eighteenth century.[45] They included guessing and catching games (games involving predictions of marriage and other forms of divination are discussed in Chapter 10). In *korshin* (minotaur), one girl tried to catch the other girls, who ran round her in a line asking her a set of questions; to the fourth question about what she used her bag for she replied that it contained 'stones to break your heads' and tried to catch one of the line, who in turn became the minotaur. Young peasants played a form of Aunt Sally (*sviaka*) throwing stones at a spike on the ground. Wrestling and other contests of strength were also popular with young male peasants. Guthrie recorded life in Russian villages, but similar games must have been played in the streets of towns. Certainly, games involving hitting or knocking over blocks of wood, which were found in towns, were similar to the Aunt Sally games played in villages in Russia, and, for that matter, everywhere in Europe. In many towns, semi-organized fights took place between different sections, streets or 'walls', which could lead to injuries and even death. Organized fights, however, could also take place in villages.

The dances of Russian peasants could take different forms, depending on local customs. Adam Olearius commented in the 1630s that:

> ... the Russians do not join hands while dancing, but each one dances by himself. Their dances consist chiefly of movements of the hands, feet, shoulders, and hips. The dancers, particularly the women, hold varicoloured, embroidered handkerchiefs, which they wave about while dancing although they themselves remain in place almost all the time.[46]

Although dancing was associated mainly with peasants, nobles could also be familiar with country dances ('Tis by no means uncommon to see Masters and Slaves mingle in the same dance,' commented Martha Wilmot[47]) and traditional round dances (*khorovody*) also took place in towns. Nevertheless, the popularity of the latest foreign dances amongst noble and, to a lesser extent, urban society distinguished them from the peasants. Dancing evenings became common in towns in the 1730s and 1740s, for which participants paid a small entrance fee. These dances, however, were western ones, and although a mixed population of the towns attended, including lesser nobles, merchants and clerks, this was an exclusively urban entertainment in which peasants did not participate.

44. Parkinson, *A Tour of Russia*, p. 92.
45. BL, Add. MS 14,390, Matthew Guthrie, *Noctes Rossicae, or Russian Evening Recreations*, ff. 102–102v, 104v.
46. *The Travels of Olearius in Seventeenth-Century Russia*, ed. by Samuel H. Baron (Stanford, 1967), pp. 48–9.
47. *The Russian Journals*, p. 48.

Foreign travellers noted how often, and well, ordinary people sang. Coxe commented in the late eighteenth century that:

> The postillions *sing* . . . from the beginning to the end of a stage; the soldiers *sing* continuously during their march; the countrymen sing during the most laborious occupations; the public-houses re-echo with their carols; and in a still evening I have frequently heard the air vibrate with the notes from the surrounding villages.[48]

At the same time, Russian folk songs became themes in instrumental pieces and comic operas during the eighteenth century, that is, in music enjoyed, and sometimes played, not by peasants but by the cultured nobility.

Great open-air fairs were held in St Petersburg, Moscow and other large towns and public holidays were held on days of religious festivals, Imperial birthdays and to celebrate military and naval victories. In addition, each town had its own special festival days; in Voronezh, for example, a holiday took place on 1 August. Amongst the entertainments on offer on such occasions were peep shows, puppet shows, shadow shows, fireworks, clowns, jugglers, conjurors, gymnasts, acrobats, performing animals (including elephants and monkeys), dwarfs, giants, bear-baiting and swings. Short plays were staged in booths at major fairs. In St Petersburg at the end of the eighteenth century such plays could be repeated as often as thirty times a day; spectators paid 5 copecks entrance fee. Foreign artistes, theatre groups and circuses frequented the major fairs.

In Moscow (unlike St Petersburg, see below), the theatre developed slowly (part of the explanation for low theatre audiences in Moscow was the hostility of the large Old Believer community). In the early eighteenth century it was mostly artisans from the foreign quarter who attended the public theatre. Even in the mid-century the Moscow theatre attracted an audience from a low stratum of society, and one whose behaviour was not always exemplary. As the playwright Aleksandr Sumarokov bitterly complained they:

> . . . sit beside the very orchestra chewing nuts and think that, after paying the entrance money for a spectacle, they may indulge in fisticuffs in the pit, or in a loud voice relate the week's adventures in the boxes while munching peanuts. . . . You travellers, who have been in London or in Paris, tell me! Do they munch nuts there during the presentation of a play; and when the performance is at its fullest height, do they whip the drunken coachmen who are quarrelling amongst themselves to the consternation of the entire pit, the boxes and the stage?[49]

Little is known about entertainment within the home within the merchant community. The wealthy Dmitrov merchant Ivan Tolchenov dined out with other wealthy merchants, nobles and major office-holders on average every

48. Coxe, *Travels into Poland, Russia*, vol. II, p. 27.
49. M. Burgess, 'Russian Theatre Audiences in the Eighteenth and Nineteenth Centuries', *Slavonic and East European Review* 37 (1958), pp. 172–3.

six or seven days. But the comment by Robert Lyall on merchant wives in the early nineteenth century suggested an element of 'oriental' indolence:

> The wives of the Russian merchants, whose circumstances permit it, pass their lives in little else than ordering the preparation of food, eating and drinking, and repose and sleep. They do no work themselves, they take almost no charge of their children, whom they commit to the guidance of wet nurses immediately after birth; and as they are surrounded by servants, they contract the most indolent habits. A number of them very frequently meet together and make merry; and even when alone, many of them get intoxicated.[50]

A separate gentry culture?

The court and the ruler played a key role in transmitting culture in Russia. Tsar Alexis's main passion was hunting and falconry and he also enjoyed the staging of mock fights between animals of different species, and firework displays. Alexis, however, also enjoyed theatical performances and the first secular plays were staged at court during his reign. The play *Judith and Holofernes*, written by Simeon Polotskii and consisting of twenty-nine scenes divided into seven acts, was staged at court in 1674. It was followed by other plays, all of which combined high drama with entertaining sets (*The Little Comedy of Bayazet and Tamerlane*, for example, included battle scenes, complete with the appearance of a horse on the set and appropriate loud sound effects) as well as presenting simple moral messages about matters such as true love, betrayal and loyalty (to the ruler as well as to one's husband).

Peter I, who set out to regulate so many aspects of the life of Russian nobles, also determined how they should enjoy themselves. The highly ritualized social ceremonies of Muscovy, amongst other things, segregated the sexes. Amongst the Muscovite elite, women had separate living quarters and ate apart from their husbands. Peter challenged this tradition with his usual combination of energy and brutality. He invited some aristocratic ladies to a concert and ball in Lefort's palace in Moscow; the reluctant and bashful ladies were forced to stay and guards were posted at the door to stop the unhappy guests from leaving early! Seclusion at court was ended; Peter's daughters entertained in mixed company on their name days and other social occasions. It took longer, of course, for customs at court to become the accepted norm in noble society. But Peter was prepared to force modern social habits on his subjects. In 1718, he instructed that social 'assemblies' should take place in the late afternoons and evenings (but finish by 10 p.m.) at noble houses in which the sexes would mingle and play games and dance.

At first, lesser nobles mixed with merchant society in these assemblies, but as the century developed grander, private, balls took place, which excluded not only non-nobles but also poorer gentry, thus creating a social gulf within

50. Lyall, *The Character of the Russians*, pp. cxviii–cxix.

noble society as well as between noble and non-noble society. Moscow and St Petersburg were the obvious centres for grand balls and spectacular masquerades. Vigel' commented that the Moscow balls not only attracted the Moscow nobility 'but also the nobles of almost all the Great Russian provinces gathered there every winter, in order to amuse their wives and daughters at them'.[51]

The cultural life of St Petersburg was firmly associated with the court and developed in a far more sophisticated way than elsewhere in the empire. The first opera was performed and the first orchestra assembled in the reign of Anna. In the reign of Elizabeth the first *Russian* opera was performed and the first permanent Russian theatre opened. In 1750 the court of Elizabeth staged 18 French comedies, 14 Russian tragedies and comedies, four Italian and German interludes and one opera. By the mid-eighteenth century, with the direct encouragement of Elizabeth, it became customary for members of high society to appear at the St Petersburg Opera House, to hear performances of mainly Italian opera. Ballet and theatrical productions also began in her reign, as did public concerts.

Operas, comic operas and plays increased not only in popularity but also in quality, and pieces by Russian playwrights (of whom Aleksandr Sumarokov is the most celebrated) began to replace foreign imports. By the late eighteenth century theatres in St Petersburg had become a fashionable place to meet and exchange gossip, to the extent that foreign visitors complained that young officers in the pit were so noisy that it was impossible to hear the play. Catherine II wrote libretti for five comic operas, two historical operas and comedies which, irrespective of their merit in artistic terms, served to ensure the performances were well publicized, elaborately staged and attended by the best of Russian and foreign society. By the end of the century theatre had also become much more popular with members of high society in Moscow, although it was never as fashionable as in St Petersburg. In 1778, Miss Katherine Harris described the performance of *Dmitrii the Impostor* by Aleksandr Sumarokov in Moscow:

> Went to the Russian Play the False Demetrius. That part said to be well written. The Actor performed it perfectly well, and had much change of countenance and good action, tho in the last act he failed at the death when he gave a box in the Ear to a friend who was rather tardy in his assistance . . . After it was over, they gave one of Bachs Concertos an old acquaintance of mine. Then follow'd a Farce.[52]

In the late eighteenth and early nineteenth centuries more provincial towns developed as social and cultural centres. Lyall commented in the early nineteenth century that 'The Italian opera is much liked at Odessa, at which we need not be surprised, since the Italian language is generally spoken there'[53]

51. F.F. Vigel', *Zapiski* (Cambridge Mass., 1974), vol. I, p. 116.
52. Quoted in Anthony Cross, *Anglo-Russica* (Oxford, Providence, 1993), p. 36.
53. Robert Lyall, *Travels in Russia, the Krimea, the Caucacus and Georgia* (London, 1825), vol. I, p. 182.

(street signs in Odessa were in Russian and Italian). In distant Tobol'sk, in Siberia, John Parkinson attended the theatre in 1793 and found it not entirely displeasing:

> There was an opera in the evening at the theatre which did not go off ill. Their prettiest and best actress was a common girl taken from the Streets. An old Abbé accompanied by a younger religious came and sat with us in Balikoff's box.[54]

Even in remote Ufa Vinskii found some well-read people and a not uncongenial lifestyle: 'In the winter we lived in the town, where [there was] sledging, gatherings, balls, and card games for me, our life was extremely pleasurable.'[55]

At home, foreign card games became popular. Yet traditional customs changed slowly. It had been customary for nobles in the seventeenth and early eighteenth centuries to keep fools or dwarfs to entertain visitors. Dwarfs were so highly valued, commented Weber in Peter's reign, that 'they take particular care in *Russia* to propagate by marrying them together, so that there is scarcely a Man of Quality but keeps a Man or Woman Dwarf for his Lady'.[56] As late as 1771, the *St Petersburg Gazette* contained an advertisement for the sale of a 25-year-old dwarf, of 'honest disposition, nimble and amusing'. Despite Peter's attempt to break the segregation of the sexes, foreign travellers commented that, in practice, men and women continued rarely to mix, even in high society. Noble houses, for example, often had specifically 'male' and 'female' quarters, which paralleled the arangements within peasant huts. Even by the beginning of the nineteenth century Martha Wilmot could comment that:

> The truth is refinement is coming on, but has not yet taken up its abode amongst them [the Russians]. The Men and Women divide into separate society.[57]

Many nobles only participated to a limited extent in the social and cultural events in Russian towns. The less wealthy nobles were excluded by cost, and many provincial nobles rarely visited even the provincial capital, sometimes only at the three-yearly noble elections. Even those wealthy nobles who did maintain an urban residence often left for the countryside in the summer and stayed there on their country estates. Parkinson commented:

> Two thirds of the Nobility visit their estates in the summer, even to the distance of 1,000 Versts, and pass three months there. The women amuse themselves with working and teaching their Children to work. The men with hunting . . .[58]

54. Parkinson, *A Tour of Russia*, p. 140.
55. Vinskii, *Moe vremia*, p. 139.
56. Weber, *The Present State of Russia*, vol. I, p. 285.
57. *The Russian Journals*, p. 37.
58. Parkinson, *A Tour of Russia*, p. 103.

The outdoor pursuits of the provincial nobility, and of the elite nobles who moved to their estates in the summer, differed little from those enjoyed by peasants, although the nobles, of course, had far more leisure in which to pursue these pleasures. Hunting and fishing were the most popular pursuits. Bears and wolves were hunted as well as hares and birds. The nobleman I.A. Raevskii described the simple pleasures of his childhood on the estate in winter in the early nineteenth century:

> In winter we used to harness three or four sledges one by one and go sledging . . . Sometimes we built a snow house with the help of the servants and turned it to ice by pouring water over it . . . On winter evenings we gathered together by the stove in the great hall to drink *sbiten'* [a drink of hot water, honey and spices] which we children all loved. Usually one of us had to recite some French or Russian verses. Neighbours came little to us in the county, there were no calling hours.[59]

SUMMARY: DEVELOPMENTS 1650–1825

In many ways, the lifestyle of the peasants changed little in this period. Their houses, dress, diet and pastimes remained essentially the same and were affected by government policy to a very limited degree only. Life in the towns underwent greater change – through town planning, the erection of new buildings, importation of new foodstuffs and beverages, introduction of western fashions, opening of theatres, etc. But changes were most noticeable in large towns and provincial centres, and most of all in St Petersburg (itself a new town) and Moscow.

In contrast, this period witnessed a transformation of the lifestyle of Russian nobles. Firstly by force, under Peter I, and then by choice, the nobility changed its dress, diet and social habits to such an extent that it became almost indistinguishable from any other European nobility of the time. In the process, the Russian nobility distanced itself from the social habits of the peasantry and the Russian townspeople. Nevertheless, the divorce between the 'Europeanized' nobility and the 'Russian' ordinary people in terms of the subject of this chapter – social behaviour and material culture – should not be exaggerated. First, even before the eighteenth century although many nobles lived modestly this did not mean that their lifestyle was identical to that of peasants and townspeople. Second, this chapter has shown that nobles still shared at least some of the pastimes and social habits of ordinary people, particularly when resident in the countryside, and that even in matters such as diet and housing some nobles did not differ fundamentally from commoners. Finally, the divisions within the nobility between the wealthy, sophisticated aristocrats and poor provincials in terms of lifestyle and social behaviour could be at least as sharp as those between nobles and non-nobles.

59. I.A. Raevskii, 'Iz vospomianii I.A. Raevskago', *Istoricheskii vestnik* (1905), no. 8, p. 396.

CHAPTER 9

The family

The basic social unit in the Russian empire was the family. This chapter will look at family size, household size and the relationships between family and household members. Marriage, family rituals and inheritance are also discussed. The two main themes are, first, the extent to which noble, urban and peasant families and family matters differed and, second, the extent to which changes occurred over this period. Most of the evidence given below is of relevance only to Great Russia.

THE FAMILY AND THE HOUSEHOLD

In the absence of accurate and full statistics of birth, marriage and death rates for the Russian empire in this period it is hard to generalize about the determinants of family size. According to one set of figures for all Russian Orthodox male children just under 555 out of every thousand children survived to the age of five in the period 1798–1805, which dropped to 550 in the period 1804–1814 (comparative figures in the period 1798–1814 were 532 in Sweden and 584 in France). Death rates were partly determined by region; children had better chances of reaching adulthood in the central, northern and western regions than in the more newly settled southern and eastern provinces. Family size depended as much on the birth rate as the death rate, and the former was partly dependent on the age of marriage (and number of marriages; the Orthodox Church permitted people to marry up to three times).

The peasant family

Infant and child mortality was high amongst peasants but, in general, slightly lower than in the towns. On the Petrovskoe estate (Tambov province) in the early nineteenth century in the region of 450 out of every thousand children died before the age of five. On the other hand, the young age of marriage (see below) meant that child-bearing started early and could last for a long time. If the children survived this could lead to enormous families. The peasant F. Vasil'ev, aged 75, claimed in 1755 to have fathered 87 children!:

... from which only four died, and all the rest were healthy. With his first wife, F. Vasil'ev begat 4 quadruplets, 7 triplets, 16 twins; with his second wife – 2 triplets, 6 twins.[1]

This, if true, was exceptional, but families of up to eight surviving children were common. In the village of Baki (Kostroma province) it was recorded in 1799 that the Fedorovs (husband and wife both aged 36) had children aged 2, 4, 6, 8, 10, 13, and 15 and had since had another baby and the Mikhailovs (both aged 41) had children aged 3, 7, 10, 12, 17 and 18 and had also had another child since the census had been taken.[2]

There were economic reasons for peasants to have a lot of children, and, in particular, to have sons, not only for their labour in what was a labour-intensive agricultural system but also to meet the fiscal and other obligations imposed by the landowner or state. As Martha Wilmot commented:

> 'Tis here the custom for the Peasantry to live *together* as their riches consist in themselves, their own labour etc. . . . the more numerous a family is the richer they become.[3]

Both landowner and peasant commune (serf and state peasant) shared the assumption that large households were more productive and wealthier. The incentive for noble landowners was to increase the number of serfs on their estates, to benefit either from their labour or from the increased *obrok* capacity. This may account for the fact that, on the whole, serf families were larger than those of state peasants. The peasant commune shared the economic interests of the landowner in its concern about the tax capacity of each family unit and discouraged the dissolution of households into small, economically unviable units. Small peasant households were vulnerable as the loss of one able worker could mean economic disaster, not only for the family concerned but also for the whole village through its collective responsibility for taxes. Indeed, the elimination of small households could be deliberately engineered by the commune through the selection of the remaining able-bodied male, or males, for conscription. In the village of Baki in the early nineteenth century, when there were frequent levies due to the Napoleonic Wars, the death of the head of the household was often followed by the conscription of his sons.

The peasant household

The peasant household could include different generations, families of brothers, sisters, uncles and aunts and people unrelated to the family. The household, therefore, was often, but not always, larger than the nuclear family. Unlike the size of the family, which depended on the fertility of the woman, the health

1. L.N. Semenova, *Ocherki istorii byta i kul'turnoi zhizni Rossii pervaia polovine XVIII v* (Leningrad, 1982), p. 85.
2. BL, Add. MS 47421, ff. 115, 118, Lieven papers, census returns of the village of Baki, 1799.
3. *The Russian Journals of Martha and Catherine Wilmot 1803–1808*, ed. by the Marchioness of Londonderry and H.M. Hyde (London, 1934), p. 103.

and sex of her offspring and on factors largely outside the control of the individual, the size of the peasant *household* could to an extent be determined to best meet the economic needs of the peasants. This has led historians to attempt both to determine the 'optimal' size of the peasant household and to find economic explanations for fluctuations in the size of the peasant household according to period and region. Statistics for this period are incomplete, but recent studies by historians of household structure on particular estates have increased our understanding of the dynamics involved.[4]

It has been estimated that the average number of males in peasant households in 1678 was 3.96, and in cotter (*bobyli*) households, without land or holding only small plots, 3.18. Within both categories there were regional variations, probably reflecting the availability of land (large family units of peasants were found in particular in Belgorod and Voronezh provinces, south of Moscow, and of landless peasants in Belgorod and Nizhnii Novgorod provinces). In general, where land was good, such as the black-earth regions, labour was more in demand and households tended to be larger and multi-generational. For the same reason, households on *barshchina* estates tended to be larger than those on *obrok* estates. During the Great Northern War (1700–21), there is evidence that households combined and grew larger, possibly because the heavy wartime tax burden was levied on the household rather than on the individual. The introduction of the poll tax at the end of the war in principle shifted the assessment of taxation from the household to the individual male peasant. In practice, however, peasants still paid tax according to the ability of the household to pay and not just according to the number of male members, which, as it included all males from babies to old men, might not necessarily be an indication of wealth. The size of the household depended more on the agricultural economy of the village than on the fiscal demands of the state. As a result, the average size of the peasant household remained fairly stable for the eighteenth century, at about 4 males, or 8 persons per household. There is some evidence to suggest that very large households declined in the early nineteenth century. On the estate of Mishino (Riazan' province, black earth), a *barshchina* estate, households had a mean size of 10 persons in 1782, which fell to just over 9 persons in the early nineteenth century. In the village of Petrovskoe (Tambov province, black earth), also a *barshchina* estate, the mean household size in 1813–34 reached a high of 9 persons in 1818 and a low of 7.7 in 1824 (after the crop failure of 1821–22).

There was significant regional diversity in household size within the Russian empire. In Siberia, households tended to be smaller than in European Russia in the late seventeenth and early eighteenth century. At the beginning of the eighteenth century, the average in Siberia was between 1.5 and 2.4 males

4. For example, S.L. Hoch, *Serfdom and Social Control in Russia: Petrovskoe, a Village in Tambov* (Chicago and London, 1986), on Petrovskoe; Peter Czap, Jr, 'The Perennial Multiple Family Household, Mishino, Russia 1782–1858', *Journal of Family History* 7, 1 (1982), pp. 5–26; Rodney D. Bohac, 'Peasant Inheritance Strategies in Russia', *Journal of Interdisciplinary History* 16, 1 (1985), pp. 23–42, on the Manuilovskoe estate.

per peasant family (or 3 to 5 persons).[5] In particular, the nuclear family was the dominant household structure in newly settled areas of Siberia. During the first half of the eighteenth century, larger and complex households grew but they declined in the second half of the century, partly because Siberian peasants were almost all state peasants who had *obrok* and not labour dues (where the number of able-bodied household members was crucial) and because recruit obligations fell more heavily on large households of state peasants. Household size grew again in the early nineteenth century, when it approached that of peasants in European Russia as the land became more populated and family units combined. In the Baltic provinces, the large peasant farms included orphans, some of whom were formally adopted, but most of whom worked as labourers. Statistics on the *odnodvortsy* in the southern frontier provinces are incomplete, but it seems that they had smaller families than peasants (slightly less than 4 male members in the second half of the eighteenth century). It was reported from Elets province that 'the *odnodvortsy* for the most part are people of small families'.[6]

While it is possible to establish some general determinants for the size of the peasant household, it is impossible to account fully for its composition from economic factors. Individual circumstances, and factors beyond human control, meant that within villages household size and structure could vary enormously. The village of Baki (Kostroma province), a serf *obrok* estate, included both complex and nuclear families, families with one parent and single occupants. To give some examples of the diversity of household type in this one village in 1799: the Larionovs (husband aged 48 and wife aged 58) lived with their nephew, his wife and two children; Stepan Fedorov, a widower, lived with his daughter-in-law and her three children; the widow Nikitina lived with her five children aged 5, 8, 12, 13, and 15; Stepanova, a widow, lived with her unmarried son; the Semenovs (aged 52 and 49) lived with their four sons, two of whom had wives, and four grandchildren; the two Borisov brothers lived together with their wives and children, ten persons altogether; Trofimov, a widower, lived with his unmarried sister (aged 45), three children from his first marriage, and the wife and three children of his eldest son; the Ivanovs (aged 37 and 43) lived with their seven children, and the wife of their eldest son; Efim Ivanov (aged 47) lived with his sister (aged 39), his wife (aged 52), three children and five 'maidens' aged 49, 54, 59, 62 and 69; the Vasil'evs (husband aged 65, wife aged 72) lived with one daughter, two sons, one of whom had a wife and three children, and a widow with three children.[7]

Most orphans were taken in by relations but peasant communes could be instructed by landowners to make provision for orphans and illegitimate children within the village. V.G. Orlov instructed his stewards that orphans

---

5. I.V. Vlasov, 'Sem'ia i semeinyi byt Sibirskogo krest'ianstva', in V.A. Aleksandrov (ed.), *Etnografiia russkogo krest'ianstva Sibiri XVII–seredina XIXv* (Moscow, 1981), p. 19.
6. V.I. Semevskii, 'Domashnii byt i nravy krest'ian vo vtoroi polovine XVIII veka', *Ustoi* (1882), no. 2, p. 70.
7. BL, Add. MS 47421, ff. 120v, 123r&v, 126v, 132, 136v, 149, 174, 200.

should be looked after on his estates by relations or 'trustworthy' peasants. Male orphans were vulnerable and could be chosen by the household as recruits in place of the sons of the head of household. Widowhood was common; it has been estimated that on the estate of Manuilovskoe (Tver' province) almost three-quarters of households included a widow at some point in the period 1813–61.[8] Some widows had sufficient property, or adult sons, to be able to live independently (and see below), but many were obliged to move into the households of their sons or other relations or to marry again.

A particular problem was posed by soldiers' wives, who could be abandoned with small children when their husbands were recruited. Few wives of recruits followed their husbands to the regiment; indeed, in 1821 wives were forbidden from joining field armies with the exception of the Caucasus corps, as it was felt that their presence was a burden. The village of Baki in 1799 included a household comprising a soldier's wife (a *soldatka*), aged 42, with three children, aged 14, 17 and 20.[9] In this case, the children were old enough to provide labour and sustain the household economically, but often wives were left with small children and could not do so. In 1814 and 1815 it was recorded in the same village that the recruitment of three young men had left behind eight young children. Under these circumstances soldiers' wives had to hope that they would be taken into the household of a relation, and in some cases were forced to remarry, although, strictly speaking, they were not widows despite the fact that their husbands were for most practical purposes regarded as dead. Some peasant communities built special simple huts for soldiers' wives and issued them with a small amount of grain for their subsistence.

In peasant households the head of the household was the *bol'shak* in Russia (*starshii* in the Ukraine; *bats'ka, dziadz'ka* in Belorussia). The head was normally the eldest male, but could be a younger male member of the household or a woman. The head dominated the lives of other members of the household. He determined which members performed *barshchina* obligations (and could ensure that the young males undertook this) and often had considerable discretion over household division and the selection of household members as recruits. It was rare for peasants under the age of 40 to become heads of household; on the Mishino estate, for example, the median age of heads of household was approximately 50 years. Sons of heads of household were most likely to become heads themselves. Even the power of the *bol'shak*, however, could be undermined by the peasant commune if he failed to farm the land effectively. In 1771, a peasant head of household was deprived of his land on the estate of I.S. Golovin because of drunkennesss, and the land was passed to his nephew. Conflicts were common between peasant heads of household and other male members of the household. Peasants – usually younger sons or

8. Rodney D. Bohac, 'Widows and the Russian Serf Community' in Barbara Evans Clements, Barbara Alpern Engel and Christine D. Worobec (eds), *Russia's Women. Accommodation. Resistance. Transformation* (Berkeley, Oxford, 1991), p. 99.
9. BL, Add. MS 47421, f. 224v.

brothers of the head – who sought to form a separate household cited such factors as 'constant fighting' and 'disgraceful behaviour' as reasons.

Wealthy peasant widows of *bol'shaki* could become heads of household, and could be just as domineering over their children and their daughters- and sons-in-law as a male head of household. In 1813, the peasant commune of Nikol'skoe (Orlov estate) put the wife of a peasant in charge of the household, because of her husband's 'weak behaviour' and the consequent 'exhaustion and extravagance' of the home, but it was an exception for any woman except a widow to head the household.[10] In the estate of Manuilovskoe (Tver' province) one third of households had a woman, always a widow, as head of household in the period 1813–61. As heads of household these widows also had the right to attend the peasant commune. Such widows could also be attractive as marriage prospects, although this might be resisted by other members of the household as it would mean a loss of property within the widow's lifetime and complications over inheritance for the children of her first marriage.

The urban family and household

It has been estimated that in 1678 the average urban household comprised 3.3 males (or about 7 persons). This meant that the average size of urban households was a little smaller than that of peasant households at this date. Nuclear families (parents and children) were more commonly found in towns. In Tomsk (Siberia) in 1700, 72 of the 79 households of members of the legally defined townspeople were nuclear families, and in 1701, over 90 per cent of the households in the Siberian towns of Tara, Turinsk and Tiumen' were nuclear families.[11] The majority of households (nearly 70 per cent) in the town of Ustiuzhna (Vologda province) in the early eighteenth century were nuclear families comprising parents and children. In Kadeshev (Moscow province) in the period 1766–67, almost half the households of merchants contained only one male, 27.9 per cent had 2 males and 12 per cent had 3 males (the average number of males in a peasant family was 4).

Nevertheless, large urban households also existed, including grandparents, brothers and their families, widows, orphans, hired labourers, apprentices and servants. In the town of Balakhna (Nizhnii Novgorod province) in 1678, for example, the average household size was 3.8 males, but of the 575 urban households 112 were one-generational households, 413 were two-generational and 50 comprised three generations. Large urban family units continued into the eighteenth century. In the small town of Ustiuzhna in the early eighteenth century the household of the wealthy Kitaev family, which dominated the economic life of the town, comprised 17 members, including several generations, uncles, aunts, nephews and nieces. Household units of 2 or more brothers and their families were also found in Ustiuzhna among poorer townspeople or

10. V.A. Aleksandrov, *Sel'skaia obshchina v Rossii (XVII–nachalo XIX v)* (Moscow, 1976), p. 296.
11. N.A. Mineneko, 'Gorodskaia sem'ia Zapadnoi Sibiri na rubezhe XVII–XVIIIvv' in *Istoriia gorodov Sibiri dosovetskogo perioda (XVII–nachalo XX v)* (Novosibirsk, 1977), pp. 170, 180.

landless peasants resident in the town – the Plotnikov household, for example, comprised 3 brothers and their wives and offspring, 12 persons in all.[12]

There seems to have been a link in towns between wealth and size of household. The wealthy families of Balakhna in the late seventeenth century had large households, which could include hired labourers or people in *kabala* relationships (see Chapter 3) as well as family members. Almost one hundred years later, in 1766–67, the wealthiest families in the town of Kadashev had the largest households. The average size in this town of the household of first-guild merchants was 2.64 males, and just over half of these households included two generations (45.2 per cent were one-generational households and 3.3 per cent three-generational); the households of second-guild merchants averaged 1.94 males (61.1 were one-generational, 35.2, two-generational and 3.7 three-generational); the households of the third-guild merchants averaged 1.58 males (65.2 per cent were one-generational, 34.8 per cent two-generational; there were no three-generational households). In Ustiuzhna, however, it has been noted above that although the wealthiest family (the Kitaevs) had the largest household, extended families also could be found among poorer inhabitants.

It has been estimated that the birth rate in towns was higher than in the countryside, but that the death rate was also higher. This also led to smaller family sizes than in the country (indeed, towns depended on a constant influx of new inhabitants from the countryside to maintain their population). In Russian towns, 25–30 per cent of children died before their first birthday and 57–58 per cent died before they reached the age of five (conditions were slightly better in the Baltic provinces, Belorussia and the Ukraine). Poor sanitation and population density particularly affected the urban poor, but epidemics also had devastating effects on towns, especially on the most vulnerable inhabitants. In 1747, it was recorded by the St Petersburg Clerical Consistory that 968 out of 3,211 boys born in the city had died before the age of one. Ivan Tolchenov, son of a prosperous merchant in Dmitrov, was one of ten children, six of whom died before their first birthday, including two who died at birth. He had five sons and three daughters, of whom all the daughters and one of the sons died.

The gentry family and household

Families and households of nobles could also be large. Nobles who wrote memoirs include Mar'ia Nikolaava, who was born at the beginning of the nineteenth century, the sixth daughter and ninth child, but, in her words, 'in those days . . . a large family was not considered a burden, but a great blessing'; her parents had three more children, and her father had been one of eight

12. M.G. Rabinovich, 'K strukture bol'shoi sem'i i russkikh gorozhan v nachale XVIII v (po materialam g. Ustiuzhny Zheleznopol'skoi'), in *Russkie semeinyi i obshchestvennyi byt* (Moscow, 1989), pp. 84–90.

children.[13] Infant mortality was also high for the children of the nobility, even though their living conditions and diet were better than those of townspeople and peasants. The wife of Efim Chemesov had seventeen children in twenty-four years, eight of whom died at birth or in childhood (several in the same year, which suggests that they were victims of an epidemic). Chemesov held various posts in local administration and became the provincial marshal of the nobility in Penza province, but the terse list at the end of his memoirs of the births and deaths of his offpring demonstrates the fragility of life even for someone who was relatively prosperous:

1767: birth of Nikolai
1768: birth of Anna
1770: birth of Aleksandra
1771: birth of Evgraf
1772: birth of Varvara 'died aged three'
1773: birth of Petr
1774: birth of Elizabet, died at birth
1775: birth of Ekaterina, died 1778
1777: birth of Efim, died 1778
1778: birth of Pavel, died at birth
1778: birth of Andrian, died in 1783
1780: birth of Efim, died in 1783
1782: birth of Mar'ia, died in 1783
1784: birth of Ivan
1785: birth of Natal'ia
1790: birth of Marfa
1791: birth of Varvara[14]

Noble households, like those of peasants and townspeople, could include near and distant relations, including widows, maiden aunts and orphans. In the case of the nobles, the size of the household was only indirectly linked to economic needs in the sense that it was expected that the wealthiest family members would provide for relations who were impoverished or who had suffered misfortunes. But there was also a habit of hospitality and an acceptance of the extended family which was more a matter of tradition than of simple economics. Children were habitually sent to study, or simply to spend the summer months, in the houses of cousins or other relations of a similar age. It was also common for widows to send their sons to be educated with relatives while retaining their daughters at home. In addition, the family lived under the same roof as the people whom they owned or employed – houseserfs, wet-nurses, tutors, etc.

13. 'Cherty starinnago dvorianskago byta. Vospominaniia Mar'i Sergeevny Nikolaevoi', *Russkii arkhiv* (1893), no. 9, pp. 107, 111, 115.
14. 'Zhizn' Efima Petrovicha Chemesova 1723–1801 gg', *Russkaia starina* 72 (1891), pp. 1–10.

MARRIAGE

The age of marriage

Foreign travellers remarked on the fact that 'Russians in the Towns, as well as the Country, marry very young, and their Houses are stocked with Children'.[15] The Code of 1649 recommended that marriages should not take place under the age of 15, but in practice children as young as 12 married and betrothals took place at an even earlier age. In the village of Baki in 1799, Fedor Filatov, aged 25, had a wife who was 15 years old, and was already the mother of two children, aged one and two; the Egorov household included Ivan, aged 12, and his wife, aged 15, and the Petrov household included Vasilli Petrov, aged 29, and his 14-year-old wife, already the mother of a three-year old child and a six-month-old baby.[16] The peasant Nikolai Shipov recalled in 1819 that when his father married a second time it was to a 14-year-old neighbour, with the result that he was three years older than his new stepmother. Some of the statistics about ages in Baki may be suspect (the wife of Petrov, for example, would have had to have given birth to her first child at the age of 11) but clearly brides could be very young. On other estates, peasants married slightly later but were still young. On the Gagarin estate at Mikhailovskoe (Riazan' province) in the late eighteenth and first half of the nineteenth century, most brides were aged between 15 and 17, and most grooms between the ages of 16 and 18. It was rare on this estate to find unmarried women over the age of 17 and unmarried men over the age of 20. The young age of peasant marriages was partly regional; in eastern Siberia, where there was no pressure on peasants from landowners, it was more common for peasants to marry in their twenties.

 Early marriage was also common among other members of society. Andrei Bolotov was betrothed to a 12-year-old girl and married her the following year. G.S. Vinskii, a minor Ukrainian nobleman, was born in 1752; his mother was 16 and his father 21 at the time. Anna Labzina, a noblewoman, was 13 at the time of her marriage. In general, townspeople, especially boys, married at a slightly older age than peasants. The wealthy merchant from Dmitrov, Tolchenov, for example, married at 19.

It was, of course, in the interest of the landowner that his peasants should marry young and start to produce offspring as soon as possible so that the number of his peasants – in effect his wealth – should increase. In 1777, V.G. Orlov instructed that females on his Sidorovskoe estate should marry by the age of 20. In 1790 he extended this rule to his newly acquired estate of Simbilei. If within six months, girls over the age of 20 remained unmarried, their families were to be fined between 10 and 15 roubles, depending on the prosperity of the household; if the household were too poor to pay the fine, the girl's father was to be beaten with rods in front of the villagers. If this failed,

---

15. Friedrich Christian Weber, *The Present State of Russia* (London, 1968), vol. I, p. 120.
16. BL, Add. MS 47421, ff. 136, 153v, 187v.

the estate manager and elders were to choose a suitable groom themselves. On the Iusupov estates not only were unmarried girls aged over 15 fined but also young widows under 40 years old who did not remarry, a practice which yielded the large sum of 2,599 roubles in fine money in 1816. At the turn of the century, the Lieven family instructed their steward in the village of Baki to make a list of all unmarried women aged between 20 and 35 and all unmarried males aged between 18 and 25. The steward was then instructed to fine all non-married peasants over the age of 25 the sum of 5 roubles (which would increase to 10 roubles if they were still unmarried by the following February), although exceptions could be made for daughters if their parents could prove that they were needed in the household.[17] On some occasions, landowners forced peasants to marry 'by lots', something which happened on Suvorov, Orlov and A.B. Golitsyn's properties in the late eighteenth century. Some landowners simply forced peasants to move to other villages on their estates where spouses could be found for them. In 1773 A.B. Golitsyn moved 12 unmarried peasant girls to another estate to find spouses for them.

Such procedures took place under the auspices of the peasant commune, which suggests that the leading members of at least some peasant communities shared the interests of the landowners in increasing the population of the village and, perhaps, in controlling and interfering in the lives of other peasants. Indeed, it was in the interests of most peasants to increase the labour of the household by encouraging early marriage without any prompting by the landowner; the only exception was poor households without sons, where it was essential to retain the labour of the daughters (brides normally entered the household of their spouse). There were cases when peasants welcomed pressure by their landowners to force reluctant girls to marry. On the Sidorovskoe estate, mentioned above, the prevalence of Old Belief was one factor which discouraged marriage (many Old Believers refused to accept the validity of the marriage ceremony conducted by Orthodox priests). Male peasants appealed to Orlov for help because local woman refused to marry. Orlov purchased female serfs for unmarried serfs on his estates when there was a shortage of local women.

Within peasant communities, not only was it customary for peasants to marry young but it was also not uncommon to marry young boys to older women or widows for economic reasons, to gain their labour or their property. In the late eighteenth century William Coxe observed peasant boys as young as seven or eight married to far older girls so that the family could gain a domestic servant. In the village of Baki, the Fedotov household included the son of the head of household, aged 16, and his wife, aged 30.[18] In 1753, in a western Siberian village, S. Tokerev arranged to marry his son Konstantin, aged 10, to a 20-year-old peasant girl. The retention of their property rights by widows (see below) meant that they could be sought as brides for other

17. BL, Add. MS 47428, f. 22, Lieven papers, miscellaneous estate papers.
18. BL, Add. MS 47421, f. 182v.

members of society as well as peasants. Olearius commented in the mid-seventeenth century on the marriages between widows and orphans as young as 12: 'In this manner, they can keep their property, and do not have to depend on friends and guardians.'[19] Large age differences could also be found in the arranged marriages for the nobility, although it was more customary for older men to marry young noble girls. Seventeen-year-old Anastasia Trubetskaia was married to 54-year-old Prince Dmitrii Kantemir in 1717. Praskov'ia Tatlina (born 1812) was married to a widower who was 17 years older than her; she described him as 'terrible' and 'coarse' but kind to her.[20] The high mortality rate in Russia meant that second and even third marriages were common at all levels of society.

Some Russians, of course, never married. In 1804, a survey of the villages in the Kostroma estates, owned by the Lieven family, found 129 unmarried males and 225 unmarried female peasants. Many of the women were quite elderly (and probably widows); of 46 unmarried women in the village of Saraust'ia, 11 were in their forties, 5 in their fifties, 4 in their sixties and 3 in their seventies. Most of the unmarried men, however, were under 30. It is not clear to what extent economic factors accounted for these bachelors and spinsters, although several groups of unmarried sisters were listed in some villages, suggesting that households where only, or mainly, girls survived may have resisted the loss of female labour through marriage.[21] Certainly there was resistance in the village of Baki to attempts by the steward to force girls to marry, and girls were hidden by their parents. Poverty, and the cost of dowries, could be a significant factor in stopping girls from marrying, and impoverished young male peasants could not attract brides to enter their households.

Choice of spouses

In small villages there was only a limited choice of spouses who were of the right age and who were not excluded by the Church on the grounds of consanguinity. However, parental choice based on economic considerations could be decisive. Shipov, the son of a wealthy peasant, had his bride chosen for him in the early nineteenth century by a family council from amongst the three girls deemed to be suitable candidates, none of whom was known to him. Special matchmakers (*svakhi*) were also used to match couples in the village and to negotiate the size of the bride's dowry, which could include bedding, livestock and land and the contribution made by the groom's family to the wedding expenses.

There was particular pressure from landowners, and from the peasant commune, for peasants to marry within the villages of their estates, so that they would not lose a source of labour and income to a neighbour. Landowners

19. *The Travels of Olearius in Seventeenth-Century Russia*, ed. by Samuel H. Baron (Stanford, 1967), pp. 94–5.
20. 'Vospominaniia Praskov'i Nikolaevny Tatlinoi (1812–1854)', *Russkii arkhiv* (1899), no. 10, p. 198.
21. BL, Add. MS 47428, ff. 131–4.

imposed a special 'exit payment' (*vyvod*) or fines on peasants who let their daughters marry outside the estate. In the 1770s, V.G. Orlov charged a fee of 15 roubles if female serfs married outside the village. By the 1790s the fee had risen to 50 roubles and by the early nineteenth century peasants were paying 100–150 roubles for the privilege of marrying outside his estate. Much larger fees were levied when peasants married members of other social estates. In 1779, Orlov charged 300 roubles for a woman to marry the servant of a government official. The state shared the same economic interests as the landowner and the peasant commune. State peasants were forbidden to marry outside their social estate until 1800, when peasant girls were allowed to marry artisans and merchants. Only in 1817 were state peasant girls and widows allowed to marry into serf families.

In practice, however, fines did not deter peasants from marrying peasants from outside their village or members of other social estates. In 1820, the wealthy peasant, V.D. Voronin, from the village of Baki in the Lieven estate paid 300 roubles to enable his daughter to marry an artisan.[22] In Siberia marriages across social estates were more common than in European Russia, and the state peasant commune gave permission for peasants to marry into other social estates, and to marry non-Russians, more easily than the serf commune. The historian Minenko found examples in the late eighteenth century of villages where up to 30 per cent of spouses were not state peasants (postdrivers, artisans, serfs, clergy, exiles, etc.). It was particularly difficult to keep track of peasants who traded in the towns and, to all intents and purposes, had become part of the urban population. In the late eighteenth century, I.S. Tochenov, from a prominent Dmitrov merchant family, married a landless peasant; one of the sisters of Ivan Men'shii, a state peasant, married a merchant in the early nineteenth century. Indeed, marriage by peasants to women from the urban estates could assist their own registration into the urban community. Three peasants who applied for registration in the Iaroslavl' urban community in 1744 were married to 'native Iaroslavl' women'. After the plague of 1771 it was common for the daughters of ruined merchant families to marry rich peasants in an attempt to save the family economically, and the same pattern emerged after the economic dislocation caused by the Continental System and the Napoleonic invasion of 1812. Furthermore, some peasants resisted the choice made for them by their parents, commune or landowner. Young couples eloped, married in secret or bribed priests to perform the ceremony for them. The short stories of Gogol', written in the 1830s and 1840s, are full of tales of poor peasants who manage to marry the daughters of rich peasants through some trickery or magic.

Among the nobility it was equally common to marry within the noble estate. The upper strata of the nobility tended, not surprising, to forge links with similar families through marriage. The wealthiest families often intermarried; in Peter's reign Vice-Chancellor M.G. Golovkin (owner of 30,000

22. BL, Add. MS 47431, ff. 82–82v, 87–8, Lieven papers, estate papers 1819–25.

serfs) married Princess E.I. Romodanovskaia (20,000 serfs). In 1730, 85 out of the 125 nobles in the top four civil, military and court ranks were related to each other by blood or marriage. It was the newcomers who had not yet formed these marriage links; 81 per cent of the children of these upper nobles in 1730 married into old families which had been ennobled before the accession of Peter I. Some nobles married their sons to the daughters of wealthy merchants (see Chapter 2) for primarily economic reasons, but by doing so they retained their noble surname while acquiring merchant capital or industrial plant.

In the seventeenth century spouses of the Muscovite elite were chosen by their parents and bride and groom often did not meet until the wedding day. As part of his attempt to break the constraints of Muscovite society, Peter I instructed in 1702 that there should be an engagement period of at least six weeks before marriage. During these six weeks the groom and bride could meet and either side could terminate the betrothal; the groom, but not the bride, was given the right to refuse to marry the bride if her ugliness or disfigurements had been disguised at the time of betrothal. Marriages without the consent of both parties were outlawed in 1722. But in practice, the children, and especially the daughters, of the nobility were still largely dependent on the choice of their spouse by their parents. It was also the parents who determined the size of the daughter's dowry and, in effect, her eligibility. Anna Labzina (born 1758) was not even informed about the choice of husband, which was determined by her mother, her uncle and her aunt when it became clear that her mother was dying: 'the matter was resolved without me'.[23] She became trapped in an unhappy marriage until the death of her husband almost twenty years later. As a widow, aged 35, she then married again, this time a man eight years younger than herself, and her second marriage proved happy although childless. A husband was also found for Praskov'ia Tatlina (born 1812) and the marriage took place two weeks later.   *sense.*

Some sons were as pragmatic in the choice of their wives as their parents. Andrian Denisov, from a prominent Cossack family, liked a girl who was 'kind and bright, but not rich'. But he married a wealthy bride.[24] Noble boys were, however, more able to resist parental pressure than their sisters. Petr Rumiantsev refused to marry a bride of his parents' choice in the mid-eighteenth century, although she possessed over 2,000 serfs and houses in Moscow and St Petersburg, and despite being advised by his father not to let her go as 'it is difficult to find [one of] her wealth'.[25] In the late eighteenth century, I.M. Dolgorukov married the daughter of a poor nobleman for love, even though 'everyone was against my marriage to Smirnaia for the reason that she was poor and so was I'.[26]

23. *Vospominaniia Anny Evdokimovny Labzinoi 1758–1828* (St Petersburg, 1914), p. 19.
24. 'Istoriia kazaka Voiska Donskago, atamana Andriana Karpovicha Denisova, 1763–1841', *Russkaia starina* (1874), no. 10, pp. 29–30.
25. Semenova, *Ocherki istorii byta*, p. 77.
26. *Zapiski kniazia I.M. Dolgorukova: Povest' o rozhdenii moem, proiskhozhdenii i vsei zhizni. 1764–1800* (Petrograd, 1916), pp. 91–2.

Divorce

Divorce was rare, particularly outside the nobility, but could legally take place according to canon law on the grounds of adultery, desertion, impotence or incurable diseases. In 1722 P.I. Iaguzhinskii, Procurator-General of the Senate, successfully petitioned the Synod for divorce from his wife on the grounds of her infidelity and dissolute behaviour (which included wandering around the house naked and desecrating a church). Women could, at least in principle, initiate divorce proceedings and wives were also released from their vows if their husbands were convicted of serious crimes. Annulment of marriages was extremely rare, and usually only happened if it could be proved that the marriage had been illegal in the first place (for example, if it were bigamous, a fourth marriage or outside the bounds of consanguinity laid down by the Church). Marriages between Old Believers were not recognized by the state and many of these took place in secret. Since wives granted a divorce took back their dowry property, it was often easier in practice, and less economically damaging, for nobles and townspeople of some means, to force an unwanted wife to take vows in a convent and provide her with the necessary endowment for entry, than formally to divorce her. Taking vows automatically dissolved the marital bonds in the eyes of the Church.

FAMILY RITUALS: WEDDINGS, CHRISTENINGS, FUNERALS

Weddings

Olearius described the wedding ceremonies of Russians in the mid-seventeenth century. At this time the rituals were similar for all classes, the only difference being in the extravagance of the dress, the cost of the presents exchanged between bride and groom and the elaborateness of the feast given to the guests. The bethrothal and exchange of gifts constituted a formal commitment to marriage and a breach of promise could result in legal proceedings for compensation. On the day of the wedding itself, the bride and groom were assisted in the preparation of their dress and hair by special helpers, or matchmakers (*svakhi*), and special songs were sung by the female friends of the bride. The priest came to the house of the bride and blessed a mixture of hops, barley and oats; bride and groom would then exchange rings. These rituals were followed by a church ceremony, which commenced with the priests receiving offerings of food, and then holding icons over the heads of the bride and groom while they were blessed:

> The priest then takes into his hands the groom's right hand and the bride's left, and thrice asks them if they wish to have one another and to live together. When they answer "Yes", he leads them around in a circle, while singing the 128th Psalm. They sing the verses after him and dance. After the dance, pretty garlands are placed on their heads. . . . Then the priest says, "Be fruitful and multiply", and unites them with the words "Whom

God has joined together let no man part", and so forth. Throughout the ceremony all the guests in the church burn small candles. The priest is given a gilded wooden cup or a drinking glass of red wine. He drinks some of it in honour of the married couple, and the groom and bride must drink three draughts. Then the groom throws the glass to the ground and he and his bride trample it into little bits, saying, "Thus let any who wish to arouse enmity and hatred between us fall under our feet and be trampled". The women then shower them with flax and hemp seed and wish them happiness. They also pull and push the newly married bride, as if to separate her from the groom, but the two hold fast to each other.[27]

The couple then retired to a private room to consummate the marriage (in some cases, after the consummation of the marriage the bridal shift 'bearing the honourable marks of Virginity' was displayed to the guests). The wedding would then be followed by feasting and festivities which could last several days. Amongst the rituals of the wedding ceremony in the late seventeenth century was one described by Samuel Collins which was a poignant reminder of the future subservience, and sometimes painful, relationship of the wife to her husband:

The Bridegroom has a Whip in one Boot, and a Jewel or some Money in the other, he bids the Bride pull them off, if she happens upon the Jewel, he counts her lucky, and bestows it upon her; but if she lights upon the Boot with the Whip in it, she is reckon'd amongst the unfortunate, and gets a Bride-lash for her pains, which is but the earnest-penny of her future entertainment.[28]

The theological content of the church service for marriage remained much the same in the eighteenth and early nineteenth centuries for all Orthodox Christians (but in Siberia, where priests could be few and many peasants were Old Believers, marriages took place in practice without church ceremonies). But by the late eighteenth century foreign travellers commented on the pre- and post-wedding ceremony rituals as a particular feature of peasant weddings, where the elaborateness of the ceremonials had remained largely unchanged, albeit with regional variations in the songs, dances and rituals. Wedding ceremonies in the countryside also involved pre-Christian rituals well into the nineteenth century. For example, on the road from the bride's house the best man (the *druzhka*) might have to overcome small obstacles on the road (barricades or bonfires) with small offerings to placate evil spirits, or he might shoot into the air and crack his whip to ward off evil. Catherine Wilmot described in the early nineteenth century the ritual bathing of the bride, who was a household serf of the Princess Dashkova (on her Belorussian estate), by her female friends on the day before the wedding:

27. *The Travels of Olearius*, pp. 167–8.
28. Samuel Collins, *The Present State of Russia* (London, 1671), p. 8.

We then attended her to the Bath with all her young Companions amounting to between 30 and 40 Girls who assisted in undressing her in the outer Chamber & then led her in a flood of tears naked into the Bath. They then took off their own Cloaths & after scouring her to their hearts' content danced round about in all their National Dances Clapping their hands & drinking Wine which was dispensed by another Eve who sat with a bottle in one hand and a glass in the other, her long tresses falling down about her Shoulders which like all the others was the only Covering they could boast . . . I believe we stay'd about an hour at the Bath which became the most festive scene imaginable. They Colour'd themselves for sport in the most ridiculous manner and sang & danced like a Troop of Bachanals while the Bride continued mute and in a flood of tears.[29]

Catherine Wilmot describes this exotic scene as a peasant custom; yet it is interesting that it was considered a suitable occasion for a foreign noble lady to attend.

Birth and baptism

Children of peasants were normally born in the bathhouse, which at least was private and relatively clean, accompanied by rituals of cleansing, the application of herbs, and the use of amulets to guard against the many misfortunes which could take place at this time (see Chapter 10, p. 247). In noble families too, children were also commonly born in the warmth of a steam bath, although this would be in a private bathroom. According to Grigorii Kotoshikhin, even the wife of tsar Alexis chose to give birth in the bathhouse in the company of her female attendants. It seems that it was more common for peasants to give birth in a kneeling position, while the nobility and merchant class were more likely to give birth lying on a bed or the floor. Infants could be swaddled but this was not as common as in western Europe. Children were often left naked so that they learned to roll and then walk easily. An English guide to educational methods in 1744 commented favourably on Russia that:

The *Muscovites* too are inur'd to Hardships even from the Womb. They use their Children to endure the Extremities of Heat and Cold, Hunger, Thirst, and Labour. They wash their new-born Infants in cold Water, and roll them upon Ice, and amongst Snow. . . .[30]

After the birth the child was usually named on the eighth day and christened on the fortieth day (but the baby would be baptized immediately if in danger of dying). Baroness Elizabeth Dimsdale, writing in 1781 noted that: 'To conclude the ceremony, a little Gold or Silver Cross, or one of inferior value,

29. *The Russian Journals*, pp. 239–40.
30. Anon., *The Common Errors in the Education of Children, and their Consequences* (London, 1744), p. 10.

211

according as the circumstances of the Parent will best admit, is hung about the Infants neck, and is the badge or token of his Baptism.'[31]

Funerals and burials

Funerals and burials were also accompanied by elaborate ceremonies and laments. According to the description given by Olearius in the seventeenth century, the dead were laid in coffins in church for several days (eight days in the winter if the deceased were a noble) and then carried to the grave by four or six persons:

> Before the body walk several veiled women from among the closest friends of the deceased, giving forth extremely sad laments and cries. By turns they cry very loudly, quiet down, and resume bewailing the untimely departure of their friend, wishing he could have lived longer, since he was so pious and dear a person.[32]

A so-called 'passport', bought from the clergy, in which it was confirmed that the deceased had received absolution for his sins and could be admitted to heaven was put in the hands of the deceased. Olearius commented that Russians mourned their dead for six weeks, and that wealthy Russians held great feasts during this period for the friends of the deceased and the priests who were present at the funeral.

Rituals surrounding burials changed little for peasants during this period. Peter I banned lamentations in St Petersburg but during Peter's reign Weber heard in a village 'the most lamentable Cries on a Burying, which not only the Relations of the Deceased, but also old Women hired of purpose for it, made out of the Windows of the House whence the Corpse was carried, that the whole Village resounded with it'. At graveyards he found people 'with the most lamentable Cries and Howlings, ask the Dead, how they do; why they died; what ailed them; and the like'.[33] In towns, the practice of lamentations declined in the course of the eighteenth century, but funerals could still be elaborate. The funeral of the father of Tolchenov, a wealthy merchant in Dmitrov, took place in 1779, and was a very public affair. The service was conducted by the Father Superior and attended by 20 priests and 10 sacristans and friends.

There is some evidence, however, that at least some of the nobility replaced the more emotional and vocal expression of their grief with something more formalized. Martha Wilmot commented in the early nineteenth century that it was the custom for noble ladies to send out mourning cards the day after the death of their husband and to receive guests all day, for fear of being 'accused of indifference and disrespect to her husband's memory and no creature wou'd

---

31. *An English Lady at the Court of Catherine the Great* ed. by A.G. Cross (Cambridge, 1989), pp. 59–60.
32. *The Travels of Olearius*, p. 275.
33. Weber, *The Present State of Russia*, vol. I, pp. 121–3.

have believ'd her sorrow genuine or have visited her in future'.[34] Individual nobles had to cope with the strain of bereavement in their own way once the elaborate ritualization of death was no longer practised. Margarita Tuchkova, a noblewoman from the Naryshkin family, built a chapel on the site where her husband fell at the battle of Borodino. After her son also died in 1826 she moved to the chapel and formed a commmunity of female recluses and thereafter devoted herself to a life of prayer and simple work.

RELATIONSHIPS WITHIN THE FAMILY

Husbands and wives

Wife-beating affected all classes. In 1757, a peasant woman in Siberia, Araf'ia Ivanova, left her husband because he 'constantly beat and maimed [her] for no reason'. Matrena Andreeva (a Siberian peasant) used 'impertinent words' to her husband; he, in response, 'beat her with a switch and when the switch broke in the impatience of his fury he took an axe from the axe store and beat her three times with the blunt end on her head and shoulders . . .'.[35] The aristocrat V.F. Saltykov, brother-in-law of Peter I's second wife, had beaten his wife (Princess Aleksandra Dolgorukaia) 'nearly starved her to death, and subjected her to such base abuse and persecution . . . that he treated her not as a wife but as a lowly, subject orphan'. In his defence, Saltykov claimed he 'never beat her without cause, but when she showed me some opposition, then I beat her with my own hands'. Furthermore, she was not blameless herself, for through her 'unpleasantness and disobedience . . . she never listened to me'.[36] I.A. Raevskii, a nobleman, wrote of his grandmother that 'Grandmother greatly feared her husband; he was short-tempered and, they say, often beat her.'[37] An anonymous English account of Muscovy in the late seventeenth century claimed that 'when Marry'd, the Wife Loves her Husband the better if sometimes he Corrects her; and concludes, he Loves her not, if he altogether declines it'.[38] This assertion was made in foreign travel accounts from the sixteenth century onwards; it seems borne out by the twentieth-century Russian proverb: 'Not to beat the wife is not to be loved by her.'

Violence was not grounds for divorce. Princess Dolgorukaia failed in her attempt at divorce, made on her behalf by her father, as wife-beating (and, for that matter, her husband's adultery) was not regarded as sufficient grounds. The case lasted several years and only ended when she entered a convent (which automatically meant that the marriage was dissolved). Sometimes the

34. *The Russian Journals*, p. 73.
35. N.A. Minenko, 'K izucheniiu semeinoi etiki Sibirskago krest'ianstva vtoroi poloviny XVIIIv', in *Krest'ianstvo Sibiri XVIII–nachala XX v. Klassovaia bor'ba, obshchestvennoe soznanie i kul'tura* (Novosibirsk, 1975), pp. 79–80.
36. Brenda Meehan-Waters, *Autocracy & Aristocracy. The Russian Service Elite of 1730* (Princeton, 1982), p. 125.
37. I.A. Raevskii, 'Iz vospominanii I.A. Raevskago', *Istoricheskii vestnik* (1905), no. 8, p. 391.
38. Anon., *A New and Exact Description of Moscovy* (London, 1698), p. 9.

violence had a sinister purpose. In 1718, Agaf'ia Visleneva was almost whipped to death by her husband, a noble landowner, and stepson, and then obliged to renounce her property and forced to take vows in a convent against her wishes. Women did, however, have some limited rights in the law. The Code of 1649 laid down the punishments and compensation for dishonouring women 'with unseemly words'. But the Code did not impose a penalty for the murder of a wife by her husband, although wives who murdered husbands were to be buried up to the neck and left to die. The law was changed by Peter I, who determined that an equal penalty (knouting) should apply for the murder of either spouse. Murders of wives by husbands were investigated and brought before the courts. In 1797 the Tobol'sk Criminal Chamber sentenced a peasant to 400 blows of the knout (in all probability a death sentence), to have his nostrils split and exile with hard labour for poisoning his wife. Rape cases were also brought before the ecclesiastical courts, partly because the dishonour of rape meant that the girl was no longer able to marry. In Peter's reign, those convicted of rape could be executed or dispatched to the galleys.

Russian husbands could be domineering and brutish. The noblewoman Praskov'ia Tatlina wrote that the general attitude of the Russian husband (including her own husband) towards his wife, was 'a woman was an object'.[39] Anna Labzina found her first husband and his young niece together in bed shortly after her marriage to him and was forced to accept his adultery. Wives could be humiliated by the preference given by their husbands to young female household serfs, who had little defence against their masters. Nevertheless, some marriages were loving ones. Mar'ia Sergeevna Nikolaeva wrote in her memoirs that 'My father passionately loved his wife.'[40] Wives chose to follow their disgraced husbands to Siberia and share in their hardships. Anna Labzina followed her disgraced second husband to Siberia in 1822. Participants in the Decembrist revolt who were exiled to Siberia were also often accompanied by their wives.

Parents and children

Parents had almost unlimited rights over the lives of their children. The Code of 1649 laid down mild punishments for infanticide (imprisonment for father or mother for one year, although mothers and their accomplices who murdered children born from adulterous relations were punished by death), which suggests an admission that extreme poverty could be at the root of this action (and possibly that such children had little chance of survival anyway). Peter I, however, introduced the death penalty for infanticide, including for those who murdered illegitimate children. A Senate resolution of 1715 acknowledged the prevalence of child-abandonment and infanticide of illegitimate

39. 'Vospominaniia Praskov'i Nikolaevny Tatlinoi (1812–1854)', *Russkii arkhiv* (1899), no. 10, p. 199.
40. 'Cherty starinnago dvorianskago byta', p. 117.

children, whose mothers 'because of shame, cast away the unfortunate little ones, whence they die or are murdered'.[41]

Children who disobeyed, or in some way dishonoured, their parents could be punished by law. The Law Code of 1649 specified that children who stole, failed to maintain or acted disrespectfully towards their parents should have inflicted on them 'a severe punishment . . . for such deeds of theirs, beat them mercilessly with the knout, and command them to attend to their father and mother in all obedience'. In 1701 a son who was found guilty of beating his parents and stealing from them was sentenced to be 'whipped mercilessly with rods'. In 1768 a Siberian peasant appealed to the local peasant office (*izba*) to whip his sons 'mercilessly' for saying offensive words in front of him. In 1801 Khristofor Aladzhalov, an Armenian merchant trading in Rostov-on Don, noted in his diary that 'a certain son who spoke impertinent words and raised his hand to his father' was punished with 50 blows of the rod in the market.[42] Disputes between children and their parents were brought before the peasant commune, which usually found in favour of the parents, and could authorize corporal punishment of younger members of the household for disobedience. Children were also supposed to provide for their parents and could be punished by the commune if they failed to do so.

Russian childhood could be harsh. Peasant children were normally only suckled for a short time, after which they were given solid foods, and pacified with a *soska*, a cloth filled with partially chewed foods to suck. The *soska* was particularly unhygienic as the food soon became putrid or mouldy. The feeding method was partly determined by the almost immediate return of Russian peasant women to work in the fields; death rates of infants were highest in the summer months when mothers were most active in the harvest. In the Crimea, in contrast, Mary Holderness, whose motherly instincts were not touched by the sight of Tatar children ('its dress, the ugliness of its features, and, more than all, the scorbutic humours . . . make it, of all the infants I ever saw, the most disgusting and uninteresting') noted that babies were suckled for two or three years.[43] The consequence of this, along with greater cleanliness of Tatar houses and the lack of physical labour demanded from Tatar women, meant that the survival rate of Tatar children was higher than that of Russian ones (although Tatar mothers, partly through exhaustion from suckling, had a lower life expectancy than Russians). The babies of the nobility were more likely to be breast-fed, but often by a peasant wet-nurse rather than by the mother.

In noble households, boys and girls were brought up by females until the age of seven and enjoyed considerable freedom during these years. In their early years, noble children depended largely on household serfs for their care and companionship. In particular, the wet-nurse, or *niania*, became their constant

41. James Cracraft, *The Church Reform of Peter the Great* (London, 1971), p. 96.
42. A. Dzhivelegov (comp.), 'Cherty provintsial'no zhizni na rubezhe XIX veka', *Golos minuvshago* (1913), no. 7, p. 189.
43. Mary Holderness, *New Russia. Journey from Riga to the Crimea* (London, 1823), pp. 224–5.

companion. After the age of seven, it was assumed that boys would be educated by their tutors or fathers, or with other male companions in schools, and girls were to be instructed in household affairs by their mothers and, in general, prepared for their marital duties. Corporal punishment was common for children in all social groups. In peasant (and urban) households, children were expected to contribute to the household economy as soon as they were able. Boys tended cattle from the age of five or six and worked in the fields from the age of seven or eight. By the age of 15 they were performing a full workload. Peasant girls helped in the home and in weaving and spinning from an early age. Peasant and town children could be hired out by their parents to other families for a period. In the Crimea and Caucasus, poverty could even lead to the sale of children. In the Crimea in the 1790s, Maria Guthrie was shocked to see young Circassian women for sale in the market, and was told by the local inhabitants that this was the 'only method which parents had of bettering the state of their handsome daughters, *destined at all events to the haram*'.[44] In Mingrelia (Georgia) in the early nineteenth century Julius von Klaproth found that the 'inhabitants subsist by some little agriculture, and by the sale of their own children'.[45]

There is some evidence that parents, particularly fathers, greeted the birth of a son with more enthusiasm than that of a daughter. Amongst peasants, sons provided the necessary labour in the fields, could help the household meet *obrok* and recruiting obligations and would, in the normal course of things, help to increase the size of the family by bringing a spouse into the household. Girls, although they also performed useful labour, would normally be lost to the household on marriage, and, in addition, would require a dowry. Baroness Elizabeth Dimsdale recalled a tale of a peasant who, when informed of the birth of a daughter 'fell into a violent Passion, and really went home and beat her [his wife], then went away and left her'. The wife, however, 'was determined to be even with him, therefore made free with the strong Liquors which were provided for rejoicing, and for him to get drunk with, and got drunk herself'.[46]

Sons were also favoured amongst the nobility, partly for economic reasons as suitable partners would have to be found for daughters. Sergei Aksakov reconstructed his view of his grandfather's attitude towards his daughters and son:

> . . . he kissed his children and gave them his blessing – his four young daughters and the infant son who was the single scion and sole hope of an ancient and noble family. The daughters he thought of no importance: 'What's the good of *them*? They look out of the house, not in; if their name is Bagroff [pseudonym of Aksakov] to-day, it may be anything on earth tomorrow; my hopes rest entirely on my boy. . . .

44. Maria Guthrie, *A Tour performed in the Years 1795–6, through the Taurida, or Crimea* (London, 1802), p. 154.
45. Julius von Klaproth, *Travels into the Caucasus and Georgia, performed in the years 1807 and 1808, by the Command of the Russian Government* (London, 1814), p. 402.
46. *An English Lady*, p. 61.

216

On the birth of a granddaughter 'he was seriously annoyed' and upon her infant death commented, 'No reason to tear one's hair over *that*! There will be plenty more girls.'[47] The grandfather may have been an extreme example, but Aksakov commented that both his parents would have preferred a son.

High infant mortality in all sectors of society led to forms of emotional self-protection or a deliberate lack of emotional investment in offspring. Baroness Dimsdale claimed that there was 'a Prejudice usually entertained by the Parents, that if one of the first die young, their Children are not born to live, which makes them careless of those they have afterwards'.[48] But this seeming callousness may have been a form of self-protection and did not mean that parents, of whatever social background, did not love their children. Porter commented on Russian peasants that:

> These people are particularly fond of children . . . You will more frequently see the men, when returning from toil, taking their infants in their arms and caressing them, than seeking the company of their wives.[49]

Memoirs of nobles also comment on the love between parents and children, even if this was constrained by the disciplinarian and formal atmosphere which prevailed in many households. It was written of P.I. Buliubash, a Ukrainian nobleman, in the early nineteenth century that 'He loved his children passionately and, although treating them with extreme tyranny, at the same time he took to heart all their grief'.[50] Infant and child mortality was all too common but this did not mean that parents took their death or suffering lightly. Bolotov, a minor nobleman, wrote of his feelings when his eldest son died of smallpox at the age of five:

> I cannot describe the pity we all felt for our child and the feelings of compassion as we looked at him during the few days of his excruciating suffering . . . We all loved him greatly and washed his coffin with our warm tears.

A few years later, he described his 'sorrow and grief' during the illness of his daughter and the great love he felt for her during this time (she recovered after a month).[51]

The daughter-in-law

The household, as has been seen above, often included members of the extended family. Within the peasant household it was accepted that the young wife, the daughter-in-law (*snokha*), who entered the household was often in the most unfortunate position. The wife of the head of household ruled over the other females and children in the house and could make life difficult, if

47. Sergei Aksakov, *A Russian Gentleman*, trans. J.D. Duff (London, 1976), pp. 18, 215, 219.
48. *An English Lady*, p. 59.
49. Robert Ker Porter, *Travelling Sketches in Russia and Sweden during the Years 1805, 1806, 1807, 1808* (London, 1809), vol. I, p. 295.
50. 'Iz proshedshei zhizni malorusskago dvorianstva (Zapisano so slov razskazchika)', *Kievskaia starina* 23 (1888), p. 150.
51. *Zhizn' i prikliucheniia Andreia Bolotova* (Cambridge, 1973), vol. III, pp. 125, 376.

not impossible, for the newcomer (and potential rival). In 1797, Agrafena Epifanova, a state peasant in Omsk region (in western Siberia), brought a case against her mother-in-law for hitting her with the result that she miscarried. The case was investigated by the Tobol'sk Criminal Chamber, which found the story to be untrue and sentenced Agrafena to a birching. Problems with mothers-in-law were not confined to the peasant household of course. Kalashnikov, a clerk, recalled that his sister, who married a townsman, suffered 'cruelties and the most severe tortures' from her mother-in-law until the time of the death of her persecutor.[52]

More seriously, it was not uncommon for new young peasant brides to be sexually abused by their fathers-in-law, who would often be the head of household and could therefore not be challenged. Much of this abuse must have taken place privately, but there were examples of cases involving state peasants which reached the courts. In Tver' province (between Moscow and St Petersburg) a state peasant, Solomonida Iadrova, complained that her father-in-law had raped her twice. The case went from the Lower Rasprava (court of first instance for state peasants) to the Tver' Consistory (a church court) and then was returned to the Tver' Criminal Chamber. In 1779, the Chamber sentenced the father-in-law to be whipped 'mercilessly', but Solomonida was also beaten with rods on the grounds that the court believed she had consented to this act. The practice of marrying young peasant boys to far older girls was a contributory factor in sexual relationships between father-in-law and daughter-in-law, with or without consent. In Radishchev's *Journey from St Petersburg to Moscow* this practice is condemned by using the words of a poor peasant girl:

> They were going to marry me off into a rich house, to a ten-year-old lad, but I didn't want that . . . They say that his father sleeps with his young daughters-in-law until his sons grow up.[53]

THE FAMILY AND PROPERTY

The composition of the household and the relationships between family members within it can be partly explained by the laws governing the family and inheritance in Russia. (In Belorussia and parts of the Ukraine, where Magdeburg law applied in towns, inheritance laws differed from those in Great Russia and widows inherited one-third of the property of their husbands; the situation in Old Finland and the Baltic provinces was also different.)

Inheritance and state law

In the second half of the seventeenth century there was a fundamental distinction in the type of land held by the nobility – *votchina* was hereditary land and *pomest'e* was land granted by the tsar in return for service. Nobles could hold

---

52. 'Zhizn' neznamenitago Timofeia Petrovicha Kalashnikova prostym slogom opisannaia s 1762 po 1794 god', *Russkii arkhiv* (1904), no. 10, p. 153.
53. Harold B. Segel, *The Literature of Eighteenth-Century Russia* (New York, 1971), vol. I, p. 377.

both forms of land but, at least in principle, service lands were only granted for military service and could be reclaimed by the crown if service were not rendered. The tsar also had a claim on the land and could reallocate it at the time of the death of the servitor if there were no suitable heir. Nobles who only had service estates, therefore, were in a more vulnerable position than those who held hereditary estates. As the century progressed the amount of hereditary land held by the nobility expanded at the expense of service lands, and the distinction between the two types of land became blurred. In practice, service lands were bought and sold and passed on to heirs, and many holders of such lands failed to perform any service.

The Code of 1649 (and subsequent supplementary laws of 1677 and 1679) established different, and complex, rules for inheritance for both hereditary and service land. Hereditary land was divided equally among sons; if there were no sons it passed in equal shares to daughters. Widows were entitled to retain their dowry, which could include land and serfs as well as movable property. They also inherited one-quarter of the movable property (money, jewels, furniture, etc.) and purchased estates could be bequeathed to them. Widows were not allowed to sell service land, mortgage it, or give it to a religious institution, but they could retain a certain amount of it as a life settlement (one-fifth, three-twentieths or one-tenth of the estate, depending on whether the husband had been killed, died on a campaign or died at home). Each daughter received one-half of the widow's share and the rest of the service lands passed to the sons in equal shares. In 1676 it was decreed that 'females of the first degree of blood relation' should inherit equal proportions as 'males of the second degree'.

What were the consequences of property law? Partible inheritance could lead to the division of estates into tiny, economically unviable, plots. In 1686, for example, Antrop Sarychev left his service estate of 38 *cheti* (some 18 hectares) in equal shares to his six sons, which meant that they inherited just over 6 *cheti* each. Although the sons managed to increase their landholdings by service to 23 *cheti*, it was generally accepted that an estate of 100 *cheti* was required to support a cavalryman. Women retained rights over their dowries, including property which they brought with them, which could not be sold or mortgaged by their husbands and which reverted to the wife's family on her death if there were no heirs. In practice, however, it was difficult for wives to prevent their husbands forcing them to sell this property, despite the fact that the Boiar Duma condemned this practice in 1677 and three years later instructed that both spouses had to sign documents disposing of the wife's property. On the other hand, the study of the Vladimir-Suzdal' region (east of Moscow) in the seventeenth century by the American historian Kivelson showed that it is difficult to generalize about the inheritance of widows and daughters in the seventeenth century, which seemed to depend as much on the wish of the householder as it did on the law. In 1671, Aleksei Kablukov gave his daughter Mar'ia as a dowry a hereditary estate of 42 *cheti*, that is one-sixth of his property (he had five other children). In 1684, Agaf'ia Bitiagovskaia only inherited 14 per cent of her father's land – a miserly 6 *cheti* – but even this was more than the law prescribed for daughters (in which a maximum should have been 10 per cent). In fact, Kivelson found that it was quite common in this region for daughters to receive more than 10 per cent of the land.

In 1714, Peter I attempted to break the practice of noble (and mercantile) inheritance by abolishing partible inheritance and decreeing that in future property had to be passed in its entirety to one son (not necessarily the eldest one). At the same time, Peter simply merged the categories of hereditary and service lands. Under this law, a widow did not inherit land at all except when there were no children, in which case she could inherit all the land, retaining it until she remarried or died. A daughter could inherit all the land if there were no sons. In 1716, Elena Saltykova successfully inherited all her father's land, defeating the claims of her male cousin, by citing the law of 1714. Peter's law provoked great opposition from the nobility, and legal confusion (for example when second wives were left childless but there were sons from a previous marriage) and in practice it was often circumvented, with the result that the law was revoked in 1731. It was then decreed that widows were to inherit one-seventh of the property and to retain rights over their dowries, while daughters were to inherit one-fourteenth of the property (husbands could also inherit one-seventh of their wives' property).

The rights of widows after 1731 could in themselves lead to the use of violence and force against unwanted or infertile wives. The violent case of 1718 cited above of a husband who beat his wife, forced her to sign over her property to her stepson and then put her in a convent and made her take vows against her will stemmed from the very fact that she had the right to dispose of her property as she wished. Indeed, among the nobles and merchants, confinement of women in convents could be a convenient means to gain control over their property, which could be disposed of irrespective of their wishes. According to Weber (writing in the reign of Peter I), they were forced to enter convents 'either by their Parents for Disobedience, or by their Brothers and Relations out of Interest to keep the Estate to themselves'.[54] There is less evidence, however, of this happening later in the eighteenth century. Noblewomen had some security and, at least in the case of wealthier widows and wives, a measure of independent wealth. Martha Wilmot commented in the early nineteenth century, conscious perhaps that Russian women enjoyed rights not shared by her own countrywomen, that:

> The full & entire dominion which Russian Women have over their own fortunes gives them a very remarkable degree of liberty & a degree of independence of their husbands unknown in England . . . Here a Woman's power to dispose of her wealth is a great check on her husband's inclination to forsake her or to Tyrannize. If she dies without children her entire property

54. Weber, *The Present State of Russia*, vol. I, p. 136.

returns to her own family unless She makes it over by will to him or you or I or John or Molly which she has equal power to do.[55]

The restoration of partible inheritance did not prevent numerous legal disputes between the nobility concerning inheritance rights to property. The extent of second marriages which could produce stepchildren, and the claims of illegitimate children and other relations were a constant source of dispute and litigation over property ownership (and a source of poverty as land was divided into economically unviable plots). The formal designation of the noble's estate as his private property in the Charter to the Nobles in 1785 did not end these disputes, partly because the Charter continued to make the distinction between land which the nobleman acquired through service or purchase (which he could dispose of and bequeath as he wished) and inherited land (which had to be disposed of according to the law of 1731).

Inheritance: customary law

Amongst peasants, whether state peasants or serfs, customary law applied and this could vary from area to area, or even between villages on a particular estate. (outside Great Russia it was different). The state, which interfered directly in the inheritance and property rights of nobles, played little role in the customary law of the peasants. This was partly because 'landed property' was *used* by the peasants but not actually *owned* by them (although in the peasants' minds the use of land in effect meant the ownership of it). In practice, the land worked by the peasants was seen by the landowner, the state and the peasant commune as a *tiaglo*, or tax unit. In view of this, it was in everyone's interest that the land worked by the peasant household had to remain an economically viable unit and this, above all, determined inheritance practice.

It was customary for the peasant wife to retain rights over her dowry (which was normally left in equal parts to her children on her death, or reverted to her family if she died childless) and also to be granted a share of her husband's property. This normally amounted to one-seventh of his land and one-quarter of his movable property (that is, the same as the amount inherited by noblewomen before 1714 and after 1731). Daughters normally had half the rights of wives, that is the right to one-fourteenth of the land. The rest of the movable and immovable property was divided equally amongst the sons. But different customs could apply in peasant communities and it was quite common for property to pass through the male line only. The records of the commune of the (serf) village of Nikol'skoe from the 1780s to the 1820s showed that property passed from fathers to sons, normally but not always in equal shares, but without any provision for wives or daughters. Peasant communities often maintained different customary laws on inheritance

55. *The Russian Journals*, p. 271.

of non-*tiaglo* land which had been leased or 'bought' (see Chapter 3) by peasants. Peasants who were not relatives but who had joined the household as labourers could also have some limited rights of inheritance on the grounds that they had worked the land and therefore had acquired a claim to it. Stepchildren and illegitimate children could also have some claims on the property. Customary rights over items of movable property were weak. In practice, valuable items such as fur coats could be bequeathed to children or other relatives, usually by means of a written document, although it could also be done through purely verbal agreements.

The peasant commune, as we know, had the ultimate power to redistribute land and to determine the composition of the household in order to ensure economic productivity and capacity to pay taxes, sometimes irrespective of the wishes of the head of the household and contrary to the customary law on inheritance. Recent scholarship by the Russian historian Aleksandrov has shown that, in practice, the peasant commune dealt with great flexibility with matters such as land use and inheritance and could override custom on grounds of economic expediency or simple common sense. In 1803, the commune on one of the Orlov family estates allowed Iakov Alekseev to leave his father's household and to take one-quarter of the property with him, on the grounds of the father's 'oppressive' behaviour towards him and the son's own blameless behaviour. The commune could also interfere in property and inheritance disputes between family members, and could determine the outcome according to the particular circumstances of the family and the productivity of individual members. This meant that the commune could forcibly take land from unsuitable heads of household and give it to other household males.

In particular, the commune was concerned that dependants should be cared for within the family so that the community as a whole should not have to shoulder an additional burden. This meant, on occasions, that communes determined that a widow should receive a share equal to that of her sons, or should have rights over the property during her lifetime. The commune could also insist that widows, or elderly parents, were maintained by their children within the household and could make special provisions for daughters, daughters-in-law or mothers-in-law. In 1824 an arrangement was made in the village of Rukavovo that a widow, Anna Belova, divided her husband's lands and possessions between her three married sons, but remained in the home of the eldest son, who also undertook to pay her debts of 425 roubles. On occasions, the heirs according to custom were passed over if they were too young, or otherwise unable to fulfil the *tiaglo* function of the land. In 1788, the serf commune on one of the Orlov estates agreed that the land of Ivanov should pass not solely to his nephew, which would have been according to custom, but be divided between his widow, her four daughters and the nephew on the grounds that one of the daughters could bring a son-in-law into the household and so be able to fulfil the *tiaglo* obligations.

Landowners could also interfere with customary rights and impose their own regulations. A.M. Cherkasskii instructed in 1719 that peasant land on his

Moscow estate should be divided in such a way that sons inherited three-quarters of the land (in equal shares) and daughters, irrespective of how many there were, no more than one-quarter of the land (also in equal shares). No provision was made for widows. Amongst state peasants in north Russia, the state (which was as concerned as the commune to maintain economic *tiaglo* units) actively intervened in the eighteenth and early nineteenth century to force redistribution and equalization of land holdings, something which, *inter alia*, could also interfere with customary rights over inheritance of property.

SUMMARY: DEVELOPMENTS 1650–1825

The family customs of nobles, like other aspects of their lives, were affected by the policies of Peter I. More freedom, at least in principle, was given to young nobles of both sexes to choose their spouses. Partly as a result of Peter's strictures, the ceremonials surrounding weddings and funerals also underwent changes in the course of the eighteenth century for nobles, and, to a lesser extent, for townspeople. However, the most important change which Peter made – namely the ending of partible inheritance in 1714 (which affected townspeople as well as nobles) – had to be abandoned because of opposition from the nobility. Government legislation did not have a decisive impact on the size or structure of the peasant family or on peasant family rituals and no attempt was made to interfere with peasant customary law. In fact, the study of this period shows us that, with the partial exception of property law, government legislation could make an only limited intrusion into the family life of all social groups. First, we see how little the composition of the family and the household, marriage customs and ceremonials in fact changed over the period. Second, the differences in the family life of nobles, townspeople and peasants remained less striking than the similarities, irrespective of legislation or economic and cultural backgrounds. In the most fundamental areas – age of marriage, relations between spouses and between other family members, etc. – aristocrat and serf alike could share the same experiences. Above all, mothers (and fathers), of whatever social estate, shared the same fears and sorrows at a time when infant and child mortality was a constant presence and reminder of the fragility of life.

CHAPTER 10

Belief: religion, magic and paganism

This chapter looks at the Orthodox Church, the clergy and religion and belief in Russia. A fundamental problem addressed here is the complex relationship between religion, magic and paganism. In Russian, the term *dvoeverie* (double faith) has been used to describe a religious system in which pagan beliefs and practices survived under a veneer of Christianity. To pre-Revolutionary Russian scholars this term described the parallel existence of Christianity and popular pagan and magical practices which, despite the vigorous attempts of the Church, were never fully extirpated. Some scholars argue that the Church was only able to secure the allegiance of the people by deliberately incorporating pre-Christian, pagan practices into Christian ritual. Marxist and feminist historians have also seen the relationship between the official Church and popular pagan practices in terms of conflict – the former seeing Christianity as a tool for social control and pagan practices as a form of popular protest against the imposition of a 'new', alien, ideology of the upper classes, the latter seeing the imposition of an essentially 'male' value system of Christianity on a more 'female' pagan system of belief. But recent historiography has suggested that a reassessment of popular religious practice in Russia is needed and challenges the assumption that the relationship between pagan or magical practices and Christianity has to be seen as one of conflict, or, indeed, that Russia was exceptional in this respect. Not only did the Church condone certain popular practices but such practices have to seen within the *mentalité* and world-view not only of the common people but also of the more educated people, and of the Orthodox parish clergy, many of whom were ambivalent about superstitious and magical beliefs.

THE RUSSIAN ORTHODOX CLERGY

The white (parish) clergy

No doubt there were pious and conscientious parish priests, but, in general, the parish clergy had a reputation for drunkenness and disorderly behaviour.

The 'Spiritual Regulation' of Peter I included instructions for bishops to curb the 'disorderly behaviour' of priests and ensure that 'priests and deacons are not disorderly and that lesser clerics are not noisy and drunk in the streets or, what is worse, rowdy in church' and that they should not 'lie down in the streets to sleep nor drink in the taverns nor boast of their capacity for drink when visiting'.[1] The peasants of a Siberian village complained in 1774 that their priest, Ivan Zagibalov:

> ... is found daily physically incapable, drunk and in such vileness, that he cannot walk, but crawls on the ground with his hair undone like some extraordinary beast.[2]

The Synod took action against extreme cases. In the 1770s a deacon, Ivan Gavrilov, was subjected to corporal punishment and confined for six months in a monastery becaue 'he leads a bad life, always drinking and visiting taverns, plays cards, and indulges in other needless acts'. He was finally defrocked after further bouts of drunkenness (he confessed that 'I had drunk myself into an unconscious stupor') and theft of money from the church.[3] Petr Levshin, as Archbishop of Tver', had priests defrocked for drunkenness in the 1770s.

The shortcomings of the seminary education (see Chapter 6) were exposed in practice. In the early eighteenth century the Archpriest Matvei Dobronravov, in Tambov, only read with difficulty and could not write. Lyall, writing in the 1820s, was shocked by the 'extreme ignorance' of the clergy he met 'who themselves had very confused notions about the respect, reverence, or adoration of the holy images'. 'What can be expected of a clergy so low in the scale of society as in Russia?' he asked acutely.[4] Most parish priests lived in poverty, scarcely better than the peasants. William Coxe described the residence of the priest of the village of Bronitsa, near Novgorod, in the 1780s 'which in no wise differed from the other buildings either in size or goodness', while the priest 'was dressed like the peasants, and was only distinguished from them by his hair, which hung loose over his shoulders to a considerable length'.[5] But many priests had no land and were dependent on fees or gifts in kind, which they charged for performing ceremonies. It has been estimated that the average income for priests in the eighteenth century was 25–40 roubles a year, a miserly sum. Small parishes fared worse. Indeed, the Bishop of Pereslavl' (north-east of Moscow) said in 1754 that 'it would be better to be in the peasantry than a churchman at such small parish churches'.[6] The lower ranks

1. James Cracraft, *The Church Reform of Peter the Great* (London, 1971), p. 246.
2. Iu.S. Bulygin, 'Nekotorye voprosy kultury pripisnoi derevni Kolyvan-Voskresenskikh gornykh zavodov XVIII v', in *Krest'ianstvo Sibiri XVIII–nachala XX v. Klassovaia bor'ba, obshchestvennoe soznanie i kul'tura* (Novosibirsk, 1975), p. 74.
3. Gregory Freeze, *The Russian Levites. Parish Clergy in the Eighteenth Century* (Cambridge, Mass., 1977), p. 71.
4. Robert Lyall, *Travels in Russia, the Krimea, the Caucasus and Georgia* (London, 1825), vol. I, pp. 6–7.
5. William Coxe, *Travels into Poland, Russia, Sweden and Denmark* (Dublin, 1784), vol. II, p. 15.
6. Freeze, *The Russian Levites*, p. 133.

of the clergy (sacristans and deacons) earned even less than priests (in the 1770s and 1780s sacristans earned 10–20 roubles a year). In Siberia, clergy could earn even less; it was not unusual for a deacon to earn as little as 4 roubles and a priest 8 roubles, plus a food allowance.

Clergy who were unable to find posts could be reduced to undignified competition in offering their services. It was reported in the 1760s that:

> An inordinately great number of idle priests and other ecclesiastical personnel are loafing around in Moscow . . . These people cause great scandals through competing with each other and, when undercut by one another, instead of assuming a humbly pious attitude becoming a priest, indulge in profane swearing, with great show of animosity, or even go so far as to fight among themselves. Having completed the agreed service they repair to government taverns or eating-houses, for they have neither home nor shelter of their own. Others, having drunk themselves into a stupor, wander around in the streets, acting in a scandalous manner.[7]

The clergy were exempt from the poll tax (although church peasants had to pay) but they were still liable to other taxes and obligations and were forcibly conscripted on occasions; in Peter's reign, parish priests were even instructed to break the sanctity of the confessional and report 'treasonable acts' to the state.

The result of this was that the parish clergy, in the words of Lyall, 'are rarely seen in genteel society, and by no means receive that attention or deference to which their holy calling, and a better education, might entitle them'.[8] Andrei Bolotov's family (minor provincial nobility) entertained the local parish priest, but the latter was exceptional as, in Bolotov's words, he was 'not a ordinary village priest'. Lack of respect for clergy could result in violence against them. The Bishop of Rostov (north-east of Moscow) complained to Peter I that 'the rural clergy are worse off than beggars, because many are subjected to the beatings of tax collectors and cannot pay'.[9] Matters did not improve as the century progressed. In 1779 Fedor Matorin, a peasant in a village in Tambov province (in the black-earth region), swore at the priest and dragged him by his hair in the street while passers-by watched.[10] Priests were particularly vulnerable to the actions of local landowners. In 1774 Nikita Ivanov, the sacristan in the village of Tarkhan (Shatsk district, Tambov), was forced into serfdom by the landowner Tatarinov. After Ivanov's death, his son, daughter and other family members were sold to other landowners. The Shatsk (Tambov province) landowner Chubarov had an elderly sacristan whipped to death in 1795.[11]

7. K.A. Papmehl, *Metropolitan Platon of Moscow (Petr Levshin, 1737–1812): The Enlightened Prelate, Scholar and Educator* (Newtonville, 1983), p. 57.

8. Robert Lyall, *The Character of the Russians, and a Detailed History of Moscow* (London, 1823), p. cxxviii.

9. Freeze, *The Russian Levites*, p. 28.

10. I.I. Dubasov, 'Iz Tambovskikh letopisei', *Istoricheskii vestnik* (1880), no. 9, p. 120.

11. I.I. Dubasov, 'Tambovskii krai v kontse XVIII i nachale XIX stoletiia', *Istoricheskii vestnik* (1884), no. 9, pp. 573–5.

Despite the lack of respect for priests, they played a vital role in local life (except, of course, in priestless Old Believer villages). Priests could refuse to give the sacrament and could determine who had the right to marry and the right to divorce. Indeed, the Church tightened up control over marriage and divorce in the second half of the eighteenth century and asserted more control over these areas of people's lives. But abuses could also take place here. Priests were accused of charging excessive fees for performing these ceremonies, and of taking bribes to marry under-age couples. Fees were fixed by the Synod in 1765 (for example 3 copecks for a baptism and 10 copecks for a marriage) but in practice larger sums were levied (in Moscow in the late eighteenth century priests charged between 1 and 2 roubles for a marriage). In the early nine-teenth century, Martha Wilmot recorded that, following a false rumour about a forthcoming conscription of unmarried peasant *girls* into the army, peasants tried to marry off young girls in panic, a situation made worse by the priests who 'redoubled the alarm in order to increase their wedding fees'. In some villages the priests 'say'd that the peasants had no time to lose as a fresh Ukase [decree] was expected to stop all Marriages till the regiments were compleat'.[12]

Clergy were also known to participate in acts of disobedience by serfs, sometimes helping to write petitions. Some members of the lower clergy greeted Razin's and Bulavin's armies with bread and salt and conducted prayers and religious processions on behalf of the rebels; a few clergy even actively joined the revolts. In 1767 a priest, G. Borisov, encouraged serfs on the estate of A. Tolstoi, following rumours that they would be freed, and signed their petition; the investigation found that he 'gave most cause for that rebellion and disobedience'.[13] Andrei Bolotov recalled in his memoirs that one of the chief brigands during the Pugachev revolt in the vicinity of his estates was a sexton who, according to Bolotov, assumed he would not be punished as an ordinary thief because of his clerical estate. Conditions during the Pugachev revolt were exceptional, but clergy were also actively involved in peasant disturbances in 1796–97 and in November 1825 it was reported that 'in many places the priests endorsed and led the peasants into disobedience'.[14]

Gov't fears of clergy involvement w/ Pugachev!

The black clergy

The upper hierarchy of bishops and archbishops was recruited from the mon-asteries; unlike the parish clergy, who had to marry before ordination, these priests were unmarried and often better educated. There were some scholarly bishops in eighteenth-century Russia, for example, Simon Legov of Riazan' and Arsenii Vereshchagin of Rostov in the early part of the century and

12. *The Russian Journals of Martha and Catherine Wilmot 1803–1808*, ed. by the Marchioness of Londonderry and H.M. Hyde (London, 1934), p. 355.
13. M.F. Prokhorov, *Krest'ianskoe dvizhenie v tsentral'noi Rossii v tret'ei chetverti XVIII v (po materialam Moskovskoi gubernii)* (Moscow, 1993), p. 74.
14. Gregory L. Freeze, 'The Orthodox Church and Serfdom in Pre-Reform Russia', *Slavic Review* 48, 3 (1989), p. 377.

Metropolitan Platon of Moscow later in the century. Many of the bishops were of Ukrainian origin and had been educated in the Kiev Academy; in 1762 only 12 out of the 26 bishops were Great Russians. Members of the higher clergy and monks could mix in high society; some were of noble origin. Tolchenov, a wealthy merchant, dined with the Father Superior and monks of the Borisoglebsk monastery. However, even amongst the upper hierarchy there could be examples of poor behaviour. Parkinson reported from Astrakhan' at the end of the eighteenth century that:

> The Archbishop's disorder was indolence and Drunkenness. When in the country he devotes himself to those vices. He [is] obliged in the Town to be more on the reserve and therefore prefers the country.[15]

Peter I tried to restrict the number of young men entering monasteries. He instructed that monks should be at least 30 years old and had to serve a three-year probation before taking vows (some monks were also drafted into the army). He fixed, and in so doing reduced, the incomes of some monasteries in Russia and limited the number of monks who were to be maintained within each monastery. Women living in convents were not allowed to take the veil until the age of 40 (raised to 60 in 1722). Nuns were also supposed to be occupied in useful occupations; in 1722 seamstresses were sent to Moscow convents to teach nuns how to spin. Following Catherine's secularization of church land in 1764 (and the transfer of church peasants into economic, or state, peasants) monasteries were categorized and the number of residents and income of each category were determined by the state.

Nevertheless, young men continued to enter monasteries from a sense of vocation, and at a younger age than Peter had decreed. In practice representatives from all social groups, including the nobility, could decide to enter monasteries. Petr Levshin, who became Metropolitan Platon of Moscow, was born in 1737, the son of a sexton. He studied at the Slavonic-Greek-Latin Academy and entered a monastery at the age of 20 when he was already a teacher at the Academy. St Seraphim of Sarov, born in 1759, the son of a Kursk merchant, became a monk at the age of 18. Georgii Mashurin, born 1789, a nobleman who served in the cavalry for eleven years, entered a monastery at the age of 29. Some monasteries created distinguished schools of translators; other monks wrote influential devotional and mystical works. Women's reasons for entering convents were mixed. Only some did so out of a sense of vocation and many of the women in convents did not take vows. The wife of the sacristan Afanasii Sil'vestrov entered a convent with her daughter when her husband became a monk.[16] Some women were forced to enter convents by their relatives in order to secure their property (see Chapter 9). Other women, who had some property with which to endow the convent, chose to live there, sometimes in considerable comfort, for security and companionship.

15. John Parkinson, *A Tour of Russia, Siberia and the Crimea 1792–1794* (London, 1971), p. 178.
16. A.B. Smirnov, 'Zhizn' Afanasiia Sil'vestrova, sel'skago sviashchenika, v inochestve Zakhariia', *Russkaia starina* (1889), no. 2, p. 374.

In the early nineteenth century Robert Ker Porter found about 150 women in the Novodevichii convent in Moscow, of whom only 75 had taken vows, but each of whom had 'a separate apartment and every reasonable comfort'.[17]

THE REJECTION OF ORTHODOXY?

Schismatics and sectarians

The Russian Orthodox Church underwent a schism in the mid-seventeeth century as a consequence of the attempt of the Patriarch Nikon to reform Church texts and liturgical practice. Those who did not accept these changes and rejected the official Orthodox Church became known as Old Believers, or schismatics, and were formally excommunicated by the Church in 1667. On the surface, the split arose over relatively trivial matters of ritual and outward forms (the use of three fingers instead of two when making the sign of the cross, the number of alleluias, the simplification of certain rites, spellings of certain words in texts) but the passionate feelings which these changes aroused can only be understood within the context of the deeply held belief that Russian Orthodoxy alone was pure (as Russia was seen as the 'Third Rome' after the collapse of Constantinople) and this purity could only be maintained through the preservation of existing rituals, form of words and other traditions. This therefore went beyond a scholarly attack on the wording of the texts (although there were grounds for challenging some of the translations used by Nikon); instead the 'incorrect form' of texts could be perceived as the 'incorrect content' and thus heretical. In this context, the fact that the changes were 'Western' in origin was particularly offensive, to the extent of being regarded as the work of the devil, and seen as an attempt to corrupt the eastern Church. Old Believers also found new forms of icon painting and singing to be heretical challenges to sacred symbols. For simple people, the rituals of the Orthodox Church were an essential part of their faith, and the attack on the form of crossing oneself aroused particular passions as this was the most frequently repeated gesture in Orthodox services and in everyday life (see below). In this respect, women were amongst the fiercest supporters of Old Belief; in the initial stages, Archpriest Avvakum (who became the leader of the Old Believers) received considerable support from elite noble ladies, some of whom had developed a passionate attachment to religious ritual.

The struggle took on an apocalyptic flavour as Old Believers believed that the implementation of Nikon's reforms would herald the destruction of the true Muscovite Church and hence the fall of mankind. It was of particular significance in this context that Nikon was active in the year 1666, which contained the number 666, which the Book of Revelation had promised was

---

17. Robert Ker Porter, *Travelling Sketches in Russia and Sweden during the years 1805, 1806, 1807, 1808* (London, 1809), vol. I, p. 241.

the key to the identity of the 'great beast', that is, the Antichrist. This magic number could also be reached by adding the numerical equivalents of letters of the names of tsar Alexis and Nikon. Old Believers soon split into two main groups; the 'priestists' who accepted priests who had been ordained in the Orthodox Church and the 'priestless' who rejected priests altogether (no bishops had gone over to the schismatics, so they could have no validly ordained clergy of their own).

The schism proved to be permanent. The number of Old Believers has been a matter of dispute (see Chapter 1, p. 15). Many Old Believers lived, or fled to, the periphery of the empire, to the north, Siberia, the Cossack communities in the south and the Polish borders. Most Old Believers were peasants or Cossacks, but Old Belief also had an appeal within the merchant community. There were two vigorous and large Old Believer communities in Moscow, which flourished economically. The attraction of Old Belief did not diminish with time. An attempt in Catherine II's reign to reabsorb the Old Believers into mainstream Orthodoxy by allowing them to retain their own rituals while acknowledging the authority of the Orthodox Church (the so-called *edinoverie*, or community of religion, movement) only had limited success with some of the 'priestist' communities. As late as the early nineteenth century, Archbishop Filaret reported that 'The Old Believers . . . exploit the lack of knowledge among the Orthodox to seduce them into the raskol [schism].'[18]

The passion with which many Russians (including priests and parishioners) opposed the reforms of Nikon can be seen by the willing sacrifice of their lives made by Old Believers for their faith. This was normally by means of self-immolation (made easier perhaps by their conviction of the imminent end of world, which initially they predicted would take place in 1691 or 1692, and their belief that salvation would be attained through suicide). The first major resistance to the state took place in the Solovetsk monastery (on the White Sea), which, in defence of the old faith, underwent an eight-year siege by tsarist forces. When the monastery was finally taken in 1676, all but 14 of the 200 or so defenders were killed. In the 1687, Old Believer peasants took over the Paleostrov monastery in Olonets province in the north; as the tsarist troops were about to enter about 2,700 Old Believers burnt themselves to death in the chapel. The following year, the monastery was taken over again and this time about 1,500 Old Believers committed self-immolation as the troops moved in. Such practices continued into the eighteenth century, particularly in Siberia. The reign of Elizabeth saw an increase of self-immolation as persecution revived. A mass self-immolation took place in Tiumen' (in western Siberia) in 1750. In 1756, 200 Old Believers burnt themselves to death in Tomsk province, declaring that:

> In the church is heresy; they serve with five wafers, they stamp the wafers with a Latin cross, they shave, they smoke tobacco, and the priests do not

18. Gregory L. Freeze, 'The Rechristianization of Russia: the Church and Popular Religion, 1750–1850', *Studia Slavica Finlandensia* 7 (1990), p. 107.

hold that to be a sin. What are you doing standing and listening to the servants of Antichrist?[19]

These mass suicides became less common after the accession of Peter III, as he and his successors followed a policy of toleration, but in 1763 over 52 peasants and postdrivers in Tiumen' burnt themselves to death.

Acts of self-immolation only took place when Old Believer communities were directly challenged by the authorities, and were most common in remote parts of the north. Most Old Believers practised their faith without interference by the Church or the government. In addition, there were some well-known communities which were tolerated, most notably those in Moscow and the Vyg community in the north. And the fact that Old Believers were capable of passionate and self-destructive acts does not mean that they were not also capable of spiritual debate or spiritual activity. The Vyg community became established as a cultural centre for Old Belief, and produced new liturgical forms and prayers, learned sermons, historical works and copies of sacred texts as well as developing musical traditions and its own style of icon painting.

The existence of Old Believers created fundamental problems for the Russian Orthodox Church and for the government. For the Church, it meant that a large proportion of the Orthodox population, particularly in the more remote regions, were outside its control and influence – indeed, after the official espousal of tolerance by Catherine II the Church also had officially to tolerate the existence of Old Belief. In addition, the ability of Old Believers to manage without priests threw into question the whole authority and status of the parish clergy. Priests were supposed to inform the Church authorities of the existence of Old Believers, but sometimes those in predominantly Old Believer areas did not dare to do so. Indeed, as parishes had considerable control over the election of priests, they could choose ones who they knew were unlikely to reveal this information, or who could be bribed to perform marriages and baptisms for 'priestist' Old Believers. From the government's point of view, Old Believers could become a rallying-point for the discontented and Old Belief played an important part in *strel'tsy* uprisings and Cossack rebellions (see Chapter 5). Old Believers could also become involved in revolts in factories in the Urals and in the north. Individual Old Believers who professed apocalyptic visions or who denounced tsars as Antichrist could also provoke disorder.

Religious sects

Some Russians sought spirituality within extreme sects. The khlysty ('flagellants', who referred to themselves as 'God's people') originated in the late seventeenth century, as the followers of Daniel Filippov and, in the early eighteenth

19. R.O. Crummey, *The Old Believers & the World of the Antichrist. The Vyg Community and the Russian State 1694–1855* (Madison, Milwaukee, London, 1970), pp. 191–2.

century, Ivan Suslov. The services of the sect commenced with songs and incantations but ended with a whirling, frenzied dance which involved ritual incantations and mutual and self-flagellation. The Molokany (or 'milk-drinkers') sect, so-called because they continued to drink milk during Lent, arose in Tambov province. They also tried to return to a more simple form of Christianity in an attempt to reach a more spiritual way of life; their communities endeavoured to establish equality of wealth. Most extreme were the late eighteenth-century Skoptsy ('self-castrators') sect, who were driven in a state of ecstasy to self-castration during the flagellation process. While most sects appealed to simple peasants, the Skoptsy included amongst their number some wealthy merchants and army officers who felt excluded from Catherine II's inner circle. In the second half of the eighteenth century priestless communities of Dukhobors ('spirit wrestlers') established themselves in Tambov province. Dukhobors rejected the Bible and icons and tried to recreate a simple and moral faith based on simple catechisms and a frugal and moral lifestyle. Despite the peaceful lifestyle of the Dukhobors, they could be persecuted (in part because they rejected conscription). Senator I.V. Lopukhin reported in 1801 on the dukhobors that:

> No sect until now has been so severely prosecuted as the Dukhobors . . .
> Many have been tortured; and whole families have been exiled with hard
> labour and have been incarcerated in the cruellest of prisons. Sometimes
> there has been no room in their cells for them to stand upright or to lie
> down full length . . .[20]

Freemasonry

Old Belief and extreme sects normally held little charm for the aristocratic elite, although N.I. Novikov (the satirist, educationalist and publisher) used the Old Believer habit of using the pre-Petrine system of counting dates from the creation rather than from the birth of Christ and published some Old Believer documents and an apologia for the actions of the Solovetsk defenders. Educated young men who felt unfulfilled by the Orthodox Church, or repelled by the ignorance of the parish clergy, looked to the West for alternatives. Freemasonry was one such movement to which many turned. The attractions of freemasonry were not purely spiritual. Many found lodges to be congenial social and cultural gatherings, which gave them opportunities for intellectual self-development and for involvement in secular charitable activities. Freemasonry circles provided the Russian nobility with a sense of fellowship and belonging and provided a forum for intellectual debate and creative thought.

For others, however, becoming a mason was an experience not dissimilar to a 'religious conversion'. The oath of initiation taken for the highest level of the Harmonia lodge read:

20. George Woodcock, Ivan Avakumovich, *The Dukhobors* (London, 1968), p. 32.

I, - -, freely and after serious consideration, promise: (1) for all my life to worship the eternal, omnipotent Jehovah in spirit and truth; (2) to try as much as possible to know His power and wisdom through nature; (3) to abstain from the vanity of the world; (4) in so far as my ability permits, to strive to promote the well-being of my brothers, to love them and help them, both by advice and action, in all their needs; and finally, (5) to observe unbreakable silence as truthfully as God is immortal.

Many young nobles found comfort in the rituals of freemasonry, in a way which parallels the popularity and importance given to rituals in Orthodoxy. To others, freemasonry offered a seemingly pure and moral set of ethical standards which, although they were based on Christian precepts, they felt they had not been able to practise satisfactorily within the Orthodox Church. The didactic and humanitarian elements of Russian freemasonry – providing help, education, dissemination of useful information, translation activity and charity for all those who needed it – seemed to fill a gap. Finally, freemasonry seemed to offer to some a solution to the conflicting influences of western rational thought and the desire for a more personal, spiritual, experience. 'Finding myself at the crossroads between Voltarianism and religion', wrote Novikov, 'I had no basis on which to work, no cornerstone on which to build spiritual tranquillity, and therefore I fell into the society.'[21]

The first grand master of Russian freemasonry was the Scot James Keith, whose lodge was founded in 1741–42. Keith left Russia in 1747 and information about freemasonry in Elizabeth's reign is patchy, although her favourite, I.I. Shuvalov, was reputed to have been a leading mason, and masonic symbols and motifs began appearing in Russian literature in the 1750s and 1760s. Peter III was reputed to have become a mason and several leading figures at his court were masons. However, freemasonry only became popular amongst the nobility in the reign of Catherine II. This was partly because freemasonry was one of many manifestations of the cultural influence of western and central Europe on the nobility at the time, and partly because, after their freedom from compulsory service in 1762, they had the leisure and opportunity to become involved in private social activities of this nature, both in the capitals and in the provinces.

Russian lodges were based on English, German or Swedish systems. Ivan Elagin, an influential figure at court in the early years of Catherine II, founded the Russian Grand Provincial lodge in 1771, modelled on the English system, which involved progression through three degrees within the lodge. Some 14 lodges were opened in St Petersburg, Moscow and the provinces based on this model. Many Russians, however, were attracted to lodges which had more complex degrees and mystical elements. Baron P.B. Reichel established the Apollo lodge in 1771, which depended on the Grand Lodge of Zinnendorf in Berlin, and soon controlled 8 lodges, including lodges in Geman-speaking

21. James H. Billington, *The Icon and the Axe. An Interpretive History of Russian Culture* (London, 1966), pp. 247–8.

Riga and Reval. In 1776 the Reichel and Elagin lodges merged and accepted the leadership of the Berlin lodge, and Elagin became the grand master of the new united Grand Provincial lodge. Almost immediately, members of this new lodge became influenced by the Swedish Order of the Temple, a lodge which comprised ten degrees, and whose elaborate robes and knightly degrees particularly appealed to a Russian nobility which lacked knightly orders and traditions of medieval chivalry. In 1778 the first Swedish-style lodge, the Phoenix, was set up in St Petersburg, followed in 1780 by the Swedish Grand National lodge under the direction of Prince G.P. Gagarin. In the early 1780s there were 14 Swedish lodges in St Petersburg and Moscow and a few more in the provinces. Most of the Elagin lodges, however, did not join the Swedish system, partly because a direct association with Sweden at a time of diplomatic tension between Russia and Sweden seemed inappropriate.

Adherents of freemasonry continued to seek new models to help them in their search for further illumination or for more satifying rituals and structures. I.G. Schwartz, a member of the Harmonia lodge in Moscow, founded by Nikolai Novikov in 1781, brought Russian freemasonry into close association with the strict observance lodge of the grand master Duke Ferdinand of Brunswick. The lodge became the VIIIth province of the Brunswick lodge, under the acting head of Prince N. Trubetskoi. It is not known how many of the Elagin lodges joined the VIIIth province. Within the VIIIth province there emerged a small esoteric group of masons who were heavily influenced by the Rosicrucian movement, knowledge of whose charters and seven degrees had been brought back to Russia from Berlin by Schwartz. Masonic and Rosicrucian literature spread through Russia, largely as a result of the activity of the private printing presses set up by Novikov (until the 1790s when masonic publications were censured and banned). Lodges were also set up in the provinces, particularly when provincial governors were masons. Governor-General A.P. Mel'gunov, for example, opened a lodge in Iaroslavl'. Vigel' founded a lodge in remote Penza in the late eighteenth century. Even where there was no lodge, provincial nobles could become acquainted with masonry through subscriptions to publications such as Novikov's *Morning Light*.

Who became freemasons? The Russian historian G. Vernadsky estimated that in 1777 4 of the 11-member Council of State, 11 of the 31 gentlemen of the bedchamber, 2 of the 5 senators of the first department of the Senate, 2 of the 5 members of the College of Foreign Affairs and the vice-president of the Admiralty College were masons (there were none known at this date in the War College). A large number of the noble deputies in the Legislative Commission were masons. Members of the high aristocracy and prominent figures at court were attracted to freemasonry, including the Repnins, Trubetskois, Vorontsovs and Panins. Special lodges attracted army officers (like the Mars lodge, founded at Iaşi in Bessarabia in 1774) and naval officers (like the Neptune lodge, founded in 1781 in Kronstadt). There were masons amongst the governors of provinces established after 1775 (including A.P. Mel'gunov in

234

Iaroslavl' and J.E. Sievers in Tver'), and amongst senior officials in central and provincial institutions. Almost all Russian poets, playwrights, authors and academics were masons. Other lodges had a predominantly foreign membership, which included academics, members of professions, bankers and merchants.

Some of the rituals of freemasonry have been recorded. In Reichel's Apollo lodge, a postulant had to remove metallic objects, take off his coat, bare his left breast and right knee and wear a slipper on his left foot. He was then left blindfolded in a vault-like room hung with black, which contained an open grave with a skeleton and a table draped in black cloth. On this was placed a skull holding a burning lamp and a Bible opened at St John's gospel. Meetings of the higher degrees of the Rosicrucians also took place in rooms hung with black cloth. When a new member had been received, the leader of the lodge would distribute bread and wine in the same way as a communion service.

Catherine II had little sympathy for the mystical elements of freemasonry and their educational work and feared that lodges could become venues for conspiracies against the throne. In the 1790s, at a time of international tension following the French Revolution, Catherine became move suspicious of freemasonry, following rumours that Grand Duke Paul, a potential rival centre of power, was being induced to join a Moscow lodge. In 1792 (shortly after the assassination of Gustavus III of Sweden), Novikov's house was searched and masonic books were found which had been banned as harmful in 1786. Novikov was arrested and sentenced, without any formal trial, to fifteen years imprisonment, though he was freed when Paul came to the throne in 1796. In 1794, Catherine ordered the closure of all lodges. Freemasonry continued, however, to attract young educated Russians in the early nineteenth century. The movement was encouraged by the rumours, which cannot be substantiated, that Alexander I became a mason (he certainly visited lodges in Russia and Germany); his younger brother Constantine certainly was a mason. Regional lodges continued to flourish and young army officers who accompanied Russian forces through Europe in 1813 and 1814 also attended, and were influenced by, lodges in the territory through which they passed. The constitutions of secret societies which were formed by army officers in the wake of the Napoleonic Wars, like the Order of the Russian Knights and the Union of Salvation and Welfare, copied some of their rules and hierarchical organization from masonic lodges. In 1815, the higher orders of masonry in Russia were subordinated to the Astrea grand lodge.

Protestant Pietism had an influence in Russia from the early eighteenth century. Pietists were concerned to recreate what they called 'true Christianity' (a phrase from the title of an influential book by Johann Arndt) by replacing dogma with a more emotional personal commitment within the established Church. This developed into an evangelical, missionary movement, based at Halle University, which aimed to establish an inter-confessional and international Christian brotherhood. Pietism was influential in the theological academies in Moscow and Kiev in the early eighteenth century and Pietists set up a number of short-lived schools in Russia in the reign of Peter I. In the 1720s a Pietist 'Herrnhut' community was established in Saxony, from which a missionary religious fraternity, the Moravian Brethren, emerged, with the aim of establishing similar communities throughout the world, including Russia. Taking advantage of Catherine II's decrees encouraging foreign settlement in the early 1760s, the Brethren founded such a community at Sarepta on the Volga. By the 1790s, Pietism had become popular with the Russian aristocracy, in particular because it seemed to offer an alternative to the abstract rationalism of the French Revolution. After the French Revolution Pietism became more closely associated with freemasonry and increasingly mystical; some Pietists and masons sought a new universal inner church and a new society of 'true Christians'. At the beginning of the reign of Alexander I, Pietism became fused with masonry in Russia through the mystical writings of Ivan Lopukhin, a former mason, whose work, written in 1798, *Several Characteristics of the Inner Church, or the one Path to the Truth and the Different Paths to Error and Damnation* supported the idea of a universal church and inner spiritual regeneration, became immensely popular. Following the kind of spiritual conversion experienced by first Prince Aleksandr Golitsyn and then, with his encouragement, by Alexander I in 1812, such ideas were given official backing. This meant actively promoting the activities of the Bible Society, which originated in English Methodism, and which the Moravian Brethren dominated in Russia. Pietists played a particularly active role in establishing provincial masonic lodges, in which German was the main language. But the sudden fall from grace of Golitsyn in 1824 brought an abrupt end to the influence of Pietists and the Bible Society.

MANIFESTATIONS OF RELIGIOUS BELIEF

Crosses, icons, relics

The attraction of Old Belief, sects and, to some extent, freemasonry demonstrated that many Russians failed to find spiritual satisfaction within the official Orthodox Church. Yet travellers to Russia frequently commented on the extent of the outward manifestions of religious belief amongst Russians. (Some of the customs described below, of course, could be practised by Old Believers as well as by mainstream Orthodox believers, and, for that manner, by many Christians in other parts of Europe.) The most obvious public manifestation of popular faith was the frequency and, to the minds of Protestant travellers from western Europe, excessive physical exertion with which peasants crossed themselves. As Catherine Wilmot remarked:

> At the rising & setting of the Sun & on other occasions they begin to cross themselves, but so *obstreperously* that the operation does not finish under qrtr of an hour. They bow their heads down almost to the ground, & then not only *recover their ballance* but throw themselves proportionably back again, crossing themselves at arms length. The old women comfortably

kneel down & kiss the ground (taking the precaution to slip their hands between it & their Lips).[22]

All peasant huts contained an icon corner, which could contain several icons, before which peasants bowed and crossed themselves when they entered the room. As William Coxe noted in the 1780s:

All the members of the family the moment they rose in the morning, and before they retired to sleep in the evening, never omitted standing before the saint; they crossed themselves during several minutes upon the sides and on the forehead; bowed very low, and sometimes even prostrated themselves on the ground. Every peasant also, upon entering the room, always paid his obeisance to this object of worship before he addressed himself to the family.[23]

Noble houses also contained icon corners in the main room, and it was common for icon corners also to be found in the bedrooms, particularly those of the ladies of the house. 'After rising from the table the Russians first cross themselves and bow to their images and then to each other' commented John Ledyard from Siberia in the 1780s.[24] It was common for nobles to own their own personal icons.

Holy relics and icons in churches were also venerated. An icon for which miraculous healing powers were claimed was brought to Moscow, under escort, for Alexis to see in 1647. In Peter's reign, the aristocrat Boris Sheremet'ev proposed to Fedor Apraksin that he should visit the miracle-working icon of the Virgin on his way to visit him on his estate. Holy icons were regularly taken into battle by Russian forces up to 1917. Miracle cults were also common, particularly in the second half of the seventeenth century. In 1666, 'Many sick, deaf and blind people and paralyzed in the arms, and lame, and paralyzed, and bothered by unclean spirits and possessed by various passions were cured and became healthy' at a site at Shuia, near Suzdal'. An investigation by the Archbishop of Suzdal' led to the denunciation of a woman.[25] Religious processions were particularly well attended at times of natural disasters, such as plagues, when holy relics and miracle-working icons would also be paraded. It was the attempt to remove an icon which had became the subject of miraculous stories and a focus for unruly crowds during the plague of Moscow in 1771 that led to the terrible riots and the murder of Archbishop Amvrosii.

Ceremonies and devotion

There were numerous public holidays for religious celebrations (most of which fell outside the main harvest period) including: Epiphany (6 January), the

22. *The Russian Journals*, p. 176.
23. Coxe, *Travels into Poland, Russia*, vol. II, p. 21.
24. *John Ledyard's Journey through Russia and Siberia 1787–1788*, ed. and intro. by Stephen D. Watrous (Madison, Milwaukee, London, 1966), p. 156.
25. P. Bushkovitch, *Religion and Society in Russia. The Sixteenth and Seventeenth Centuries* (New York and Oxford, 1992), pp. 95–6.

Blessing of the Waters (17 January), Candlemas (2 February), the Annunciation (25 March), Palm Sunday, Easter Day, the Ascension of Christ, Pentecost, the Transfiguration (6 August), the Assumption of the Holy Virgin (15 August), Festival of the Holy Virgin's Birth (8 September), the Raising of the Cross (14 September), the Presentation of the Holy Virgin to the Temple (21 November), Christmas (25 December). These were simply the main festivals; Johann-Georg Korb, an Austrian diplomat, stated that 'There are almost as many festivals in Russia as there are days in the year: but the festivals alternate between the different quarters of the city; so that while one quarter is keeping holiday, the other is working.' He claimed that most Russians 'get through their sacred functions in the dark', so that the rest of the day 'they consecrate, if not to work, at least to debauchery'![26]

Travellers commented in particular on the mass participation in public religious ceremonies. The ceremony of the blessing of the waters took place throughout Russia and was described by Olearius in the seventeenth century:

> When he [the priest] had finished, the women grabbed their children, large and small, in their nightshirts or without, and submerged them three times in the stream. Some of the adults also jumped in. Finally they brought the horses, too, to drink of the holy, health-giving water. Afterward, they returned to the church to be blessed.[27]

All sectors of society participated enthusiastically in the Easter celebrations. Captain James Jefferyes commented in 1719 that 'After a Lent, as long as it is rigorous, their appetite is so ravenous that there are very few houses where they do not commence feasting at the very arrival of Easter day and go to such excess that many make themselves ill and have to keep to their beds while others are amusing themselves.'[28]

In addition, saints' days were keenly observed, as in Catholic Europe. As Baroness Dimsdale noted:

> The Russians apprehend that every Day of the Year is consecrated to some particular Saint and believe that every individual is under the peculiar Protection of that holy Person on whose Day they happen to be born, and it is usual to name them after the Saint, I believe all of them carry a small metal Picture of their tutelary Saint about their Persons . . . A Russian Woman of the lower ranks would not go a Journey without her tutelary Saint and in case she was to forget it, would expect some great Misfortune to befall her before she returned home.[29]

26. [Jonann-Georg Korb], *Diary of an Austrian Secretary of Legation at the Court of Czar Peter the Great*, trans. by Count Mac Donnell (London, 1863), vol. II, pp. 182–3.
27. *The Travels of Olearius in Seventeenth-Century Russia*, ed. by Samuel H. Baron (Stanford, 1967), p. 53.
28. *Historical Manuscripts Commission. Report on the MSS of Lord Polwarth, preserved at Mertoun House Berwickshire* (London, 1916), vol. II, pp. 116–17, Jefferyes to Polwarth, 3 April 1719.
29. *An English Lady at the Court of Catherine the Great. The Journal of Baroness Elizabeth Dimsdale, 1781*, ed. by A.G. Cross (Cambridge, 1989), p. 47.

In 1799 after the battle of Zurich:

> ... there was hardly one of the mortally-wounded Russians who had not clutched at the image of the patron saint which he wore about his neck, and pressed it to his lips before drawing his last breath.[30]

Russians attended church regularly. Aleksandr Menshikov attended services almost daily while he was on military service in the Ukraine in 1720. The merchant Ivan Tolchenov recorded his frequent visits to church in his diaries. In May 1776, for example, he recorded seven attendances, including two processions with the cross; in January 1805 he attended the liturgy almost every day, a pattern which continued throughout the year. The level of attendance by peasants is hard to determine, but several noble landowners instructed their stewards to keep a record, which perhaps suggests that it cannot be assumed that all peasants automatically went to church.

Travellers commented on the fervour of the congregation which, to British travellers in particular, was seen as excessive and uncivilized. Collins, writing in the late seventeenth century, commented that 'upon some great Vigils they stay all night in their Churches, at certain times prostrating and crossing themselves, and knocking their heads against the Ground'.[31] On the other hand, the Russian clergy complained that churches, and church services, were not always treated with respect. In 1759 the Metropolitan of Moscow found that:

> At many churches in important parishes, during the summer holidays, eating tents are set up and wine and beer are sold. This is very indecent. For, having been drinking in the tent, the common people are a source of much noise and shouting during the vespers and matins, and even liturgy ...

Twenty years later, a priest complained that 'Young men and women, on holidays and Sundays during church services, conduct idle conversations and, standing inside the church, laugh indecently, and say shameful words.'[32] This comment relates to the behaviour of the common people but in Peter I's reign the elite were obliged to participate in rowdy mock religious ceremonies. This could lead to curious hybrid behaviour. On Christmas Day 1716, Prince Aleksandr Menshikov rose at 5 a.m. for morning prayers, attended mass in the morning and dined until 3 p.m. He then visited the home of Ivan Buturlin, the mock 'Bishop of St Petersburg', sang bawdy carols at the house of the mock Prince-Pope and returned to Buturlin's house for supper.

In the seventeenth century, nobles founded churches or private chapels as a mark of devotion. The founding of private chapels was discouraged by the government in the eighteenth century as it led to an uncontrollable expansion in posts for clergy. But nobles continued to donate money to monasteries and churches and to build chapels and churches and bell towers on their estates.

---

30. Christopher Duffy, *Russia's Military Way to the West: Origins and Nature of Russian Military Power 1700–1800* (London, 1981), p. 135.
31. Samuel Collins, *The Present State of Russia* (London, 1671), pp. 3–4.
32. Freeze, *The Russian Levites*, p. 176.

Aleksei Kablukov, a wealthy provincial noble in the second half of the seventeenth century in Suzdal' and Shuia, regularly donated money to the Shuia Trinity-Saviour Monastery 'to pray for the souls of his relatives' and contributed sums for the construction of the church of the Virgin of Kazan' in Shuia. After the Iankov home had been destroyed in the Napoleonic invasion of 1812 the family rebuilt the chapel first as:

> We thought that God had punished us because we had built the [new] house and not finished decorating the church, so now we decided to finish at least one of the chapels, and then worry about the house.[33]

Merchants also donated money to build and restore churches and to have icons painted. The new welfare institutions established by Catherine II in 1775 had to compete with more traditional recipients of charitable donations. Governor-General A.P. Mel'gunov was only able to get a donation of bricks from the merchants of Iaroslavl' for his new charitable home in the 1780s when he threatened otherwise to demolish for this purpose a brick tower which held a precious icon. Convents were also maintained at the expense of local laymen, partly as a refuge for elderly or unmarried female relations. In 1765, that is, after Catherine II's secularization of Church property, the gentry and merchants of the town of Bolkhov Rozhdestvo petitioned the Metropolitan of Moscow and the Synod to be allowed to continue to support the convent which maintained their relations.

The act of Christian charity, particularly the giving of alms to beggars, was encouraged by the Orthodox Church and was an accepted popular custom, to the extent that the actions of the state in establishing institutional structures for poor relief (see Chapter 5), and in imposing fines on almsgivers in 1718 and 1720, could be regarded as an encroachment on the moral obligations of the individual and as an unwelcome attempt to graft a 'western' (Catholic and Protestant) concept of state charity onto different, Orthodox, traditions. In 1647 tsar Alexis gave 10 copecks each to 100 beggars and 3 copecks each to a further 100. Bishop Tikhon of Zadonsk (1724–83) stated that it was 'the duty of the rich man to give, the beggar to accept gratefully, and to shower the giver with zealous prayers'. In the early eighteenth century Count Sheremet'ev fed up to 50 people a day at an 'open table' on his estate. In the second half of the eighteenth century, Anna Labzina, a minor noblewoman, recounted that her parents gave gifts and food to beggars for three days to celebrate her birth. Later, she accompanied her widowed mother on weekly visits to the prisons, bringing gifts of money and clothing and caring for the sick. The philanthropic activities of the freemasons followed this Orthodox tradition – N.I. Novikov established two schools for poor children and Governor-General A.P. Mel'gunov opened an orphanage in Iaroslavl'. In the early nineteenth century some of this charitable work became chanelled through formal charitable

---

33. Priscilla Roosevelt, *Life on the Russian Country Estate. A Social and Cultural History* (New Haven and London, 1995), p. 271.

and mutual aid societies but the practice of individual donations of alms to pilgrims, prisoners, convicts and beggars continued, despite the state's attempt to outlaw the latter activity.

Devout Russians of all social backgrounds went on pilgrimages within and outside the Russian empire. This included the tsars, who, admittedly, often managed to combine pleasure with piety. Immediately after Alexis's coronation he went to pray at Mozhaisk, Zvenigorod and Borovsk; in 1650 he spent over a month on a pilgrimage (although hunting parties were arranged at the same time). Elizabeth regularly visited the Tikhvin monastery to pray to the Virgin of Tikhvin and visited the Kiev caves. But as the future Catherine II recorded with irony:

> The empress spent much time at the stops, also went on foot and often rode to the hunt . . . There was constantly music, balls and gambling, which went so far that sometimes forty to fifty thousand roubles were lost at gaming tables.[34]

The father of Mother Angelina (she was born in 1809 and set up a religious community in the mid-nineteenth century), a wealthy nobleman, frequently went on pilgrimages, including several visits to Kiev. Matrona Naumovna Popova (born 1769), daughter of a sacristan, was a pilgrim to Zadonsk, the Solovetsk monastery (a distance of 1500 kilometres) and Kiev; she returned to Zadonsk and established a mission to care for other pilgrims. Anastasiia Logacheva (born 1809), from a peasant background, lived most of her adult life as a hermit and had a reputation locally for her piety and wisdom, but also spent nine months on a pilgrimage to Jerusalem. Khristofor Aladzhalov, an Armenian merchant in Rostov-on-Don, noted in his diary for 1798 the passage of pilgrims through the town who had attempted to reach Jerusalem to visit the holy places but who had turned back at Jaffa. Pilgrims were respected figures and were often given shelter, food and alms at noble estates.

Fasts

The seriousness with which Russians kept their fasts was remarked upon by many travellers, often with incredulity. 'I have seen with Astonishment how zealous they are in observing their Fasts, and some of the Peasants are even so superstitious, that in those Times they refuse to sell Milk or Eggs to Travellers', commented Weber.[35] Fasting could take place for over 30 weeks of the year. The main fasts were at Christmas and Lent (seven weeks) but outside fast periods, Wednesday and Fridays were normally also fast days. In practice, the peasant diet included only a limited amount of meat so that fasting did not necessarily mean a complete transformation of their normal diet. The great fast in Lent also coincided with the greatest shortage of foodstuffs

---

34. Quoted in Evgeny V. Anisimov, *Empress Elizabeth. Her Reign and Her Russia 1741–1761*, ed. and trans. by John T. Alexander (Gulf Breeze, 1995), p. 177.
35. Friedrich Christian Weber, *The Present State of Russia* (London, 1968), vol. I, p. 121.

following the winter before the spring crops were harvested. But this practical side to fasting should not be exaggerated. Of particular concern to the state was the refusal of peasant soldiers and sailors to abandon their fasts on campaign, with dire results, at least in the early eighteenth century. Weber commented in Peter I's reign that many soldiers died through disease 'and the more, because their Superstition will not allow them to break their long Fasts'.[36] Christopher Hermann von Manstein found that during the Ochakov campaign in the 1730s 'though the synod grants them a dispensation for eating flesh during the actual campaign, there are few that choose to take the benefit of it, preferring death to the sin of breaking their rule'.[37]

It does seem, however, that wealthier members of society became less conscientious about fasts during the eighteenth century and that this marked a division between the customs of nobles and the rest of Russian society. Weber commented in Peter's reign that 'Those Persons who have seen foreign Countries have pretty well broke through this cruel Custom of fasting, but the Common People, and others who affect an extraordinary Devotion, are strict Observers of it, and look upon breaking the Fast as a most heinous Crime.'[38] In the early nineteenth century Robert Pinkerton remarked that:

> The merchants and middle classes observe the fasts with nearly equal rigour: but the nobles in general do not subject themselves too strictly to these privations; except the aged females among them . . .[39]

Even when the nobility did observe fasts, this did not necessarily mean that they suffered overmuch. Martha Wilmot noted that at the sound of the cathedral bell 'those who are engaged in eating their last supper of substantial food drop their knives and forks' and 'All are forsaken in a moment', yet, she continued 'the variety of fast dishes is incredible, we had 23 to-day'![40]

Personal faith

Of course the external manifestations of religious belief do not reveal the depth and extent of religious understanding of the individual. Many travellers, especially Protestant ones, denounced superstitious ignorance on the part of the Russians simply through prejudice towards religious practices which seemed excessive and strange to their eyes. A fundamental problem in determining the genuineness of the Christian elements of faith as opposed to magical or pagan practice is that it is impossible to be sure of the motivation behind the actions of individuals. To give one example, the crossing of oneself, so much commented upon by travellers, could be either an example of genuine

36. Weber, *The Present State of Russia*, vol. I, p. 54.
37. Christopher Hermann v. Manstein, *Contemporary Memoirs of Russia from the year 1727 to 1744*, ed. by David Hume (London, 1856), pp. 170–1.
38. Weber, *The Present State of Russia*, vol. I, p. 344.
39. Robert Pinkerton, *Russia: or, Miscellaneous Observations on the Past and Present State of that Country and its Inhabitants* (London, 1833), p. 72.
40. *The Russian Journals*, pp. 85, 97.

devotion, or an unthinking habit, or a means to ward off evil spirits – or a mixture of all three. The same can be said of the invocation of saints and the worship of icons.

Most Russians would have to comply with the accepted religious practices whatever their inner beliefs, although an odd case came before the Secret Chancellery in 1755, in the reign of Elizabeth, of an *odnodvorets* who, it was claimed (he was denounced by his wife), never went to church, stated that God did not exist, threw the icons in his house on the floor and removed his cross, as well as accusing Elizabeth of being 'worse than a simple woman' – presumably this was the reason the case reached the court. However, this was an exception and was likely an attempt to blacken further the character of someone accused of treason.[41] Memoirs give some insight into the depth of the beliefs of members of the nobility, but the evidence remains inconclusive. The writer Alexander Herzen (born in 1812) stated that 'I took the sacrament after the early service in Holy Week, and, after devouring eggs coloured red, *paskha* and Easter cakes, I thought no more of religion for the rest of the year'.[42]

Other memoirists could record a rather different picture. Praskov'ia Tatlina (born 1808) was constantly made aware of the 'fear of God' as a child: 'My mother described herself as filled with the suffering of Job, and said that a man without religion was lost, and my father repeated: do not bow to anyone except God.' That this was becoming rather old-fashioned for the time, however, can be seen by the fact that she described this childhood as 'Old Russian' and that 'A completely different atmosphere was found in the house of my uncle and aunt', which she herself was attracted to in 'spirit'.[43] It is even more difficult to ascertain the depth of religious feeling in other social groups where memoirs are sparse. The monk, Nikolai Il'inskii, described the faith of his great-grandmother:

> She always had her rosary on her belt . . . She, having them in her right hand, prayed morning and evening . . . Often she woke up at night and, having got up without a fire, prayed to God with this rosary, bowing to the ground sometimes one hundred times, sometimes two hundred times and more'.[44]

Individual Russians, from all social backgrounds, could choose a life of prayer and devotion. Matrona Naumovna Popova, daughter of a sacristan, who later set up a mission in Zadonsk to help pilgrims, recalled that she underwent a spiritual conversion after meeting a hermit, Melaniia:

> . . . Melaniia explained to me the limitless love of God to fallen humanity; and along with this she laid bare the different paths to salvation . . . Hearing

41. Iu.Ia. Kogan, *Ocherki po istorii russkoi ateisticheskoi mysli XVIIIv* (Moscow, 1962), p. 96.
42. *My Past and Thoughts. The Memoirs of Alexander Herzen*, trans. by Constance Garnett, intro. by Isaiah Berlin, (London, 1968), vol. I, p. 42.
43. 'Vospominaniia Praskov'i Nikolaevny Tatlinoi (1812–1854)', *Russkii arkhiv* (1899), no. 10, p. 195.
44. 'Iz zapisok Nikolaia Stepanovicha Il'inskago', *Russkii arkhiv* (1879), no. 12, p. 384.

her I cried from the tender emotion awakened in me by the edifying, almost unearthly conversation; after this, wordly life . . . although it had never pleased me, now lost for once and for all its attraction for me.[45]

Monks who devoted themselves to lives of prayer and meditation, or who became holy recluses, such as St Serafim of Sarov (1759–1833), inspired others to follow their way of life.

PAGANISM AND MAGIC

Pagan festivals and sprites

Pagan festivals coincided with the summer and winter solstices (as they did in many parts of Europe at the time). On the day of St John Kupalo, around the time of the summer solstice, peasants made a special 'nosegay of nettles, thistles and other prickly plants, as an insulting offering' to wood sprites. Peasants and their cattle then jumped over this nosegay, and over a bonfire at night, the aim being to render these wood nymphs harmless.[46] Indeed, 'On this ominous night the calves are allowed to spend the night with the cows, for fear that witches might dry up their milk; and the windows of the huts are all carefully garnished with nettles.' At the end of December (during the 12 days of Christmas) Sviatki took place (probably in pre-Christian time to celebrate the winter solstice), described as follows in the early nineteenth century:

> . . . the youths of all ranks, in almost every house, are masked, and unite in dancing and play, or in evening parties; at which enigmatical songs are sung, and many youthful tricks and gambols played off. They go and hearken at the windows of their neighbours; they pour melted wax or lead into water, and divine, from the figure it assumes, what their future fortune is to be; &c. &c.[47]

The songs (*koliadki*) concerned prosperity and luck, and contained invocations to Koliada, a personification of the season; they contained almost no Christian motifs.

Other pagan rituals took place at key points in the agricultural year but some also coincided with major Christian festivals. Holy ('Clean') Thursday involved preparation for Easter but was also a ritual purification of the farm before spring work commenced. It was customary to make magic protective rings around the farms by circling them with an icon to prevent the penetration of evil spirits. The festival of Semik, or Rusal'naia week or Trinity week, took place for a week around the time of Pentecost. According to Matthew

45. Brenda Meehan, *Holy Women of Russia. The Lives of Five Orthodox Women Offer Spiritual Guidance for Today* (San Francisco, 1993), p. 62.
46. BL, Add. MS 14,390, ff. 73v–79v, Matthew Guthrie, *Noctes Rossicae, or Russian Evening Recreations.*
47. Pinkerton, *Russia*, pp. 202–3.

Guthrie, who made a special study of peasant practices in the 1780s, a branch was prepared by villagers to represent 'the Spreading Birth' and special dances were performed and songs were sung which, amongst other things, invoked the goddess Lada. Houses and churches were decorated with branches and flowers. The ceremony came to a conclusion on Trinity Sunday when the branch 'is Conducted in great Ceremony followed by the whole joyous band, to the nearest Water, where it is dispoiled of all its gay ribbons & Streamers, and Committed to the Deep'. An important part of these ceremonies was the ritual making and destruction of a straw doll which was supposed to represent *rusalka*, a female sprite. According to Pinkerton, writing in the early nineteenth century, these ceremonies took place in 'every town and village in Russia proper', including 'the streets of Petersburg'.[48] Towns had their own festivals, in which local peasantry and peasants living in the towns would also participate. In Voronezh, for example, in the eighteenth century the festival of Iarilo was celebrated on 4 June. Someone was chosen by the townspeople and the resident peasants as Iarilo, and crowned with a special cap with little bells. This would be followed by dancing, games and drunken festivities.

Peasants had a deep-rooted belief in sprites which probably pre-dated Christianity. There were regional variations in belief about sprites, but almost all peasants believed that each home had its resident sprite, which normally lived near the stove, under the threshold or in the attic. The sprite could punish sloppy household management, abusive language and neglect and disrespect of him by causing walls to creak, pots to bang, milk to curdle, threads to tangle, etc. His power was such that peasants tried not to offend him by making loud noises or whistling for fear that he would take revenge or leave the house altogether; he was normally referred to obliquely by euphemisms. His actions could also be interpreted as omens. Gradually the house sprite became associated with the devil (having a tiny horn and a tail, for example) but this did not take place generally until the end of the nineteenth century; before this time, the purely pagan, non-Christian image of the house sprite seems to have predominated. The village bathhouse and theshing barn contained their own sprites, the *bannik* and the *ovennik*, both of whom could be harmful if offended. The forests, water and fields were also believed to have their own sprites (known as the *leshii*, *vodianoi* and *polevoi*). In addition, belief in the *rusalka*, who could be the soul of an unbaptized or stillborn baby or a drowned young girl, was common in South Russia and the Ukraine.

Magic

Pagan festivals were essentially rural affairs, and sprites were normally associated with rural life, although, as has been seen above, some ceremonies and practices were transported to the towns, which, of course, included peasant permanent or temporary residents. Many of the magical practices described

48. Pinkerton, *Russia*, p. 201.

below are also associated with matters which particularly concerned peasants (weather, harvests, etc.), but belief in sorcery, magic and omens and the practice of divination was not confined to the lower orders. Certainly in the mid-seventeenth century, religion, magic, science and superstition coexisted in the world view of all levels of society (and not just in Russia, of course). Tsar Alexis ordered the collection of magic herbs at midsummer. In 1670, as his son lay dying, Alexis sent an under-secretary to search the house of an old sorceress who had recently died 'for roots, herbs, stones and written spells which she used to help guard sick people from bewitchments' and to question her daughter 'whether she had taught her skills to anyone else'.[49]

From the time of the reign of Peter I, and the westernization and secularization which took place at the upper levels of society, magic played a less fundamental role in the life of the higher orders. It should be noted, however, that Peter I recorded his dreams and that many of the activities associated with masonry, which attracted some of the noble elite of Russia, blurred the boundaries between mysticism and magic. Yet all members of society could be influenced to some degree in their actions by magical practice and superstitions. In 1731, a *landrat* (chief administrator) of Novgorod was accused of possessing spells and prayers for childbirth and bewitching guns, dream and prediction books and a variety of herbs, roots and coloured stones. In 1754, Porfirii, Bishop of Suzdal', reported that magic and witchcraft were rife and could be found in practically every home, especially at the time of weddings and childbirth (he asked the Synod to relieve him of all his duties).[50] Such beliefs persisted into the nineteenth century. Martha Wilmot commented in 1807 that:

> The lower orders believe *rigidly* in the power & influence of Fairys, Witches, &c. &c. &c. &c. The Higher Orders to a Man to a Woman play *la bonne avanture* on the Cards & are happy or miserable according to the good or bad Omens of the fortune telling cards.[51]

Many of the practices described below have west European equivalents and it should not be thought that Russia was necessarily exceptional in this respect. Where Russia differed was in the relative freedom with which peasant society in particular pursued these practices without effective restrictions from either the Church or the government. Magicians in Russia were traditionally male (the *koldun* or wizard) but women (often the midwife) were also involved in sorcery and fortune-telling. The places most associated with magic and divination were bathhouses and crossroads, although churches, cemeteries, barns, thresholds, holes in the ice and hopfields could also be magical places. The most magical time was midnight; thus, the best conditions for magic were in the bathhouse at midnight. Almost all Russian villages had bathhouses,

49. Philip Longworth, *Alexis Tsar of All the Russias* (London, 1984), p. 198.
50. Most of the section on magic is drawn from the forthcoming publication by W.F. Ryan, *The Bathhouse at Midnight: An Historical Survey of Magic and Divination in Russia.*
51. *The Russian Journals*, p. 286.

about which there were also many superstitions (the sprite of the bathhouse, the *bannik*, was generally held to be the most malicious of all sprites). Birth normally took place in the bathhouse, as did the ritual songs and bathing of the bride before her marriage.

At its most fundamental level magic was concerned with matters of life and death, love and happiness, things which concerned all classes equally. The high rate of infant and child mortality at all levels of society led to magical and pagan practices surrounding birth and the first few years of the child. Special herbal potions, chants, spells, various objects worn by the bride at her wedding and amulets were used by peasants at the times of childbirth. Spells were also said over the new-born child by the midwife. It was thought that particular demons preyed on children, which stole or possessed them or, less seriously, kept them awake and crying at night. It was thought to be bad luck to show children a mirror, lift them above eye-level, talk to them during washing or cut their nails or hair before their first birthday. Pinkerton commented that children were not addressed by their Christian name in the presence of strangers for fear that this would put an evil spell on the child, and 'after such an inauspicious encounter, they spit several times on the ground, repeating, at the same time, prayers against the effects of the *evil-eye* and all Satanic influences'.[52] Miscarriages, stillbirths and infant death were not only suffered by peasant women. The sister of Bolotov, a provincial nobleman, lost several children in infancy and thereafter put her trust for the survival of her new infant son in such things as a particular icon and naming him after the first person she met. Such superstitions are not, of course, unique either to Russia or to the eighteenth century.

Magic, mainly in the form of love potions or spells, was used to gain or recapture the love of, usually, the husband or lover. In 1770, a peasant was accused of using a magic charm to gain the love of a widow; he had to write certain words and breathe them into a bottle of wine which she was then to drink. In 1812 Dar'ia Karganova (from Verkhne-Omsk volost', Siberia) admitted adding 'magical remedies' to her husband's food so that 'he would not torment her, but love her'.[53] Spells were also employed to ward off and cure impotence and other illnesses (at a time when medical services were in their infancy). Magic concerned survival and prosperity in all walks of life. Spells and magical rituals connected with agricultural life were common in rural communities to ensure, among other things, abundant harvests, successful hunting, the retrieval of lost livestock, good weather and to ward off natural disasters. Merchants had spells to aid success in business. Soldiers had special spells to heal wounds and to prevent the misfire of weapons.

Malefic magic (the use of spells and potions for harmful purposes) could be used to destroy the love of rivals and to harm or even kill enemies. In 1740, Il'ia Chovpilo, the servant of a colonel, was accused of writing, in blood, a

---

52. Pinkerton, *Russia*, p. 155.
53. N.A. Minenko, *Russkaia krest'ianskaia sem'ia v zapadnoi Sibiri (XVIII–pervoi poloviny XIX v)* (Novosibirsk, 1979), p. 130.

pact with the 'prince of devils'. In 1753, a group of peasants on an estate near Suzdal' were accused of acquiring a spell to kill their master (this involved bewitching a piece of wax by reading a spell-book in front of an icon, doing a somersault over a knife stuck in the floor, and rubbing the wax on the intended victim's bed, shoes and threshold). Less seriously, in 1815, a peasant, Mikhail Chukharev, was found guilty of casting a spell to inflict hiccups on his cousin; he was condemned to 35 blows of the knout and a public penance. It was common, as elsewhere in the world, to make dolls in the image of the person to be harmed. Malefic magic was not confined to the lower classes. In the late seventeenth century fear of spells directed against members of the court was common and all members of the tsarina's household had to swear not to make spells or keep herbs or roots. One of the potential brides paraded before tsar Alexis fainted and it was rumoured that witchcraft was responsible. Martha Wilmot, in the early nineteenth century, commented sarcastically that:

> New storys too are coming to light about Mme S[cherbenin] who has been plotting with *Sorcerers* the destruction of her Mother, Sister in Law, & me. A powerful Charm was to have bewitch'd us, alienated our reason or kill'd us.[54]

Much magic was used for predictions – mainly to determine future spouses (usually, but not always, husbands), but also to determine such things as the sex of children, the weather (of crucial importance to peasant farmers) or future well-being and prosperity. The future could be foretold by cards, dreams, beans, interpreting shapes of molten wax, rings and other objects in a bowl of water, the shape of smoke and flames, conjuring up images in mirrors, particular sounds and overheard words, counting odd and even numbers, chance meetings, marks left by cinders or snow, oracles concerned with animals such as grain pecked by hens, etc. Divination concerning future spouses was particularly common at Yuletide, midsummer and Semik (around the time of Pentecost). It must be remembered that amongst many peasant communities the choice of husbands was of necessity rather limited. Therefore conjuring the image or name of one's future spouse by these means would be less open-ended and unpredicable than in a more mobile society. A manuscript penitential dating from the eighteenth century condemned what seems the dangerous practice of predicting the sex of new-born children: 'pregnant women giving bread to a bear; if it growls she will have a girl; if it is silent, a boy' (semi-tamed bears were used in popular entertainment and involved in some wedding rituals).

Popular divination was not confined to peasants. The difference, however, was that such activities became merely a pleasant social pastime for other social groups rather than something which could be perceived as a serious prediction of weather or of economic and physical survival. Divinations at

---

54. *The Russian Journals*, p. 290.

Yuletide celebrations, for example, had become a matter of harmless fun for most for merchants and nobles by the mid-nineteenth century and were only taken more seriously by the elderly female peasant members of the household. Fortune-telling and divination were common to all classes. Divination which took place from coffee grounds and beans was, however, by its very nature, restricted to the classes which consumed coffee, that is, the nobility and the prosperous merchantry (John Capodistria, one of Alexander I's ministers and a native of Corfu, visited a 95-year-old Finnish woman who told fortunes from cards and from coffee cups). Published fortune-telling and dream inter-pretation books were available from the 1760s (and banned only after 1918). This meant that what was largely an oral culture amongst peasants became accessible to literate townspeople and nobles (particularly noble ladies). Parkinson commented at the end of the eighteenth century (with an unusual honesty amongst western observers in noting an English parallel!) that on 11 January:

> At Count Golofkin's they were casting lead for the purpose of telling for-tunes, a piece of superstition constantly practised on the eve of the new year. The also make use of wax for the same purpose. On this night they have also several other superstitious practices which among us are observed on St Mark's eve.[55]

In the 1820s the rediscovery of folk belief by Russian Romantics led to divina-tion becoming fashionable for the educated elite. Aleksandr Pushkin owned a dreambook and a cartomantic guide; both Pushkin and the poet K.F. Ryleev consulted professional fortune-tellers. In Pushkin's *Eugene Onegin*, the heroine, Tatiana, a provincial landowner's daughter, demonstrates her knowledge of fortune-telling from consulting cards, a vision in the mirror she puts under her pillow at night, the shapes formed by molten wax, and rings in a bowl, and believes the name of her future husband will be that of the first man whose name she asks. In particular, she relies for telling her fortune on a dream book, the dream book of Martin Zadeka, which she bought from a pedlar.

There was a general belief amongst all classes in bad omens, such as chance meetings, animals or priests crossing one's path, and meetings at crossroads and other transitional places such as bridges, porches or threshholds. Weather predictions were particularly important in agricultural life and linked with proverbs, similar variants of which can be found all over Europe. Some dates in the year and days of the week were considered lucky or unlucky. February 29th was considered a particularly unlucky date (St Cassian, whose feast was on 29 February also became associated with malefic magic and misfortune). Friday was popularly regarded as especially unlucky (a belief which had both pagan and Christian origins), as it can still be in Britain when the 13th of the month falls on a Friday. Journeys in Russia could be hazardous, and this generated a series of superstitions. Martha Wilmot commented that 'there is a

---

55. Parkinson, *A Tour of Russia*, p. 75.

Superstition in Russia that no one should begin a Journey on a Monday'.[56] In addition, travellers had to sit for a moment before setting out and it was (and still is) customary not to cross back over the threshold once one has gone through the door.

The law and magic

In 1551, Ivan IV summoned a special a council of the Church to debate a list of moral and ecclesiastical questions prepared by him. The proceedings (known as the *Stoglav*) of the council outlined the canon law precedents for dealing with sorcery and magic. They also, however, advised that magical practices should be punished not only by excommunication but also by 'political disgrace', recognizing that the secular authorities had a role to play in the eradication of such practices. This arose partly because witchcraft could be linked with conspiracy against the state. On 22 April 1670, Artamon Matveev, a senior army commander, was accused of attempting to influence the tsar's choice of bride by sorcery. In 1671, one of the tsarina's serving women was tortured on suspicion that she had intended to perform malefic magic on her mistress or to poison her by stealing mushrooms and salt. In 1689–90, Prince Golitsyn and Sil'vestr Medvedev were accused of using astrology and magic in plotting to kill the young tsar Peter. This may account for the number of court cases concerning witchcraft which were tried as treason cases (the phrase in the second chapter of the Code of 1649 on crimes against the tsar, 'if anyone should have evil designs on the health of the tsar', has been interpreted as having witchcraft and magic in mind).

Peter I introduced severe punishments for witchcraft in his Code of Military Law of 1716 (based, however, on the penalties on witchcraft in the Swedish military code). The first article reads:

> If any soldier is found to be an idol-worshipper, black magician, gun-charmer, or superstitious and blasphemous enchanter, depending on the nature of the offence he shall be placed under close arrest, put in irons, made to run the gauntlet, or be burned to death.

This was the first time that a law against witchcraft in Russia was not based on canon law (furthermore, ecclesiastical courts after this date could apply this military law in cases of heresy, witchcraft or blasphemy). It also helped to explain why so many soldiers feature in witchcraft cases in the eighteenth century. The Military Code was regularly used not just in military courts but also civil courts until the full codification of laws in the reign of Nicholas I. At a local level, the peasant commune could punish villagers for harmful witchcraft (although many magical practices would be accepted by the peasants

---

56. *The Russian Journals*, pp. 325–6.

as normal and, indeed, beneficial). In 1820, the commune of the village of Sibirtsevo in Siberia investigated a case of sorcery allegedly inflicted on thirteen peasant women and girls by a peasant woman, Dar'ia Gorchakova, and a soldier's wife, who was in possession of 'some dried herbs' (the case was referred to the district court and then the provincial criminal chamber).

The government, and the Church, objected to the music and dancing of wandering jesters, or *skomorokhi*. This was partly because these occasions often descended into drunken revelry and disorder. Jesters also had a reputation for telling satirical tales and jokes about people in authority. The dances were also supposed to induce a trance-like state and were associated with fortune-telling. And the drum used by the *skomorokhi* was similar to that used by shamans and as such was associated with sorcery and divination. In 1648, Alexis issued a decree instructing people to attend church and forbidding immoderate drinking, jesters, music, masks, divination, curses, bawdy songs, dances, devilish peformances, etc. The decree followed a report from Belgorod that:

> ... lay people of all ranks, their wives and children, do not go to God's churches during the holy singing on Sundays and the Lord's days and major festivals and drunkenness has multiplied among people of all sorts, and every sort of disorderly devilish activity, frivolity and jesters with all sorts of devilish games.[57]

Anyone indulging in such activities were to be beaten with rods and could be exiled for a third offence. *Skomorokhi* themselves were to be flogged for a first offence and flogged again and fined for a second offence. In practice, these activities continued into the early eighteenth century. In 1719, the archimandrite ordered that the traditional *skomorokhi* instruments played by monastic workers at the Aleksandr Nevskii monastery in St Petersburg were to be taken and smashed.

The Church, Christianity and magic

The relationship between the Church and magic was a complex one. Wandering holy fools posed a particular problem for the Church as they were venerated and respected by nobles and merchants as well as by simple people. Holy fools were linked with pagan shamanistic practices, in particular because some of them dressed like shamans and carried similar trinkets. They also sometimes performed ritualistic dances, fell into trances and were held responsible for inducing a state of hysteria. In the eighteenth century, a 'false holy fool', called Vassilii, aged 20, was brought before the Synod, accused of murder, rape, making the sign of the cross with two fingers (that is, Old Believer practice), performing evil magic, having devils at his command (whom he

---

57. R.E.F. Smith, David Christian, *Bread and Salt. A Social and Economic History of Food and Drink in Russia* (Cambridge, 1984), p. 150.

used to jam watermills) and bringing treasure from Greece, Turkey and Sweden! The case was referred to the Justice College because of his 'wizardry and having devils'. Holy fools continued to exist in the nineteenth century (despite Peter I declaring holy fools to be insane and forbidding them to inherit property and marry). They were apparently fashionable with the members of the aristocracy in the reign of Alexander I as mediums and clairvoyants.

It was, however, common for the Church to assimilate or tolerate, rather than seek to outlaw, pagan customs in Christian ceremonies. Many pagan and magic rituals survived in religious celebrations of all members of society (as, indeed, they still do in most 'advanced' countries today). It was customary for the best man to perform various pagan rituals, such as clearing obstacles on the path between to the bride's house, and shooting into the air and cracking a whip to ward off evil spirits. Windows were often shut in churches during weddings to keep out evil spirits. Samuel Collins noted in the late seventeenth century the popular perception of the involvement of nuns in witchcraft at weddings: 'Seldom a Wedding passes without some Witch-craft (if people of quality marry) chiefly acted as 'tis thought by Nuns, whose prime devotion tends that way.' He also cited the case of an unfortunate bridegroom who had to seek the aid of witches to 'unravel the Charm, and untie the Codpiece-point' as 'it seems some old Woman had tyed up his Codpiece-point'![58] Wizards, it was believed, could put the evil eye on weddings, so that some felt it prudent to invite them to attend the ceremony. The Abbé Chappe d'Auteroche described a merchant wedding in 1761 in Tobol'sk (Siberia) in which a wizard was in attendance 'who comes with an intent to counteract the witchcraft which might be practised by other magicians, to prevent the consumation of the marriage'.[59] In 1794 the Tobol'sk clerical consistory examined the case of Gavril Rozhnev who, it was claimed, had been:

> . . . present at peasant weddings as a druzhka [best man] ostensibly as a precaution so that no harm would occur, having fashioned a cross out of wax for the people, reading a prayer with it, so that the simple people consider him as a wizard.

Rozhnev was sentenced to three years' church penance for his activities.[60] Wizards were sometimes also present at the ritual bath of the bride. At funerals, some of the songs were pagan in origin and had associations with ancestor worship. On Christmas evening it was customary to put a large pot of boiled wheat or barley before the icon. This potage was often blessed by the priest.

The Church also 'Christianized' pagan festivals. It has been noted above that many pagan festivals coincided with major Christian festivals. The clergy participated directly in pagan rituals, as Guthrie remarked in the 1780s 'to tranquillize the minds of their ignorant parishioners' and to dissuade them

58. Samuel Collins, *The Present State of Russia* (London, 1671), pp. 7, 10–11.
59. Abbé Chappe d'Auteroche, *A Journey to Siberia* (London, 1770), pp. 305–6.
60. M.M. Gromyko, *Trudovye traditsii russkikh krest'ian Sibiri (XVIII–pervaia polovina XIX v)* (Novosibirsk, 1975), pp. 332–3.

252

from seeking the help of shamans. On 23 April (St George's day), when cows were traditionally taken out to pasture for the first time in northern Russia, the priests performed a ceremony to ward off harmful wood nymphs who attacked cattle:

> A branch of Palm preserved for the purpose since Palm Sunday, with a lighted Taper a Pot of Barsly and two Eggs (one for the Cowherd the other for a Beggar) are placed before the family image or Saint, and then carried thrice round the Group of Cattle, together with the Cross, sprinkling them each time with the Palm dipt in holy Water, after which they are driven over a hatchet buried under the threshold, by the same consecrated Palm, and from thence to pasture; after which they may defy in the opinion of the Rustics, all the Spells and Witchery of Satan and his Imps; but to secure the matter still more the holy Palm must either be thrown into running Water, or Stuck into an anthill, and the Barsly sown on the field.[61]

In the trans-Baikal region (eastern Siberia), on St John's day, a priest would read a prayer at each fence-post and make a cross of fresh tar on the gates as a protection against witches who took on the form of dogs and stole milk from cows. Not all these activities met with official approval. The 'Spiritual Regulation' of 1721 criticized practices when 'priests pray with the people before an oak; and a priest distributes the branches of that tree among the people as a blessing'.[62]

This last point suggests that the assimilation of pagan festivals into Christian acts could be seen less as a cynical attempt by the clergy to convert an essentially pagan peasantry than a reflection of the fact that many of the clergy could share the same magical or customary beliefs as their flock. Clergy, along with soldiers, were the professional groups most frequently tried for witchcraft. Part of the reason for this was that, after Peter's establishment of the Holy Synod, this was one few areas of jurisdiction still retained by ecclesiastical courts. In practice, as witchcraft could easily be associated with incitement to sedition or crimes against the state, cases regularly passed from ecclesiastical courts to civil courts. The other reason for the number of cases against clergy – black as well as white clergy – was the extent of their active participation in magical practices.

Priests were unfrocked in the eighteenth century for claiming to have miracle-working icons, for exorcizing the devil and for the possession of magical writings. Synod records after 1721 illustrate the direct involvement of clerics, especially lower clergy, in magic. In 1722, a monk was exiled to the Solovetsk monastery for possessing magical texts, which included instructions for telling fortunes by throwing dice, a divinatory Psalter and a prayer against the devil. In 1729 a priest was accused of having 'heretical letters', including a prayer to Baba Iaga (the evil old witch of Slavonic folklore). In 1731, a deacon from

61. BL, Add. MS 14,390, f. 80v.
62. *The Spiritual Regulation of Peter the Great*, ed. and trans. by A.V. Muller (Seattle and London, 1972), pp. 14–15.

Chernigov cathedral was found in possession of magic books which included instructions for calling up devils: these specified removing your cross and crushing it under your right heel, removing your belt, denying Christ, the Virgin, the Apostolic Church, the apostles, the twelve great feasts of the Church and your own parents. In 1761, in a rather sad case, a priest and his wife were accused of going to a witch for a spell to enable them to have children.

As pagan and magical elements could be present in Christian ceremonies, so Christian elements also featured in magical practices. In particular, as elsewhere in Europe, religious objects such as crosses, relics, blessed water and talismans were defences against sorcery and evil spirits (and crosses were normally removed before performing magical rites). Wizards could be revealed by religious objects; a Palm Sunday candle was believed to show wizards and witches upside down. Amulets, which were worn to ward off evil spirits, were as common as crosses and could have Christian symbols drawn on them or words from the Scriptures attached to them (pendant amulets, called *zmeeviki*, had a Christian motif on one side and a pagan motif involving serpents on the other side). Religious practices could be parodied (although not to the extent as occurred in western Europe), sometimes with magical intent, such as wearing crosses upside down, turning icons to the wall and placing candles upside down. The Yuletide celebrations included mock burials complete with false 'priests' and 'deacons'. Many magical prayers were based on Orthodox prayers.

The invocation of saints for magical, pagan or legitimate purposes is a grey area. In Russian popular belief St Nicholas (the fourth-century Bishop of Myra) was not only popularly given the status of an apostle but also was the patron saint of livestock – especially horses – the protector of grain fields and a potent power against evil spirits. His feast day of 6 December could be celebrated with the sacrifice of a three-year-old bull; after mass the priest sprinkled the cattle with holy water. Popular legends abound concerning the miracles performed by St Nicholas, in particular concerning the return of a kidnapped child to its parents. St George was considered the patron saint of livestock and shepherds, and the rituals surrounding his feast days (26 November and 23 April) were largely concerned with these. Candles were lit before his icon to protect livestock from wolves. Most popular celebrations concerning saints were associated with major points in the peasants' agricultural year. This was true of St George's day: 23 April was traditionally the day on which cattle, and sometimes horses, were put out to pasture for the first time in the year; before the mid-seventeenth century 26 November had been the day on which peasants could move freely and it then became the major day for settling accounts. Other saints assumed the personality of pagan gods, in particular the prophet Elijah, who is held by scholars to represent the thunder god Perun (Elijah was believed to ride across the sky in a fiery chariot, striking the earth with lightning bolts). During storms, candles from Holy Thursday were lit, houses were censed and black cats and dogs (who could be transformations

of the devil) were thrown outside the house. To an extent, the popular perception of saints can be seen as a grafting of Christian personages onto a pagan
base. It could also be seen as a genuine merging of pagan and Christian ideas.
This seems to have created little conflict in the mind of the peasant, although it
has exercised the minds of scholars considerably and spawned a vast literature
on the pagan-cum-Christian *mentalité* of the Russian peasant and the concept
of *dvoeverie*.

In a similar way, icons became involved in superstitious and magical beliefs.
Merchants were known to reward or punish icons to which they had prayed
for success in trade. Icon oracles were also a form of divination. Martha Wilmot
recounted the actions of the noblewoman Aleksandra Kochetova:

> . . . she wrote the word 'Yes' on one scrap of paper and 'No' on the other.
> She then gave the two papers to someone to mingle & throw behind an
> Image of a Saint which her Mother had given her, resolv'd & even *bound by
> a promise* to adopt whatever advice the Saint should give. She then pray'd
> before it & at the end of some time shut her eyes, made the sign of the
> Cross & drew out a paper. It was the answer to her question 'Should I
> marry M. de -'. The Saint answer'd 'No', & from that time she say'd no
> power on earth could ever tempt her to become his Wife. The Princess
> Alexandra Gallitzen went on a pilgrimage to know whether the Saints
> council'd her to marry General Loptoff! On this occasion they answer'd
> 'Yes', & she became his Wife.[63]

However, Martha Wilmot went on to comment sceptically that "tis true the
Lady's inclinations in both cases were the same as the tutelary Saints'!

SUMMARY: DEVELOPMENTS 1650–1825

The schism in the Orthodox Church took place at the beginning of the period
of this book and remained permanent, not just until 1825 but until the Revolution and beyond. The policies of Russia's rulers towards the Church, the
clergy (some of which are discussed more fully in other chapters) and religious matters had a significant impact. Alexis had been partly responsible for
encouraging the reforms which led to the schism in 1667; Peter I transformed
the clergy into almost a service class for the state and drastically reduced the
number of monks and nuns; Catherine II secularized church lands and formally decreed religious toleration; Alexander I's own spiritual experience led
to the encouragement of mystical and Pietist movements. Nevertheless, this
chapter has illustrated and emphasized the *continuity* in beliefs – be they religious, pagan, magical or a mixture of all three – particularly as far as peasant
society was concerned. Little change took place in this period in the rituals
and symbols of Christian belief or in the way in which popular faith was
manifested. Participation in pagan festivals, superstitions, magical practices

63. *The Russian Journals*, p. 373.

and the blending of all these with Christian practices did not seem to be greatly affected either by the passing decades or by the policies pursued by Church and state. The nobility and townspeople were less dominated by these practices than peasants, who often depended on the vagaries of climate or fortune for survival. A significant number of nobles began to feel alienated from the official Church and sought solace in masonic movements, mysticism and foreign religious movements. Despite this trend, the divide between nobles and commoners should not be exaggerated. Russian nobles, almost without exception, were Christian, most remained Orthodox (and could remain so while being masons), and most continued to share not only the religious but also many of the superstitious and magical beliefs of the common people.

Conclusion: Russia in 1825

During the period covered by this book the international position of Russia (and then the Russian empire) was transformed. In the second half of the seventeenth century Russia was perceived by the European Great Powers to be a country of little diplomatic importance on the periphery of Europe, whose strategic interests were assumed to be limited to conflicts with her immediate neighbours. By the second half of the eighteenth century Russia had become an integral member of the European diplomatic community and her military and, to a lesser extent, naval strength were fully acknowledged. By 1815 Russia was the greatest military power in Europe. This transformation had taken place through a series of wars in which Russia had been largely successful not only on the battlefield but also in asserting her claims through diplomatic negotiations and at the peace settlements. As a result, borders expanded significantly to the west (the Baltic provinces, part of the former Poland-Lithuanian Commonwealth), the south (the Ukraine, Crimea, Bessarabia, part of the Caucasus) and the north (Finland). The changed status of Russia was illustrated by the very different receptions given to the only two tsars to travel to England in this period. Peter I in 1698 was regarded as an eccentric ruler of a curious but little-known and diplomatically insignificant country; Alexander I in 1814 was hailed as the 'Christian conqueror' of Napoleon, the saviour of Europe and as the ruler of the strongest military power in Europe.

Significant internal progress and change also took place during this period, largely in consequence of initiatives taken by Russia's rulers. Most notable was the expansion of provision for education, which came about almost entirely as a result of the personal interest taken in the matter by individual rulers (in particular Peter I, Catherine II and Alexander I). Russia's rulers also deliberately stimulated the development of cultural and intellectual life. By 1825 the physical appearance, occupations, education, lifestyle and cultural perceptions of Russian nobles (and the wealthier townspeople) had been transformed. Indeed, the lives of Russian nobles, even the poorer and provincial ones, had undergone more change (by methods ranging from brute force to persuasion, depending on the inclinations of the ruler) than any other group in

Russian society. Government legislation also had a significant impact on many aspects of provincial life which affected townspeople (and the large number of peasants living and working in towns) as much as nobles, including changes to the structure of urban administration and the judicial system, the establishment of a rudimentary police force, the setting up of hospitals and other welfare institutions, and initiatives in town planning. The armed forces had also been transformed by the policies of the tsars. At the same time Russia experienced an industrial 'take-off' in the eighteenth century (at least initially in response to Peter I's direct encouragement) in areas such as iron and copper mining and textile production.

The most important areas of Russian life which did not undergo substantial change were serfdom and methods of agriculture, which remained largely untouched throughout the period. This study has shown that this did not necessarily mean that serfs were impoverished or that serfdom was necessarily a retarding economic feature. Serfdom did not restrict the development of crafts in the countryside, stop serfs from pursuing trade or travelling to market their goods, or prevent the development of industries based on serf labour. There is insufficient evidence to show whether state peasants were more economically productive or agriculturally innovative than serfs but the indications are that differences arose more from soil quality and from the communications networks than from legal status. To some extent serfdom was an administrative necessity for a country which, despite attempts to reform local administration, still lacked the necessary organs of law and order and an adequate bureaucracy to govern the countryside directly. The peasant communes (of state peasants as well as serfs) played a crucial role in every aspect of the life of the peasant as well as furnishing the state with the manpower and taxes on which its new-found military strength depended. Government legislation had an impact on peasants in terms of their obligations but there was little attempt in this period to interfere with their family customs, lifestyle, pastimes or beliefs.

Equally significant as the areas which underwent little change were those where the changes were unsuccessful or potentially destructive. It proved difficult for the government to stimulate a sense of corporate pride and identity in either urban institutions of self-government or in noble provincial assemblies. Attempts by Peter I and Catherine II to introduce guilds were unsuccessful and Russian towns remained institutionally and economically weak, unable to compete with or restrict the activities of trading peasants. In practice, it was impossible to attract the ablest and wealthiest nobles to posts in local administration or to stimulate the development of provincial society around the noble assemblies. The policies of Russia's rulers towards the Church deliberately weakened the influence of both parish and monastic clergy. Government interference in the duties of parish clergy (particularly under Peter) undermined their integrity and independence and the education imposed upon them did little to improve standards overall and resulted in the departure from the clerical estate of some of its most able members. The influence of the monastic clergy on Russian society was dramatically reduced by government restrictions on the numbers taking holy orders, followed by control over the size and functions of monasteries and finally by the secularization of church and monastic lands in 1764. The traditionally weak role which the Church had played in education was reinforced by the exclusion of priests from the national schools, with the result that the clergy provided little in the way of social or intellectual leadership in the towns or the countryside.

The problem which Russia faced by 1825, however, was not so much that Russia's rulers had failed to enact changes but the growing estrangement between the regime and a section of the educated noble elite – that is, the very people who had been most affected by educational and cultural developments stimulated by the tsars – over the present state and future direction of the country. This had become apparent by the 1790s as events began to unfold in France – the county whose culture and language Russian nobles had been brought up to admire. A prime example of this was Aleksandr Radishchev, son of a wealthy landowner and a product of the elite Russian educational system (he attended the Corps de Pages before being sent abroad to study at Leipzig University, one of the leading universities in Europe at that time). In 1790 he published his *Journey from St Petersburg to Moscow*, in the style of a sentimental journey, popular at that time in the West, in which he attacked the evil practices of serfdom, the corruption of administration and justice and, in an allegorical dream sequence, the very institution of the monarchy. Radishchev was arrested, imprisoned in the Peter and Paul fortress, tried for sedition and sentenced to death, a sentence which was later communted to ten years' exile to a remote fort in Siberia (from which he was released by Paul I).

Western ideas, pastimes and habits, many of which had been deliberately encouraged by the tsars, influenced the elite members of Russian society, like Radishchev, in the late eighteenth century. But the most direct impact of the West, both physically and intellectually, came about as a result of the Napoleonic Wars and, in particular, as a result of the Napoleonic invasion of Russia in 1812[1] and the subsequent campaigns in central and western Europe. The invasion destroyed whole towns and villages (by battle or, in the case of Moscow, by fire), devastated crops and left roads strewn with corpses of men and carcasses of horses. The town of Smolensk was almost destroyed – only 350 of 2,250 buildings remained standing – and the property and population of small villages within the province were also devastated. In the district of Gzhatsk over 8,000 buildings were damaged, while the merchant population of Gzhatsk town declined from 185 before the invasion to 52. In the province as a whole 172,566 corpses and 128,739 carcasses had to be cleared after the departure of the armies. All members of society in the path of the retreating and invading forces suffered physical losses but even people far distant from the invasion route were affected by the increased demands for recruits (there

---

1. The material concerning the invasion of 1812 is drawn from Janet M. Hartley, 'Russia in 1812 Part I: The French Presence in the *Gubernii* of Smolensk and Mogilev', 'Russia in 1812 Part II: The Russian Administration of Kaluga *Gubernija*', *Jahrbücher für Geschichte Osteuropas* 38 (1990), pp. 178–98, 399–416.

were three levies in 1812), heavier taxes and the passage of people through their land. These included new conscripts, prisoners of war (between mid-August and mid-October 1812 22,000 prisoners passed through Kaluga province, to the south of the invasion route), sick and wounded soldiers (the hospital in Kozel'sk, Kaluga province, housed 3,000–5,400 patients and received as many as 1,361 men on one day alone; Kaluga town hospital treated some 7,000 men) and not only individual refugees but whole institutions (government offices and schools) which moved east.

The invasion illustrated both some of the administrative and social problems of Russia but also a degree of resilience within state and society. The ethnic diversity of the population in the western borderlands meant that Napoleon could rally at least some Catholic Polish and Lithuanian landowners and gave the Russian government cause for concern over the loyalty of the non-Russian, and in some cases non-Orthodox, peasantry and the Jewish urban population. The invasion led to disorder in the countryside and encouraged some serfs to rise against their masters (particularly in the area near the invasion route) and the Russian government feared that Napoleon would create social chaos by declaring the freedom of the serfs. The strain of the invasion proved almost too much for local and central government offices. Nevertheless, the inherent stability of the state was demonstrated by the fact that most non-Russians in the western borderlands, of whatever social background, remained loyal (or were at least wary of committing themselves too soon to a foreigner). Most serfs showed more concern to defend their property and lives against the invader (and against roaming Cossacks) than to overturn the social order and, in any case, Napoleon did not wish to put at risk his military and diplomatic objectives by posing as serf liberator. Indeed, the year of 1812 provoked a patriotic response amongst society shown by the willingness of nobles and townspeople to donate money and services for the country. Twenty-two pupils at the Kaluga school for the nobility and two of their teachers volunteered for the militia; the Kaluga merchants contributed 205,000 roubles for the war effort. Even amongst peasants some form of national, Orthodox Russian consciousness was displayed in their violent reaction against foreign invaders. Simple people regarded Napoleon as the Antichrist (Philippe-Paul de Ségur claimed that the Orthodox clergy had told the peasants that the French were 'a legion of devils commanded by the Anti-Christ'). Peasants, artisans, minor officials and priests joined the partisan groups which harassed the retreating Napoleonic forces.

In fact, the physical destructiveness of the 1812 invasion proved less harmful to the regime than the intellectual impact of that year and of the campaigns of the following two years on the educated elite. Young army officers who fought in 1812 (either in the regular army or in partisan units) experienced a new, patriotic fervour which they felt was shared by all social groups. N.A. Bestuzhev, who later became a Decembrist and participated in the uprising following the death of Alexander I, wrote that in 1812 'Vast Russia rose as one man . . . The national fervour in Russia was great because it was a national war.'[2] These young officers then crossed Europe in pursuit of the retreating armies and during this time they saw how much better ordinary people lived than in Russia and came into contact with the educated elites of western Europe. In the process, they came to despise what they perceived to be the backwardness and lack of freedom in their own country. This was particularly hard to bear when they, and the Russian people, had in their view played such a crucial role in liberating Europe from the tyranny of Napoleon. As Mikhail Fonvizin (also a Decembrist) explained:

> During the campaigns in Germany and France our young people became acquainted with European civilization, which made a strong impression on them so that they could compare everything they had seen abroad with that which presented itself at every turn at home – the slavery of the vast majority of Russians who had no rights, the cruel treatment of subordinates by their superiors, all manner of the abuse of power, everywhere arbitrary rule – all this excited the discontent and outraged the patriotic feelings of educated Russians.[3]

The feeling of frustration was deepened by the stark contrast between Russia's newly acquired international status and the atmosphere of oppression at home created by the conservatism in educational policies and the establishment of military colonies. This, coupled with the dashed expectations of Alexander introducing a constitution into Russia (as he had in the Congress Kingdom of Poland) had led by 1825 to an almost complete divorce between the tsar and this alienated group of the educated elite.

In a sense the Russian regime was a victim of its own success. Russian rulers had created a group of well-educated nobles – in effect a 'civilized' elite which was on a par with the aristocracy of central and western Europe. In the process, however, this elite had acquired a knowledge of foreign languages and a sometimes uncritical admiration for 'western' culture which led them to find fault with the very regime which had provided and determined the content of their education. In the view of this elite the Russian ruler was failing to enact the further fundamental political and social changes necessary to bring Russia to what they had been brought up to regard as the 'civilized' level of development of the West. In the early nineteenth century, after the experience of the French Revolution and the Napoleonic Wars, this meant they demanded the introduction of a 'constitution' which would, among other things, enshrine certain inalienable rights and establish some form of national representation. Such a constitution might potentially challenge the institution of serfdom; it would certainly modify the powers of the ruler.

★★★★★★★★★★★★★★★★

The fragility of Russia's cultural progress was wittily characterized by Martha Wilmot in 1806:

2. L.Ia. Pavlova, *Dekabristy – uchastniki voin 1805–1814 gg* (Moscow, 1979), p. 94.
3. M.V. Dovnar-Zapol'skii, *Idealy dekabristov* (Moscow, 1907), p. 204.

Yes! I know all about the luxury of Moscow & the civilization of Petersburg, but have you ever seen a clumsy romping ignorant Girl of 12 years old with a fine Parisian cap upon her head? So seems to my eye this Imperial Realm. The cloister'd ignorance not only of the 12th but of the 11th Century is the groundwork of this colossal Region and 5 or 6 Centurys will no doubt produce the same effects here they have in other parts of Europe; but Time must disengage the ligaments which bind the plant before it strengthens & expands into a self supported standard. More sudden means would bend it to the Earth & so of Russian political liberty & civilization![4]

But it was all too easy for foreign travellers and young educated Russian nobles and, for that matter, it is tempting for historians, to measure Russian developments in the period covered by this book against some ideal, civilized 'Europe' which was often more a matter of myth than of reality. Martha Wilmot was not only one of the most acute commentators on Russian life but also one of the most honest. Her comments above concluded with the words:

But what business have I to shake my ears over the World, as if I held it in my clutches like an Apple elaborately to prove that the rosy side was sweet & the green side sour?

---

4. *The Russian Journals of Martha and Catherine Wilmot*, ed. by the Marchioness of Londonderry and H.M. Hyde (London, 1934), p. 223.

Select Bibliography

This is primarily a list of English-language secondary sources. Key texts in other languages and recent studies of particular interest have also been included. Primary sources (printed and non-printed) are not included here but are cited in the footnotes. See also Philip Clendenning, Roger Bartlett, *Eighteenth Century Russia: A Select Bibliography of Works Published since 1955*, Russian Bibliography Series, 2 (Newtonville, 1981).

Abbreviations of articles cited in the bibliography:

ASEER	*American Slavonic and East European Review*
CASS	*Canadian-American Slavic Studies*
CMRS	*Cahiers du monde russe et soviétique*
CSP	*Canadian Slavonic Papers*
FOG	*Forschungen zur osteuropäischen Geschichte*
JGO	*Jahrbücher für Geschichte Osteuropas*
JMH	*Journal of Modern History*
OSP	*Oxford Slavonic Papers*
RH	*Russian History*
RR	*Russian Review*
SEER	*Slavonic and East European Review*
SR	*Slavic Review*

GENERAL SOCIAL AND ECONOMIC

J.T. Alexander, *Bubonic Plague in Early Modern Russia. Public Health & Urban Disaster* (Baltimore and London, 1980).

E.V. Anisimov, 'Izmeneniia v sotsial'noi strukture russkogo obshchestva v kontse XVII–nachale XVIII veka (Posledniaia stranitsa kholopstva v Rossii)', *Istoriia SSSR* 5 (1979), 35–51.

E.V. Anisimov, *Podatnaia reforma Petra I* (Leningrad, 1982).

C. Becker, '*Raznochintsy*: The Development of the Word and the Concept', *ASEER* 18 (1959), 63–74.

H.A. Bennett, 'Evolution of the Meaning of *Chin*: An Introduction to the Russian Institution of Rank Ordering and Niche Assignment from the Time of Peter the Great's Table of Ranks to the Bolshevik Revolution', *California Slavic Studies* 10 (1977), 1–44.

W.L. Blackwell, *The Beginnings of Russian Industrialization 1800–1860* (Princeton, 1968).

M. Confino, *Société et mentalités collectives en Russie sous l'Ancien Régime* (Paris, 1991).

M. Confino, *Systèmes agraires et progrès agricole: l'assolement triennal en Russie aux XVIIIe–XIX siècles* (The Hague, Paris, 1969).

M.E. Falkus, *The Industrialization of Russia, 1700–1914* (London, 1972).

G.L. Freeze, 'The *Soslovie* (Estate) Paradigm and Russian Social History', *American Historical Review* 19 (1986), 11–36.

M.M. Gromyko and I.V. Vlasov (eds), *Russkie: semeinyi i obshchestvennyi byt* (Moscow, 1989).

R. Hellie, *Slavery in Russia 1450–1725* (Chicago and London, 1982).

V.M. Kabuzan, *Narody Rossii v pervoi polovine XIX v. Chislennost' i etnicheskii sostav* (Moscow, 1992).

V.M. Kabuzan, *Narody Rossii v XVIII veke. Chislennost' i etnicheskii sostav* (Moscow, 1990).

A. Kahan, 'Natural Calamities and their Effect upon the Food Supply in Russia (An Introduction to a Catalogue)', *JGO* 16 (1968), 353–77.

A. Kahan, *The Plow the Hammer and the Knout. An Economic History of Eighteenth-Century Russia* (Chicago and London, 1985).

A.A. Kizevetter, *Russkoe obshchestvo i vosemnadtsatom stoletii* (Rostov-on-Don, 1904).

M. Kochan, *Life in Russia under Catherine the Great* (London and New York, 1960).

B.N. Mironov, 'Consequences of the Price Revolution in Eighteenth-Century Russia', *Economic History Review* 45 (1992), 457–78.

G.E. Munro, 'Feeding the Multitudes: Grain Supply to St Petersburg in the Era of Catherine the Great', *JGO* 35 (1987), 481–508.

Ivan Pososhkov, *The Book of Poverty and Wealth*, ed. and trans. by A.P. Vlasto and L.R. Lewitter (London, 1987).

M.D. Rabinovich, 'Odnodvortsy v pervoi polovine XVIIIv', *Ezhegodnik po agrarnoi istorii vostochnoi Evropy 1971 g.* (Vilnius, 1974), 137–45.

L.N. Semenova, *Ocherki istorii byta i kul'turnoi zhizni Rossii pervaia polovina XVIIIv* (Leningrad, 1982).

Ia.E. Vodarskii, *Naselenie Rossii v kontse XVII–nachale XVIII veka (chislennost', soslovno-klassovyi sostav, razmeshchenie* (Moscow, 1977).

E.K. Wirtschafter, 'Problematics of Status Definition in Imperial Russia: the Raznočincy', *JGO* 40 (1992), 319–39.

E.K. Wirtschafter, *Social Identity in Imperial Russia* (DeKalb, 1997).

E.K. Wirtschafter, *Structures of Society. Imperial Russia's 'People of Various Ranks'* (DeKalb, 1994).

BIOGRAPHIES OF RUSSIAN RULERS

J.T. Alexander, *Catherine the Great. Life and Legend* (New York and Oxford, 1989).

M.S. Anderson, *Peter the Great* (London and New York, 1995).

E.V. Anisimov, *Empress Elizabeth. Her Reign and her Russia 1741–1761*, trans. by J.T. Alexander (Gulf Breeze, 1995).

J.M. Hartley, *Alexander I* (London and New York, 1994).

L.A.J. Hughes, *Russia in the Age of Peter the Great* (New Haven and London, 1998).

L.A.J. Hughes, *Sophia. Regent of Russia 1657–1704* (New Haven and London, 1990).

C.S. Leonard, *Reform and Regicide: the Reign of Peter III of Russia* (Bloomington and Indianapolis, 1993).

P. Longworth, *Alexis. Tsar of all the Russias* (London, 1984).

P. Longworth, *The Three Empresses: Catherine I, Anne and Elizabeth of Russia* (New York, 1972).

A. McConnell, *Tsar Alexander I: Paternalistic Reformer* (New York, 1970).

R.E. McGrew, *Paul I of Russia 1754–1801* (Oxford, 1992).

I.M. de Madariaga, *Catherine the Great: A Short History* (New Haven and London, 1990).

I.M. de Madariaga, *Russia in the Age of Catherine the Great* (London, 1981).

A. Palmer, *Alexander I. Tsar of War and Peace* (London, 1974).

H. Ragsdale (ed.), *Paul I: A Reassessment of his Life and Reign* (Pittsburgh, 1979).

WOMEN AND THE FAMILY

B.E. Clements, B.A. Engel, C.D. Worobec (eds), *Russia's Women. Accommodation, Resistance, Transformation* (Berkeley, 1991).

P. Czap, 'The Perennial Multiple Family Household, Mishino, Russia, 1782–1858', *Family History* 7 (1982), 5–26.

A. Dallin, G.W. Lapidus (eds), *Women in Russia* (Stanford, 1977).

P.P. Dunn, '"That Enemy is the Baby": Childhood in Imperial Russia', in L. deMouse (ed.), *The History of Childhood* (London, 1976).

B. Farnsworth, L. Viola (eds), *Russian Peasant Women* (Oxford and New York, 1992).

G.L. Freeze, 'Bringing Order to the Russian Family: Marriage and Divorce in Imperial Russia, 1760–1860', *JMH* 62 (1990), 709–46.

N.S. Kollman, 'The Seclusion of Elite Muscovite Women', *RH* 10 (1988), 170–87.

E. Levin, 'Infanticide in Pre-Petrine Russia', *JGO* 34 (1986), 215–24.

N.A. Minenko, *Russkaia krest'ianskaia sem'ia v zapadnoi Sibiri (XVIII–pervoi poloviny XIXv)* (Novosibirsk, 1979).

C.J. Pouncey (ed. and trans.), *The Domostroi: Rules for Russian Households in the Time of Ivan the Terrible* (Ithaca and London, 1994).

D.L. Ransel (ed.), *The Family in Imperial Russia: New Lines of Historical Research* (Urbana, 1978).

D.L. Ransel, *Mothers of Misery. Child Abandonment in Russia* (Princeton, 1988).

J. Tovrov, *The Russian Noble Family. Structure and Change* (New York and London, 1987).

PASTIMES, CUSTOMS, AND LIFESTYLE

J.T. Alexander, 'Medical Developments in Petrine Russia', *CASS* 8 (1974), 198–222.

R.P. Bartlett, 'Britain, Russia, and Scurvy in the Eighteenth Century', *OSP* 29 (1996), 23–43.

M. Burgess, 'Fairs and Entertainers in Eighteenth-Century Russia', *SEER* 38 (1959), 95–113.

D. Christian, *'Living Water'. Vodka and Russian Society on the Eve of Emancipation* (Oxford, 1990).

A.G. Cross, 'The Russian *Banya* in the Descriptions of Foreign Travellers and in the Depictions of Foreign and Russian Artists', *OSP* 24 (1991), 34–59.

H.W. Dewey, K.B. Stevens, 'Muscovites at Play: Recreation in Pre-Petrine Russia', *CASS* 13 (1979), 189–203.

M. Glants, J. Toomre (eds), *Food in Russian History and Culture* (Bloomington and Indianapolis, 1997).

L.G. Ivanits, *Russian Folk Belief* (New York and London, 1992).

A. Lindenmeyr, *Poverty is not a Vice. Charity, Society, and the State in Imperial Russia* (Princeton, 1996).

A.F. Nekrylova, *Russkie narodnye gorodskie prazdniki, uveseleniia i zrelishcha konets XVIII–nachalo XX veka* (Leningrad, 1984).

P. Roosevelt, *Life on the Russian Country Estate: A Social and Cultural History* (New Haven, 1975).

W.F. Ryan, *The Bathhouse at Midnight: An Historical Survey of Magic and Divination in Russia* (forthcoming).

W.F. Ryan, 'The Witchcraft Hysteria in Early Modern Europe: Was Russia an Exception?', *SEER* 76, 1 (1998), 49–84.

R.E.F. Smith, 'The Russian Stove', *OSP* 18 (1985), 83–101.

R.E.F. Smith, D. Christian, *Bread and Salt: A Social and Economic History of Food and Drink in Russia* (Cambridge, 1984).

F. Wigzell, *Reading Russian Fortunes: Print Culture, Gender and Divination in Russia from 1765* (Cambridge, 1998).

J.C. Zacek, 'The Imperial Philanthropic Society in the Reign of Alexander I', *CASS* 9 (1975), 427–36.

CHURCH, CLERGY AND RELIGION

S.K. Batalden (ed.), *Seeking God: The Recovery of Religious Identity in Orthodox Russia, Ukraine, and Georgia* (DeKalb, 1993).

C.B. Becker, 'The Church School in Tsarist Social and Educational Policy from Peter to the Great Reforms', unpublished PhD thesis, Harvard University, 1964.

W.L. Blackwell, 'The Old Believers and the Rise of Private Industrial Enterprise in Early Nineteenth-Century Moscow', *SR* 24 (1965), 407–24.

S. Bolshakoff, *Russian Mystics* (London, 1977).

P. Bushkovitch, *Religion and Society in Russia. The Sixteenth and Seventeenth Centuries* (New York and Oxford, 1992).

M. Cherniavsky, 'The Old Believers and the New Religion', *SR* 25 (1966) 1–39.

J. Cracraft, *The Church Reform of Peter the Great* (London, 1971).

R.O. Crummey, *The Old Believers & the World of the Antichrist. The Vyg Community and the Russian State 1694–1855* (Madison, Milwaukee, London, 1970).

G.L. Freeze, 'The Disintegration of Traditional Communities: the Parish in Eighteenth-Century Russia', *JMH* 48 (1976), 32–50.

G.L. Freeze, 'Handmaiden of the State? The Church in Imperial Russia Reconsidered', *Journal of Ecclesiastical History* 36 (1985), 82–102.

G.L. Freeze, 'The Orthodox Church and Serfdom in Prereform Russia', *SR* 48 (1989), 361–87.

G.L. Freeze, *The Parish Clergy in Nineteenth-Century Russia: Crisis, Reform, Counter-Reform* (Princeton, 1983).

G.L. Freeze, 'The Rechristianization of Russia: the Church and Popular Religion, 1750–1850', *Studia Slavica Finlandensia* 7 (1990), 101–36.

G.L. Freeze, *The Russian Levites: Parish Clergy in the Eighteenth Century* (Cambridge, Mass., 1977).

G.L. Freeze, 'Social Mobility and the Russian Parish Clergy in the Eighteenth Century', *SR* 33 (1974), 641–62.

G.A. Hosking (ed.), *Church, Nation and State in Russia and the Ukraine* (London, 1991).

B. Meehan, *Holy Women of Russia. The Lives of Five Orthodox Women offer Spiritual Guidance for Today* (San Francisco, 1993).

B. Meehan-Waters, 'Russian Convents and the Secularization of Monastic Property', in R.P. Bartlett, A.G. Cross, K. Rasmussen (eds) *Russia and the World of the Eighteenth Century* (Columbus, Ohio, 1988), 112–24.

A.V. Muller (ed. and trans.), *The Spiritual Regulation of Peter the Great* (Seattle and London, 1972).

R.L. Nichols, T.G. Stavrou (eds), *Russian Orthodoxy under the Old Regime* (Minneapolis, 1978).

K.A. Papmehl, *Metropolitan Platon of Moscow (Petr Levshin, 1737–1812): The Enlightened Prelate, Scholar and Educator* (Newtonville, 1983).

P. Pera, 'Theoretical and Practical Aspects of the Debate on Marriage among the Priestless Old Believers from the End of the Seventeenth Century to the Mid-Nineteenth Century', unpublished PhD thesis, University of London, 1986.

M.A. Thomas, 'Muscovite Convents in the Seventeenth Century', *RH* 10 (1983), 230–42.

E.M. Thompson, *Understanding Russia. The Holy Fool in Russian Culture* (Lanham, New York and London, 1987).

G. Woodcock, I. Avakumovic, *The Doukhobors* (London, 1968).

J.C. Zacek, 'The Russian Bible Society, 1812–1826', unpublished PhD thesis, Columbia University, 1964.

N.D. Zol'nikova, *Soslovnye problemy vo vzaimootnosheniiakh tserkvi i gosudarstva v Sibiri (XVIII v.)* (Novosibirsk, 1981).

EDUCATION, CULTURE, INTELLECTUAL LIFE

J. Billington, *The Icon and the Axe. An Interpretive History of Russian Culture* (New York, 1966).

J.L. Black, *Citizens for the Fatherland. Educators and Pedagogical Ideas in Eighteenth Century Russia* (New York, 1979).

J.L. Black, 'Educating Women in Eighteenth-Century Russia: Myths and Realities', *CSP* 20 (1978), 23–43.

M. Burgess, 'Russian Public Theatre Audiences of the 18th and Early 19th Centuries', *SEER* 37 (1958), 160–83.

A.G. Cross, 'The Eighteenth-Century Russian Theatre through British Eyes', *Studies on Voltaire and the Eighteenth Century* 119 (1983), 225–40.

D.W. Edwards, 'Count Joseph de Maistre and Russian Educational Policy, 1803–1828', *SR* 36 (1977), 54–75.

J.T. Flynn, 'The Universities, the Gentry, and the Russian Imperial Services, 1815–1825', *CASS* 2 (1968), 486–503.

J.T. Flynn, *The University Reform of Alexander I 1802–1835* (Washington, 1988).

J.G. Garrard (ed.), *The Eighteenth Century in Russia* (Oxford, 1973).

N. Hans, *History of Russian Educational Policy (1701–1917)* (London, 1931).

J.M. Hartley, 'The Boards of Social Welfare and the Financing of Catherine II's State Schools', *SEER* 67 (1989), 211–27.

W.G. Jones, 'The Morning Light Charity Schools 1777–80', *SEER* 56 (1978), 47–67.

W.G. Jones, *Nikolay Novikov, Enlightener of Russia* (Cambridge, 1984).

D.M. Lang, *The First Russian Radical: Alexander Radishchev, 1749–1802* (London, 1959).

W.B. Lincoln, 'A Re-examination of some Historical Stereotypes: An Analysis of the Career Patterns and Backgrounds of the Decembrists', *JGO* 24 (1976), 359–68.

A. McConnell, *A Russian Philosophe: Alexander Radishchev, 1749–1802* (The Hague, 1964).

I.M. de Madariaga, 'The Foundation of the Russian Educational System by Catherine II', *SEER* 57 (1979), 369–95.

I.M. de Madariaga, 'Freemasonry in Eighteenth-Century Russia' in her *Politics and Culture in Eighteenth-Century Russia* (London, 1998).

G. Marker, *Publishing, Printing, and the Origins of Intellectual Life in Russia 1700–1800* (Princeton, 1985).

G. Marker, 'Who Rules the Word? Public School Education and the Fate of Universality in Russia, 1782–1803', *RH* 20 (1993), 15–34.

A.G. Mazour, *The First Russian Revolution 1825* (Berkeley, 1937; reprinted Stanford, 1961).

C.S. Nash, 'Educating New Mothers. Women and the Enlightenment in Russia', *History of Education Quarterly* 21 (1981), 301–16.

C.S. Nash, 'The Education of Women in Russia, 1762–1796', unpublished PhD thesis, New York University, 1978.

M.J. Okenfuss, *The Discovery of Childhood in Russia. The Evidence of the Slavic Primer* (Newtonville, 1980).

M.J. Okenfuss, 'Education and Empire: School Reform in Enlightened Russia', *JGO* 27 (1979), 41–69.

M.J. Okenfuss, 'Education in Russia in the First Half of the Eighteenth Century', unpublished PhD thesis, Harvard University, 1970.

M.J. Okenfuss, 'From School Class to Social Caste. The Divisiveness of Early-Modern Russian Education', *JGO* 33 (1985), 321–44.

M.J. Okenfuss, 'Technical Training in Russia under Peter the Great', *History of Education Quarterly* 13 (1973), 325–45.

K.A. Papmehl, *Freedom of Expression in Eighteenth Century Russia* (The Hague, 1971).

A.N. Pypin, *Obshchestvennoe dvizhenie v Rossii pri Aleksandre I* (Petrograd, 1918).

M. Raeff, *The Decembrist Movement* (Englewood Cliffs, 1966).

H. Rogger, *National Consciousness in Eighteenth-Century Russia* (Cambridge, 1960).

G. Seaman, 'Folk-Song in Russian Opera of the Eighteenth Century', *SEER* 41 (1962–63), 144–57.

V.I. Semevskii, *Politicheskiia i obshchestvennyia idei dekabristov* (St Petersburg, 1907).

C.H. Whittacker, *The Origins of Modern Russian Education: An Intellectual Biography of Count Sergei Uvarov, 1786–1855* (DeKalb, 1984).

J.C. Zacek, 'The Lancastrian School Movement in Russia', *SEER* 45 (1967), 343–67.

THE NOBILITY

W.R. Augustine, 'Notes Toward a Portrait of the Eighteenth-Century Russian Nobility', *CASS* 4 (1970), 373–425.

M. Bogoslovskii, *Byt i nravy russkago dvorianstva v pervoi polovine XVIII veka* (Moscow, 1906).

M. Confino, *Domaines et seigneurs en Russie vers la fin du XVIIIe siècle* (Paris, 1963).

M. Confino, 'A propos de la notion de service dans la noblesse russe aux XVIIIe et XIXe siècles', *CMRS* 34 (1993), 47–58.

N.W. Cornell, 'The Role of the Nobility in Agricultural Change in Russia during the Reign of Catherine II', unpublished PhD thesis, University of Illinois at Urbana-Champagne, 1972.

worth citing?

R.O. Crummey, *Aristocracy and Servitors. The Boyar Elite in Russia 1613–1689* (Princeton, 1983).

R.O. Crummey, 'Peter and the Boiar Aristocracy, 1689–1700', *CASS* 8 (1974), 274–87.

R.O. Crummey, 'Reflections on Mestnichestvo in the Seventeenth Century', *FOG* 27 (1980), 269–81.

P. Dukes, *Catherine the Great and the Russian Nobility* (Cambridge, 1967).

T. Esper, 'The Odnodvortsy and the Russian Nobility', *SEER* 45 (1967), 124–34.

R.D. Givens, 'Servitors or Seigneurs: The Nobility and the Eighteenth-Century Russian State', unpublished PhD thesis, University of California, Berkeley, 1975.

J. Hassell, 'The Implementation of the Table of Ranks during the Eighteenth Century', *SR* 29 (1970), 283–99.

L.A.J. Hughes, *Russia and the West, the Life of a Seventeenth-Century Westernizer, Prince Vasily Vasil'evich Golitsyn (1643–1714)* (Newtonville, Mass., 1984).

R.E. Jones, *The Emancipation of the Russian Nobility 1762–1785* (Princeton, 1973).

A. Kahan, 'The Costs of "Westernization" in Russia: the Gentry and the Economy in the Eighteenth Century', *SR* 25 (1966), 40–66.

V.A. Kivelson, *Autocracy in the Provinces. The Muscovite Gentry and Political Culture in the Seventeenth Cenury* (Stanford, 1996).

S.A. Korf, *Dvorianstvo i ego soslovnoe upravlenie za stoletie 1762–1855 godov* (St Petersburg, 1906).

D.C.B. Lieven, *The Aristocracy in Europe, 1815–1914* (Basingstoke, 1992).

I.M. de Madariaga, 'The Russian Nobility in the Seventeenth and Eighteenth Centuries' in H.M. Scott (ed.), *The European Nobilities in the Seventeenth and Eighteenth Centuries*, vol. II, *Northern, Central and Eastern Europe* (London and New York, 1995), 223–73.

B. Meehan-Waters, *Autocracy & Aristocracy. The Russian Service Elite of 1730* (New Brunswick, 1982).

B. Meehan-Waters, 'The Muscovite Noble Origins of the Russians in the Generalitet of 1730', *CMRS* 12 (1971), 28–75.

B. Meehan-Waters, 'The Russian Aristocracy and the Reforms of Peter the Great', *CASS* 8 (1974), 288–302.

N.I. Pavlenko, 'Odvorianivanie russkoi burzhuazii v XVIII v.', *Istoriia SSSR* (1961), no. 2, 71–87.

N.I. Pavlenko *et al.* (eds), *Dvorianstvo i krepostnoi stroi Rossii XVI–XVIII vv. Sbornik statei, posviashchennyi pamiati Alekseia Andreevicha Novosel'skogo* (Moscow, 1975).

M. Raeff, 'La noblesse et le discours politique sous le règne de Pierre le Grand', *CMRS* 34 (1993), 33–46.

M. Raeff, *Origins of the Russian Intelligentsia: The Eighteenth-Century Nobility* (New York, 1966).

M. Raeff, 'The Russian Nobility in the Eighteenth and Nineteenth Centuries: Trends and Comparisons' in I. Banac, P. Bushkovitch (eds), *The Nobility in Russia and Eastern Europe* (New Haven, 1983), 99–120.

A. Romanovich-Slavatinskii, *Dvorianstvo v Rossii ot nachala XVIII veka do otmena krepostnago prava* (St Petersburg, 1870; reprint The Hague, Paris, 1968).

S.O. Shmidt, 'Obshchestvennoe samosoznanie *noblesse russe* v XVI–pervoi treti XIX v.', *CMRS* 34 (1993), 11–32.

H.-J. Torke, 'Adel und Staat vor Peter dem Grossen (1649–1689)', *FOG* 27 (1980), 282–98.

THE URBAN POPULATION

A.I. Aksenov, *Genealogii Moskovskogo kupechestva XVIIIv. Iz istorii formirovaniia russkoi burzhuazii* (Moscow, 1988).

A.I. Aksenov, *Ocherki genealogii uezdnogo kupechestva XVIIIv* (Moscow, 1993).

S.H. Baron, 'The Fate of the *Gosti* in the Reign of Peter the Great', *CMRS* 14 (1973), 488–512.

S.H. Baron, 'Who were the *Gosti*?', *California Slavic Studies* 7 (1973), 1–40.

D.R. Brower, 'Urbanization and Autocracy: Russian Urban Development in the First Half of the Nineteenth Century, *RR* 42 (1983), 377–402.

P. Bushkovitch, 'Towns, Trade, and Artisans in Seventeenth-Century Russia: the View from Eastern Europe', *FOG* 27 (1980), 215–32.

W. Daniel, 'The Merchantry and the Problem of Social Order in the Russian State: Catherine II's Commission on Commerce', *SEER* 55 (1977), 185–203.

W. Dowler, 'Merchants and Politics in Russia: The Guild Reform of 1824', *SEER* 65 (1987), 38–52.

D. Griffiths, 'Eighteenth-Century Perceptions of Backwardness: Projects for the Creation of a Third Estate in Catherinian Russia', *CASS* 13 (1979), 452–72.

M.F. Hamm (ed.), *The City in Russian History* (Lexington, 1976).

J.M. Hartley, 'Town Government in Saint Petersburg Guberniya after the Charter to the Towns of 1785', *SEER* 62 (1984), 61–84.

P. Herlihy, *Odessa: A History, 1794–1914* (Cambridge, Mass., 1986).

M. Hildermeier, *Bürgertum und Stadt in Russland 1760–1870. Rechtliche Lage und soziale Struktur* (Cologne and Vienna, 1986).

M. Hildermeier, 'Was war das Mesčanstvo?' *FOG* 36 (1985), 15–57.

J.M. Hittle, 'Catherinean Reforms, Social Change, and the Decline of the *Posad* Commune' in D.K. Rowney, G.E. Orchard (eds), *Russian and Slavic History* (Columbus, 1977).

J.M. Hittle, *The Service City. State and Townsmen in Russia 1600–1800* (Cambridge, Mass. and London, 1979).

H.D. Hudson, Jr, 'Urban Estate Engineering in Eighteenth-Century Russia: Catherine the Great and the Elusive *Meshchanstvo*', *CASS* 18 (1986), 393–410.

R.E. Jones, 'Jacob Sievers, Enlightened Reform and the Development of a "Third Estate" in Russia', *RR* 36 (1977), 424–38.

A.A. Kizevetter, *Posadskaia obshchina v Rossii XVIII stoletiia* (Moscow, 1903; reprint Newtonville, 1978).

Iu.R. Klokman, *Ocherki sotsial'no-ekonomicheskoi istorii gorodov severno-zapada Rossii v seredine XVIII v.* (Moscow, 1960).

Iu.R. Klokman, *Sotsial'no-ekonomicheskaia istoriia russkogo goroda vtoraia polovina XVIII veka* (Moscow, 1967).

J.M. Lauber, 'The Merchant-Gentry Conflict in Eighteenth-Century Russia', unpublished PhD thesis, University of Iowa, 1967.

W.B. Lincoln, 'The Russian State and its Critics: A Search for Effective Municipal Government, 1786–1842', *JGO* 17 (1969), 531–41.

D.H. Miller, 'City and State in Muscovite Society: Iaroslavl', 1649–1699', unpublished PhD thesis, Princeton University, 1974.

B.N. Mironov, *Russkii gorod v 1740–1860-e gody: demograficheskoe, sotsial'noe i ekonomicheskoe razvitie* (Leningrad, 1990).

D. Morrison, *'Trading Peasants' and Urbanization in Eighteenth-Century Russia: the Central Industrial Region* (New York and London, 1987).

F.Ia. Polianskii, *Gorodskoe remeslo i manufaktura v Rossii XVIII v.* (Moscow, 1960).

M.G. Rabinovich, *Ocherki etnografii russkogo feodal'nogo goroda. Gorozhane, ikh obshchestvennyi i domashnii byt* (Moscow, 1978).

P.G. Ryndziunskii, *Gorodskoe grazhdanstvo doreformennoi Rossii* (Moscow, 1958).

L.N. Semenova, *Rabochie Peterburga v pervoi polovine XVIII veke* (Leningrad, 1974).

V.I. Shunkov (ed.), *Goroda feodal'noi Rossii: Sbornik statei pamiati N.V. Ustiugova* (Moscow, 1966).

THE RURAL POPULATION

There are many important Soviet archive-based studies of peasant communities of which only a few have been included here; several others are cited in the footnotes.

V.A. Aleksandrov, *Sel'skaia obshchina v Rossii (XVII–nachalo XIX v.)* (Moscow, 1976).

R. Bartlett (ed.), *Land Commune and Peasant Community in Russia: Communal Forms in Imperial and Early Soviet Society* (Basingstoke and London, 1990).

J. Blum, *Lord and Peasant in Russia from the Ninth to the Nineteenth Century* (Princeton, 1961).

R.D. Bohac, 'The Mir and the Military Draft', *SR* 47 (1988), 652–66.

R.D. Bohac, 'Peasant Inheritance Strategies in Russia', *Journal of Interdisciplinary History* 16 (1985), 23–42.

G. Bolotenko, 'Administration of the State Peasants in Russia before the Great Reforms of 1838', unpublished PhD thesis, University of Toronto, 1979.

I.A. Bulygin, *Monastyrskie krest'iane Rossii v pervoi chetverti XVIII veka* (Moscow, 1977).

J. Bushnell, 'Did Serf Owners Control Serf Marriage? Orlov Serfs and their Neighbors, 1773–1861', *SR* 52 (1993), 419–46.

E.D. Domar, M.J. Machina, 'On the Profitability of Russian Serfdom', *Journal of Economic History* 44 (1984), 919–55.

N.M. Druzhinin, *Gosudarstvennye krest'iane i reform P.D. Kiseleva*, vol. I, *Predposylki i sushchnost' reformy* (Moscow and Leningrad, 1946).

S.A. Grant, '*Obshchina* and *Mir*', *SR* 35 (1976), 36–51.

S.L. Hoch, *Serfdom and Social Control in Russia: Petrovskoe, a Village in Tambov* (Chicago and London, 1986).

E.I. Indova, *Krepostnoe khoziaistvo v nachale XIX veka. Po materialam votchinnogo arkhiva Vorontsovykh* (Moscow, 1955).

P. Kolchin, *Unfree Labor: American Slavery and Russian Serfdom* (Cambridge, Mass., 1987).

I.M. de Madariaga, 'Catherine II and the Serfs: a Reconsideration of Some Problems', *SEER* 52 (1974), 34–62.

E. Melton, 'Enlightened Seignorialism and its Dilemmas in Serf Russia, 1750–1830', *JMH* 62 (1990), 675–708.

E. Melton, 'Household Economies and Communal Conflicts on a Russian Serf Estate, 1800–1817', *Journal of Social History* 26 (1993), 559–86.

N.A. Minenko, *Russkaia krest'ianskaia obshchina v zapadnoi Sibiri XVII – pervaia polovina XIX veka* (Novosibirsk, 1991).

D. Moon, 'Reassessing Russian Serfdom', *European History Quarterly* 26 (1996), 483–526.

J. Pallot, D.J.B. Shaw (eds), *Landscape and Settlement in Romanov Russia 1613–1917* (Oxford, 1990).

L.S. Prokof'eva, *Krest'ianskaia obshchina v Rossii vo vtoroi polovine XVIII pervoi polovine XIX veka (na materialakh votchin Sheremetevykh)* (Leningrad, 1981).

N.L. Rubinshtein, *Sel'skoe khoziaistvo Rossii vo vtoroi polovine XVIII v. (istoriko-ekonomicheskii ocherk)* (Moscow, 1957).

V.I. Semevskii, *Krest'iane v tsarstvovanie Imperatritsy Ekateriny II* 2 vols (St Petersburg, 1901).

W. Sutherland, 'Peasants on the Move: State Peasant Resettlement in Imperial Russia, 1805–1830s', *RR* 52 (1993), 472–85.

W.S. Vucinich (ed.), *The Peasant in Nineteenth-Century Russia* (Stanford, 1968).

INDUSTRIAL WORKERS

I. Blanchard, *Russia's 'Age of Silver'. Precious Metal Production and Economic Growth in the Eighteenth Century* (London and New York, 1989).

A.S. Cherkasova, *Masterovnye i rabotnye liudi Urala v XVIII v.* (Moscow, 1985).

H.D. Hudson, Jr, *The Rise of the Demidov Family and the Russian Iron Industry in the Eighteenth Century* (Newtonville, 1986).

J. Mavor, *An Economic History of Russia* 2 vols (London and Toronto, 1914).

A.M. Pankratova, *Formirovanie proletariata v Rossii (XVII–XVIII vv.)* (Moscow, 1963).

R. Portal, *L'Oural au XVIIIe siècle. Étude d'histoire économique et sociale* (Paris, 1950).

F.N. Rodin, *Burlachestvo v Rossii: istoriko-sotsiologicheskii ocherk* (Moscow, 1975).

M.I. Tugan-Baranovsky, *The Russian Factory in the Nineteenth Century*, trans. by A. and C.S. Lewis (Homewood, 1970).

S.P. Turin, *From Peter the Great to Lenin: A History of the Russian Labour Movement with Special Reference to Trade Unionism* (London, 1968).

OFFICIALS, ADMINISTRATION AND THE LAW

V.A. Aleksandrov, *Obychnoe pravo krepostnoi derevni Rossii XVIII–nachalo XIX v.* (Moscow, 1984).

J. Alexander, *Autocratic Politics in a National Crisis: the Imperial Russian Government and Pugachev's Revolt, 1773–1775* (Bloomington, 1969).

J.M. Hartley, 'Catherine's Conscience Court – an English Equity Court?' in A.G. Cross (ed.), *Russia and the West in the Eighteenth Century* (Newtonville, 1983), 306–18.

J.M. Hartley, 'Philanthropy in the Reign of Catherine the Great: Aims and Realities', in R. Bartlett, J.M. Hartley (eds), *Russia in the Age of Enlightenment: Essays for Isabel de Madariaga* (London, 1990), 167–202.

R. Hellie, 'Early Modern Russian Law: the Ulozhenie of 1649', *RH* 15 (1988), 155–80.

R. Hellie, *The Muscovite Law Code (Ulozhenie) of 1649*, part I, *Text and Translation* (Irvine, 1988).

R.E. Jones, *Provincial Development in Russia: Catherine II and Jacob Sievers* (New Brunswick, 1984).

M. Kovalevsky, *Modern Customs and Ancient Laws of Russia* (London, 1891).

J.P. LeDonne, *Absolutism and Ruling Class: the Formation of the Russian Political Order, 1700–1825* (New York and Oxford, 1991).

J.P. LeDonne, 'The Judicial Reform of 1775 in Central Russia', *JGO* 21 (1973), 29–45.

J.P. LeDonne, 'The Provincial and Local Police under Catherine the Great, 1775–1796', *CASS* 4 (1970), 513–28.

J.P. LeDonne, *Ruling Russia. Politics and Administration in the Age of Absolutism 1762–1796* (Princeton, 1984).

I.M. de Madariaga, 'Penal Policy in Eighteenth-Century Russia' in her *Politics and Culture in Eighteenth-Century Russia* (London, 1998).

C. Peterson, *Peter the Great's Administrative and Judicial Reforms* (Stockholm, 1979).

W.M. Pintner, 'The Social Characteristics of the Early Nineteenth-Century Russian Bureaucracy', *SR* 29 (1970), 429–43.

W.M. Pintner, D.K. Rowney (eds), *Russian Officialdom: The Bureaucratization of Russian Society from the Seventeenth to the Twentieth Century* (Chapel Hill, 1980).

M. Raeff, 'The Well Ordered Police State and the Development of Modernity in Seventeenth and Eighteenth Century Europe', *American Historical Review* 80 (1975), 1221–43.

H.J. Torke, 'Continuity and Change in the Relations between Bureaucracy and Society in Russia, 1613–1861', *CASS* 5 (1971), 457–76.

S.M. Troitskii, *Russkii absoliutizm i dvorianstvo v XVIII v. (formirovanie biurokratii)* (Moscow, 1974).

G.G. Weickhardt, 'Due Process and Equal Justice in the Muscovite Codes', *RR* 51 (1992), 463–80.

R.S. Wortman, *The Development of a Russian Legal Consciousness* (Chicago and London, 1976).

G.L. Yaney, *The Systematization of Russian Government: Social Evolution in the Domestic Administration of Imperial Russia 1711–1905* (Urbana, 1973).

THE ARMED FORCES

J. Alexander, *Emperor of the Cossacks* (Larrami, 1973).

L.G. Beskrovnyi, *Russkaia armiia i flot v XIX veke. Voenno-ekonomicheskii potentsial Rossii* (Moscow, 1973).

L.G. Beskrovnyi, *Russkaia armiia i flot v XVIII veke (ocherki)* (Moscow, 1958).

C.A.G. Bridge (ed.), *History of the Russian Fleet during the Reign of Peter the Great by a Contemporary Englishman [1724]* Naval Records Society, vol. 15 (1899).

C. Duffy, *Russia's Military Way to the West: Origins and Nature of Russian Military Power 1700–1800* (London, 1981).

W.C. Fuller, Jr, *Strategy and Power in Russia 1600–1914* (New York, 1992).

G. Gajecky, *The Cossack Administration of the Hetmanate* 2 vols (Cambridge, Mass., 1978).

J.L.H. Keep, 'Catherine's Veterans', *SEER* 59 (1981), 385–96.

J.L.H. Keep, 'The Russian Army's Response to the French Revolution', *JGO* 28 (1980), 500–23.

J.L.H. Keep, *Soldiers of the Tsar: Army and Society in Russia 1462–1874* (Oxford, 1985).

E. Kimmerling [Wirtschafter], 'Soldiers' Children, 1719–1856: A Study of Social Engineering in Imperial Russia', *FOG* 30 (1982), 61–136.

J.P. LeDonne, 'Outlines of Russian Military Administration 1762–1796. Part I: Troop Strength and Deployment', *JGO* 31 (1983), 321–47.

J.P. LeDonne, 'Outlines of Russian Military Administration 1762–1796. Part II: The High Command', *JGO* 33 (1985), 175–204.

P. Longworth, *The Cossacks* (London, 1969).

P. Longworth, 'Transformations in Cossackdom 1650–1850' in B.K. Király, G.E. Rothenberg (eds), *War and Society in East Central Europe*, vol. I, *Special Topics and Generalizations in the Eighteenth and Nineteenth Centuries* (New York, 1979), 393–407.

R. Pipes, 'The Russian Military Colonies, 1810–1831', *JMH* 22 (1950), 205–19.

M.D. Rabinovich, 'Sotsial'noe proiskhozhdenie i imushchestvennoe polozhenie ofitserov reguliarnoi russkoi armii v kontse Severnoi Voiny', in N.I. Pavlenko, L.A. Nikiforov, M.Iu. Volkov (eds), *Rossiia v period reform Petra I* (Moscow, 1973), 133–71.

M. Raeff, 'Pugachev's Rebellion' in R. Forster, J. Greene (eds), *Preconditions of Revolutions in Early Modern Europe* (Baltimore and London, 1970), 161–201.

E.K. Wirtschafter, *From Serf to Russian Soldier* (Princeton, 1990).

NON-RUSSIANS IN THE RUSSIAN EMPIRE

R.P. Bartlett, *Human Capital. The Settlement of Foreigners in Russia 1762–1804* (Cambridge, 1979).

R.P. Bartlett, 'The Russian Nobility and the Baltic German Nobility in the Eighteenth Century', *CMRS* 34 (1993), 233–44.

M. Branch, J.M. Hartley, A. Mączak (eds), *Finland and Poland in the Russian ·Empire: A Comparative Study* (London, 1995).

A.G. Cross, *By the Banks of the Neva. Chapters from the Lives and Careers of the British in Eighteenth-Century Russia* (Cambridge, 1997).

D.M. Crowe, *A History of the Gypsies of Eastern Europe and Russia* (London and New York, 1995).

A.S. Donnelly, *The Russian Conquest of Bashkiria 1552–1740* (New Haven and London, 1968).

S.M. Durnow, *History of the Jews in Russia and Poland from the Earliest Times until the Present Day*, vol. I, *From the Beginning until the Death of Alexander I* (Philadelphia, 1916).

J.R. Gibson, 'Russian Occupance of the Far East, 1639–1750', *CSP* 12 (1970), 60–78.

A.W. Fisher, *The Crimean Tatars* (Stanford, 1978).

A.W. Fisher, 'Enlightened Despotism and Islam under Catherine II', *SR* 27 (1968), 542–53.

J. Forsyth, *A History of the Peoples of Siberia. Russia's North Asian Colony 1581–1990* (Cambridge, 1992).

G.F. Jewsbury, *The Russian Annexation of Bessarabia, 1774–1828. A Study of Imperial Expansion* (New York and Guildford, 1976).

J. Kahk, H. Palli, H. Uibu, 'Peasant Family and Household in Estonia in the Eighteenth and the First Half of the Nineteenth Centuries', *Journal of Family History* 7 (1982), 76–88.

A. Kappeler, *Russland als Vielvölkerreich: Entstehung, Geschichte, Zerfall* (Munich, 1992) (trans. into French as *La Russie. Empire Multiethnique* (Paris, 1994)).

M. Khodarkovsky, *Where Two Worlds Met. The Russian State and the Kalmyk Nomads, 1600–1771* (Ithaca and London, 1992).

J.D. Klier, 'The Ambiguous Legal Status of Russian Jewry in the Reign of Catherine II', *SR* 35 (1976), 804–17.

J.D. Klier, *Russia Gathers her Jews: The Origins of the 'Jewish Question' in Russia, 1772–1825* (DeKalb, 1986).

Z.E. Kohut, *Russian Centralism and Ukrainian Autonomy: Imperial Absorption of the Hetmanate 1760s–1830s* (Cambridge, Mass., 1988).

Z.E. Kohut, 'The Ukrainian Elite in the Eighteenth Century and Its Integration into the Russian Nobility', in I. Banac, P. Bushkovitch (eds), *The Nobility in Russia and Eastern Europe* (New Haven, 1983), 65–97.

I.S. Koropeckyj, *Ukrainian Economic History: Interpretive Essays* (Cambridge, Mass., 1991).

D.M. Lang, *A Modern History of Georgia* (London, 1962).

G.V. Lantzeff, *Siberia in the Seventeenth Century: A Study of the Colonial Administration* (Berkeley and Los Angeles, 1943).

D.F. Lynch, 'The Conquest, Settlement and Initial Development of New Russia (The Southern Third of the Ukraine), 1780–1837', unpublished PhD thesis, Yale University, 1965.

B. Nolde, *La formation de l'Empire russe. Études, notes et documents*, 2 vols (Paris, 1952–53).

R. Pipes, 'Catherine II and the Jews: The Origins of the Pale of Settlement', *Soviet Jewish Affairs* 5 (1975), 3–20.

A. Plakans, 'Peasant Farmsteads and Households in the Baltic Littoral, 1797', *Comparative Studies in Society and History* 17 (1975), 2–35.

A. Plakans, 'Seigneurial Authority and Peasant Family Life: the Baltic Area in the Eighteenth Century', *The Journal of Interdisciplinary History* 5 (1975), 629–54.

M. Raeff, *Siberia and the Reforms of 1822* (Seattle, 1956).

T.U. Raun, *Estonia and the Estonians* (Stanford, 1987).

D.G. Rempel, 'The Mennonite Commonwealth in Russia: A Sketch of its Founding and Endurance', *The Mennonite Quarterly Review* 47 (1973), 259–308; 48 (1974), 5–54.

I.L. Rudnytsky (ed.), *Rethinking Ukrainian History* (Edmonton, 1981).

D. Saunders, *The Ukrainian Impact on Russian Culture 1750–1850* (Edmonton, 1985).

S.F. Starr (ed.), *Russia's American Colony* (Durham, N. Car., 1987).

O. Subtelny, *Ukraine: A History* (Toronto, Buffalo and London, 1994).

R.G. Suny, *The Making of the Georgian Nation* (Bloomington and Indianapolis, 1988).

R.G. Suny, 'Russian Rule and Caucasian Society in the First Half of the Nineteenth Century: The Georgian Nobility and the Armenian Bourgeoisie, 1801–1856', *Nationalities Papers* 7 (1979), 53–78.

F.W. Thackeray, *Antecedents of Revolution: Alexander I and the Polish Kingdom, 1815–1825* (Boulder, 1980).

E.C. Thaden, *Russia's Western Borderlands, 1710–1870* (Princeton, 1984).

P.S. Wandycz, *The Lands of Partitioned Poland, 1795–1918* (Seattle and London, 1974).

A. Wood (ed.), *The History of Siberia: From Russian Conquest to Revolution* (London and New York, 1991).

D.B. Yaroshevski, 'Imperial Strategy in the Kirghiz Steppe in the Eighteenth Century', *JGO* 39 (1991), 221–4.

J.J. Zatko, 'The Organisation of the Catholic Church in Russia, 1772–84', *SEER* 43 (1965), 303–13.

S.J. Zipperstein, *The Jews of Odessa. A Cultural History, 1794–1881* (Stanford, 1986).

Ia. Zutis, *Ostzeiskii vopros v XVIII veke* (Riga, 1946).

Chronology

REIGN OF ALEXIS (1645–76)

1648   Urban riots in Moscow and other towns
           Zemskii sobor convened in Moscow
           Skomorokhi banned
1649   *Ulozhenie* or Law Code
1654   Treaty of Pereiaslavl'; Cossacks in the Ukraine recognize the suzerainty of the tsar
1666   Patriarch Nikon deposed; beginning of the schism in the Orthodox Church
1667–71 Revolt of Stenka Razin
1667   Treaty of Andrusovo; acquisition of Smolensk and Kiev
1668–76 Siege of the Old Believers in the Solovetsk monastery

REIGN OF FEDOR III (1676–82)

1678   Census (of population of both sexes)
1682   *Mestnichestvo* (precedence system) abolished

REIGN OF PETER I (1682–1725)
(REGENCY OF SOPHIA 1682–89; JOINT RULE WITH IVAN V 1682–96)

1682   *Strel'tsy* revolt
1687   Opening of the Moscow Slavonic-Greek-Latin Academy
1697   Ban on the import and use of tobacco lifted
1698–99 *Strel'tsy* revolt
1699   Decree reforming urban administration
1701   Foundation of the School of Mathematics and Navigation (closed 1752)
1702   Decree on marriage and on betrothal period for groom and bride
1703   Foundation of St Petersburg

1705	Fines imposed on men who retained their beards
1707–8	Bulavin revolt
1714	Decrees for the establishment of cipher schools
	Decree abolishing partible inheritance
1715	Opening of the St Petersburg Naval Academy
1716	Code of Military Law
1718	Establishment of social 'assemblies' for the nobility
1719–24	Reform of tax assessment leading to the introduction of the poll tax
1719	First census (of male population)
1719	Introduction of passports
1721	Establishment of town magistracies and urban reform
	Treaty of Nystad; acquisition of Estonia, Livonia, Ingria and Vyborg
	Issue of the Spiritual Regulation and establishment of the Holy Synod
1722	Promulgation of the Table of Ranks
1724	Division of monasteries into three categories, each with designated philanthropic functions

REIGN OF CATHERINE I (1725–27)

1726	Foundation of the St Petersburg Academy of Sciences (opened 1727)
	Foundation of the St Petersburg Gymnasium

REIGN OF PETER II (1727–30)

1727–28	Collection of the poll tax becomes the responsibility of landowners

REIGN OF ANNA (1730–41)

1731	Restoration of partible inheritance
1732	Establishment of the Noble Cadet Corps
1736	Compulsory state service limited to twenty-five years
c.1740	Establishment of the Imperial Ballet Corps at court

REIGN OF IVAN VI (1740–41)

REIGN OF ELIZABETH (1741–62)

1743	Treaty of Åbo; acquisition of more territory in southern Finland
1744–47	Second census (of male population)
1753	Internal tariffs and tolls within the empire abolished
1755	Foundation of Moscow University
1756	Opening of the first public theatre
1758	Merchants instructed to sell their serfs
1759	Establishment of the Corps de Pages school

1760   Noble landowners, urban communities and state peasant communes given the right to exile unruly serfs, townspeople or state peasants to Siberia as settlers

REIGN OF PETER III (1762)

1762   Manifesto of freedom from compulsory service for the nobility
        Decree on the secularization of Church land

REIGN OF CATHERINE II (1762–96)

1762–64 Third census (of male population)
1764   Confirmation of the secularization of Church lands
         Opening of the Foundling Hospital in Moscow
         Foundation of Smolnyi girls' school
         Abolition of the Hetmanate (Left-Bank Ukraine)
1767   Opening of the Legislative Commission
1771   Moscow plague riots
1772   First Partition of Poland
1773–75 Pugachev revolt
1775   Taxation reform; ends the collective *tiaglo* responsibility of the whole urban community
         Abolition of the Zaporozhian Cossack host
         Statute on Provincial Administration
1782   Fourth census (of male population)
         Promulgation of the Police Code
1783   Decree permitting the establishment of private printing presses
         Acquisition of the Crimea
1785   Charter to the Nobles
         Charter to the Towns
1786   Statute on National Education
1790   Publication of A.N. Radishchev's *Journey from St Petersburg to Moscow*
1793   Second Partition of Poland
1794   Closure of masonic lodges in Russia
1795   Fifth census (of male population)
1795   Third Partition of Poland

REIGN OF PAUL (1796–1801)

1797   Recommendation that serfs should work no more than three days a week on their masters' estates

REIGN OF ALEXANDER I (1801–25)

1803   Decree on Public Education
        Free Cultivators' Law

1804	Statute on the Jews
1806	Mining Statute
1808	Reform of the seminaries
1809	Decree on examinations for the civil service
	Treaty of Fredrikshamn; acquisition of the rest of Finland
1810	First military colony set up in Mogilev province
1811	Sixth census (of male population)
1812	Treaty of Bucharest; acquisition of Bessarabia
	Opening of the Imperial lycée at Tsarskoe selo
1812	French invasion of Russia
	Moscow destroyed by fire
1813	Establishment of a branch of the Bible Society in Russia
1815	Treaties of Vienna; creation of the Congress Kingdom of Poland
1816	Formation of the Union of Salvation
	Decree emancipating the serfs in Estonia
	Formation of the Imperial Philanthropic Society
1817	Decree emancipating the serfs in Courland
1818	Formation of the Union of Welfare
1819	Decree emancipating the serfs in Livonia
	Revolt in Chuguev military colony
1822	Formation of the Northern and Southern Societies
1824	Guild reform
1825	Decembrist revolt

Glossary

arshin   linear measurement; 72.12 cm (28 in)

assignat   paper rouble; worth less than a silver rouble (set at a value of 25 copecks in 1812–15)

barshchina   corvée, obligatory labour, performed in particular by serfs

belye mesta   'white property' in towns, which was not subject to the *tiaglo*, that is, urban fiscal and labour obligations; abolished in theory in 1649

bobyl', bobyli   cotter/s, either landless peasants or peasants holding only small plots

boiar   the highest rank of the service aristocracy in sixteenth- and seventeenth-century Muscovy

boiarskaia duma   the Boiar Council; an executive body, comprising the aristocratic elite, which advised the tsar and supervised the administrative chancelleries; lapsed under Peter I

burmistr, -ry   urban elected official/s; also serf official/s, appointed with the approval of the commune or elected, who acted as a peasant manager for the landowner

chet', -ti   as *chetvert'*

chetvert'   as grain measure, 57.33 kg (126.39 lb); as land measure usually 0.54 hectares (1.35 acres), that is, half a *desiatina*

chetverik   grain measure, 7.11 kg (15.8 lb)

chin   rank in the Table of Ranks

denga   Muscovite coin, equal to half a copeck

desiatina, -ny   land measure of 1.08 hectares (2.7 acres)

dvorianstvo   collective word for the Russian nobility, used from the time of Peter I

gost', gosti   the richest group of merchants in Muscovy, which also acted as government agents in collecting state dues and in administration; the category declined under Peter I and was merged with the merchantry

gostinaia sotnia   the second richest category of merchants in Muscovy, which also carried out administrative and fiscal obligations; the category declined under Peter I and was merged with the merchantry

hetman   elected or appointed leader of the Ukrainian and Zaporozhian Cossacks

iamshchik, -ki   postdriver/s; a special category of state peasants which had to carry the mail and provide transport for official and private travellers on the major post roads

kabala   debt servitude, a contract of service for a period of time, or for life, in place of paying interest for a monetary loan

kholop, -py   male slave/s; slaves and slavery (*kholopstvo*) as a separate institution gradually disappeared after slaves were made subject to the poll tax, which they paid at the same rate as serfs

kupets, kuptsy   merchant/s; organized into merchant guilds after 1721

meshchanin, meschane   sometimes used as a broad term to denote the people involved in commercial and artisan activities; after the Charter to the Towns in 1785 the category (the third) of artisans registered in craft guilds

mestnichestvo   system of 'place order' or precedence based on family and service; abolished in 1682

obrok   quitrent, usually money dues but sometimes payments in kind, paid by peasants

odnodvorets, -rtsy   one-homesteader/s; the descendants of Muscovite petty service men settled on the southern and eastern frontiers; the category was abolished in 1868

pomeshchik, -chiki   holder/s of *pomest'e* land

pomest'e, -t'ia   land granted in return for military service; after 1762 such land became regarded as full private property of private persons

posad, -dy   urban settlement/s in Muscovy. *Posadskie liudi* could be used as a collective term to denote all the *tiaglo*-paying town dwellers or could refer to the poorer and less-skilled inhabitants; in the Charter to the Towns of 1785 the *posadskie* were classed as the sixth (and last and least prestigious) category of urban inhabitants, comprising unskilled workers and hired labourers

prikaznye liudi   people working in government offices or *prikazy*; also junior clerical staff in posts below the Table of Ranks

pripisnye   'assigned' state peasants attached to a specific industrial enterprise

pud   unit of weight; 16.38 kg (36.11 lb)

ratman, -ny   elected urban official/s

raznochinets, -ntsy   'people of various ranks', in this period mainly people who had left the social estate of their parents but had not formally entered another legal social category

sazhen   linear measurement; 2.133 metres (7 feet)

skhod   assembly of the peasant commune

skomorokh, -khi   travelling minstrel/s

starosta   elder

strelets, strel'tsy   'musketeer/s', armed militiamen in infantry regiments in Moscow; they grew in military importance in the seventeenth century, when the category became lifelong and hereditary, but the regiments were disbanded by Peter I after riots and revolts

tiaglo   the sum of fiscal and other obligations levied usually on an individual in the seventeenth century and on a unit (usually an adult couple) in the eighteenth and nineteenth centuries; the term was also used to designate the capacity of taxpayers to meet their obligations

tsekh, tsekhi   craft guild/s

Ulozhenie   code of laws of 1649, which, *inter alia*, institutionalized serfdom

versta, -sty   linear measurement, 1.067 km (0.663 miles)

voevoda   military governor in charge of a province from the time of Peter I; post abolished in 1775

votchina   hereditary landed estates or property

zemskii sobor   'assembly of the land'; consultative elected body; declined in the second half of the seventeenth century

Maps

Map 1   European Russia: ethnic composition

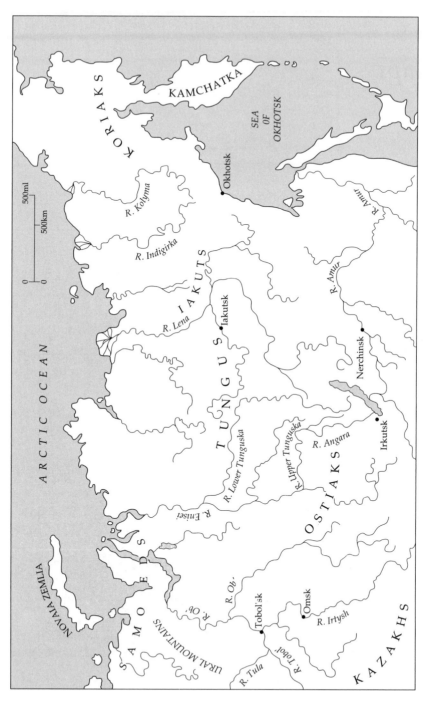

Map 2   Siberia: ethnic composition

Index